International Conference e-Learning (EL2020)

Held at MCCSIS 2020 (Held online due to COVID-19)

Lisbon, Portugal
21 - 25 July 2020

ISBN: 978-1-7138-2275-2

Printed from e-media with permission by:

Curran Associates, Inc.
57 Morehouse Lane
Red Hook, NY 12571

Some format issues inherent in the e-media version may also appear in this print version.

Printed with permission by Curran Associates, Inc. (2021)

International Association for Development of the Information Society (IADIS)
Rua Sao Sebastiao Da Pedreira
No. 100, 30, 1050-209
Lisbon, Portugal

Phone: 351 21 3151373
Fax: 351 21 3151244

secretariat@iadis.org

Additional copies of this publication are available from:

Curran Associates, Inc.
57 Morehouse Lane
Red Hook, NY 12571 USA
Phone: 845-758-0400
Fax: 845-758-2633
Email: curran@proceedings.com
Web: www.proceedings.com

TABLE OF CONTENTS

USE OF HYBRID CLASSROOM AND OPEN EDUCATIONAL RESOURCES: EXPERIENCE GAINED FROM A UNIVERSITY IN HONG KONG

Nikolina Dragicevic, Ioanna Pavlidou and Eric Tsui
The Hong Kong Polytechnic University, Hung Hom, Kowloon, Hong Kong SAR

ABSTRACT

Hybrid classroom, which combines face-to-face and online learning, is becoming a popular way of delivering courses in higher education and a subject of growing interest in academic literature. At the same time, the ongoing development of digital educational resources and a trend of openness in systems and education gives open educational resources an increasingly important role in democratising learning. The purpose of this study is to present the approach that combines hybrid classroom and open educational resources developed at one higher education institution in Hong Kong and to investigate the students' views towards the approach. A questionnaire inquiring students' affection towards hybrid classroom and open educational resources has been administered to postgraduate students of the knowledge management programme and related critical factors have been identified and discussed. Results show that the adopted approach enriches students' learning experience by providing a variety of benefits, such as allowing diverse methods and modes of delivery and enabling more flexible, self-controlled, and self-paced learning. Particularly promising seems to be the positive experience from joining the co-located and distance learners, with providing potential advantages such as cross-cultural learning. Moreover, students reported that their learning experience was enhanced with open educational resources. However, some challenges, of technical and pedagogical nature, have been identified, which require further considerations of curriculum design to facilitate hybrid classroom (and use of open education resources) optimally.

KEYWORDS

Hybrid Classroom, Open Educational Resources, Higher Education, Hybrid Learning

1. INTRODUCTION

The development of information and communication technologies generated digital affordances that allowed organising, sharing and storing knowledge online and streaming high-quality media that can efficiently simulate the physical environment. At the same time, the pervasiveness of digital devices used in workplaces and daily lives and the ubiquity of data created the need to develop a set of digital competences such as learning in networks, learning from diversified media sources and leveraging on technologies (e.g., Gallardo-Echenique et al., 2015; Germaine et al., 2016; Muller, 2015; Siemens, 2008). The availability of technological resources and the necessities of this rapidly changing world require to revisit teaching and learning in education.

For these reasons, in recent years, there has been an emergence of a variety of new pedagogies that incorporate digital technologies and online learning (Bower et al., 2017; Kemp and Grieve, 2014). Within these approaches, classrooms are not bounded by walls but can extend to virtual environments, giving rise to the hybrid classrooms (HC), i.e., the considerate symbiosis of the face-to-face (F2F) and online learning experiences (Bersin, 2004). Technology also provides an opportunity to make education more open, such as to share knowledge and learning materials in a digital format, giving prominence to open educational resources (OER), i.e., freely available digital resources (D'Antoni, 2009).

In this paper, building on these trends in higher education and practice, we present our approach that combined HC and OER in knowledge management (KM) postgraduate courses at The Hong Kong Polytechnic University (PolyU) and report students' attitudes towards hybrid learning and using open resources in learning.

There are two main research objectives for this study:

1) To ascertain how HC and OER are used in one higher education institution in Hong Kong;
2) To understand students' affection towards the use of HC and OER.

To answer these questions, first, in section 2, we provide a short theoretical background on the concepts of HC and OER. Then, in section 3, we introduce the approach that is used at the postgraduate academic programme. Next, in section 4, we report and discuss the results from the questionnaire inquiring students' inclination towards joining F2F and online learning environment and using OER in comparison to traditional textbooks. Last, in section 5, we conclude with some implications for further research.

2. THEORETICAL BACKGROUND

2.1 Hybrid Classroom – Definition and Types

HC is a type of course that combines the traditional face-to-face (F2F) learning with online (web-based) learning. Online learning can be synchronous, as in the case of live lectures, or asynchronous, as in the case of pre-recorded lectures and presentations with voice. Apart from online lectures, it can consist of other online methods and tools, such as online teaching materials, online pre-lecture assignments and discussion forums (Zhao and Breslow, 2013). "Hybrid" as a term is many times used interchangeably with "blended", in most studies having identical meaning (Zhao and Breslow, 2013). In this sense, a course is hybrid or blended when F2F learning is supplemented by web-based facilitation of delivering the lecture (and not merely supported by digital means such as computers or presentation tools) (Helms, 2014; Zhao and Breslow, 2013). Such an understanding of HC, where F2F is combined with the online lectures, we also adopt in this paper.

Zhao and Breslow (2013) classify HC according to the degree of usage of online learning: replacement model, where a portion of the F2F lectures is reduced and replaced by online learning; supplemental model, where the number of F2F classes remains the same, but the students are recommended to engage in online learning; emporium model, where the courses are delivered exclusively online but with access to a physical learning and resource centre; and, last, the buffet model, that offers all the options of F2F and online learning and every student can create a personalised combination on their individual taste. Other scholars attempted to categorise hybrid classrooms by suggesting the exact portion of online learning that is adopted. For example, Allen et al. (2007) propose that boundaries of the online part of the course are between 30-79%; a lower percentage would be considered as a web-facilitated course and a higher as a fully online course.

2.2 Applications of Hybrid Classroom

At the practical level, there can be numerous combinations and applications of HC. A few examples include a classroom that consists of only distant students connected in a virtual environment, only co-located students or a mix of both (Bower et al., 2017). The technologies reported in the literature are also diverse, from online chat, live video, quizzes and breakout rooms to blended reality with 3D media (Bower et al., 2017).

One of the benefits of HC is in breaking the classroom boundaries which allows a broader students' participation, such as of disengaged university students, individuals that have big distance from the institution and vulnerable groups (Bower et al., 2015; Bowyer and Chambers, 2017). HC also creates a significant opportunity to enrich the learning experience. For example, the formation of an educational ground that is diverse in activities, experiences or even cultures, as it can occur in a cross-institutional HC, has a potential to satisfy the needs of different learner's personalities (Picciano, 2009), enhance interest and healthy competition (Bower et al., 2015; Milheim, 2014), stimulate critical thinking (Loes et al., 2012) and support the development of working skills for diverse teams (Gomez et al., 2009).

2.3 Open Educational Resources

OER is a term related to a broader set of entities, processes and systems that are based on openness, depicted by the concepts such as open-source, open access, open data, open innovation and open government. The first definition of OER was coined by UNESCO (2002) as "The open provision of educational resources, enabled by information and communication technologies, for consultation, use and adaptation by a community of users for non-commercial purposes." According to Smith and Seward (2017), this openness has three dimensions: production, distribution and consumption. In this sense, OER can be described as a result of open, collaborative production of people who are willing to add value; as a product of open distribution, since they are located in the public domain and not channelled to the users by traditional commercial distribution channels; and as a learning resource available for open consumption, as anyone can access and enjoy their value.

With the developments of information and communication technologies, on the one hand, and a need for the democratisation of knowledge, on the other, the use of OER becomes more and more important in educational environment (D'Antoni, 2009). OER materials can be used for teaching, learning, assessment and research purposes as well as for curriculum development. Some of the benefits include access to cost-free materials, the flexibility to combine different resources, use of diversified resources, control over which resource(s) to use (Wiley et al., 2014).

Most of the research focuses on identifying the impact directly on students' performance, such as GPA, engagement or assessment scores (Hilton, 2016), while several scholars studied the perceptions from teacher's perspective in using them (Pitt, 2015).

3. DESCRIPTION OF THE APPROACH

This paper describes an approach that combines HC and OER in the quest to equip students with digital competences at the KM programme at PolyU. Both HC and OER are implemented in the context of the open pedagogy tendencies of the PolyU, characterised by the learner centricity, knowledge sharing, technology enablement, connectedness and openness of resources (Figure 1).

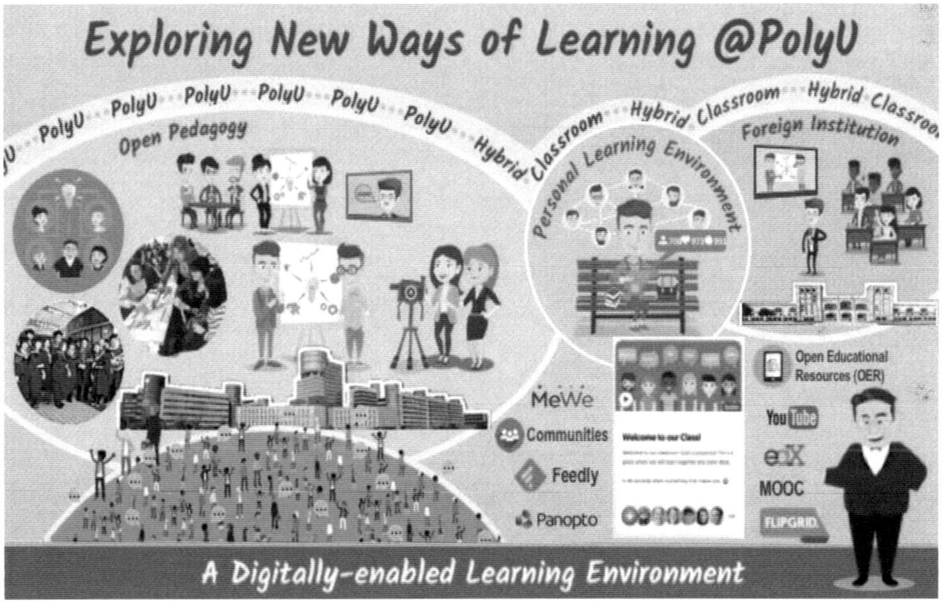

Figure 1. Hybrid classroom and OER are adopted in line with the open pedagogy tendencies at PolyU

Table 1 provides a summary of ways hybrid classroom is utilised at the KM programme at PolyU. In its simplest form, a subject teacher, apart from F2F conducts some of the classes online (typically around 30%), consistent with the replacement model of HC (Zhao and Breslow, 2013).

The approach also allows more complex forms, such as a collaboration between host university and universities from abroad. In the latter case, for example, the teacher would set up an online class where he would co-lecture with his/her colleague from other university and invite students from both universities to participate and collaborate via Blackboard collaborate (or potentially other platforms). Since the subject teacher of the KM programme is a leader of the two Massive Open Online Courses (MOOCs) (edX, 2020), MOOC learners are also invited to join the online classrooms when the topic is suitable.

Enactment of HC consists of two components. One is a personal learning environment and network (PLE&N) which refers to the peer-based learner-centric platform and online discussion forum set up by a teacher, which aims to foster self-regulated, network-based, and lifelong learning (Tsang and Tsui, 2017). For organising HC, a MeWe community platform is used, and relevant articles are automatically located and sent to the students, members of the forum. Students review, discuss and further annotate these articles.

Table 1. Types of HC used at KM programme at PolyU

Types of hybrid classrooms	**Facilitator(s)**	**Style of interaction (Online/ F2F/ Both)**	**Mode of interaction (Synchronous/ Asynchronous/ Both)**	**Attendees and mode of attendance**		
				PolyU students	**Students from an overseas university**	**MOOC learners**
Basic	PolyU staff	F2F classroom (70%); online environment (30%)	Both	Yes Co-located (PolyU classroom) and remotely	No	When a suitable topic Remotely
Extended	PolyU staff Guest lecturer	F2F class + real-time Q&A over the online platform	Both	Yes Co-located (PolyU classroom) and remotely	No	When a suitable topic Remotely
Linked	PolyU staff + staff from a different institution	Each facilitator takes a turn to present; students from both sides ask questions	Both	Yes Co-located (PolyU Classroom) and using the online platform during F2F	Yes Co-located (Home institution's classroom) and using the online platform during F2F	When a suitable topic Remotely
	PolyU staff + staff from a different institution	Mini-lecture, Q&A, assignment, mutual projects etc.	Both	Yes Remotely	Yes Remotely	When a suitable topic Remotely

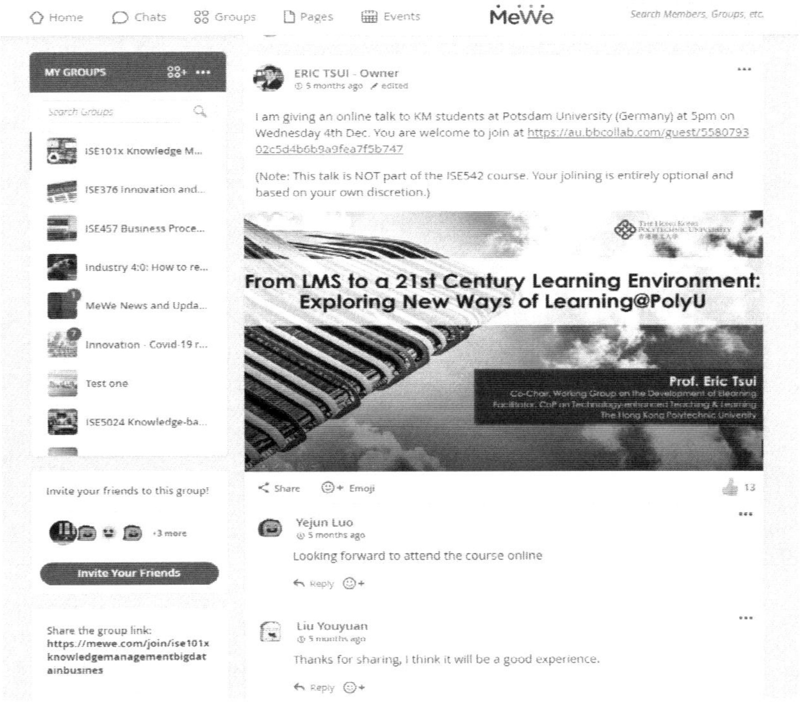

Figure 2. Using the social network of MeWe as part of the PLE&N

The other component of HC is the organisation of an online classroom by using a combination of Panopto, Blackboard Collaborate, and MeWe platforms. A range of activities are designed to reflect various teaching and learning pedagogies which, among others, include: 1) teachers from different institutions presenting on a topic of common interest via live or pre-recorded sessions; 2) teachers organising joint live sessions with Q&A; 3) students engaging in role-playing exercises and taking turns to ask and answer questions; 4) students from multiple universities engaging in common assignments; 5) students from multiple universities engaging in common projects; 6) students forming joint, multi-institutional teams to collaborate and co-produce the subject deliverables. Both synchronous and asynchronous collaborations are used since students from different institutions do not share the same class schedule or time zone.

Figure 3. PolyU OER library

An important part of HC is the use of OER, the purpose of which is to be a supplementary learning material to pre-designed course content. A subject teacher helps to identify relevant OER resources for his hybrid classes by working with a librarian and his students. An increasingly important role in providing resources for the enactment of HC plays the OER library (https://oer.lib.polyu.edu.hk/home.html) set up by PolyU. PolyU library endeavours both into the production of its resources and relying on the world-wide commons-based peer production model (e.g., the model used by Wikipedia) of OER (Wiley et al., 2014).

Students are also encouraged to identify, share and use relevant and good quality OERs (with a teacher's endorsement) with their peers. Teacher assesses the quality and usefulness of OER materials, which are in the form of, among others, articles and videos posted into the chosen platforms, for example, Blackboard Collaborate, MEWE community, or in PLE&N. A subject teacher incorporates selective OER materials to update course content and informs the library to update the OER portal.

OER used for the HC purposes cover, among others, Massive Open Online Courses (MOOC), YouTube videos, MIT Open Courseware, MERLOT repository, RSS feeds, industry news and articles, industry and academic reports.

4. METHOD

4.1 Participants, Data Collection and Analysis

The 74 students who participated in the first semester of the 2019/2020 KM postgraduate course were asked to participate in the study and complete an online questionnaire about their attitude towards HC and use of OER. The final number of students who completed the survey is 40. A questionnaire has been adapted based on Lin, (2008) and Bliss et al. (2013). HC teacher has transmitted the questionnaire in an online form. The questionnaire consists of two main components – one related to HC and the other to OER. In the HC section, students were asked to share their views and behaviours regarding computer access and their HC background, different features of the technology used, and their attitude towards the HC. In the OER section, students were asked to compare the use of OER to commonly used traditional textbooks on a variety of factors, such as cost, quality, outcomes and ways of use.

The collection and analysis of data were of qualitative and quantitative nature, consisting of multiple-choice, Likert-type, multiple-select, constructed response items, and open-ended questions that asked students about each of the themes mentioned above. Data were analysed by congruently using quantitative and qualitative procedures. Descriptive analytics were employed to analyse the data quantitively in terms of percentages. Qualitative data was analysed by using comparative method grounded theory methodology (Corbin and Strauss, 1990; Kolb, 2012), which utilises an analytic procedure of constant comparison and relies on the researchers` ability to interpret data, discover patterns in it, and create relevant themes.

4.2 Results and Discussion

Table 2 presents some descriptive statistics regarding the technology usage of the students and their prior experience with HC. The results regarding the first questionnaire element, which is about the devices that students use to participate in HC, shows a clear tendency in using personal mobile devices (laptop, smartphone and tablet) over desktop computers. Such finding comes in line with the current global trend of using mobile devices over computers for a growing number of tasks (Biddix et al., 2015; Dolch and Zawacki-Richter, 2018; Eurostat, 2015). At the same time, the majority of the students also show high usage of their computer with 60% exceeding the 3 hours daily. A clear preference from students to access the online delivery of the HC from home was noted (85%), while a smaller percentage chose to join from a library or dormitory. Last, it is noteworthy to mention that the greater part of the students (67.5%) involved in this survey has never participated in a hybrid classroom in the past.

Table 2. Descriptive Statistics of Student Technology and HC Usage

Device Used (%)	%
Desktop	12.5
Laptop	62.5
Smartphone	35
Tablet	25
Other	
Computer Access (%)	
At computer lab	0
At home	85
In the dorm	2.5
In the library	13.5
Frequency Using Computer (%)	
3- 5 hours per week	15
Daily more than 3 hours	60
Every day 1-2 hours	25
Less than 1-2 hour per week	0
Hybrid Classroom Taken (%)	
Yes	32.5
No	67.5

4.2.1 Views on Hybrid Classroom

In the questionnaire, students were asked to reflect their affection toward HC, and the results are depicted in Table 3 categorised in positive, negative and overall items. The discussion of the findings presented in the table incorporates the results from several open-ended questions in which the authors asked the students about their best experiences and issues or concerns they might have regarding HC.

Overall, students expressed positive attitudes towards using HC and would recommend hybrid learning to friends (47.5%).

Table 3. Student Affection Toward Hybrid Classroom

Survey items					
Positive items	**1**	**2**	**3**	**4**	**5**
I could control the pace of my own learning	0	0	22.5	50	27,5
Online assignments were helpful in understanding the course content	5	5	27.5	52.5	10
The connection between what I did online and in-class was clear	2.5	15	30	37.5	15
I didn't have any difficulty in managing my time for the online part of the course	0	25	27.5	37.5	10
Negative items	**1**	**2**	**3**	**4**	**5**
The online course materials were difficult to follow.	10	15	47.5	27.5	0
The time I spent online would better have been spent in class.	15	27.5	32.5	17.5	7.5
I found participating in the online messaging system useless for my learning.	10	25	27.5	30	7.5
I was unable to share ideas with other students on a regular basis.	7.5	27.5	35	25	5
Overall items	**1**	**2**	**3**	**4**	**5**
I would recommend taking the hybrid classroom to a friend	7.5	15	30	30	17.5
I would take another course that incorporates BB Collaborate	2.5	15	37.5	30	15

Diverse learning approaches

Overall, the students expressed positive attitudes towards making use of the diversity of learning methods provided by HC. Furthermore, 62% of the students found the online assignments to be helpful to understand the syllabus and 25% were confident to deal with the online materials, but 27% perceived the online materials were hard to follow.

Nevertheless, several students reported that they found the experience of online learning useful since they got the chance to practice skills which would help them to adapt to digital working environments. This finding supports the argument that the adopted approach aids with developing digital competences in students.

Self-control and self-paced learning

77.5% of the students reported that they felt able to learn on their own pace, and 47.5% managed their time successfully in the online activities of the course. Confirming this finding, most of the students in their open-ended comments emphasised that online classes are particularly "convenient" due to "flexible time management for having lectures" or "flexibility of time and place to study." This result is satisfactory; a student's independence and self-configuration is a critical element of a successful hybrid classroom (McGee and Reis, 2012). Furthermore, the availability of enough time within a lecture allows students to comprehend information and develop their critical views (Westermann, 2014).

Connectivity and interactivity

Some students stressed that the online interactions stimulated them to engage more; for example, one of the respondents acknowledged that "some classmates who are less active in F2F lecture are more active in an online course." Reasons for students' higher engagement could be found in the online environment-specific teaching, and learning circumstances which minimise the power distance between students and teachers and are by design more learner-centric than F2F environments (Ku and Lohr, 2003). For example, traditionally, in eastern societies, teachers exhibit a more authoritative instruction style, and students tend to save face and avoid conflict, influenced by the Confucius' philosophy (Chiu, 2009). However, online learning practices seem to mitigate some of these cultural aspects and empower students to engage without fear of negative evaluation.

The students also found value in continuing to engage in the F2F classes, particularly due to the opportunity to socialise in person with their peers and the opportunity to discuss and comprehend the ideas more deeply. F2F learning is recognised to facilitate the socialisation aspect of learning better than online learning (Bower et al., 2015).

Technology and structure

Most of the students (45%) expressed satisfaction from using the online teaching system BB Collaborate, although they did not find as useful its online messaging system. The students also mentioned that few technological challenges, such as audio and video quality and usage - disconnectedness, interruptions, and distortions, undermined the flow of the lecture.

Regarding the pedagogical challenges, the students emphasised that some of the learning materials were not adjusted appropriately for the online presentation and that it was hard to follow the content. Some of the students also stressed that they would favour more structured peer-to-peer interactions in the online classroom and that it was hard for them to keep concentration and attention online. 30% of the students reported that it was difficult to share ideas in HC setting with their peers. Nevertheless, a significant percentage of students felt that there was a clear connection between what they have learned in the physical and online classroom (52.5%) and would not change the online part of the course for a physical classroom (42.5%).

Table 4. Students' affection towards the participation of another university

Participation of the faculty from a third party institution adds value to a class	**%**
Significant value	27.5
Good value	52.5
Medium value	20
Little value-added	0
No value-added	0
Participation of the students from a third party institution adds value to a class	
Significant value	22.5
Good value	47.5
Medium value	30
Little value-added	0
No value-added	0

Lastly, as shown in Table 4, the students highly valued the interaction and communication with international students and faculty, with most of the students reporting that they were of good or significant value. In the open-ended questions, they stressed that they had enjoyed the opportunity to "communicate with Professor far from Hong Kong," "sharing the knowledge," and "interaction with foreign scholars."

These results come in line with prior research which reports about the positive benefits of joining the remote and co-located students is HC, such as the exposure to different teaching and learning styles of the participants from the guest institution (Milheim, 2014).

4.2.2 Views on Open Educational Resources

Within the framework of HC and curriculum expansion, OER were used as a supplementary learning material to traditional textbooks. Table 5 shows that most of the students used OER resources or 2-3 times a month (35%) or 2-3 times a week (27.5%).

Table 5. Descriptive statistics on OER usage

Frequency of using OER	%
Never	0
2-3 times a semester	25
2-3 times a month	35
2-3 times a week	27.5
Daily	12.5

We have further asked students to reflect their experience in using OER in terms of perceived quality and perceived usefulness for learning, the results of which are shown in Table 6 and Table 7, respectively. In general, OER are assessed as having a similar quality to the traditional textbooks (77.5%), with a significant percentage of students finding them better (15%) and a smaller part finding them worse than the textbooks (7.5%). This finding comes in line with prior research that explores students impressions of OER having comparable or better quality than textbooks (Watson et al., 2017).

Noteworthy is the finding that the majority of students (75%) think that OER and public internet articles have about the same quality, while 15% find OER better and only 2.5% worse than internet articles. More studies are required to understand whether such results correspond to the objective value of the two types of resources, or they arise from students' inability to appraise and compare the two critically.

A high percentage of the participants (37.5%) assesses textbooks cost as too excessive, the majority (45%) has a neutral opinion, and 17% think that the cost is not "too much". Commercial textbooks cost is broadly accepted both by students and institutions as an essential downside and as a significant factor for the adoption of OER in higher education (Hilton, 2016; McGreal, 2019).

Table 6. Students perceptions of the quality of OER

Overall, what do you think of the OER materials used in this course?	%
Worse than the quality of the traditional textbooks	7.5
About the same as the quality of the traditional textbooks	77.5
Better than the quality of the traditional textbooks	15
How do you rate the quality of the OER materials adopted in this course in relation to public internet articles?	%
Worse than the quality of the public internet articles	2.5
About the same as the quality of the public internet articles	75
Better than the quality of the public internet articles	22.5
In general, textbooks and course materials cost too much	%
Strongly disagree	10
Disagree	7.5
Neither agree nor disagree	45
Agree	20
Strongly agree	17.5

At the same time, the vast majority of students regards that OER indeed improves their learning experience from moderate (65%) to high (7.5%) degree. In comparison, 10% finds OER did not contribute at all and 10% that even decreased their learning experience. Only a small part of the course audience (7.5% of students) did not perceive any connection of OER to their learning experience.

Table 7. Students perceptions on the usefulness of OER for learning

How do you rate the quality of the OER materials adopted in this course in relation to traditional textbooks?	**%**
OER materials were detrimental to my learning experience	10
OER materials did not enhance my learning experience at all	10
OER materials have not been used for my learning experience	7.5
OER materials have mildly enhanced my learning experience	65
OER materials have greatly enhanced my learning experience	7.5
Imagine you have the freedom to choose one out of two courses with the same syllabus (one course uses OER materials, and the other one uses traditional published textbook(s), what would be your likely decision?	%
I would enrol in the course that uses a traditionally published textbook	10
I would enrol in the course that uses a digital textbook	55
I would have no preference	35

5. CONCLUSION

In this paper, we have presented the approach that combines HC and OER and applied it in a postgraduate course at the Hong Kong Polytechnic University. We have distributed a questionnaire to capture the students' affection towards HC and OER. The data analysis helped us to understand the advantages, challenges and possible future studies.

Consistent with the previous studies, the students' overall attitude towards HC is positive (Bower et al., 2015; Lin, 2008; Zydney et al., 2019). Most of the students thought that HC enriches their learning experience by providing a variety of benefits, such as the utilisation of diverse methods and modes of delivery, more flexible, self-controlled, and self-paced learning. Particularly promising seems to be the positive experience from joining the co-located and distance learners, with providing potential advantages such as cross-cultural learning. Future larger-scale studies (employing rigorous methods of investigation) would need to be deployed to explore the particulars of the online interactions (e.g., differences in learning styles in different cultures) among the co-located and distance learners, to understand and facilitate their learning in HC in optimal ways. The role of domain, cultural or other types of diversity in cross-institutional hybrid classrooms and how it affects students' satisfaction, interest and engagement, performance, needs to be investigated.

Apart from the diverse benefits, enacting HC brings also diverse challenges that lie in the technological and pedagogical dimensions (Raes et al., 2019). The technological challenges stem from the audio and video disruptions. The pedagogical challenges emerge from the issues regarding the redesigning traditional lectures in a hybrid context, creating a continuum between the F2F and online learning and providing an inclusive and engaging experience for remote users by facilitating at the same time a connection between the F2F and the remote participants (Bower et al., 2017; Gomez et al., 2009).

Most of the students reported that their learning experience was enhanced with OER, and in general, provided positive attitudes to using OER in comparison to traditional textbooks and internet resources. The study on the benefits of OER in HC is, however, very limited in scope. Further studies are required which would investigate whether students` contributions in the learning assignments were generated by using OER as references and to which extent they contributed to students' comprehension of the subject topic.

Overall, consistent with the previous studies, our research shows that the experience of students is not undermined through teaching but is mainly influenced by the content and the quality of the teaching itself (Aly, 2013; Nortvig et al., 2018). However, the experience of the students' that join the online classroom from different physical locations might be different than in the traditional, F2F classroom (Raes et al., 2019; Szeto, 2014; Zydney et al., 2019). Consecutively, HC cannot be based on the adjusted curriculum of a traditional classroom but need to be designed from scratch, a recommendation that is widely accepted in the literature (e.g., Bowyer and Chambers, 2017). To facilitate HC optimally, a further investigation of different curriculum designs, practices and experiences becomes vital.

ACKNOWLEDGEMENT

The work covered in this paper is funded by a Teaching and Development Grant (Project code: GYF18-19/PT1/ISE01) by The Hong Kong Polytechnic University. Support by the university is gratefully acknowledged.

REFERENCES

Allen, I.E., Seaman, J., Garrett, R., 2007. Blending in: The Extent and Promise of Blended Education in the United States, Sloan Consortium (NJ1). Sloan Consortium.

Aly, I., 2013. Performance in an Online Introductory Course in a Hybrid Classroom Setting. Canadian Journal of Higher Education 43, 85–99.

Bersin, J., 2004. The blended learning book: Best practices, proven methodologies, and lessons learned. John Wiley & Sons.

Biddix, J.P., Chung, C.J., Park, H.W., 2015. The hybrid shift: Evidencing a student-driven restructuring of the college classroom. Computers & Education 80, 162–175. https://doi.org/10.1016/j.compedu.2014.08.016

Bliss, T., Robinson, T.J., Hilton, J., Wiley, D.A., 2013. An OER COUP: College Teacher and Student Perceptions of Open Educational Resources. JIME 2013, 4. https://doi.org/10.5334/2013-04

Bower, M., Dalgarno, B., Kennedy, G.E., Lee, M.J.W., Kenney, J., 2015. Design and implementation factors in blended synchronous learning environments: Outcomes from a cross-case analysis. Computers & Education 86, 1–17. https://doi.org/10.1016/j.compedu.2015.03.006

Bower, M., Lee, M.J.W., Dalgarno, B., 2017. Collaborative learning across physical and virtual worlds: Factors supporting and constraining learners in a blended reality environment. British Journal of Educational Technology 48, 407–430. https://doi.org/10.1111/bjet.12435

Bowyer, J., Chambers, L.C., 2017. Evaluating blended learning: Bringing the elements together. Cambridge Assessment, Research Matters.

Chiu, Y.-C.J., 2009. Facilitating Asian students' critical thinking in online discussions. British Journal of Educational Technology 40, 42–57. https://doi.org/10.1111/j.1467-8535.2008.00898.x

Corbin, J., Strauss, A., 1990. Grounded theory research: Procedures, canons and evaluative criteria. Zeitschrift für Soziologie 19, 418–427.

D'Antoni, S., 2009. Open Educational Resources: reviewing initiatives and issues. Open Learning: The Journal of Open, Distance and e-Learning 24, 3–10. https://doi.org/10.1080/02680510802625443

Dolch, C., Zawacki-Richter, O., 2018. Are students getting used to Learning Technology? Changing media usage patterns of traditional and non-traditional students in higher education. Research in Learning Technology 26. https://doi.org/10.25304/rlt.v26.2038

edX, 2020. Eric Tsui [WWW Document]. edX. URL https://www.edx.org/bio/eric-tsui (accessed 5.1.20).

Eurostat, 2015. Being young in Europe today - 2015 edition.

Gallardo-Echenique, E.E., de Oliveira, J.M., Marqués-Molias, L., Esteve-Mon, F., 2015. Digital Competence in the Knowledge Society 11, 17.

Germaine, R., Richards, J., Koeller, M., Schubert-Irastorza, C., 2016. Purposeful Use of 21st Century Skills in Higher Education. Journal of Research in Innovative Teaching 9.

Gomez, E.A., Dezhi Wu, Passerini, K., 2009. Traditional, Hybrid and Online Teamwork: Lessons from the Field. Communications of the Association for Information Systems 25, 395–411. https://doi.org/10.17705/1CAIS.02533

Helms, S.A., 2014. Blended/hybrid courses: a review of the literature and recommendations for instructional designers and educators. Interactive Learning Environments 22, 804–810. https://doi.org/10.1080/10494820.2012.745420

Hilton, J., 2016. Open educational resources and college textbook choices: a review of research on efficacy and perceptions. Education Tech Research Dev 64, 573–590. https://doi.org/10.1007/s11423-016-9434-9

Kemp, N., Grieve, R., 2014. Face-to-face or face-to-screen? Undergraduates' opinions and test performance in classroom vs online learning. Front Psychol 5. https://doi.org/10.3389/fpsyg.2014.01278

Kolb, S.M., 2012. Grounded theory and the constant comparative method: Valid research strategies for educators. Journal of emerging trends in educational research and policy studies 3, 83–86.

Ku, H.-Y., Lohr, L.L., 2003. A case study of Chinese student's attitudes toward their first online learning experience. ETR&D 51, 95–102. https://doi.org/10.1007/BF02504557

Lin, Q., 2008. Student Views of Hybrid Learning: A One-Year Exploratory Study. Journal of Computing in Teacher Education 10.

Loes, C., Pascarella, E., Umbach, P., 2012. Effects of Diversity Experiences on Critical Thinking Skills: Who Benefits? The Journal of Higher Education 83, 1–25.

McGee, P., Reis, A., 2012. Blended Course Design: A Synthesis of Best Practices. Journal of Asynchronous Learning Networks 16, 7–22.

McGreal, R., 2019. A Survey of OER Implementations in 13 Higher Education Institutions. The International Review of Research in Open and Distributed Learning 20, 141–145. https://doi.org/10.19173/irrodl.v20i5.4577

Milheim, K.L., 2014. Facilitation Across Cultures in the Online Classroom. International Journal of Learning, Teaching and Educational Research 5.

Muller, J., 2015. The future of knowledge and skills in science and technology higher education. High Educ 70, 409–416. https://doi.org/10.1007/s10734-014-9842-x

Nortvig, A.-M., Petersen, A.K., Balle, S.H., 2018. A Literature Review of the Factors Influencing E-Learning and Blended Learning in Relation to Learning Outcome, Student Satisfaction and Engagement. Electronic Journal of e-Learning 16, 46–55.

Picciano, A.G., 2009. Blending with Purpose: The Multimodal Model. Journal of Asynchronous Learning Networks 13, 7–18.

Pitt, R., 2015. Mainstreaming Open Textbooks: Educator Perspectives on the Impact of OpenStax College open textbooks. The International Review of Research in Open and Distributed Learning 16. https://doi.org/10.19173/irrodl.v16i4.2381

Raes, A., Detienne, L., Windey, I., Depaepe, F., 2019. A systematic literature review on synchronous hybrid learning: gaps identified. Learning Environ Res. https://doi.org/10.1007/s10984-019-09303-z

Siemens, G., 2008. Learning and knowing in networks: Changing roles for educators and designers. ITFORUM for Discussion 27, 1–26.

Smith, M., Seward, R., 2017. Openness as Social Praxis. First Monday 22. https://doi.org/10.5210/fm.v22i4.7073

Tsang, H.W.C., Tsui, E., 2017. Conceptual design and empirical study of a personal learning environment and network (PLE&N) to support peer-based social and lifelong learning. VINE Journal of Information and Knowledge Management Systems 47, 228–249. https://doi.org/10.1108/VJIKMS-03-2017-0010

UNESCO, 2002. Forum on the Impact of Open Courseware for Higher Education in Developing Countries, UNESCO, Paris, 1-3 July 2002: final report - UNESCO Digital Library [WWW Document]. URL https://unesdoc.unesco.org/ark:/48223/pf0000128515 (accessed 5.1.20).

Watson, C.E., Domizi, D.P., Clouser, S.A., 2017. Student and Faculty Perceptions of OpenStax in High Enrollment Courses. International Review of Research in Open and Distributed Learning 18, 287–304.

Westermann, E.B., 2014. A Half-Flipped Classroom or an Alternative Approach?: Primary Sources and Blended Learning. Educational Research Quarterly 38, 43–57.

Wiley, D., Bliss, T.J., McEwen, M., 2014. Open Educational Resources: A Review of the Literature, in: Spector, J.M., Merrill, M.D., Elen, J., Bishop, M.J. (Eds.), Handbook of Research on Educational Communications and Technology. Springer, New York, NY, pp. 781–789. https://doi.org/10.1007/978-1-4614-3185-5_63

Zhao, Y., Breslow, L., 2013. Literature Review on Hybrid/Blended Learning.

Zydney, J.M., McKimmy, P., Lindberg, R., Schmidt, M., 2019. Here or There Instruction: Lessons Learned in Implementing Innovative Approaches to Blended Synchronous Learning. TechTrends 63, 123–132. https://doi.org/10.1007/s11528-018-0344-z

RESPONDING TO COVID-19: RAPID ORGANISATIONAL CHANGE IN ONLINE CPD PRODUCTION A CASE REPORT

Dirk Pilat[1,2] and David Cameron[3,4]
Royal College of General Practitioners, London, UK
[1]Dr, FRCGP, PgDipGp (Otago), BSc (Open), MA ODE (Open)
[2]Medical Director for eLeaning and Accreditation
[3]Dr, MA (Oxon.), PhD
[4]Assistant Director, Professional Development

ABSTRACT

Over only a few weeks in March 2020 the COVID-19 pandemic changed health care delivery in the United Kingdom completely - not least in general practice, where over 1 million patients are already treated every day. To reduce viral spread, practices introduced remote doctor-led triage and face-to-face consultations where converted almost exclusively to telephone or video. Guidance on the management of this new, emerging disease changed frequently, so the UK's Royal College of General Practitioners (RCGP) took the strategic decision to direct a large part of the College's staff and resources to provide general practitioners (GPs) with online continuous professional development (CPD) resources around COVID-19 and the new ways of working. In this case report we describe how the RCGP's online learning team responded to the critical imperatives of the pandemic both within project management and educational practice and created a COVID-19 resource hub, covering all aspects of general practice during the pandemic.

KEYWORDS

Continuous Professional Development, e-Learning, COVID-19, Organisational Change, General Practice

1. INTRODUCTION

In December 2019 the city of Wuhan, capital of Hubei province in China, became the centre of an outbreak of pneumonia of unknown origin, with most of the initial patients working or living around the local Huanan seafood wholesale market. In the early stages of this pneumonia, severe acute respiratory infection symptoms occurred, with some patients rapidly developing acute respiratory distress syndrome (ARDS), acute respiratory failure and subsequent death. Named "Novel Coronavirus Disease 2019" (COVID-19) by the World Health Organization (WHO), the disease was identified to be caused by the severe acute respiratory syndrome coronavirus 2 (SARS-CoV-2) (Fei Zhou, 2020). Even though the Chinese central government introduced a quarantine of previously unheard severity and scaled up inpatient heath care in Hubei province, SARS-CoV-2 nevertheless spread rapidly across the world, with the first confirmed cases in the UK identified late January 2020 (Moss, Barlow, Easom, Lillie, & Samson, 2020).

During the first week of March the outbreak had spread across the United Kingdom, with 200 confirmed cases and one fatality. The Royal College of General Practitioners (RCGP), the professional body for family doctors in the UK, recognised there was an immediate need for support and guidance for its members who were facing an unprecedented challenge. A strategic decision was taken to focus a large part of the College's staff and resources onto providing this support and guidance, with immediate effect. This included summaries of guidance released by national governments across the UK and related agencies; policy positions developed to support the profession, for example on the issues of Personal Protective Equipment (PPE) and testing; a newly-created discussion forum to allow members of the College to ask and respond to queries and initiate dialogue with the College leadership; and an online repository, or Hub, of resources and learning materials to support GPs' (and other primary care professionals') professional practice in managing all aspects of the COVID-19 pandemic. The development of the 'Resource Hub' is the subject of this paper.

A small team of professional staff and clinicians was drawn together with a remit to create the first iteration of the Resource Hub within a few days. This required the development of new processes for resource development and quality assurance, the secondment of clinical expertise from across and beyond the College, as well as staff working in different ways (e.g. event managers shifting to webinar development).

The fast-changing nature of the knowledge base for COVID-19 required a significantly accelerated review and update process for any new resources that were published – in some cases, updates were required on a daily basis as rapid reviews were published by research institutions. This case report aims to outline how the RCGP adapted to and addressed the challenge of providing essential COVID-19 continuing professional development (CPD) resources for the United Kingdom's primary care sector during a critical period of professional challenge and uncertainty.

2. THE ROLE OF ONLINE CPD IN UK GENERAL PRACTICE

Patients and the wider public rightly expect the highest degree of professionalism from their physicians. The concept of professionalism encompasses a range of characteristics, including ethics, values, attitudes, judgement, knowledge, skills and 'meta-skills' (Morrow, 2014). The notion of the professional, and professional practice, relies on the ongoing maintenance of domain-specific knowledge and skills; continuing professional development (CPD) is therefore an intrinsic aspect of professionalism, best considered as a 'state of mind' or 'intellectual alignment' rather than a series of discrete events or resources (Cameron & Grant, 2017). Thus, society and the profession itself demand that family doctors not only fulfil the traditional roles of healer and source of comfort, but also operate on the basis of the latest scientific expertise and maintain the highest standards in education, training and practice. The complexity of modern medicine makes this demand ever more difficult to fulfil for the practising doctor, who has to balance his workday between patient contact, administrative tasks and CPD. Whilst newly qualified doctors are certified as safe to practice, the sheer volume of domain knowledge in medicine, and the pace of its development and revision (Densen, 2011), ensure that CPD is a career-long endeavour which is vital for patient safety. This requires both responding to educational needs that arise during patient contact, and being continuously up to date with the ever-shifting evidence base for effective diagnostic and therapeutic methods (General Medical Council (UK), 2012). Family doctors, or general practitioners (GPs), face a particular challenge in their specialism which requires a very broad range of knowledge across many areas of medicine, as exemplified by the GP Curriculum (RCGP, 2020).

A recent survey showed that GPs are using online resources for CPD often and that these are well accepted, valued and likely driven by the need to meet users' identified learning needs and the positive influence of GP appraisal and revalidation (Cunningham, Alexander, Luty, & Zlotos, 2019). However, attitudinal differences to online CPD resource utilisation between different GP groups and technical barriers are still present: frequent internet users and doctors under 45 were shown to more comfortable using online resources and finding the experience more enjoyable and cost-effective, compared to low volume users (MacWalter, McKay, & Bowie, 2016).

The rapid emergence of a global pandemic caused by a novel coronavirus brought into sharp focus the need for GPs to develop and maintain their professional knowledge and skills. Working on the frontline of the national (and global) collective effort against COVID-19, GPs needed to be able to access, assimilate and put into practice a wide range of new information and guidance, which was emerging and changing on a daily basis. This included clinical knowledge related to the presentation, epidemiology and treatment of the disease, but also the necessary changes to traditional ways of working that were required, including patient consultation, practice management and end of life care.

Fortunately, online and e-learning CPD resources can contribute to the rapid upskilling of a professional workforce. E-learning offers a wide variety of formats to encompass a range of learning modes and provides the opportunity for dual coding; this variety also improves the accessibility of learning episodes which can be consumed at convenient times and settings (e.g. short audio podcasts) (VanNieuvenborg, Goossens, De Lepeleire, & Schoenmakers, 2016). E-learning is therefore particularly suitable to meet the professional learning needs of GPs in the context of an emerging healthcare crisis; as learners, they are self-directed and highly motivated to learn, whilst also extremely time-poor and in need of immediate, relevant and results-oriented knowledge and skills.

3. THE RCGP'S ONLINE CPD PROVISION

The Royal College of General Practitioners was founded in 1952 as an academic body to support good standards of practice, education and research. It represents and supports general practitioners (GPs) on licensing, education, training, research and clinical standards. It sets the curriculum and training needs for GP trainees, holds the mandatory qualification exams and runs a CPD scheme for its 57,000 members (Royal College of General Practitioners, 2012). As part of its commitment to CPD it has been running e-learning programmes since 2008, with various methods of content development, quality assurance and delivery.

3.1 Essential Knowledge Updates (EKU)

The Essential Knowledge Updates (EKU) programme was initiated in 2008 to provide GPs with a quick and accessible way to update their knowledge on new evidence relevant to primary care, to encourage effective application of that knowledge in clinical practice, and to enhance their skills and ultimately patients' experience and care. EKU e-learning modules are released on a quarterly basis and are authored by practising GPs under the supervision of an EKU Fellow with experience in effective online learning development. The topics for each individual update are chosen from a literature search on primary care journals and resources by one of the RCGP's information scientists and is reduced by the lead GP for the programme from ca 300 papers and guidelines covering the last six months to about fifty, only choosing papers that are applicable for front-line general practice. These are then voted upon by a panel of senior academic general practitioners. Each new Update undergoes a five-step quality assurance process, including literature reviews and topic refinement on the basis of frontline relevancy and content revision by a group of senior academic GPs. EKU modules are accessed by about 38,000 GPs per year. (Pilat, Content development for 72,000 Learners: an online learning environment for general practitioners; a case study, 2016).

3.2 Online Learning Environment

The Online Learning Environment (OLE) is a collection of distance and blended CPD courses. Delivered via the whole palette of e-learning including screencasts, podcasts, blogs and modules, it produces content written by GPs for GPs, mapped against the GP curriculum. Responding to the needs of the GP workforce, it produces e-learning based on areas identified by both the learners and current academic literature in which primary care is struggling, such as early cancer diagnosis. The use of a combination of different media elements that cater to the various learning preferences reinforces the take home messages, promotes reflection, identifies knowledge gaps and helps to demonstrate learning. Working in close cooperation with its partners in academia, public health, non-governmental and commercial organisations it has found acclaim both from its learners and external organisations such as the National Institute for Health and Care Excellence (NICE) and has won two national eLearning awards.

With currently over 120,000 registered learners, its content is consistently rated highly by its users. (Royal College of General Practitioners eLearning Department, 2017). The success of the OLE is closely associated with its content development model which guarantees content accuracy and appropriateness for its audience: each course follows a six step quality assurance workflow, starting with a scoping call or meeting of a peer review group , in which interested general practitioners, hospital specialists, a GP author and a GP editor decide on the content and produce a scoping document. After the scoping document is signed off by the peer review group, a GP author in cooperation with an eLearning fellow produces a first draft which is forwarded to the group for the first round of comments. After incorporation of comments and suggestions, the course production moves on to reflect the instructional design, after which it undergoes a second round of peer reviews. The course is then adapted to incorporate additional comments from the peer review group, thereafter the course is built before it is quality assured by the medical director for eLearning and launched (Royal College of General Practitioners eLearning Department, 2017). While tried and tested over ten years, this model unfortunately was not responsive enough for the challenge that COVID-19 presents, as the involvement of external stakeholders often leads to prolonged periods of discussion around the content during peer review, resulting in typical turnaround time of four months from inception to release.

4. ONLINE CPD IN RESPONSE TO THE COVID-19 PANDEMIC

The COVID-19 pandemic emerged at a moment when general practice in the UK is facing a number of structural and demographic challenges, including increased demand due to an ageing patient load with an ever increasing range of comorbidities (Pilat, Access and the great socioeconomic divide, 2015). As an urgent and spreading threat whose clinical and epidemiological characteristics are still being documented, upskilling the primary care workforce to address the challenge of COVID-19 was urgently needed. In addition, public health measures imposed by the UK Government, including social distancing, isolation and shielding, required an immediate shift in ways of working, with in-person consultation almost entirely replaced by remote (phone or video) consultation in a very short timeframe. Clinicians were thus faced with a new disease and a new way of interacting with patients (Greenhalgh, Covid-19: a remote assessment in primary care, 2020). It was therefore necessary to create online resources to not only to keep members of the primary care team informed about the rapidly changing evidence base but also introduce them to best practice in new ways of working. An example for how the evidence base evolved was the use of the Roth Score in suspected COVID-19 presentations: initially, it was thought to be a helpful tool to assess patients with breathlessness remotely during a phone consultation. Guidance on its use was rapidly reproduced and circulated on social media, professional distribution lists and through both local and national guidelines. A review just a few days later established that it was not sufficiently accurate for GPs to use in patients with suspected COVID-19, so existing online guidance needed to be rewritten to avoid patient harm (Greenhalgh, Question: Should the Roth score be used in the remote assessment of patients with possible COVID-19?, 2020).

As part of the RCGP's response to the COVID-19 pandemic, in early March the College set up a COVID-19 Resource Hub, with the intention of hosting both RCGP-generated content and external guidance. Making use of an existing Moodle 3.5 platform, the web development team was able to publish the first iteration of the Hub within a few days and subsequently respond rapidly to requests for edits or the addition of new material, usually within a matter of hours. Moodle's flexibility as a content delivery platform allowed the production of a variety of learning activities: SCORM packages, screencasts, podcasts and a variety of webinars were all used to cover the emerging knowledge. With increasing content and increased usage by health care professionals, the Moodle team was able to adapt the site daily and respond to the needs of both learner and the content developers, resulting in various design iterations of the Resource Hub over 12 weeks (see Figure 1).

Figure 1. Screenshot of COVID-19 resource hub as of 22/06/2020

Due to the novel nature of the COVID-19 threat, new guidance for GPs had to be produced on an unprecedented scale. This required cross-sector cooperation with other Royal Colleges and professional organisations, with initial contacts quickly generating a large volume of new guidance and content for potential publication. It quickly became apparent that the existing model of content production and quality assurance was not responsive or prolific enough to keep up with the requirements of this project, so the Resource Hub team drew in staff and clinicians from other departments across the College. In addition, clinical expertise was requested (and quickly offered) from external organisations including universities, public health agencies and research institutions. This allowed new guidance to be highlighted very rapidly and new content developed on the basis of this guidance and new evidence, as it emerged. In addition, the College's existing clinical networks allowed resources relating to specialist areas to be developed, including managing COVID-19 in secure environments, palliative care, respiratory medicine and diabetes.

The pace of delivery and the volume of work meant that the quality assurance process for the development of new materials needed to be extremely streamlined and efficient, whilst maintaining high standards of output. In addition, there was a need to ensure that any new CPD resources published under the aegis of the RCGP was aligned with the policy position of the College. A small leadership group was set up with oversight of both clinical and policy aspects of the College's COVID-19 response. This group met frequently (initially three times per week) to review proposals for new resources and check the alignment of newly-created resources prior to publication. Between these stages, the e-learning and webinar development team managed a compressed quality assurance process that produced new content within days instead of months. The previous six step quality assurance was reduced to three steps with a significant reduction in turnaround time of new content: authors were supported by experienced e-learning fellows in the development of new materials and draft resources were checked by the College's medical director for e-learning. Within two months, the newly-formed team created sixty new individual eLearning items and vetted and hosted seventy external resources, spread over 9 different subgroups. Usage of the OLE increased significantly: compared to the previous 3 months there was an increase of 170% of individual visitors to the website.

This demonstrates the importance of operational agility in response of a crisis such as the COVID-19 pandemic: department heads were able to quickly change workflows in short iterations with constant feedback from the assigned project teams. As the OLE's content management system was not outsourced or subject to a service-level agreement, the Moodle administration team was able to respond immediately to requests for changes from their clinical colleagues. Administrators worked continuously on breaking down silos, fostering collaboration across teams and made sure the relationship to external stakeholders was kept close. As a consequence of the pandemic, work in a number of areas of the College had been paused, particularly those relating to face-to-face events or clinical topics that were now a lower priority for GPs. This allowed staff to be temporarily seconded to the College's COVID-19 response, with clear areas of responsibility. Small, focused groups were established which met virtually on a frequent basis; this allowed intelligence and guidance to cascade from the College's leadership, through senior managers to the project delivery teams, and reports on progress to pass back to the leadership. The project manager for the OLE released a daily, up to date list of content that was in production which gave all stakeholders an overview over the current state of the Resource Hub and development pipeline, from the College president to project officers and administrators. Since the inception of the RCGP's COVID-19 response in early March 2020 a high level of review, reflection and iteration went into the Resource Hub project across all hierarchical levels. As the timeline of the pandemic and the College's response proceeded, processes were adapted and shifted to address both the changing circumstances and lessons learned. Teams evolved, with new individuals brought in and others released as necessary. Quality assurance and approval processes were tweaked to avoid development bottlenecks or overloading specific individuals. The focus of support shifted; for example, in early March resources relating to good practice in remote consultation were a priority, whereas by late May there was a growing need for CPD related to the respiratory management of recovering COVID-19 patients.

5. DISCUSSION

This case demonstrates how an environmental trigger can create rapid organisational change, both through adapting formal staffing structures and informally through negotiated changes in staff roles. These changes were not limited to organisational aspects: andragogical and educational practice had to adapt as well, with some paradigms needing re-evaluation. A key feature of this case, which is likely to have been experienced by other organisations, is how the critical imperatives of the pandemic forced very rapid adjustments in modes of project delivery and management. Nevertheless, there was a clear and shared vision at all levels of the organisation; an appreciation of the need to deliver results to meet the challenge; small, agile teams were drawn together whose individuals were selected for their talent, self-motivation and good will; the project was managed with rigid control systems replaced by looser, super-productive processes.

This mirrors the fundamental changes in practice that GPs were facing, which the RCGP was attempting to support. Traditionally, attempts to effect organisational change would face significant inertia and perhaps resistance; in March/April 2020 there was a universal recognition across the College for the need to work differently. Warren Buffet spoke of the "institutional imperative" as an often-unrecognised force which can resist radical learning and change to existing structures and systems (Buffet, 1989). The urgent need to provide resources and guidance for frontline GPs – within a matter of days – overrode this imperative in the case of the RCGP. The confluence of circumstances meant that the RCGP saw, almost without explicit intention, the emergence of the key principles behind what Alan Kay has described as the 'power of context' which drove the success of the Xerox PARC programme of the 1970s (Kay, 2004) and which for the RCGP created a new resource that accompanies all members of the primary care team as a reliable source of CPD through the next stages of the pandemic.

ACKNOWLEDGEMENTS

Many thanks to Damian Bardiger and Sabeen Altaf for their suggestions for this paper.

REFERENCES

Abbasi, K. (2020, May 1). The many uncertainties of COVID-19. Journal of the Royal Society of Medicine, 113(5), 167.

Ahmed, W., Vidal-Alaball, J., Downing, J., & Lopez Segui, F. (2020, April 18). Dangerous Messages or Satire? Analysing the Conspiracy TheoryLinking 5G to COVID-19 through Social Network Analysis. Retrieved from Journal of Medical Internet Research: preprints.jmir.org/preprint/19458

Buffet, W. (1989). Letter to the shareholders of Berkshire Hathaway Inc. Retrieved from https://www.berkshirehathaway.com/letters/1989.html

Cameron, D., & Grant, A. (2017). The role of mentoring in early career physics teachers' professional identity construction. International Journal of Mentoring and Coaching in Education, 128-142.

Cunningham, D., Alexander, A., Luty, S., & Zlotos, L. (2019, May 8). CPD preferences and activities of general practitioners, registered pharmacy staff and general practice nurses in NHS Scotland – a questionnaire survey. Education for primary care, 30(4), 220-229.

Densen, P. (2011). Challenges and opportunities facing medical education. Transactions of the American Clinical and Climatological Association,, 122, 48-58.

Fei Zhou, T. Y. (2020, March 9). Clinical course and risk factors for mortality of adult inpatients with COVID-19 in Wuhan, China: a retrospective cohort study. The Lancet.

General Medical Council (UK). (2012, June). Continuing professional development. Retrieved from General Medical Council: https://www.gmc-uk.org/-/media/documents/cpd-guidance-for-all-doctors-0316_pdf-56438625.pdf

Glaveanu, V. P. (2017). Editorial Psychology in the Post-Truth Era. Europe's Journal of Psychology, 13(3), 375-377.

Greenhalgh, T. (2020, March 20). Covid-19: a remote assessment in primary care. British Medical Journal, 368.

Greenhalgh, T. (2020). Question: Should the Roth score be used in the remote assessment of patients with possible COVID-19? Oxford: Oxford COVID-19 Evidence Service Team, Nuffield Department of Primary Care Health Sciences, University of Oxford.

Kay, A. (2004). The Power of Context: remarks upon receipt of the Draper Award, National Academy of Engineering, 24 Feb 2004. Retrieved from http://www.vpri.org/pdf/m2004001_power.pdf

MacWalter, G., McKay, J., & Bowie, P. (2016). Utilisation of internet resources for continuing professional development: a cross-sectional survey of general practitioners in Scotland. BMC Medical Education, 16(24).

Morrow, G. e. (2014). Professionalism in healthcare professionals. HCPC.

Moss, P., Barlow, G., Easom, N., Lillie, P., & Samson, A. (2020, February 27). Lessons for managing high-consequence infections from first COVID-19 cases in the UK. The Lancet, e46.

Pilat, D. (2015). Access and the great socioeconomic divide. In R. Charlton, Compassion, Continuity and Caring in the NHS (pp. 15-20). London: RCGP.

Pilat, D. (2016). Content development for 72,000 Learners: an online learning environment for general practitioners; a case study. Proceedings of the international conference e-learning 2017 (pp. 28-34). Lisbon: IADIS.

RCGP. (2020, May). GP Curriculum: an overview. Retrieved from RCGP: https://www.rcgp.org.uk/training-exams/training/gp-curriculum-overview.aspx

Royal College of General Practitioners. (2012, March). History of the College. Retrieved May 2020, from Royal College of General Practitioners: https://www.rcgp.org.uk/about-us/the-college/who-we-are/history-heritage-and-archive/history-of-the-college.aspx

Royal College of General Practitioners eLearning Department. (2017). Learning Technologies Award; Best learning technologies project public & non profit sector; Submission. London: RCGP.

VanNieuvenborg, L., Goossens, M., De Lepeleire, J., & Schoenmakers, B. (2016, April). Continuing medical education for general practitioners: a practice format. Postgraduate Medical Journal, 92(1086), 217-222.

THE STUDENTS PERSPECTIVE ON USING AN E-LEARNING PLATFORM: E-OWL

Isabel Araújo[1,2] and Pedro Miguel Faria[1]
[1]*Instituto Politécnico de Viana do Castelo, Viana do Castelo, Portugal*
[2]*Centre for Studies in Education and Innovation (CI&DEI), Instituto Politécnico de Viseu, Portugal*

ABSTRACT

The evolution of ICT and its adoption in higher education is driving greater interactivity in teaching and learning processes. The teaching/learning paradigm has been changing. Both educational actors, teacher and student, are increasingly adapting to use technologies. This article presents a study that enhances how technologies can be used in the teaching and learning process, through a mathematics content platform, for higher education students. A survey of the state of the art was made in order to demonstrate some advantages of the teaching-learning process, the teacher's and student's behavior' profiles and their role in relation to the use of new technologies. The main objective of this study is to analyze the student's view on the use of the E-OWL platform in the learning process, and thus contribute to the development of more interactive and motivating learning environments. The privileged instrument in this study was the questionnaire, applied after the use of the platform in an educational context, to students of the Computer Graphics and Multimedia Engineering degree. The results obtained revealed that students demonstrate ease in using the E-OWL platform and that was useful in supporting the course, stimulating continuous study and allowing self-regulation of learning, confirming the relevance of an increasing adoption of ICT in an e-learning context.

KEYWORDS

E-learning, ICT, LMS, Virtual Learning Environments, Higher Education, Engineering Teaching

1. INTRODUCTION

Developments in technology allow a faster access to a greater number of people, which drives changes in a number of areas, including the higher education concerning its educational context. The use of information and communication technologies (ICT) in the educational context is a reality in higher education, boosting interactivity in the learning process (Daniela, Strods, & Daiga, 2019; Kirkwood & Price, 2014). However, the teaching-learning process in higher education Institutions sometimes cannot keep pace with technological changes. The current students, born of the digital generation, have a greater ability with the new technologies, while part of the teachers still reluctant to use ICTs (Lobo & Maia, 2015). According to Moran (2007) technologies are important in an educational context, but they don't solve the fundamental issues because "if teaching only depended on technologies, we would have found the best solutions a long time ago" (Moran, 2007:12). In this sense, several studies have been carried out (Nortvig, Petersen & Balle, 2018) highlighting the relevance of using ICTs, both at the students' level (Paechter, Maier & Macher, 2010; Al-Rahmi et al 2018) and at the teachers' level (Al-Samarraie, 2018). According to Ricoy and Couto (2014) the use of good pedagogical practices through the use of ICT is an innovative situation, related to the integration of strategies involving dynamism and interactivity that allow significant learning with high educational value. Moreover, it enhances good academic results when associated with the satisfaction of students and teachers.

This article presents how technologies can be used in the teaching learning process, through the usage of a Web platform with mathematical content, focused in higher education students. The objective of this article is to describe a first study on using the E-OWL platform in an educational context, highlighting the student's point of view on using it in their learning processes. The article is organized in six sections starting by the introduction, followed by a context of using technologies in the teaching-learning process in higher education, then a brief introduction the -E-OWL platform is made, the method used in this study is described and a section focused in the analysis of results is detailed before the conclusions.

2. ICT IN HIGHER EDUCATION IN AN EDUCATIONAL CONTEXT

The influence of ICT in education has contributed to the evolution of conventional classes, essentially based on the expositive method, which are being overcome. The teacher, who holds the knowledge and the student who is the receiver, i.e. the concept of the teacher transmitting the knowledge and the student memorizing it to carry out the assessment tests is evolving to a context in which the teacher acts as a supervisor, i.e. being a knowledge facilitator and the student constructs his own knowledge, in a more active and critical way. It should be noted that conventional teaching methods do not appeal to students.

In order to arouse interest and attention it is necessary to be attentive to their daily lives and, furthermore, integrated with technological changes (Antunes, 2010). The expansion of professional performance, mainly the HEI teachers, is related to a continuous pedagogical improvement, carrying out a reflection on their theoretical and practical knowledge, observing difficulties and needs for the qualification of teaching, seeking a teaching that is more participatory, meaningful and innovative (Carabetta Júnior, 2010). However, the use of the Internet, or the computer, for example, is no guarantee that a student will build knowledge. It is up to the teacher to know how to explore the educational potential offered by these resources and to create situations so that the student can mean and understand the information obtained, generating new knowledge Valente (2002, 2003).

Information and communication technologies (ICTs) present new possibilities for the individual to experience creative processes, establishing unexpected approximations and associations, bringing together previously disconnected meanings and expanding the capacity of interlocution through the different languages that such resources provide (Martinsi, 2008). In this sense, seeking new methodological strategies, involving ICT, which are part of students' daily lives, from a very early age, is essential for professionals in the educational field. Thus, it is fundamental to know the methodological possibilities that technologies bring to work the content, through creative activities, a process of conscious and reflective development, using pedagogically the technological resources, with a perspective of transforming school learning (Pereira & Freitas, 2010).

The use of technology alone does not represent pedagogical change, if it is used only as technological support to illustrate the classes. What becomes necessary is that it be used as a learning mediation so that there is an improvement in the teaching learning process. The simple access to technology itself is not the most important aspect, but the creation of new learning environments and new social dynamics from the use of these new tools (Moraes & Varela, 2007). For Moran (2007) technologies have not replaced teachers but will enable various tasks and functions of teachers to be transformed. Freire and Shor (1986) state that the task of passing information can be left to databases, books, videos or programs (...) In this way, it is possible for the teacher to become a stimulator of student learning, arousing in them the curiosity to know, to research, and to seek the most relevant information.

Thus, the new higher education teacher, facing ICTs, must have content knowledge, teaching methodology, know how to deal with emotions, be committed to the production of knowledge through research and extension and, above all, break the paradigms of conservative ways of teaching, learning, researching and evaluating with technological innovations (Bertoncello, 2010).

3. THE E-OWL PLATFORM

Several online platforms to support higher education have been developed in the last two decades, namely in the area of Mathematics, such as Imathematics, MathYou, GCSE Maths, PMate, M@t-Educate-with-success, among others.

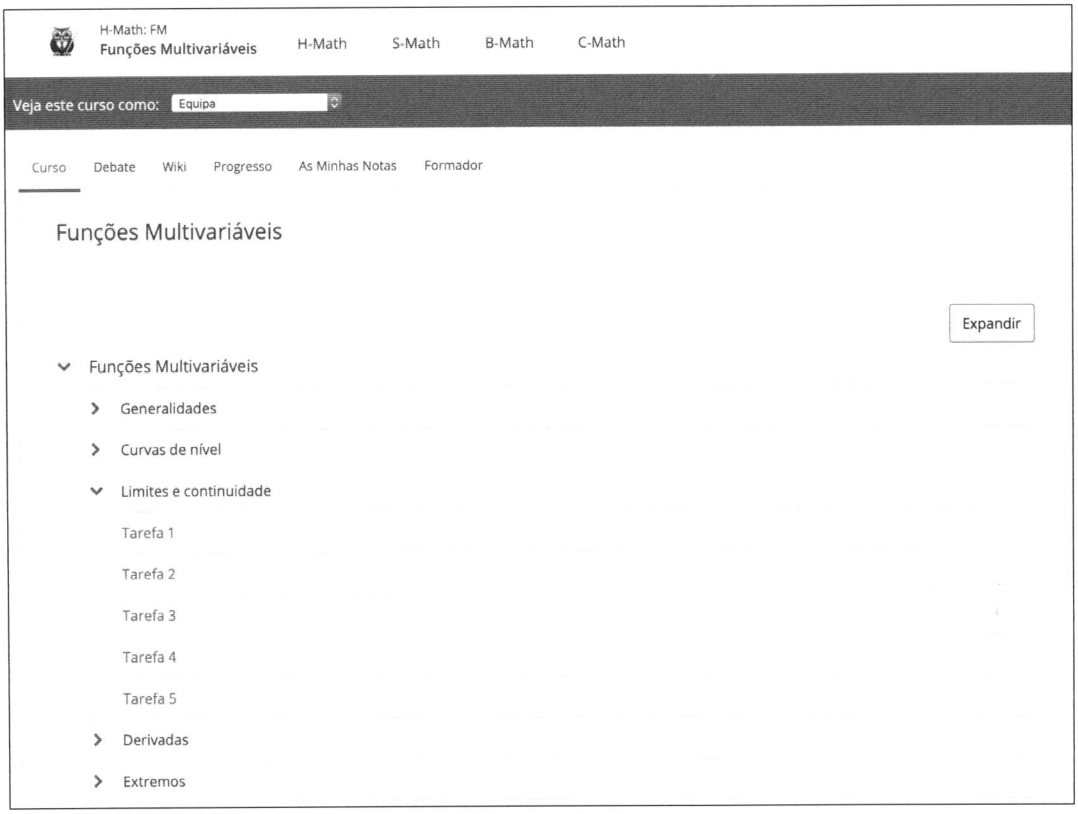

Figure 1. The E-OWL platform interface

More recently, this year, a new platform was developed supported on the Open Edx LMS and named: E-OWL. This platform provides a set of "chapters" that correspond to the themes of a mathematical course. Each chapter is organized with a set of tasks that the student must perform. All tasks give feedback to the student, regardless of whether the answer is correct or not. If it is correct, a positive feedback is given with the resolution, in order the student may verify its resolution. If the answer is not correct the feedback alerts the student that the answer is wrong, as well as indicates suggestions for resolution. Additionally, some tasks present hints that are considered relevant for the execution of them. One of the things to note is that the tasks are arranged in such a way that the theoretical contents appear throughout their completion.

4. METHOD

In order to evaluate the platform in an educational context it was used with students enrolled in the 1st year of the Computer Graphics and Multimedia Engineering degree of a higher education institution in the North of Portugal, in the Mathematics course. Students were asked to use the E-OWL platform, in particular, to perform tasks available on it, either in the classroom or in extra-class periods. Moreover, due to the pandemic period related with Covid-19 virus, half of the classes were face-to-face, and the rest were carried out virtually, using the Zoom and Moodle platforms. Subsequently, after the end of the 1st chapter, students were asked to answer a questionnaire about the E-OWL platform, in order to get opinions from the students about the platform they used. The questionnaire consisted of 5 sections. The first section characterising the respondents (age, gender, among others). The following three sections, concerning the characterisation of the E-OWL platform, its classification in an educational context and the use of the platform in teaching/learning processes, were made up of multiple questions using Likert scales. Finally, the last section consisted of an open question, asking students to indicate some advantages and possible disadvantages of using the platform.

5. PRESENTATION AND DATA ANALYSIS

A questionnaire was applied to 35 students aged between 18 (17.1%) and 30 (2.9%), of which 75% are up to 23 years old. Also, 80% of the respondents were male and 45.7% had already attended this course (Figure 2).

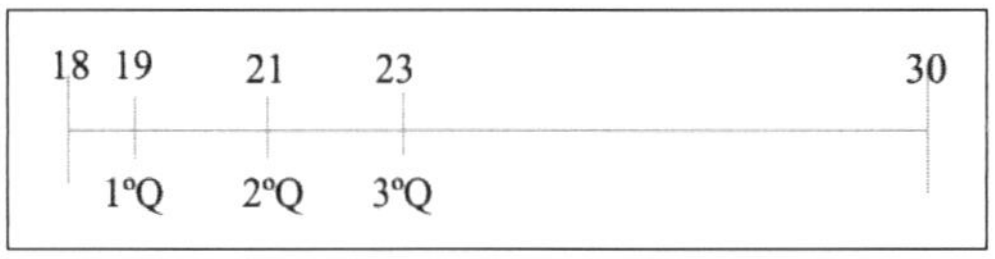

Figure 2. Age of respondents to the questionnaire

Moreover, 34% had already used online learning platforms, in addition to Moodle (the institutional platform) as one of the following: Virtual School, BitDegree, M@t-Educate-with-success and Udemy. Regarding the E-OWL platform, 51.4% of the respondents indicated that they accessed up to 2 hours a week and between 2 and 4 hours 48.6%, and before the pandemic, which forced social isolation and confinement at home, 71% accessed the E-OWL platform only at school.

The remaining (29%) accessed from the school and the place where they lived at home or in an academic residence. Concerning the difficulty in accessing the E-OWL platform in the process of registering/creating an account and starting to use it, on a scale of 1 (very difficult) to 6 (very easy) 86% rated between 4 and 6 (Figure 3).

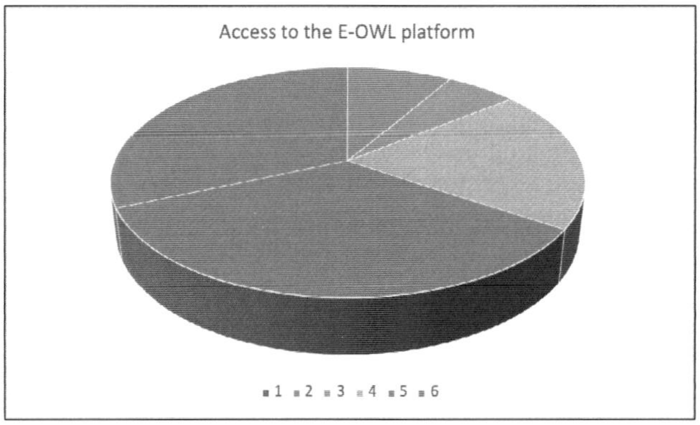

Figure 3. Access quality to the E-OWL platform

Considering the access speed to the platform, on a scale from 1 (very slow) to 6 (very fast), 88% of the respondents rated it between 4 and 6 (Figure 4).

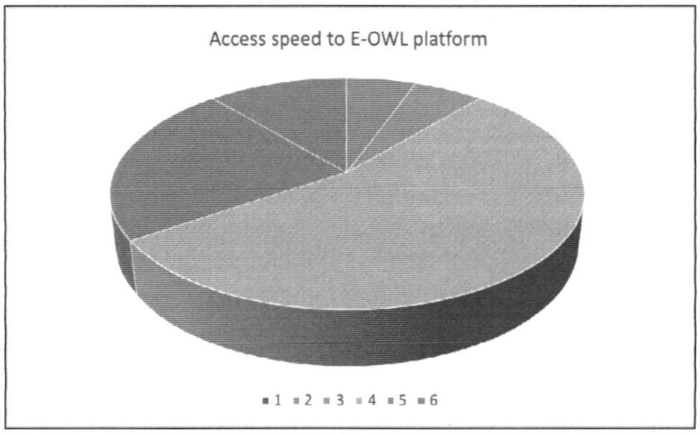

Figure 4. Access speed to E-OWL platform

As shown in Figure 5, the vast majority of students (more than 90%) classified the E-OWL platform as reasonable or Good/ Very Good ease of use, accessibility to information, usefulness in supporting autonomous study, usefulness in supporting the course in general, amount of information provided, simple and intuitive organisation, as well as understanding and functioning. It should be noted that more than 40% considered Good/Very Good the user-friendliness, usefulness in supporting the autonomous study, usefulness in supporting the course in general, amount of information provided, simple and intuitive organization, as well as understanding and functionality. However, 20%, 17% and 14%, respectively, indicated a mediocre diversity of functionalities, usefulness in supporting the updating of relevant information and clarity of language. However, 20%, 23% and 29%, respectively, indicated from Good/Very Good the diversity of functionalities, utility in supporting the updating of relevant information and clarity of language.

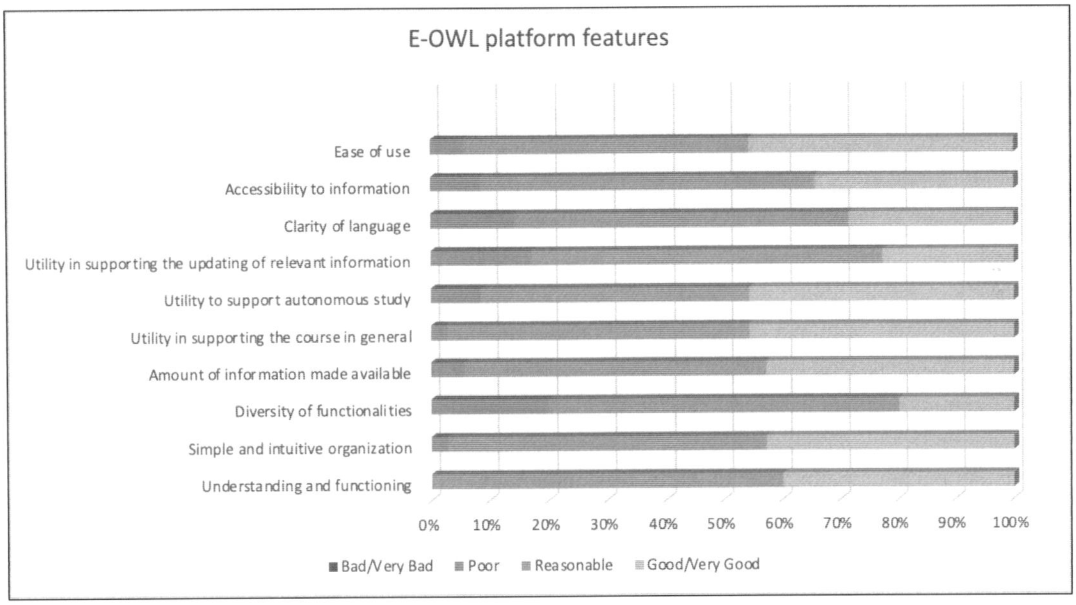

Figure 5. Characterization of some features of the E-OWL platform

Analysing Figure 6, it is observable that almost all students (between 97% and 100%) rated as Agree or Strongly Agree this platform allows access to information anytime and anywhere as long as access to the Internet be available, the tasks proposed in the E-OWL platform are relevant, the feedback given to the option indicated helps in understanding the issues involved and the possibility to navigate between "theory" and "practice" is an added value for learning. It is observable that 26% and 60% of students, respectively, rated as Strongly Agree and Agree that using the platform has helped to understand the contents. In accordance with the previous classification, (1) 91% rated as Strongly Agree or Agree with the use of this platform it is possible to better follow the subject in study, as well as indicated as Strongly Agree or Agree (2) 74% and 89%, respectively, this platform stimulates continuous study and allows self-regulation of learning. Regarding the statements "The contents of the E-OWL platform are well structured" and "The language of the contents of the E-OWL platform is perceptible and clear" 94% and 89% indicated Strongly Agree and Agree, respectively. Also, 20% of respondents Disagree that this platform respects the learning pace of each. However, 54% and 26% indicated Agree and Strongly Agree, respectively. It should be noted that 80% Disagree or Strongly Disagree that this platform does not facilitate autonomous study. Only 17% Agreed and 3% Strongly Agree. Regarding the statement this platform does not oblige to study more, 69% Disagree or Strongly Disagree, verifying that 26% and 6% Strongly Agree and Agree, respectively. Concerning the tasks presented on E-OWL platform not being enough, 60% Strongly Disagree, despite 9% Strongly Agree.

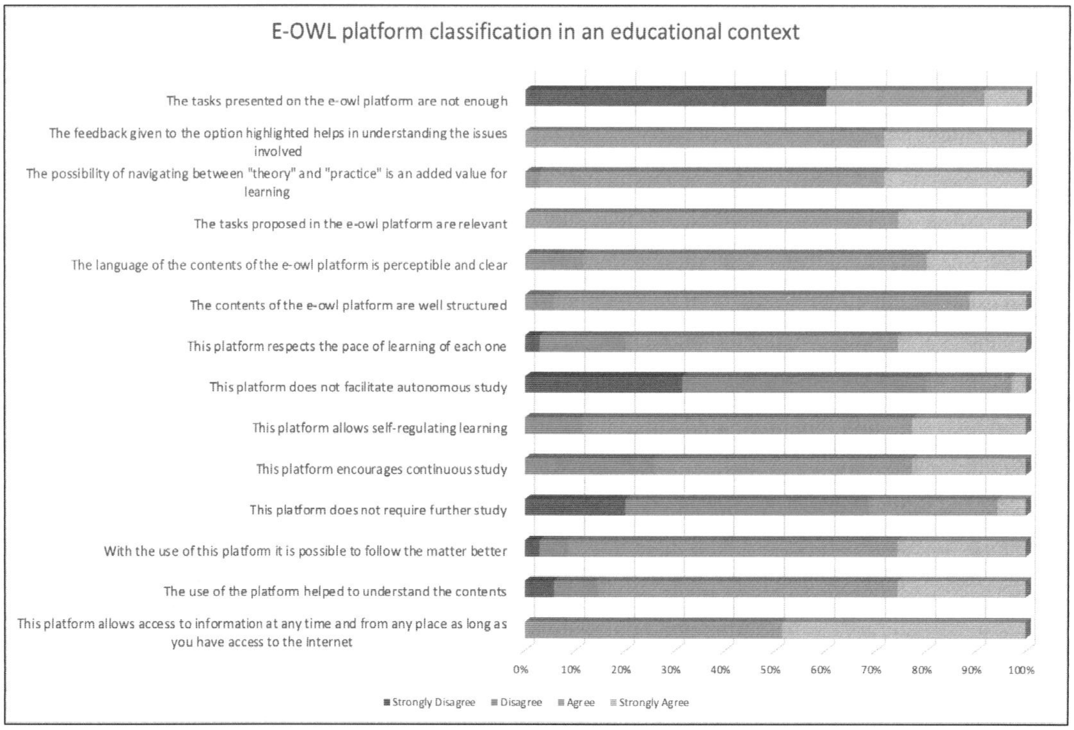

Figure 6. E-OWL platform classification in an educational context

Almost all (94%) of the surveyed students indicated Agree or Strongly Agree so that the exploration of the tasks proposed in the E-OWL platform facilitates the monitoring of classes and the use of the platform allows the development of mathematical aptitudes. The statement of greatest disagreement (23%) was the learning methodology supported in the use of the E-OWL platform promotes autonomous learning, although also 23% Strongly Agree. Considering the statement "The methodology adopted based on the use of the E-OWL platform facilitates the transfer of acquired knowledge to other tasks (exercises, problems)", 71% Agree and 17% Strongly Agree. Summarizing, the students considered that the E-OWL platform supported them in their study and facilitated the construction of knowledge.

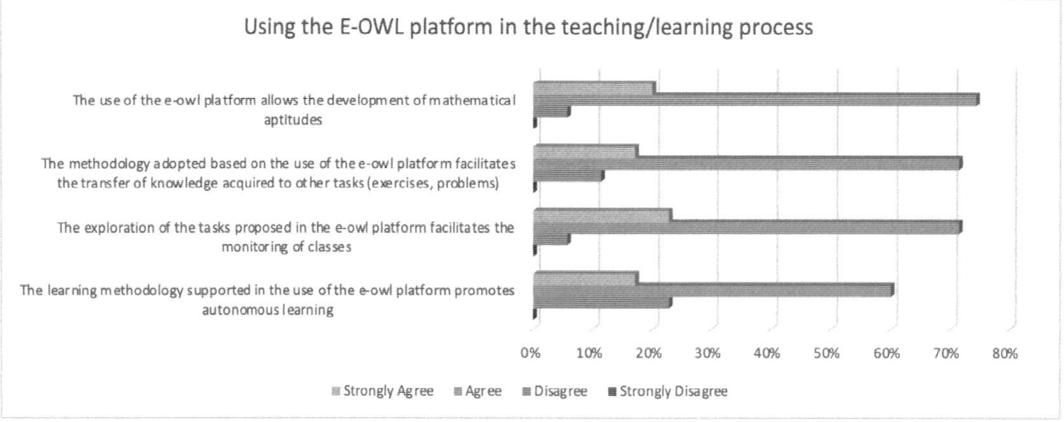

Figure 7. Classification of using E-OWL platform in a teaching/learning process

On last question, the most frequently mentioned opinion was that the exercises were solved, feedback was given to the student and that they were user-friendly. Some comments in this regard:

- "The access to the platform is easy, it keeps us up to date with the subjects taught in class, it has complementary exercises and their solution to promote a more individualized study. In general, it is a support tool for a continuous student study".
- "It's a good platform for learning. The access to exercises with explanation of the subject helps to understand things better".
- "It explains the essential points to understand the contents, explains the theory while practicing, gives feedback on the exercises, allows more practical learning and therefore closer to an evaluation situation".

The second most quoted opinion is related to self-study/self-learning, as evidenced by the following comments:

- "Easy accessibility, help in self-study, help in understanding the subject and gives important examples of certain points of the subject".
- "Using the platform allows us to study a little more independently. It allows us to apply theory to the resolution of exercises, and at the same time the feedback that is given at the end of the answer is very important, because it helps us to understand better the theory that we may not know so well yet".
- "This platform allows self-learning and the discovery of new concepts".

Lastly, as a whole, the students considered that this platform was a strong support to the classes at distance, providing the contents in a more appealing and interactive way.

6. CONCLUSION

According to the diagnostic analysis carried out, the E-OWL platform is easy to use, useful in supporting the courses, as well as in supporting autonomous study, stimulating continuous study and allowing self-regulation of learning and respecting the learning rhythm of each student, both during the classes in person and during the period when all the classes were online. It should be noted that the students considered that the feedback given to the option indicated helps in understanding the issues involved, and almost all the students agreed that the possibility of navigating between "theory" and "practice" constitutes an added value for learning, and with the use of this platform it is possible to better follow the course contents. In this sense it can be said that the platform facilitates the construction of knowledge and it is an interesting support in the learning process. We believe that in a current context, given the young students who are very familiar with the technologies, investment should continue to be made in the creation and evolution of interactive online platforms for teaching and learning in order to meet students' needs and interests.

This article is a first study on the E-OWL platform. Further studies may be carried out at a later stage, including a comparison of the differentiating features of this platform and others that already exist.

REFERENCES

Al-Rahmi, W., Alias, N., Othman, M., Alzahrani, A., Alfarraj, O., Saged, A. & *Rahman, N.*, 2018. Use of E-Learning by University Students in Malaysian Higher Educational Institutions: A Case in Universiti Teknologi Malaysia. *IEEE Access*, Vol. 6, pp. 14268-14276.

Al-Samarraie, H., Teng, B., Alzahrani,A. & Alalwan, N., 2018. E-learning continuance satisfaction in higher education: a unified perspective from instructors and students. *Studies in Higher Education*, Vol 43, Nº 11, pp 2003-2019.

Antunes, C. (2010). Utilizando a tecnologia a seu favor. 17ª Ed. Petrópolis, RJ: Vozes.

Carabetta Júnior, V., 2010. Rever, pensar e (re)significar: a importância da reflexão sobre a prática na profissão docente. Revista Brasileira de Educação Médica, Vol. 34 Nº 4, pp 580–586.

Bertoncello, L., 2010. A utilização das TIC e sua contribuição na educação superior: uma visão a partir do discurso docente da área de letras. Disponível em: https://www.recursos.portaleducoas.org/publicaciones/utiliza-o-das-tic-e-sua-contribui-o-na-educa-o-superior-uma-vis-o-partir-do-discurso?audience=3&area=&country=

Daniela, L., Strods, R., Daiga, K., 2019. Technology-enhanced learning (tel) in higher education: Where are we now? In Lytras, D., Miltiadis, Daniela, L. & Visvizi, A.(orgs); 2019. *Knowledge-intensive economies and opportunities for social, organizational, and technological growth*, Igi Globa Publisher of timely Knowledge, pp. 12-24

Freire, P.; Shor, I. A, 1987. *Pedagogy of Liberation: Dialogues for Transforming Education*. Boston: Bergin and Garvey.

Kirkwood, L. Price, 2014. Technology-enhanced learning and teaching in higher education: What is 'enhanced' and how do we know? A critical literature reviews

Learning, *Media and Technology*, Vol. 39, pp. 6-36

Lobo, A., Maia, L., 2015. O uso das TICs como ferramenta de ensino-aprendizagem no Ensino Superior. *Caderno de geografia*, Vol. 25, Nº44, pp 16-26

Moraes, C.R., Varela, S., 2007. A motivação do aluno durante o processo de ensino-aprendizagem. Revista eletrônica de educação. Vol.1, Nº 1, pp 1-15.

Moran, J. M.; Masetto, M. T.; Behrens, M. A., 2007. *Novas tecnologias e mediações pedagógicas*. 13. ed. São Paulo: Papirus.

Martinsi, M.C., 2008. Situando o uso da mídia em contextos educacionais. *Portal do MEC.*

Nortvig, A.; Petersen, A.; Balle, S., 2018. A Literature Review of the Factors Influencing E-Learning and Blended Learning in Relation to Learning Outcome, Student Satisfaction and Engagement. *Electronic Journal of e-Learning*, Vol 16, Nº 1, pp 46-55.

Paechter, M., Maier, B. & Macher, D., 2010. Expectativas e experiências dos alunos em e-learning: sua relação com as conquistas da aprendizagem e a satisfação com o curso. *Computadores e Educação*, Vol. 54, pp 222-229.

Pereira, B.T.; Freitas, M.C, 2010. *O uso das tecnologias da informação e comunicação na prática pedagógica da escola.* Disponível em: http://www.diaadiaeducacao.pr.gov.br/portals/pde/arquivos/1381-8.pdf

Ricoy, M. & Couto, M., 2014. As boas práticas com TIC e a utilidade atribuída pelos alunos recém-integrados na universidade. Educação e Pesquisa, Vol. 40, Nº 4, pp 897–912.

Valente, J., 2002. Uso da internet em sala de aula. *Educar em Revista*, Curitiba, Nº 19, pp 131-146.

Valente, J. A., 2003. Curso de especialização em desenvolvimento de projetos pedagógicos com o uso das novas tecnologias: Descrição e fundamentos. In: Valente, J., Prado, M. & Almeida, M. (orgs), 2003. *Educação a Distância Via Internet*. São Paulo: Avercamp. pp 23-55.

HYBRID RECOMMENDATION APPROACH BASED ON A VOTING SYSTEM: EXPERIMENTATION IN AN EDUCATIONAL CONTEXT

Mohammed Baidada[1, 2], Khalifa Mansouri[3] and Franck Poirier[1]
[1]*Lab-STICC, Bretagne-sud University, France*
[2]*LIMIE, ISGA Rabat, Morocco*
[3]*SSDIA, ENSET, Hassan II University, Morocco*

ABSTRACT

We present in this paper the results of a second experiment that was recently conducted to evaluate a hybrid recommendation approach in an online learning environment. The approach consists of mixing the two approaches of content-based filtering and collaborative filtering to improve the relevance of the educational resources recommended to learners. A first experiment was carried out in 2019 and gave convincing results, which led us to repeat a second experimentation in order to confirm the results, on the one hand, and on the other hand, to modify the way learners evaluate the resources by transforming the "like" by a vote from one to five, in order to verify whether this will bring an improvement in the recommendations. This second experiment was also an opportunity to integrate an engine that guides learners' searches by adding criteria relating to their preferences and to check their satisfaction with the use of this engine. The results were globally positive.

KEYWORDS

E-Learning, Recommendation System, Content-Based Filtering, Collaborative Filtering, Hybrid Filtering, Experimentation

1. INTRODUCTION

Recommendation systems (RS) are increasingly used in the field of personalization in online learning environments, given their ability to determine the educational resources best suited to learners (Garrido et al., 2016; Segal et al., 2019; Souali et al., 2011). Based on filtering methods, several approaches, including hybridization, have been proposed with the aim of improving the relevance of the recommendations (Baidada et al., 2018). These approaches have also tried to exploit all kinds of interactions between learners and the learning system.

Our contribution consists of a hybrid recommendation approach that mixes the two methods of content-based filtering and collaborative filtering, to offer the educational resources best suited to a learner's preferences. We conducted a first experiment in which learners evaluated the teaching resources in a binary way with "like/dislike". The convincing results of this first experiment encouraged us to repeat it by modifying the method of evaluation by replacing the like/dislike by an evaluation on a Likert scale from 1 to 5 (vote). In this paper we present the results of the second experiment which confirmed the improvement in the relevance of the recommendations. Before that we will present a background of our work, then a state of the art of RSs in online learning environments, and a general presentation of our approach and the protocol of experimentation.

2. BACKGROUND OF OUR WORK

Our research focuses on RSs for personalization in online learning environments. We have proposed a hybrid approach mixing the two methods of content-based filtering and collaborative filtering, with the aim of improving the relevance of the educational resources recommended to learners (Baidada et al. 2018). Our approach was tested between April and May 2019, and the results were conclusive. They shown that the hybrid recommendation approach gives better results than the content-based filtering and collaborative filtering separately, except for the private institute where we had obtained almost similar results.

In order to confirm our results, we conduct a new experiment, with two essential extensions:

1. Change the binary evaluation mode (like/dislike) for the shared resources by the learners used in the first experiment, by an evaluation method on a Likert scale with a voting system ranging from 1 to 5;
2. Propose an integrated search engine which helps the learners to find external resources corresponding to their preferences.

These two points, relating to the second experiment, are the subject of our paper and will be detailed in the section reserved for the presentation of our contribution.

3. STATE OF THE ART

3.1 Recommendation Systems

RSs are increasingly used on the web. With the aim of offering the most suitable content to users, they are found in e-commerce (Amazon, Ebay), video streaming sites (YouTube, Netflix), social networks (Facebook, Twitter, Linkedin) (Burke et al., 2011; Klašnja-Milićević et al., 2011). They have also been used in e-learning to guarantee the personalization of the learning process by recommending the most suitable content for the learners. D. Herath and L. Jayarathne (2018) used an RS based on data mining techniques to predict learners' performance. M. Tadlaoui et al. (2015, 2018) exploited the social links connecting the learners to recommend educational resources to them; they were interested in popular, useful and recently viewed resources. A. Klasnja-Milicevic et al. (2011) proposed a system which recommends sequences of pedagogical activities to learners by considering their learning styles.

3.2 Filtering Methods

Filtering methods are the basis of RSs. Often they are classified as follows (Isinkaye et al., 2015):

- Content-based filtering: it offers the user similar items and which have the same values for a set of attributes which describe them, it requires knowledge of a description of the items and user preferences;
- Collaborative filtering: which considers the similarities of the user to a group of users to whom he or she can be linked. There are two subtypes: user-based and item-based. The one that was used in the experiment is user-based collaborative filtering, which considers the similarity of the user to a group of users with whom he or she shares interests.
- Hybrid filtering: This is a combination of two or more filtering methods.

4. OUR CONTRIBUTION

As mentioned in the background, this new experiment brings to the first one the two extensions already mentioned, namely, modifying the resource evaluation mode by replacing the like/dislike with an evaluation on a Likert scale from 1 to 5 (vote), and also to offer learners the possibility of searching for external educational resources relating to their preferences through an integrated search engine.

The purpose of this new experiment through the integration of the discrete-scale evaluation method is to verify its impact on the recommendations of the educational resources. And then its purpose, through the proposal of the integrated search engine, is to exploit the learner's profile to filter the educational resources that he or she is likely to look for and make them correspond as closely as possible to his or her preferences.

The 2nd experiment will therefore allow us to verify the following hypotheses:

- The 2nd experiment must confirm the results of the 1st experiment by showing that hybrid filtering gives better recommendations than the other filtering approaches applied separately;

- The evaluation of educational resources with a discrete scale of 1 to 5, must have an impact on the recommendations (best values for the precision and recall indicators);
- Learners will appreciate the external resources proposed by the integrated search engine.

A technical description of the platform used in the first and second experiment will be given in the following section.

5. DESCRIPTION OF THE EXPERIMENT

For the first experiment we used the Moodle platform, to which we added SocialWall as a plugin which transforms the format of the courses into a social network appearance (Post, Comment, Like, etc). We have also developed recommendation modules related to the different filtering approaches used, which we have integrated into the platform. Figure 1 presents the diagram of our platform for the first experiment.

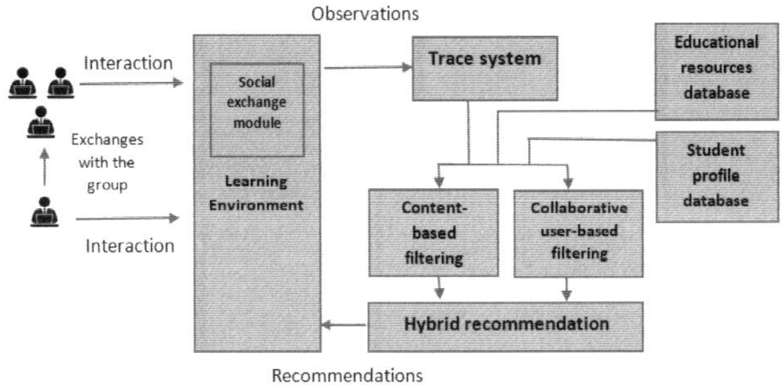

Figure 1. Diagram of the platform used for the 1st experiment in the case of the hybrid recommendation

The method of calculating recommendations according to each filtering method is described in our previous work (Baidada et al., 2018). Recall that we used a weighted hybridization approach (Burke, 2007), i.e. the results of the two filtering methods were combined numerically with a mean with equal coefficients.

Regarding the notion of the profile, we are based on the reference models IEEE PAPI (Public and Private Information for Learners) and IMS LIP (Learner Information Package) (Pavlov and Paneva, 2006; Wei and Yan, 2009), and we considered the "Preferences" component.

Subsequently, through the study of standards relating to Learning Object Metadata (LOM), namely IEEE LOM, CanCORE LOM and Dublin Core Metadata (Roy et al., 2010), we retained 3 elements relating to preferences of the learner who are General, Technical and Educational. The following table (table 1) gives a description of the final criteria retained with their possible values:

Table 1. Learner preferences metadata

Section	Element retained	Values
General	**Language**	English, French, Arabic
Technical	**Resource format**	Video, Document (pdf, slides, …), Web article
Educational	**Resource type**	Course, Tests or exercises, Forum

For the second experiment, the diagram was retained in its entirety, making two essential modifications:
- Changing the like / dislike rating system by a voting system;
- Proposal of a search engine for external educational resources (Figure 2).

Our integrated search engine is based on the CURL resource extractor module. It is a module that uses the CURL extension (Client URL) of PHP to send http requests to remote servers. These requests are initiated by the learners and enriched with the criteria related to their profiles before being launched on these servers. For example, for a learner who searches for the key words "initiation en PHP", and knowing that in his or her profile we retained his or her preferences for videos as types of resources, courses as type of activity, and language French, then the final request which will be launched will be:

"http://www.google.com/search?q=Intiation+en+PHP+cours+video&lr=lang_fr".

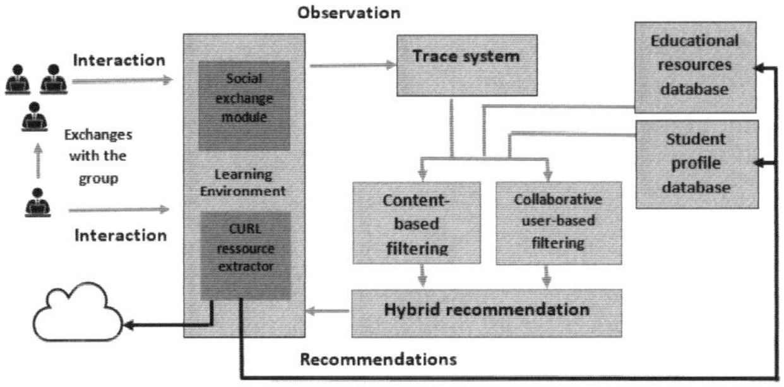

Figure 2. Diagram of the platform used for the 2nd experiment in the case of the hybrid recommendation

The experiment targeted two groups of engineering students in two different public and private institutes in Morocco. For the private institute, it is a group of 3rd year computer engineering of 33 students. For the public institute, this is a group of 1st year computer engineer cycles of 64 students. The average age of the groups is 21.1 with a standard deviation of 1.36. There are 32% female and 68% male.

Each group was divided into three subgroups:

- Subgroup 1: to whom we proposed a content-based filtering approach;
- Subgroup 2: to whom we proposed a collaborative filtering approach;
- Subgroup 3: to whom we have proposed a hybrid approach to the previous methods.

Table 2 below shows the distribution of the different groups:

Table 2. Size of groups

	Sub-group 1	Sub-group 2	Sub-group 3	Total
Public	21	21	22	64
Private	11	11	11	33
Total	32	32	33	97

Students were enrolled in a web programming course for the private institute, and an object-oriented programming course for the public institute. The experiment took place between the beginning of January and mid-February 2020.

We chose an online evaluation method with real users. This evaluation method guarantees better results than the offline evaluation method with datasets.

6. EVALUATION METHOD

To assess our recommendation system, we used the three indicators commonly used in this area (Isinkaye et al.., 2015; Portugal et al., 2017), namely:

- Precision: means the percentage of results which are relevant, it measures the quality of the recommendations (the accuracy). It is given by the following report: Number of relevant recommended resources / Number of recommended resources;
- Recall: refers to the percentage of total relevant results correctly classified by the algorithm, it measures the quantity of recommendations (completeness). It is given by the report: Number of relevant recommended resources / Total number of relevant resources;
- F-measure: It is a harmonic average of the two previous indicators.

We used the same indicators for the evaluation as for the first experiment, with an essential difference in the choice of the relevance threshold. For the first experiment we considered a binary evaluation with like / dislike and we therefore considered a relevant resource any resource on which a learner has like. For this second experiment, we considered a voting system for resources with values ranging from 1 to 5. It was therefore necessary to determine the relevance threshold for resources. Instead of setting a value between 1 to 5 (Ben Ticha, 2018), we chose the average of the votes of a resource by the learners, which generated a different relevance threshold for each resource.

Regarding the analysis method, we opted for the ANOVA (ANalysis Of VAriance) method which allows us to test the significant differences between the means. It is used to measure changes in a metric variable by one or more nominai explanatory factors. In our case, we chose the ANOVA1 variance analysis to explain the variation of a single dependent metric variable by a single explanatory factor. More precisely, we seek to test the effect of the qualitative variable "group" successively on each of the quantitative variables "Precision", "Recall" and "F-measure". We applied ANOVA1 to each institute separately, and then applied it to both institutes.

Finally, we tested the effect of the qualitative variable "Institute" on each of the indicators. For this we used the Student T-test, which compares the means of two sample groups.

In order to test the equality of the means between the three groups, we used the null hypothesis:

- H_0 : there is no difference between the three groups
- H_1 : at least one group is different from the others

We used the Tukey test which proposes a significance level of 0.05, called sig (Tukey significant difference). The hypothesis 0 will be rejected if the threshold obtained is lower than 0.05, and therefore we will deduce that at least one group is different from the others.

Note that we have adopted the same methods and analytical approaches as for the first experiment, in order to confirm the results.

7. RESULTS

7.1 ANOVA1 for the Two Combined Institutes

We used SPSS software to get the results. As a first step, we considered the two institutes together and an inter-group analysis was performed. This analysis gave a significance level (sig) of 0.00. Hypothesis 0 was rejected, and we deduced that at least one group is different from the others. This required a multiple comparison of the means to see which group is different. Table 3 summarizes the results for the three indicators precision, recall and F-measure:

Table 3. Multiple comparison of the three indicators - the two institutes grouped

	Sig(G1 vs G2)	Sig(G1 vs G3)	Sig(G2 vs G3)
Precision	0.29	0.00	0.00
Recall	0.25	0.00	0.00
F-measure	0.26	0.00	0.00

We find that group 3 compared to the other two groups 1 and 2 have a significance level (sig) equal to 0, confirming that it is different from the other two groups. We then proceeded to a classification in homogeneous subsets, to find the groups which present similarities and the groups which differ, this by considering the harmonic averages. Table 4 presents the results:

Table 4. Classification into homogeneous subsets for the three indicators - the two institutes grouped

		Precision		Recall		F-measure	
		Subset		Subset		Subset	
Groups	Size of group	1	2	1	2	1	2
Group 1	32	0.38		0.24		0.29	
Group 2	32	0.42		0.27		0.33	
Group 3	33		0.59		0.43		0.49

For the three indicators, group 3 has a harmonic mean much higher than the other groups, and it is classified each time in a single subset, while the other two groups are classified in the same subset.

7.2 ANOVA1 for the Private and Public Institute Separately

For the two institutes considered separately, the inter-group analysis gave a significance level sig less than 0.05. It has once again been deduced that at least one group is distinguished from the others.

Following the same approach, the multiple comparison of the three indicators respectively for the two institutes gave the results presented in Tables 5 and 6:

Table 5. Multiple comparison of the three indicators - Private Institute

	Sig(G1 vs G2)	Sig(G1 vs G3)	Sig(G2 vs G3)
Precision	0.621	0.001	0.014
Recall	0.955	0.000	0.001
F-measure	0.849	0.001	0.003

Table 6. Multiple comparison of the three indicators - Public Institute

	Sig(G1 vs G2)	Sig(G1 vs G3)	Sig(G2 vs G3)
Precision	0.378	0.000	0.000
Recall	0.147	0.000	0.000
F-measure	0.216	0.000	0.000

For the two institutes group 3 presents a difference compared to the others with significance thresholds lower than 0.05. We must proceed to the classification into homogeneous subsets given by Tables 7 and 8:

Table 7. Classification into homogeneous subsets for the three indicators - private institute

		Precision		Recall		F-measure	
		Subset		Subset		Subset	
Groups	Size of group	1	2	1	2	1	2
Group 1	11	0.33		0.23		0.27	
Group 2	11	0.37		0.24		0.29	
Group 3	11		0.49		0.35		0.41

Table 8. Classification into homogeneous subsets for the three indicators - public institute

		Precision		Recall		F-measure	
		Subset		Subset		Subset	
Groups	Size of group	1	2	1	2	1	2
Group 1	21	0.40		0.24		0.30	
Group 2	21	0.45		0.29		0.35	
Group 3	22		0.63		0.45		0.53

For the two institutes separately, each time group 3 has a better harmonic mean and is classified in a subset while the two groups 1 and 2 are classified in another.

7.3 T-Student Test between the Two Institutes

We used T-Student test to check whether the variable "Institute" has an influence on each of the indicators. Referring to the results table (Table 9), we note that the significance level sig, for the three indicators, is less than 0.05, which leads us to confirm a difference between the two institutes.

Table 9. T-Student test

		sig
Precision	equal variances hypothesis	0.002
	unequal variances hypothesis	0.001
Recall	equal variances hypothesis	0.016
	unequal variances hypothesis	0.009
F-measure	equal variances hypothesis	0.007
	unequal variances hypothesis	0.004

According to the statistics table provided by SPSS (Table 10), we get higher values for the public institute compared to the private institute. It's especially the precision that makes a big difference.

Table 10. Group statistics

	Institute	Size	Average	Standard deviation	Mean standard error
Precision	Private	33	0.40	0.12	0.02
	Public	64	0.50	0.15	0.18
Recall	Private	33	0.27	0.09	0.15
	Public	64	0.33	0.11	0.14
F-measure	Private	33	0.32	0.10	0.17
	Public	64	0.40	0.13	0.16

7.4 Questionnaire Results

To support the results obtained, a questionnaire was distributed to the learners who participated in the experiment. 66 responded, here are some of the statistics that emerged:

- For the satisfaction with the experiment platform : 59% respond "very good"
- For the satisfaction with the exchange module : 50% respond "very good"
- For the relevance of shared resources in the group : 54% respond "good"
- For the relevance of recommended resources : 64% respond "very good"
- For matching recommended resources to their preferences : 54% respond "a lot"

With regard to the use of the search engine, out of 48 who evaluated it, 62% confirm that the resources proposed correspond "a lot" to their preferences (Figure 3).

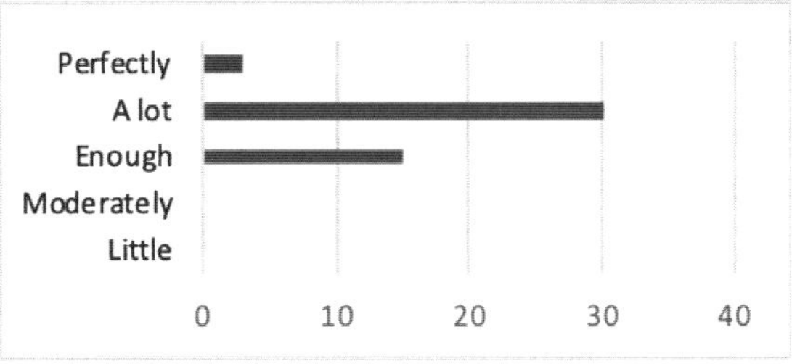

Figure 3. Matching of researched resources to preferences

8. DISCUSSION

Through the results obtained, this second experiment confirms the results of the first, by showing that group 3 to which we applied the hybrid recommendation approach presented better results compared to the other two groups, for the case of the two combined institutes, and for the public institute and this time also for the private institute. On the other hand, the public institute always presents better results, the thing that we had explained for the first experiment also, by the overall level of students in the public sector which is generally better, the thing which influences the quality of shared resources and their relevance when evaluating these resources.

One of the objectives of this second experiment was to check whether the evaluation with a voting system would improve the quality of recommendations compared to a binary evaluation with like / dislike. The results obtained rather show a slight improvement for the recall indicator, which leads us to confirm that we have gained in terms of the completeness of the recommended resources rather than in their quality.

The questionnaire made it possible to confirm the general appreciation of the learners, both with regard to the use of the platform, the social exchange module, and the relevance of the resources recommended by the system, and that these corresponded very much to their preferences. Learners also appreciated the integrated search engine, confirming that the results it generated correspond to their preferences.

9. CONCLUSION

We have verified through the first experiment that the hybridization of the two methods of content-based filtering and collaborative filtering improves the relevance of the recommendations in an online learning context. The second experiment was an opportunity to confirm this result, but also to verify the impact of the evaluation method on the relevance of the recommendations. It was also an opportunity to extend the platform to a proposal of external resources that best matched the learners' preferences, through the integrated search engine, and to check their satisfaction with the results returned.

The results were positive, the hybrid recommendation always gives better results, the evaluation method with a scale from 1 to 5 impacts the Recall indicator, and finally the learners were globally satisfied with the use of the integrated search engine and the results it offers.

This will encourage us to develop our platform by taking full advantage of learners' interactions with the system to better understand their needs and interests. This can be achieved by exploiting the queries made on the search engine, by analyzing those that most interest the learners.

REFERENCES

Baidada, M., Mansouri, K., Poirier, F. 2018. Hybrid Recommendation Approach in Online Learning Environments, In: Rocha Á., Serrhini M. (eds) Information Systems and Technologies to Support Learning. EMENA-ISTL 2018. Smart Innovation, Systems and Technologies, vol 111. Springer, Cham. pp 39-43. https://doi.org/10.1007/978-3-030-03577-8_5

Ben Ticha, S. 2018. Recommandation personnalisée hybride, Phd Thesis, University of Lorraine, France in joint supervision with the University of Tunis El Manar, Tunisia

Burke, R. 2007. Hybrid web recommender systems. *Lecture Notes in Computer Science (Including Subseries Lecture Notes in Artificial Intelligence and Lecture Notes in Bioinformatics), 4321 LNCS*, 377–408.

Burke, R. et al., 2011. Recommender systems: An overview. *AI Magazine*, *32*(3), 13–18. https://doi.org/10.1609/aimag.v32i3.2361

Garrido, A. et al., 2016. On the use of case-based planning for e-learning personalization. *Expert Systems with Applications*, *60*, 1–15. https://doi.org/10.1016/j.eswa.2016.04.030

Herath, D. and Jayarathne, L. 2018. Intelligent Recommendations for e-Learning Personalization Based on Learner's Learning Activities and Performances, *International Journal of Computer Science and Software Engineering*, Vol.7, Issue 6, pp.130-137. https://doi.org/10.13140/RG.2.2.27785.34406

Isinkaye, F. O. et al., 2015. Recommendation systems: Principles, methods and evaluation. *Egyptian Informatics Journal*, *16*(3), 261–273. https://doi.org/10.1016/j.eij.2015.06.005

Klašnja-Milićević, A. et al., 2011. E-Learning personalization based on hybrid recommendation strategy and learning style identification. *Computers and Education*, *56*(3), 885–899. https://doi.org/10.1016/j.compedu.2010.11.001

Pavlov, R. and Paneva, D. 2006. Personalized and adaptive learning–approaches and solutions. *In the Proceedings of the Third CHIRON Open Workshop "Visions of Ubiquitous Learning"*, 20 June, 2006, Stockholm, Sweden, pp. 6-19

Portugal, I. et al., 2017. The use of machine learning algorithms in recommender systems: A systematic review. *Expert Systems with Applications*, *97*, 205–227. https://doi.org/10.1016/j.eswa.2017.12.020

Roy, D. et al., 2010. A Comparative Study of Learning Object Metadata, Learning Material Repositories, Metadata Annotation & an Automatic Metadata Annotation Tool. *Boley & Akerkar*, *2*, 103–126.

Segal, A. et al., 2019. A difficulty ranking approach to personalization in E-learning. *International Journal of Human Computer Studies*, *130*(October 2017), 261–272. https://doi.org/10.1016/j.ijhcs.2019.07.002

Souali, K. et al., 2011. A new recommender system for e-learning environments. *International Conference on Multimedia Computing and Systems -Proceedings*, 1–4. https://doi.org/10.1109/ICMCS.2011.5945630

Tadlaoui, M. et al., 2015. Approche pour recommandation de ressources pédagogiques basée sur les liens sociaux, EIAH'2015, June 2015, *7ème Conférence sur les Environnements Informatiques pour l'Apprentissage Humain*, Agadir, Morocco, pp.192-203

Tadlaoui, M. 2018. Système de recommandation de ressources pédagogiques fondé sur les liens sociaux formalisation et évaluation, PhD Thesis, INSA Lyon, France, in joint supervision with Tlemcen University, Tlemcen, Algeria

Wei, X. and Yan, J. 2009. Learner profile design for personalized E-learning systems. *Proceedings - 2009 International Conference on Computational Intelligence and Software Engineering, CiSE 2009.* https://doi.org/10.1109/CISE.2009.5363560

USING FORMAL CONCEPT ANALYSIS TO EXPLORE HIDDEN KNOWLEDGE IN THE ASSESSMENT OF A MATH COURSE

Francisco Pérez-Gámez, Manuel Ojeda-Hernández, Ángel Mora Bonilla,
Domingo López-Rodríguez and Nicolas Madrid
Departamento de Matemática Aplicada - E.T.S.I.Informática – Universidad de Málaga, Spain[*]

ABSTRACT

Since the emergence of COVID-19, online teaching and e-Learning has become essential in education. Actually, in at our University, we have had to move to a complete online teaching framework through the Moodle e-learning system. As a result, we have had to deploy new material as videos in Youtube channels, new exercises, tasks, live teaching, etc that have generated a huge amount of data that contains interesting information. In particular, we have used randomly generated exams from a bank of quizzes to evaluate the students. In this paper, we analyze the results of these quizzes using Formal Concept Analysis tools in order to check the hidden knowledge in the assessment process with the goal of improving the developed material for next years. In addition, we will analyze how the different exercises and tests relate to each other so that we can use this information in the following courses to improve our lectures.

KEYWORDS

e-Learning Assessment Tools, Formal Concept Analysis, Knowledge Mining, Concepts, Quizzes, Random Exams

1. INTRODUCTION

The term *Blended Learning* (Dziuban et al., 2018) refers to every teaching style that combines traditional face- to-face lectures with an online platform where some content is uploaded, namely theoretical material, quizzes, tasks or any other kind of stuff related to the module.

e-Learning has advantages such as allowing a self-paced learning for each one of the students, availability of the content at any time and community-based support, given in the form of forums where the students can ask and solve their own questions and their partners'. Usually we could say we approach our teaching using Blended Learning, that is, we provide on-site courses with live teaching but with strong support from online systems.

However, when our Blended Learning approach turns into a completely online course, as it has been mandatory with the situation caused by the COVID-19, some disadvantages might appear, such as a lack of focus, poorly motivated students can quickly fall behind in an online course; and the feeling of isolation the students can get, the impersonality, suppression of communication mechanisms such as body language, and elimination of peer- to-peer learning can make online learning a challenging experience for some students. This is a phenomenon we have experienced since class participation has decreased even though it had a specific weight in the marking scheme.

e-Learning is an interesting approach for learning that we can use to improve the quality of the teaching and learning process. Nowadays, in the framework of Spanish Universities, the use of Moodle is widely extended (Almansa-Martinez,2019) (Cabero-Almenara,2019). Moodle (Modular Object-Oriented Dynamic Learning Environment) is, at the moment, the most popular system for e-Learning purposes. In 2002, Martin Dougiamas presented the first version of Moodle based on socio-constructivist pedagogy providing a set of tools that support an inquiry- and discovery-based approach to online learning. Furthermore, Moodle allows for collaborative interaction among students as a standalone or in addition to conventional classroom instruction".

[*] {franciscoperezgamez, manuojeda, amora, dominlopez, nicolas.madrid}@uma.es

The wide use of e-Learning platforms has brought about a huge amount of data that, with a proper processing, may bring out significant information very useful for teaching purposes. Classical techniques as Machine Learning or Data Mining can be used to extract knowledge from data. Currently, there are already many different approaches in the literature showing the advantages of using techniques of Machine Learning or Data Mining to e-Learning (Mohamad, 2013) (Romero, 2008), (Viloria, 2019). For example, it is possible to develop systems that adapt or recommend modifications of certain contents according to different students aspects defined by their behavior (Ashraf, 2020) (De Maio, 2012) (Asil Oztekin, 2013) (Hooshyar, 2020). Others applications of these kind of techniques to e-Learning are the development of tools to detect and prevent academic dropouts (Burgos, 2018), (Chung, 2019), (Chui, 2020), (Gray, 2019), the detection of problematic aspects in evaluation tasks (García 2011), the representation of feelings or preferences of students (Carmona, 2007), (Zengin, 2011) or the measurement of the student experience during an e-course (Shukor, 2015), (Hew, 2020) among others.

In our research we deal with the problem of searching for hidden patterns and relationships between different courses or lectures in university degrees. Specifically, in this paper we present some preliminary results obtained by using FCA techniques to the data collected from the course named EstMetNum (a module of Statistics and Numerical Methods) that has been taught completely in an e-Learning platform due to the COVID-19 restrictions. Data collected in this course include questions asked and debated by the alumni in the forums, quizzes answered, tasks proposed during the online lectures and knowledge bits proposed by the students in the glossaries, etc. This general problem of finding links between different lectures has been also addressed by other researchers, e.g., in (Yahya, 2019), (Buldu, 2010), but the difference with respect to our approach is that we use Formal Concept Analysis (FCA) (Ganter, 99), (Ganter, 2019) as the tool to extract the knowledge from the data, which although it has been applied in the context of e-Learning e.g., in (De Maio, 2012), to the best of our knowledge it has never been applied to this specific goal.

Formal Concept Analysis (FCA) is a solid mathematical framework to manage information, based on logic, lattice theory and Galois connections. It defines two explicit representations of the tacit knowledge present in a dataset, in the form of *concepts* (closed sets under a closure operator, that is, entities characterized by the non-formalized relationships among the attributes or features in a dataset) and *implications*, which can be seen as exact association rules.

The mechanisms used to extract concepts from a dataset in FCA allow us to hierarchically organize them in the so-called *concept lattice*. An important aspect to emphasize is that the concept lattice captures *all* the implicit knowledge that can be deduced from a formal context.

FCA provides the methods to find those representations, more precisely to extract the concepts and implications that can be deduced from the dataset, and introduces a logic to reason and infer new knowledge. In this sense, FCA allows to discover knowledge in datasets analogously to what other techniques (e.g. in Machine Learning) do, but this logic-based approach is more suitable to provide explainable answers when dealing with real-world datasets. Comparing our approach with other techniques used in machine learning and data mining such as association rules, FCA extracts more knowledge, since it gives not only the implications (exact association rules) but also the concepts organized in a hierarchical structure, the concept lattice. Moreover, our team has developed a logic to manipulate implications and to build automated methods to reason with them.

In this work, we approach using FCA the retrieval of the concepts from a dataset with the marks obtained in the different exercises and test using Moodle quizzes. In this way, Section 2 shows the material and methods we have developed in our online course explaining the generation of the quizzes using R language to build a huge bank of quizzes and how we have approached the use of FCA to extract knowledge. The results obtained are explored in Section 3 and some conclusions and future works appear in the last section.

2. MATERIALS AND METHODS

We analyze in this work the results (marks) obtained from a set of quizzes extracted from Moodle concerning the subject Statistics and Numerical Methods in the Bachelor degree of Telecommunication Systems Engineering and in the Bachelor degree of Electronic Systems Engineering. Of course, the data has been anonymized to protect the personal information of the students.

Although we have used extensively the habitual tools that Moodle provides, and due to a big number of students (70 in each course), we have decided to generate a large question bank by means of R language and the R/exams package (http://www.r-exams.org). This open-source package exams, for the R language, provides a one-for-all approach to automatic exams generation. We develop dynamic exercise models with random parameters to build patterns of exercises and generate random exams. The questions were exported to Moodle using the *exams2moodle* function of the R/exams package. We could ensure that different students tackled different tests from a question bank of about 5,000 questions.

Moreover, during the course, some similar exercises generated in the same way were solved by students using a self-assessment question bank. The traditional class in the classroom has been moved to online teaching, then we reinforced the existent material in the Moodle course with new learning units: lectures using videos via a private Youtube channel together with online live lessons using Google Meet and/or Microsoft Teams, quizzes, tasks, forums, available material online, etc.

Although we believe that the work with all this material has been very satisfactory, we need to objectively measure the students' learning processes in order to give the right marks for each student's work. And the random exams generated from R language have been the main tool for assigning the final grade/mark.

The goal in this works is on the one hand to translate the intense work done in this hard situation caused by COVID and on the other hand to communicate the results we have achieved in the course.

The csv file with the marks of the different exercise patterns has the following structure:

- Three main statistics exams and three main numerical methods exams: Descriptive Probability Test (StD in the dataset), Random Variables Test (StR) and Matlab Statistical Test (StM), Non Linear Equations Test (NtNle), Numerical Nonlinear Equations and Solving Linear Systems Test (NtNleLs), Numerical Interpolation-Approximation-Derivation-Integration Test (NtIaDi) and Numerical Matlab Test (NtM).
- Two specific exercises from statistics and five specific exercises from numerical methods: Regression Exercise (Ser), Variables Distributions (SeV), Numerical Nonlinear Equations Exercise (NeNle), Numerical Interpolation Exercise (NeI), Numerical Non Classical Interpolation (NeNci), Numerical Exercise Approximation (NeA), Numerical Matlab Exercise (NeM).
- The final mark of the students (FinalMark).

As a summary of the goal of the paper, can we extract interesting knowledge from the marks in the exercise patterns? Some questions are raised as motivation of the analysis of the results we introduce in the rest of the paper using Formal Concept Analysis, a mathematical tool to discover knowledge:

- Which exercise patterns have been more decisive in the final marks?
- Is there any hard exercise that students have not approached adequately?
- Have the specific exercises been important in the final mark?
- Is there any interaction among some categories of the specific exercises or between specific exercises and main exams?

The data to be analyzed for FCA is a binary relation between a set of objects and a set of attributes. In a first stage of the analysis we will use classical FCA then we binarize the csv considering 1 if the student passes this exam or exercise. Next figure shows the binary relation named fc_en from the the csv file (en_bin.csv):

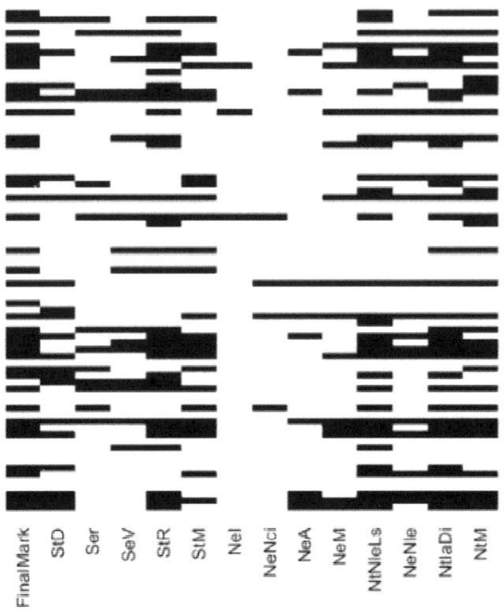

Figure 1. Binary relation

Due to the limitations of space, in this work we do not introduce an extensive summary of Formal Concept Analysis. See (Ganter, 99), (Ganter, 2019) for more details on FCA.

The binary table is named in FCA the *formal context*. It is a triple $\boldsymbol{K} = \preccurlyeq G, M, I \succ$ where G is a set of objects and M a set of attributes and $I \subseteq G \times M$ is a binary relation. $\preccurlyeq g, m \succ \in I$ means that the object g has the attribute m. Two mappings $\uparrow: 2^G \rightarrow 2^M$ and $\downarrow: 2^M \rightarrow 2^G$ named concept-forming operators, are defined as follows: for any $X \subseteq G$ and $Y \subseteq M$,

$$X^{\uparrow} = \{m \in M \mid \preccurlyeq g, m \succ \in I, for\ all\ g \in X\}$$

$$Y^{\downarrow} = \{g \in G \mid \preccurlyeq g, m \succ \in I, for\ all\ m \in Y\}$$

The meaning of $X\uparrow$ is the subset of all attributes shared by all the objects in X and $Y\downarrow$ is the subset of all objects that have the attributes in Y. Without going into details, in FCA it has been proved that these mappings constitute a Galois connection, therefore, both compositions are closure operators and it is the key point to find the fixed points in which a set of object shares a set of attributes and this set of attributes shares the same set of objects, that is, a concept.

A pair of subsets $\preccurlyeq X, Y \succ$ with $X \subseteq G$ and $Y \subseteq M$ such that $X\uparrow = Y$ and $Y\downarrow = X$ is called a *formal concept*. is named the *extent* and Y the *intent* of the concept. The formal concepts have an order relation, and the set of all the formal concepts, denoted by $(\boldsymbol{G}, \boldsymbol{M}, \boldsymbol{I})$, is a lattice, named *concept lattice*.

We have used R language to develop the analysis of the quizzes using FCA, and specifically the R package named **fcaR**(https://CRAN.R-project.org/package=fcaR). This package allows to extract the knowledge inside a binary dataset using FCA (See https://github.com/neuroimaginador/fcaR for some vignettes explaining the use of this package).

Using **fcaR** the user can extract in a easy way the concepts, the full concept lattice, relationships between attributes, etc. In the following section, we show how we can use **fcaR** to extract the hidden knowledge in the datasets with the quizzes marks.

3. RESULTS

To answer the questions that we have presented in the previous section, we have explored the dataset using FCA methods. First, from the original binary dataset, we have built its concept lattice to explore the set of items (topics, exercises, tests) which share a common behaviour among students.

Since we are interested in frequent behaviours, in many cases we have to set a threshold on the support of the concepts we are studying. The support of a set is the proportion of cases in which the set appears in the dataset, among all cases. Depending on the variability of the data, the support threshold is also variable and will depend on the number of concepts that can be considered significative.

This first approach has given a concept lattice composed by 187 concepts. With such a high amount, the lattice plot (called *Hasse diagram*) does not fit in standard paper sizes, thus we present only the lattice for concepts whose support exceeds 42% (that is, concepts appearing in at least 42% of the cases in the dataset) in the next figure:

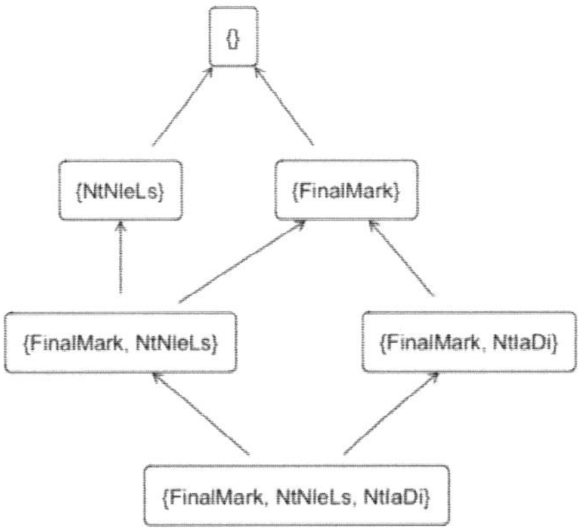

Figure 2. Concepts appearing in at least 42% of the cases in the dataset

We'll look at the so-called irreducible elements, the minimal elements needed to rebuild the whole lattice. They provide essential information about the frequent co-occurrences inside the dataset. This irreducible elements are those with only an upper-neighbour in our plot, so they are {NtNleLs}, {FinalMark}, {FinalMark, NtIaDi}. Among those, only two of the concepts contain information about the FinalMark item. The first one,

{FinalMark}, means that essentially, passing the subject can be done in multiple ways and there is no a common pattern of items that co-occur that implies passing the subject. But the other concept, {FinalMark, NtIaDi}, means that there is one fundamental test in the subject (the one about interpolation, approximation, differentiation and integration) that is key in the sense that it usually leads to the obtention of a good final mark.

This first analysis answers the questions "Which exercise patterns have been more decisive in the final marks?" and "Have the specific exercises been important in the final mark?". We expand this analysis to approach the remaining open questions.

Let us now consider two independent contexts, one for students who passed the subject and another for the students who did not. Again, the actual number of concepts in the concept lattice is high, so we must impose a threshold to only visualize the most frequent patterns, as in the next figure:

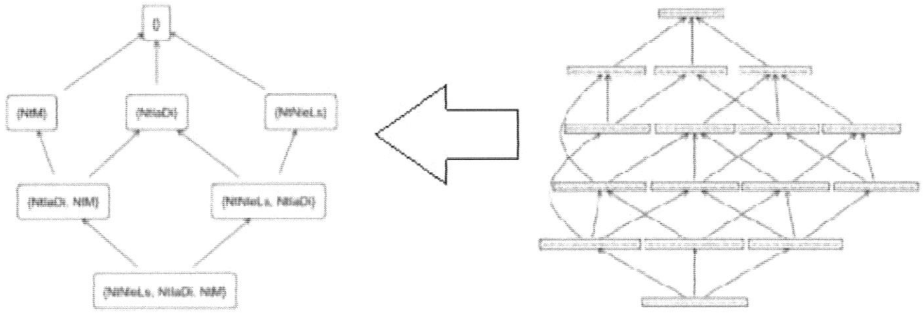

Figure 3. Left sublattice (figure 2) and right complete lattice

We can see that even imposing only frequent concepts, in the second lattice, concepts are difficult to read. This is due to the fact that concepts in that lattice contains many attributes, that is, many items (topics, tests, etc.). To have a better readability of those lattices, as before, we study the irreducible elements.

In the first case, for students which passed, the most important concepts, defining what items clearly suggest the student is performing well in the subject, are {NtM}, {NtIaDi} and {NtNleLs}. That is, we confirm that NtIaDi (the test on interpolation, approximation, differentiation and integration) is very important in the subject and thus passing it is a strong attribute of students who pass the subject. This analysis also allows us to identify the another two items (the MATLAB exam and the test on the resolution of numerical equations and systems) that are important in passing the subject.

For students who didn't pass, we study their fails, that is, in which items they failed that conducted to failing the subject. If we explore the irreducible elements of the lattice, {StM, NeI, NeNci, NeA, NeM, NeNle, NtIaDi, NtM}, {StM, NeI, NeNci, NeA, NeM, NtNleLs, NeNle, NtIaDi}, {Ser, StM, NeI, NeNci, NeA, NeM, NeNle, NtIaDi}, {Ser, SeV, StM, NeI, NeNci, NeA, NeM, NeNle, NtIaDi} and {StD, Ser, StM, NeI, NeNci, NeA, NeM, NeNle, NtIaDi}, we find that these are items that students frequently fail where they fail the subject: the students fail a lot of tests; there is not a single item which if they fail then they fail the subject. Thus, failing the subject has not a single reason *inside* the subject. It can be hypothesized that the reason can be a lack of previous mathematical knowledge and skills in part of the students.

Thus, with this analysis, we have given response to "Which exercise patterns have been more decisive in the final marks?", "Is there any hard exercise that students have not approached adequately?", and "Have the specific exercises been important in the final mark?".

The last question to answer is related to the relationship between items in the subject, that is, if there is any set of items, tests, exercises, etc., whose behaviour among students is the same. This is related to the notion of statistical correlation. We build in this case a formal context by binarizing the correlation between items in the original formal context. We can then build the lattice of *frequent correlated items* in the subject, which we present in the next figure:

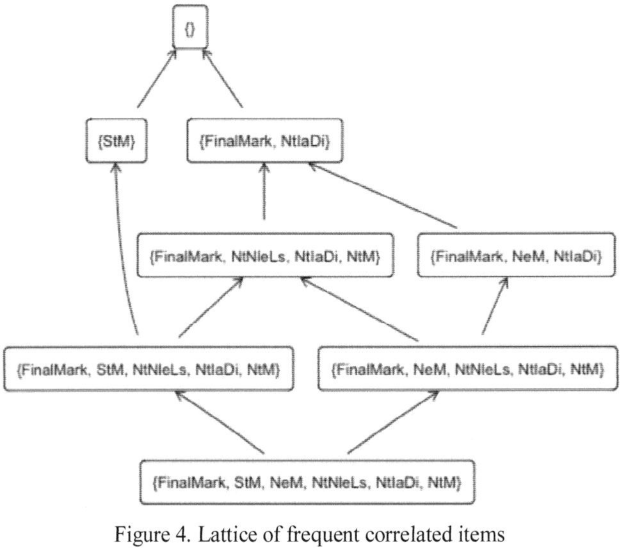

Figure 4. Lattice of frequent correlated items

The irreducible concepts in this lattice with more than one element, {FinalMark, NtIaDi}, {FinalMark, NtNleLs, NtIaDi, NtM} and {FinalMark, NeM, NtIaDi}, indicate which areas share the same behaviour among most students, that is, in every irreducible concept, all items are highly related, meaning that most students pass *all of the corresponding tests* or most students *fail all of them*. It is remarkable that in the three concepts the item NtIaDi appears accompanying the FinalMark, corroborating our previous findings: one of the key tests in the subject is the one for numerical interpolation, approximation, differentiation and integration.

4. CONCLUSIONS AND FUTURE WORK

We have presented our experience on how to evaluate a full online course in our university due to the Covid restrictions. It was necessary to implement an online assessment and the use of quizzes was the best option. A huge quiz bank has been developed using R language and the R/exams package. A random exam for each student has been done and we have evaluated the students with all the marks obtained.

We have used in this work FCA to extract knowledge from the dataset with the marks of students in the quizzes. Some interesting patterns arise from this knowledge obtaining in our analysis the important topics, exercises and tests and the relationship among them. We show the concept lattice obtained and how it is possible to use FCA to reveal significant gaps in the evaluation process. We have obtained interesting patterns concerning the assessment units used in this course: some units appear frequently for the students passing the course (numerical interpolation, approximation, differentiation and integration); some units are detected as key tests; there is no test significative enough to make a student automatically fail (when the student fails, more than one test is failed); the subject can be succeeded in several ways and there is not a common pattern of items that co-occur when the students pass the subject. In general, the knowledge appearing in the concept lattice could reveal gaps, hard tests for students, unique ways to pass the subject doing the same test, etc.

This is the first step in our study, our short-term goals we want to extend our study using fuzzy formal concept analysis, where we can grade the marks and to obtain a deeper knowledge. Also, we are going to make changes in our lectures taking the results in this study into account and we will repeat this study in order to check if we have improved or new changes could be suggested.

ACKNOWLEDGMENT

This work has been partially supported by the project TIN2017-89023-P of the Science and Innovation Ministry of Spain, co-funded by the European Regional Development Fund (ERDF), UMA18-FEDERJA-001 and PIE15-130.

REFERENCES

Almansa-Martínez,et al,2019, *Functionalities of moodle and edmodo in the middle and higher educations. In Revista de Comunicación de la SEECI, (Vol 50, 87-105).*

Asil Oztekin, et al, 2013. *A machine learning-based usability evaluation method for e-Learning systems. In Decision Support Systems (Vol 56, pp 63-73)*

Ashraf, M. et al, 2020. An Intelligent Prediction System for Educational Data Mining Based on Ensemble and Filtering approaches. *In Procedia Computer Science (Vol. 167, pp. 1471–1483). Elsevier B.V.*

Buldu, A. and Üçgün, K, 2010. Data mining application on students' data. *In Procedia - Social and Behavioral Sciences (Vol. 2, pp. 5251–5259). Elsevier.*

Burgos, C. et al, 2018. Data mining for modeling students' performance: A tutoring action plan to prevent academic dropout. *Computers and Electrical Engineering, 66, 541–556.*

Cabero-Almenara, et al, 2019. *Technical and Didactic Knowledge of the Moodle LMS in Higher Education. Beyond Functional Use. Journal of New Approaches in Educational Research,* (Vol 8, 25-33)

Carmona, C., et al, 2007. Discovering Student Preferences in e-Learning.

Chui, K. T. et al, 2020. Predicting at-risk university students in a virtual learning environment via a machine learning algorithm. *Computers in Human Behavior, 107, 105584.*

Chung, J. Y. and Lee, S., 2019. Dropout early warning systems for high school students using machine learning. *Children and Youth Services Review, 96, 346–353.*

De Maio, C. et al, 2012. RSS-based e-Learning recommendations exploiting fuzzy FCA for Knowledge Modeling. *Applied Soft Computing Journal, 12(1), 113–124.*

Dziuban, C. et al, 2018. Blended learning: the new normal and emerging technologies. *International Journal of Technology in Higher Education. 15(3)..*

Ganter, B. and Wille, R. (1999). Formal Concept Analysis: Mathematical Foundations. Springer. Ganter, B. and Obiedkov, S. (2016). Conceptual Exploration. Conceptual Exploration, 1–315.

García, E. et al, 2011. A collaborative educational association rule mining tool. *Internet and Higher Education, 14(2), 77– 88.*

Gray, C. C. and Perkins, D., 2019. Utilizing early engagement and machine learning to predict student outcomes. *Computers and Education, 131, 22–32.*

Hew, K. F. et al, 2020. What predicts student satisfaction with MOOCs: A gradient boosting trees supervised machine learning and sentiment analysis approach. *Computers and Education, 145, 103724.*

Hooshyar, D. et al,, 2020. Open learner models in supporting self-regulated learning in higher education: A systematic literature review. *Computers and Education, 154, 103878.*

Mohamad, S. K. and Tasir, Z., 2013. Educational Data Mining: *A Review. Procedia - Social and Behavioral Sciences, 97, 320–324.*

Romero, C., et al, 2008. Data mining in course management systems: Moodle case study and tutorial. *Computers and Education, 51(1), 368–384.*

Shukor, N. A., et al., 2015. An Examination of Online Learning Effectiveness Using Data Mining. *Procedia - Social and Behavioral Sciences, 172, 555–562.*

Viloria, A. et al, 2019. Determinating student interactions in a virtual learning environment using data mining. *In Procedia Computer Science (Vol. 155, pp. 587–592). Elsevier B.V.*

Waheed, H. et al, 2020. Predicting academic performance of students from VLE big data using deep learning models.

Computers in Human Behavior, 104.

Yahya, A. A. and Osman, A., 2019. Using Data Mining Techniques to Guide Academic Programs Design and Assessment.

In Procedia Computer Science (Vol. 163, pp. 472–481). Elsevier B.V.

Zengin, K., Esgi et al, 2011. A sample study on applying data mining research techniques in educational science: Developing a more meaning of data. *In Procedia - Social and Behavioral Sciences (Vol. 15, pp. 4028–4032). Elsevier.*

DIGITAL COMPETENCES FOR EDUCATORS IN THE ITALIAN SECONDARY SCHOOL: A COMPARISON BETWEEN DIGCOMPEDU REFERENCE FRAMEWORK AND THE PP&S PROJECT EXPERIENCE

Cecilia Fissore[1], Francesco Floris[2], Marina Marchisio[2], Sergio Rabellino[3] and Matteo Sacchet[4]

[1]*Department of Foreign Languages and Literatures and Modern Cultures, University of Torino, Via Giuseppe Verdi, 10, 10124 Torino, Italy*

[2]*Department of Molecular Biotechnology and Health Sciences, University of Torino, Via Nizza 52, 10126, Torino, Italy*

[3]*Department of Computer Science, University of Torino, C.so Svizzera 185, 10149 Torino, Italy*

[4]*Department of Mathematics "G. Peano", University of Torino, Via Carlo Alberto 10, 10124, Torino, Italy*

ABSTRACT

Schools are facing a new challenge in their approach to education, due to the spreading of digital technologies. New tools and new ideas take shape at an increasing rate. Educators and teachers at all levels need to be trained and keep up to date with technological opportunities. Some help comes from official EU documents providing directions, guidelines, and reference framework. This is the case of the DigCompEdu, a resource about digital competences for educators, which lists 22 digital competences divided into six main areas equally important for the development of good practices in digital education. In this paper, we want to observe the list of competences in the "Problem Posing and Solving" project, an Italian experience with teachers in STEM disciplines , supported by the Italian ministry of Education; this project makes use of digital technologies of different kinds and innovative methodologies that enhance teaching and learning in secondary schools. We will analyze the competency framework from the point of view of teachers and students participating to the project.

KEYWORDS

Digital Competences, Digital Education, Digital School, Problem Solving, Secondary Education, Teacher Training

1. INTRODUCTION

Nowadays trend in education massively involves the use of digital technologies and environments. The structures and the environments need to be prepared and suited for this digital transformation. The first structure that younger students encounter during their compulsory educational path is the school, which must adapt their approach to education according to the potentialities that digital technologies can offer. Ministries, professors, and other stakeholders started running many projects related to school and education, with different purposes:

- Integration: connect digital technologies to other topics in learning and to other specific disciplines.
- Comprehension: understand the state of the use of digital technologies at schools.
- Training: contribute to the knowledge and skills of staff and teachers.
- Inclusion: address accessibility issues or gender studies.

There are some tools that can facilitate the transition to the digital education: the so called LMS, Learning Management System. Since the beginning of the digital era, many developers have worked to create environments that encourage didactical purposes. Among these environments, one of the most renowned is Moodle, which is an open source software.

The "Problem Posing and Solving" project, PP&S, (Brancaccio et al., 2015a), headed by the Italian Ministry of Education, promotes the training of teachers of secondary schools on innovative teaching methods through the use of digital technologies, and on the creation of a culture of problem posing and problem solving, through the use of Information and Communication Technology (ICT). Teachers involved in the project have learned - and still do - how to use different kinds of digital tools, in order to enhance their daily didactics. The essential tool for professional development of teachers and for the renewal of teaching and learning is the VLE, a Moodle-learning platform, available at www.progettopps.it, integrated with an Advanced Computing Environment (ACE), an Automatic Assessment System (AAS) and a web conference system. The tools used within the PP&S project support innovative and adaptive teaching:

- the VLE allows synchronous and asynchronous discussions, collaborative learning, interactivity and interaction, integration with tools for computing and assessment, activity tracking;
- the ACE allows interactive exploration of possible solutions to a problem, different ways of representation and feedback from automatic calculations and interactive explorations;
- the AAS allows students to carry out the necessary exercises independently, to have step-by-step guided solutions to learn a method and to make repeated attempts of the same exercise with different parameters and values. The AAS promotes students' autonomy and awareness of their skills and facilitates class management for teachers.

All the actions, developed in compliance with the PP&S directions, enable collaborative learning among teachers and promote problem posing and problem solving as learning methodologies (Barana et al., 2017). Technologies are not useful without the right methodologies, and this is the reason why teachers were trained in the following areas: problem posing and solving with an ACE that supports problem resolution and generalization, automatic formative assessment with adaptive questions aimed at teaching students how to solve problems, collaborative learning among teachers in a community of practice for the exchange of ideas, and collaborative learning among students in a learning community. The PP&S Project offers various training activities that allow teachers to reconsider their day to day teaching using technologies: face-to-face training, online training modules, weekly online tutoring, online asynchronous collaboration, and collaborative learning within a learning community.

The project started following the Italian National Strategies about STEM disciplines but, as it keeps growing and developing, it can respond to even more needs. Education is changing very fast and the European Union is trying to keep up with its development. In fact, the European Commission science and knowledge service proposed a document called DigCompEdu (Punie et al., 2017) which describes what skills an educator is required to be digitally competent. This document contains a reference frame to support the development of digital competences specifically for educators at all levels of education.

Since there PP&S project acts on digital education, the aim of this work is to understand whether the strategies and the methodologies initially adopted by the project, fulfill the indications later provided by DigCompEdu. We will prove the adherence to the framework with examples and data. After Section 2, which denotes the State of the art, the following sections articulate the research questions and the analysis and discussion on the connections between the reference frame of DigCompEdu and the PP&S project actions. The results section contains some data on the training of teachers carried out within the project, referring to the academic year 2019-2020, and some data on the use of the platform by students by teachers. During the current Academic Year, there has been the global pandemic caused by Covid-19. For this reason, starting from March 2020, many training activities focusing on Online Didactics have been provided.

2. STATE OF THE ART

The state of digital education in European schools is described in the document Digital education at school (Eurydice report, 2019). In line with the European indications, many countries define digital competence as a key competence. Most countries include the development of digital competence at all levels of education. Unlike other school subjects, digital competence is not only addressed as a topic on its own, but also as a transversal subject. The curriculum is changing in half of the European education systems in relation to digital competence. All national digital competences frameworks emphasize that teachers must be aware of how to integrate digital technologies into their teaching and professional development and they must be able to put them into practice. Even if digital competences are part of the curricula, they are little assessed at school through national testing.

In addition to European directions, there are some national and international implementations of these guidelines. As an example, the Digital Schools of Europe project aims at enhancing digital integration in learning, teaching, and training (Digital Schools of Europe Final Evaluation, 2018). Moreover, the project wants to address low achievement in basic skills and to develop basic and transversal skills, both objectives by using innovative and effective methods. Another example of implementation is SELFIE (SELFIE | Education and Training), a free, easy-to-use, customizable tool to assess where a school stands in the approach to learning in the digital age.

Behind the competences framework, the professional development of teachers plays an essential role. In this sense, a European experience was provided by the Erasmus+ SMART (Science and Mathematics Advanced Research for good Teaching) project (Brancaccio et al., 2019), whose main output were two open online courses called "Mathematical Modelling" and "Observing, Measuring and Modelling in Science". These two open online courses were created to help teachers in their continuous professional development, in an open self-paced path. In order to deploy the most expressive potentialities of digital technologies, both courses use interactive materials ready to be downloaded, modified to be used in the classroom and redistributed to the community.

An important document to state the needs of competences is DigCompEdu (Punie & Redecker, 2017), a reference framework directed towards educators at all levels of education. Teachers and students are the main target, but it is important to also mention the people who train the teachers so that they improve their didactics.

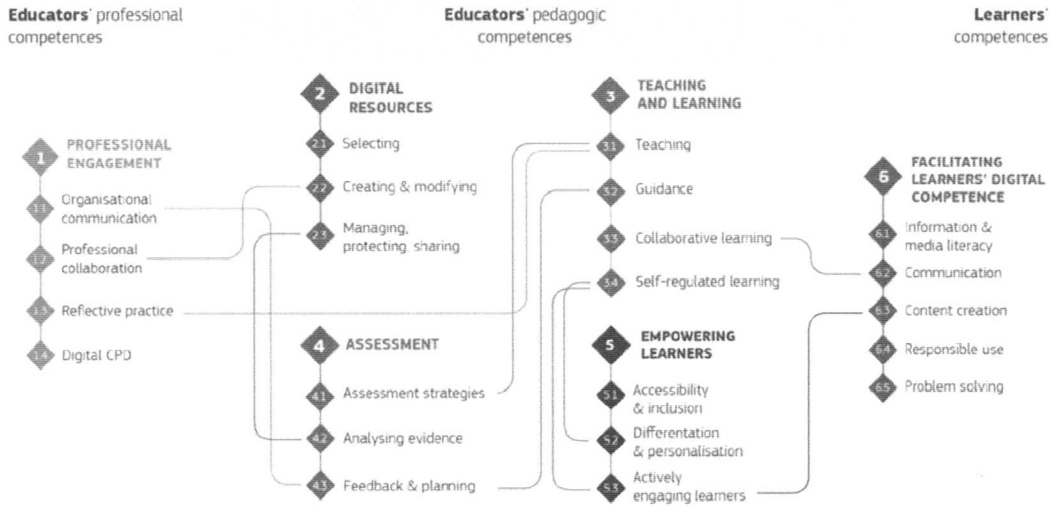

Figure 1. The DigCompEdu framework, divided into areas and sub-areas

The six DigCompEdu areas that focus on different aspects of educators' professional activities are:

- Area 1: Professional Engagement Using digital technologies for communication, collaboration and professional development.
- Area 2: Digital Resources Sourcing, creating and sharing digital resources.
- Area 3: Teaching and Learning Managing and orchestrating the use of digital technologies in teaching and learning.
- Area 4: Assessment Using digital technologies and strategies to enhance assessment.
- Area 5: Empowering Learners Using digital technologies to enhance inclusion, personalization and learners' active engagement.
- Area 6: Facilitating Learners' Digital Competence Enabling learners to creatively and responsibly use digital technologies for information, communication, content creation, wellbeing and problem-solving.

These areas are further divided into specific sub-competences that covers all the main aspects that a student, a teacher or any other actor involved in education may face.

3. PP&S TEACHER TRAINING MODEL IN COMPARISON WITH DIGCOMPEDU

Even if the PP&S project was born in 2012, that is around 5 years before the DigCompEdu (published in 2017), it seems to anticipate and address many of the areas and competences detailed in DigCompEdu. The PP&S project is not just a set of actions addressing STEM teaching, but it developed a model that combines didactical methodologies and strategies with technologies, connecting different actors and peers. The assessment of the adherence of the PP&S model to the EU guidelines can contribute to the educational community. since it is possible to export and reuse the same approach in different contexts and countries. Thus, the questions of this research paper are the following:

1. Do the actions of the PP&S project fall within the European indications of the DigCompEdu?
2. Which areas of the DigCompEdu are covered and which of them are not?

We are going to enter systematically in all the specific areas and competences to see which ones are activated and addressed by the project PP&S. Figure 1 represents a scheme of all the competences described in DigCompEdu.

3.1 Professional Engagement

Area 1 of DigCompEdu describes professional engagement. Communication is essential for the project, since in the online platform teachers interact with students and with their peers in a collaborative approach (Competence 1.1). In fact, teachers are enrolled in a virtual Community of Teachers (Competence 1.2). The main tool for collaboration is the discussion forum, in which teachers discuss different topics: curricula, usage of ACE and AAS, methodologies (like problem solving and automatic formative assessment). The interactions with teachers also take place synchronously, via web conference tools, connecting with experts in digital education at the University of Torino, providing teachers with an up-to-date training session at the frontiers of research. Within the Community, teachers can also share their products and their resources, and they can find contents for self-training, promoting the continuous professional development (Competence 1.4). Beyond the Community, every teacher manages one or more courses to share and work with students. Access to teacher's personal course is available to colleagues, so they can see how peers use technologies and apply methodologies, thus fostering reflective practices (Competence 1.3).

3.2 Resources

Area 2 of DigCompEdu describes sourcing, creating and sharing digital resources. The community of PP&S Teachers owns a shared database of contents and educational resources, one for interactive materials for teaching STEMs with an ACE and one for tests with automatic assessment. Teachers are guided in selecting the right resources: databases are organized by types of contents and degree of education (Competence 2.1), and every entry provides descriptors such as topic, objectives, prerequisites, etc. The search in the web and the use of a variety of tools, according to the purpose of didactics, is strongly encouraged, even if the project proposes a precise methodology and specific tools. Teachers are supported until they become autonomous in the modification of existing resources and in the creation of their own ones, which are strongly recommended to be interactive (Competence 2.2). The shared contents are copyrighted with the logo of the project in order to acknowledge that they were prepared by a teacher in the PP&S project (Competence 2.3). The project provided training in all aspects of digital education and the most interested teachers are aware of copyright issues, of the advantages of the use of open licenses like Creative Commons and data protection, even if, to date, these topics are not included in the "starting package" for teachers.

3.3 Teaching and Learning

Area 3 of DigCompEdu describes competences about teaching and learning, which is the core of DigCompEdu. One of the proposed teaching methods is the problem solving with an ACE, with contextualized situations in which students must apply and develop knowledge to solve problems (Brancaccio et al., 2015b). Since the project proposes the use of specific tools dedicated to problem solving methodology, teachers have the opportunity to install the ACE for free on their personal computer and in school labs, empowering their devices (Competence 3.1). In this way, students can work independently with the ACE to develop problem solving and computational thinking skills (Barana et al., 2019). Teacher can freely manage their online classes and experiment, develop new formats and teaching methods for education. Teachers learn about the use of adaptive resources, mainly questions (which will be described in the next subsection) to provide personalized feedback and action into the learner's processes (Competence 3.2).

3.4 Assessment

Area 4 of DigCompEdu describes competences about assessment. This is one of the main topics of the PP&S, since one of the selected tools to enhance learning is an Automatic Assessment System (AAS). The integration of the platform with an automatic assessment system, based on a computing environment, allows the creation of questions with variable parameters and with open answers, evaluating the process and not the result. In particular, the focus is on Automatic Formative Assessment using the model developed at the University of Torino (Barana et al., 2018; Barana, Marchisio & Rabellino, 2019) with interactive and immediate feedback, promoting adaptive teaching and self-regulated learning (Competence 4.1). The teacher can constantly monitor students' behavior on the platform and interpret all the learning data of each student. Basic analytics can be provided by the LMS and the AAS in order to evaluate the effectiveness of the resources and activities (Competence 4.2), but this is just for the more expert teachers, since it is also a quite new research topic (Marchisio et al., 2019; Barana, Marchisio & Sacchet, 2019). Some teachers use the AAS for summative assessment, too, providing important feedback and planning intervention and recovering according to the results (Competence 4.3).

3.5 Empowering Learners

Area 5 of DigCompEdu describes competences related to empowering learners. This is something strongly dependent on the teachers' approach, but technologies can provide fruitful advantages. Accessibility is addressed, which is crucial at school level, even if not very detailed in online environment. Luckily for teachers, Moodle supports accessibility as a main project goal (https://docs.moodle.org/31/en/Accessibility). To enforce the accessibility of Moodle, the platform uses EasyReading, a font suitable for dyslexia. Even personalized paths are left to the teachers' responsibility and since they provide blended learning, it is something that can happen both online and in the class. Competences of area 5 are more difficult to assess compared to those of the other areas.

3.6 Facilitate Learners

Area 6 of DigCompEdu describes how to facilitate learners' digital competence. This is the mirror of Area 1, from the learners' point of view. It is very difficult to understand whether the PP&S project reaches a standard in these competences or not. Every teacher uses the platform differently: in person with students, shown in the classroom or in the lab, or in a blended way, for online lessons, homework or flipped classroom. Moreover, some teachers facilitate students' group activities. Since students browse an online environment, they are used to search and find many information autonomously and, sometimes, they are motivated by the teacher in a personal search all over the web to look for Open Educational Resources (Competence 6.1). In this setting, collaboration is automatic (Competence 6.2) since students meet in the classroom every day. Some students, the most skilled ones, were able to create their own contents using the ACE to present a mathematical topic in a contextualized situation during their secondary school final exam (Competence 6.3).

4. RESULTS

The PP&S project operates since 2015 promoting new STEM teaching methods to teachers all over Italy, reaching many different schools and teachers.

In the absence of similar experiences, for dimension and openness, the project developed a model to sustain an introduction of the technology into the Italian secondary school. The PP&S model has evolved during these years and has been continuously improved and refined and proved effective by working with a substantial number of teachers and students who have worked on the e learning platform over the past 5 years
The following table (Table 1) presents an overview of the project scale.

Table 1. General overview of the PP&S project, last update April 2nd, 2020

	Amount		Amount
Users	**25623**	New users AY 2019/2020	**3967**
of which teachers	**1827**	of which teachers	**356**
of which students	**23796**	of which students	**3611**

In the Academic Year 2019/2020 there are 2015 courses in which teachers work with students (every teacher has got at least one course). In order to promote teacher training, material for self-training is always available on the platform. Moreover, at the beginning of the Academic Year 2019/2020 a synchronous online training module entitled "Innovative teaching methods for teaching and learning STEMs in the PP&S Project" actively involved 37 teachers who were new to the project, with four 1-hour online meetings. To obtain complete certification, each teacher had to participate in at least 3 meetings, structure and customize the course for their class and set the contents of at least one section (inserting an interactive material and a test with automatic evaluation). This module comes with weekly meetings for all teachers: ten 1-hour slot on STEM didactics with an ACE and ten 1-hour slot on automatic evaluation for STEM disciplines.

During the Academic Year, there was the global pandemic caused by Covid-19. This caused a period of emergency, during which the weekly meetings were suspended in favor of a general training on online teaching. In fact, the PP&S project decided to open enrollments to teachers of lower and upper secondary schools of all disciplines, not only STEM. The main training topics concerned the use of the Virtual Learning Environment to manage and offer students activities and resources, and automatic formative assessment to monitor and facilitate learning, creation of adaptive tests. 186 teachers participated in the extraordinary training. Table 2 shows data related to users in the PP&S project between the period Pre Covid-19 (01/09/2019 - 29/02/2020) and during Covid-19 (01/03/2020 to the present date, written in the table caption).

Table 2. Comparison between Pre and During Covid-19, last update April 2nd, 2020

Period	Pre Covid-19 01/09/2019 - 29/02/2020	During Covid-19 01/03/2020 up to date	Increase
New users	**1466**	**2847**	**+194%**
Average of new users per day	**11**	**80**	**+627%**
Average login per day	**4875**	**7727**	**+59%**
Average distinct user login per day	**117**	**1120**	**+918%**

These numbers do not only show an increased number of accesses to the platform, but they are also prove of an active engagement and collaboration in the Community of Teacher forum. In the Pre Covid-19 period (6 months), 133 forum threads and 303 posts were created, with 3351 visualizations, while during Covid-19 (1 month) 56 forum threads and 124 posts were created, with 1148 visualizations. The numbers are significant when considering the time span, since the Pre Covid-19 period of time is 6 times longer than the Covid-19 period of time.

During this period, the collaboration among teachers on the platform to overcome this emergency situation was particularly important and significant. The teachers discussed a lot about how to best propose an online teaching, to carry out synchronous online lessons and how to prepare relevant materials and resources. The teachers collaborated mainly through the forum of the Teacher Community (Table 3), where each teacher can open a discussion, write an intervention in a discussion already present or simply consult the forum. The ever-present support of the trainers was also fundamental.

Table 3. Data from the Teacher Community forum Pre and During Covid-19, last update April 2nd, 2020

Period	Pre Covid-19 01/09/2019 - 29/02/2020	During Covid-19 01/03/2020 up to date
Threads created	77	**56**
Threads read	2203	**1148**
Posts created	179	**124**

All the teachers have completely transformed their teaching into online teaching, structuring the course on the platform and inserting different types of activities and resources for the students. Figure 2 shows an example of an online course on the platform with examples of activities within one of the various sections.

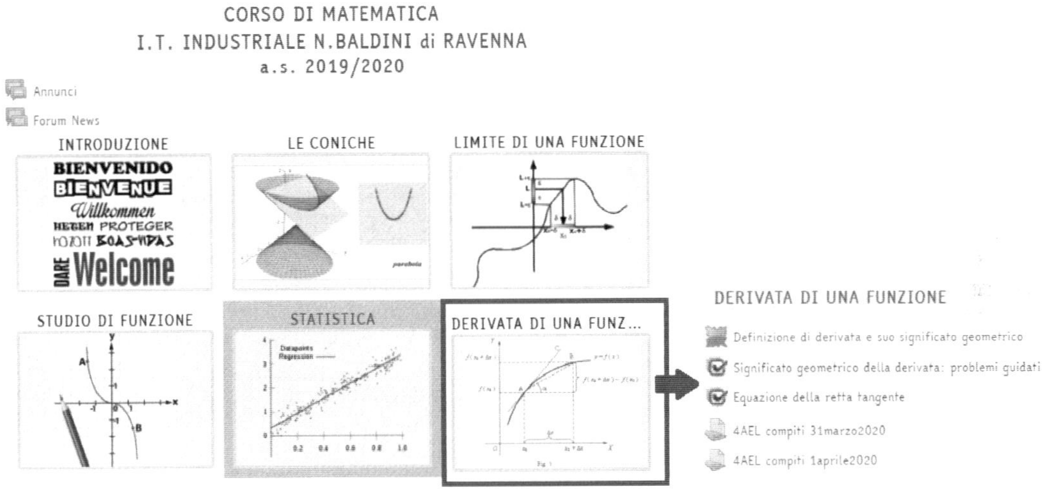

Figure 2. The DigCompEdu framework, divided into areas and sub-areas

5. CONCLUSION

Activation of competences is certainly addressed by the project PP&S, even without being the main aim of the project. Students and teachers are involved together in an online environment, pulling out some basic competences, and trained to use specific digital competences every time they interact with the LMS. Thus, the educational action provided by the project PP&S mostly adhere to the guidelines of DigCompEdu. The interested teachers cover all areas of competences, while most of them are involved in Areas from 1 to 4, which are the essential ones for good practice in teaching. As we emphasized in the paper, when the competences are addressed, they are close to research level, since teachers interact directly with experts, researchers and professors at the University of Torino. The training of teachers within the project was particularly emphasized and appreciated during the emergency period for the COVID-19 pandemic. As the results show (partial data only for the month of March 2020), the participation of teachers in the training activities and the collaboration among teachers on the platform was relevant. This period of emergency and online teaching will certainly also be relevant for students and for their development of digital skills, such as the use of information and digital media for activities and the use of technologies for communication and collaboration for educational activities.

The guidelines of the DigCompEdu framework should be followed in every country in Europe. The PP&S model could be an implementation of these guidelines that could be adopted in different educational contexts and grades. Besides the adherence to the guidelines, the availability of an online environment, where people with the same needs can share ideas and resources, and bring competences to a wider group of peers, even internationally, plays an important role to rebuild the human relations interrupted by Covid-19 .

REFERENCES

Barana, A., Conte, A., Fioravera, M., Marchisio, M., Rabellino, S. (2018). A Model of Formative Automatic Assessment and Interactive Feedback for STEM. In: Proceedings of 2018 IEEE 42nd Annual Computer Software and Applications Conference (COMPSAC), IEEE, Tokyo, Japan, pp. 1016–1025.

Barana, A., Conte, A., Fissore, C., Floris, F., Marchisio, M., & Sacchet, M. (2019). The Creation of Animated Graphs to Develop Computational Thinking and Support STEM Education. In Maple Conference (pp. 189-204). Springer, Cham.

Barana, A., Fioravera, M., & Marchisio, M. (2017). Teacher training: a model for introducing innovative digital methodologies for learning Mathematics. Proceedings of the 3rd International Conference on Higher Education Advances, HEAd'17. http://dx.doi.org/10.4995/HEAd17.2017.5303

Brancaccio, A., Demartini, C., Marchisio, M., Palumbo, C., Pardini, C., Patrucco, A., & Zich, R. (2015a). Problem Posing and Solving: Strategic Italian Key Action to Enhance Teaching and Learning of Mathematics and Informatics in High School. Proceedings of COMPSAC Symposium on Computer Education and Learning Technologies (CELT).

Brancaccio, A., Esposito, M., Marchisio, M., Pardini, C., & Sacchet, M. (2019). Open professional development of math teachers through an online course. Proceedings of the IADIS International Conference e-Learning 2019 (part of MCCSIS 2019), pp. 131-138.

Brancaccio, A., Marchisio, M., Palumbo, C., Pardini, C., Patrucco, A., Zich, R. (2015b). Problem Posing and Solving: Strategic Italian Key Action to Enhance Teaching and Learning Mathematics and Informatics in the High School. In: Proceedings of 2015 IEEE 39th Annual Computer Software and Applications Conference, IEEE, Taichung, Taiwan, pp. 845–850.

Barana, A., Marchisio, M., & Rabellino, S. (2019). Empowering Engagement through automatic formative assessment. In 2019 IEEE 43rd Annual Computer Software and Applications Conference (COMPSAC), IEEE, Vol. 1, pp. 216-225.

Barana, A., Marchisio, M., & Sacchet, M. (2019). Advantages of Using Automatic Formative Assessment for Learning Mathematics. In S. Draaijer, D. Joosten-ten Brinke, & E. Ras (A c. Di), Technology Enhanced Assessment, Springer International Publishing, Vol. 1014, pp. 180–198.

In Digital education at school in Europe – Eurydice report (2019). Retrieved from https://op.europa.eu/en/publication-detail/-/publication/d7834ad0-ddac-11e9-9c4e-01aa75ed71a1/language-en/format-PDF/source-105790537, last accessed April, 2nd, 2020.

In Digital Schools of Europe Final Evaluation (2018). Retireved from http://www.digitalschoolseurope.eu/wp-content/uploads/2018/10/DSoE-Final-Evaluation-180929.pdf, last accessed April, 2nd, 2020.

Marchisio, M., Rabellino, S., Roman, F., Sacchet, M., & Salusso, D. (2019). Boosting up Data Collection and Analysis to Learning Analytics in Open Online Contexts: an Assessment Methodology. Journal of E-Learning and Knowledge Society, 15(3), pp. 49-59. https://doi.org/10.20368/1971-8829/1135048

Punie, Y., Redecker, C., (2017). European framework for the digital competence of educators: DigCompEdu. Publications Office of the European Union. https://doi.org/10.2760/159770

In SELFIE | Education and Training. Retrieved from https://ec.europa.eu/education/schools-go-digital_en, last accessed April, 2nd, 2020.

GENDER DIFFERENCES IN ATTITUDES TOWARDS OBOW EXAMS: THE CASE OF A DEVELOPING COUNTRY

Mary Ann B. El Rassi
Saint Jospeh University, Beyrouth, Lebanon

ABSTRACT

Despite the increased research interest on the implementation of Open Book Open Web exams in developed countries, there has been very little systematic studies that investigated the difference in gender experience and the cognitive process that could affect attitude towards OBOW exams compared to the traditional ones in developing countries. This paper aims at filling this gap in knowledge by comparing OBOW and traditional exam methods. Several exams in two different contextual settings were done and in three different high schools. The exams were divided into two phases, midterms and finals and several methods were adopted. The sample included 307 students in addition to three focus groups that helped us to identify important factors. Factors such as gender, emotional tension/anxiety, technology self-efficiency, perceived ease of use were important cues that predicted academic performance. At the end of this research paper, we propose a preliminary model that could be detested further with a larger sample.

KEYWORDS

Open Book Open Web Exams, Academic Performance, Electronic Learning, Developing Countries

1. INTRODUCTION

In a world where globalization is considered as a multidimensional phenomenon, e-leaning appears to be one of the emerging trends and is increasingly weighing not only in developed economies but also in developing economies (Guàrdia, Crisp & Alsina, 2017). It is an innovative tool, mainly for subjects that necessitate multimedia and collaboration. As a result, the student profile has changed economically, culturally and socially as new online teaching techniques have emerged, encouraging students from all over the globe to enroll in e-distance learning (Joi, Camille & Krista, 2011). This has resulted in an impressive change in the educational technology. A transformation that has been of a major interest to scholars and journals recently which have led to the creation of a stream of literature that examined this topic from different angles such as blended learning techniques and wholly online techniques among others (Steve, Ferrante and Heppard, 2016). Despite this new revolution, one facet of the academic life has hardly changed at all, which is the traditional exam model for conducting exams that still dominates. Given the fact, that most of the modern academic institutions use the internet platform to communicate with their students and exchange information, they still fear conducting online exams and prefer to rely on a physical examination that is physically monitored. We cannot deny the fact that most of this new generation is an internet savvy and depend largely on the use of the net very often in their daily activities. Therefore, this paper is centered on the following question: What could possibly be the influential factors that affect the students' attitude towards Open-Book Open-Web exams? Whereas developing countries differ from developed countries in terms of culture and ICT infrastructure (El Rassi, 2020; El Rassi, 2018; El Rassi & Harfouche, 2016). Our major objective in this research is to better understand the students' attitude towards an OBOW in an era where it appears that there is a gap in literature when it comes to assessing this issue in a developing country. To accomplish the study's main objective outlined in this paper, we proceed by presenting a literature review concerning the employment of e-learning in the education system, the OBOW.

2. E-LEARNING, OBWO AND TRADITIONAL MEANS

In the following section we present an overview of the literature concerning the above mentioned subject. Our major concern is to provide an overview about e-learning and OBOW. The traditional closed book examination methods are able to investigate the student's knowledge based on their learning (Guàrdia et al., 2017). These methods are entirely based on the student's memory and is considered as an assessment instrument that is more likely to foster deep learning. Thus, sometimes, these methods are not very efficient in assessing the students' knowledge and have been questioned by many scholars. It is also found that traditional exams sometimes result in higher scores but those same students might fail to pass the competitive recruitment exams when required because they lack the freedom of analyzing (Steve et al,2016). In order to overcome this issue, some scholars have encouraged educators to reassess their traditional format by proposing an open –book-open – web exam among other options (Steve et al, 2016). Thus, a new trend had emerged where some universities for example have started to accommodate grades from traditional exams to OBOW to award program degrees. This new pattern called OBOW allows students to use electronic devices during their exam assessment. It reflects a major change and difference from the traditional format as it allows the student to take full advantage of all the available resources through the Web. Another interesting outcome of the OBOW examination is that questions represent real world problems which requires general knowledge and research and this minimizes the chance of copying or cheating by students (Steve et al, 2016). Even though this looks quite easy to be done by cheating or copying, a submission procedure such as plagiarism software could be used to detect any academic fraud. The major idea in the OBOW model is to urge the students to think in a conceptual way to analyze and solve a given problem or mini-case and that is by employing their knowledge and expertise that they have acquired during their course of studies (Miller and Young-Jones, 2012). In addition to the use of plagiarism software, and the time constraints that the student faces when conducting his exam (for a period of 2 or 3 hours), it would be impossible for them to outsource the solution as the accomplice should be first familiar with the subject which makes it more difficult for them to cheat. Therefore, may authors have considered that the OBOW exams represent an efficient way to engage students whether they are monitored for cheating as in the traditional exams or not (Steve et al,2016). Therefore, assessing the cognitive process is very crucial to understanding the factors that affect students' experience in OBOW and traditional exams as students' learning is guided by the way they are assessed.

3. LITERATURE REVIEW

The Technology Acceptance Model (TAM) that was proposed by Davis (1986) is one of the most broadly adopted models in theory that was used in different settings and contexts by many authors (Davis et al., 1989; Venkatesh, Morris, Davis, & Davis, 2003). This model was based on the general human behavior model that is called the theory of reasoned action (Fishbein & Ajzen 1975) whereas the theoretical basis was to offer an enlightenment of the human computer use behavior that was earlier proposed by Fishbein & Ajzen (1975). Moreover, this model is interesting to the current study as it has also investigated the applicability and legitimacy to examine students' intention when using e-learning technologies in several studies (Roca et al. 2006). The model considers that the perceived usefulness (PU) and perceived ease of use (PEU) are the antecedent determinant factors to use IT and are considered as the two main constructs of this model as they are able to predict the individual's attitude towards using a certain system. Perceived usefulness is defined as the extent to which an individual believes that using a certain system will improve his job performance. While the perceived ease of use is defined as the extent to which an individual believes that using a certain system will be free of mental and physical effort. PU and PEU are two antecedents that could influence a person's attitude (A) while attitude is perceived as the individual's assessment of his behavior. This attitude (A) is also expected to influence the individual's behavioral intention (BI) and consequently, BI is expected to influence the actual use (AU) of a certain system. Furthermore, the use of technology has also been of a major concern in the literature. Computer anxiety is defined as an individual's apprehension or even fear, when she/he is faced with the possibility of using computers (Simonson et al., 1987). Howard & Smith (1986) defines computer anxiety as the tendency of a person to experience a level of uneasiness over his or her impending use of a computer. In fact, students' who are using e-learning as new educational tools could have some anxiety towards presenting their exams online (OBOW). Several researches have investigated computer anxiety as a key factor in influencing the different types of technology intention such as e-mails and computer usage. Recently, several researches have been conducted in the area of e-learning intention to use to investigate the role of computer anxiety on students' intention (Ndubisi, 2004; Saadé & Kira 2006). Saadé and Kira (2006) have conducted research to assess the emotional state of students' perception towards online learning system based on the technology intention model (TAM). The authors have extended technology intention model to include Anxiety and Affect as antecedents and for both perceived usefulness and perceived ease of use. The findings from the study indicated that the perceived usefulness of using online system is not determined by the students' computer anxiety. However, it has indirect influence through the perceived ease of use on the students' intention of online learning system. Furthermore, the anxiety has a positive influence on students' intention of using online system. In conclusion, the emotional state has no direct impact on perceived usefulness of an online learning system, whereas, it has power in predicting the ease of use of the online learning system. Ndubisi (2004) has conducted research to investigate the critical factors that influence the student' intention to adopt e-learning in Malaysia. The author examined many factors on students' intention to use the Blackboard system such as users' attitude, subjective norm, perceived behavioral control, perceived usefulness and ease of use of the system. Some of those factors were used to mediate and others to test directly the proposed variables. The findings show that the computer anxiety has contributed significantly and has predicted about 22% of variation in perceived behavioral control. The findings also indicate that the students with high level of computer anxiety have less perceived behavioral control which will ultimately influences the behavioral intention to use e-learning tools. In brief, computer anxiety seems to be a crucial factor that could influence the e-learning adoption in higher education institutions. Other studies have investigated the computer self-efficacy in e-learning as an antecedent to the TAM model. In a study that was conducted by Madorin & Iwasiw (1999), the authors have investigated the effect of computer self-efficacy in e-learning in the faculty of nursing. Self-efficacy is an individual's believe about his own ability and incentive to achieve a specific task (Agarwal, Sambamurthy, & Stair 2000). In the current study it is considered as one's capacity to use a technology to complete a specific task (Venkatesh et al., 2003). The findings of Madorin & Iwasiw (1999) study revealed that while the computer self-efficacy has a strong effect on PEU, it has an insignificant effect on PU. While several studies have been conducted to examine the self-efficiency influence on the technology intention model (Madorin & Iwasiw, 1999), the results of these study were different than Venkatish et al. (2003) results. The latter authors have argued that the underlying problem might be low computer self -efficacy and in such cases, a training should be conducted to enhance the user's self-efficiency when using technology which could increase the individual's attitude.

4. METHODOLOGY

The research was conducted in a high school that has adopted the web as a support to its teaching methods. Students can connect with their teachers, consult their lessons and grades through an application called pronote. In addition to that, the school has initiated many electronic initiatives and had merged them into their learning processes for their students' access and use. Nevertheless, the traditional learning model is still valid. This paper is based on a comparison between the traditional method examination and the OBOW. Two exams were conducted during the same year and for the same courses, in addition to some focus groups where participants were selected from the students and professors who had experienced both methods that are stated in our paper. The traditional exam was conducted at school and monitored by instructors, while the OBOW exam was made outside the school on a day off and the due time limit was fixed. This had allowed the students to take the test at their convenience and from any place they may choose to be comfortable with. And as the school is an international French school that usually have 3 different campuses in the same city, the students were divided into 3 different groups sharing in common the same educational level (senior high school year) and course offerings. The total number of students that participated in this exam was 307 among which 41% were male and 59% were female students and their age range was expected to be 17-18. All three groups have taken the same exam, at the same time without knowing each other or without even knowing that the others have had a similar case. Then we compared the grades of OBOW exams of the students by the same group of students from the traditional closed book exam. As we have targeted three different campuses for the same school and the same courses taken, we have divided our groups into 3 main groups depending on their grades as mentioned before. Having three different locations have helped us a lot because students aren't supposed to be familiar with each other which could decrease the possibility of cheating when doing the first and second phase of the exam. Both exams consisted of two phases: the first phase consisted of 30 multiple choice questions and was estimated to be finished within 45 minutes, and students were given 60 minutes. While the second part consisted of a mini case where the students should be able to illustrate and analyze based on their personal knowledge. Once they start, they cannot keep it on hold or save and return to it later. While the second phase consisted of a mini-case analysis that was well-researched, well thought-out scripts along with a reflection that represents the value of this approach for the improvement of students' learning outcome. The second phase couldn't be copied as it was automatically passed through the plagiarism software and was based on their personal writing skill. After finishing the two exams, we then interviewed 3 focus groups to evaluate their experience and assessment of this new experience and compare the differences, if found, in the two adopted models in addition to their instructors. Each focus group was chosen from the three campuses based on their academic level. Sentences and verbatim were selected which had helped us in constructing a questionnaire. Then we carried on our study by sending this questionnaire by email to the same students. In an attempt to detect any possible cheating or difficulties encountered in part I of the OBOW exam, we have estimated that when a student took more than 4 minutes to answer a question, he could possibly be looking to find another alternative with other peers. Considering that 30 multiple choice questions needed between 45 to 60 minutes to be completed and there is no penalty in answering any question falsely, therefore we expected the student to pick any answer if he doesn't know it within a time frame of 3 or 4 minutes' maximum. A previous sample test was done online and in campus with the students to avoid any technical mistakes they might encounter.

5. RESULTS

In this section we will start by presenting the results of the exams conducted in both models and their grade scores. Then we proceeded by choosing a focus group that equally represents all three schools. Starting with the first phase of the exam, we have conducted two exams for the same course. One midterm that was done through traditional means, with a pen and paper, while the second was done during the final exam using the OBOW method. Table 1 explains in details the results of the first phase that consisted of a Multiple Choice Question (MCQ) exam. It included 30 questions that equally varied between difficult, medium and easy. In the traditional method, pen and paper, students were monitored in class and the supervisors were able to detect any technical or cheating problems directly on the spot. In the OBOW method, the answers were chosen randomly for each student which means that cheating is not an easy task for them to do due to the time constraints unless they waste their time and efforts to make it happen. The below table shows that the instructors participated in screening the degree of cheating during the examination period. Cheating was evaluated based on the time the students took to finish their exam whether phase one or phase two.

Table 1. QCM exam results comparison

Phase 1 : Multiple choice questions (MCQ) - 30 questions- 60 mn							
	Type of exam	Grp1-execllent >16/20	Grp2-good 14 to 16 /20	Grp3-average 10 to 14/20	Grp4-below average < 10/20	Invalid	Numbers of students
School I	OBOW	32	40	24	6	0	102
	Traditional	38	47	16	1	1*	
School II	OBOW	44	33	17	3	1*	98
	Traditional	45	30	20	2	1*	
School III	OBOW	50	37	14	4	2*	107
	Traditional	53	29	22	3	0	
Total # of students	OBOW	126 (41%)	110 (35.8%)	55 (18%)	13 (6%)	3	307
	Traditional	136 (44.22%)	106 (34.5%)	58 (18.9%)	5(2%)	2	

*Cheating

In the first and second groups, the OBOW exam performance reached 41% for Group1 compared to 44.22% for the traditional model and 35.8% for the OBOW in group 2 compared with 34.5% in for the traditional model. Summing them together, 76.8% of the grades in OBOW were slightly lower than 78.7% in the traditional model. This means that both methods were at the same level of efficiency in the MCQ exam. Cheating in the OBOW was less significant than in the traditional model as it was detected. This difference could be considered insignificant which allows us to state that the two methods we have used were credible and efficient for our study.

Table 2. Mini-case exam results comparison

Phase 2 : Mini case assessment- 90 minutes							
	Type of exam	Grp1-execllent (above 16/20)	Grp2-good\ (between 14/20 and 16 /20	Grp3-average between 10 and 14/20	Grp4-below average < 10/20	Invalid cheating	Numbers of students
School I	OBOW	35	34	31	1	1*	102
	Traditional	28	33	37	4	0	
School II	OBOW	46	32	18	2	0	98
	Traditional	44	30	20	2	2*	
School III	OBOW	41	39	22	5	0	107
	Traditional	29	32	39	6	1*	
Total number of students	OBOW	122 (40%)	105(34.2%)	71 (23.1%)	8 (2.6%)	1	307
	Traditional	101 (33%)	95(31%)	96 (31.2%)	12(4%)	3	

*Cheating

In the second phase, the students were offered a mini case and were expected to have a personal contribution. Unless the student didn't attend the previous seminars, he cannot fulfill the requirements and analyze the case study. For the same reasons as in phase I, a student that has been detected to be wasting time or encountering some technical difficulties was considered either cheating or having technical problems. The OBOW exam performance reached 40% for group1 compared to 33% for the traditional model and 34.2% in OBOW for group 2 compared to 31% for the traditional model. Summing them together, 74.2 of the grades in OBOW were scattered between group 1 and group 2 which is higher than the sum of those two groups in the traditional model (64%). While cheating in the OBOW was less significant than in the traditional model (1 student in the OBOW took more than 10 minutes in answering 2 questions). Furthermore, a higher number of failing students that scored below the average were identified in the traditional exam. We then proceeded our investigating by choosing three focus groups whereas each focus group consisted of three students and one teacher from each institution in order to evaluate their experience and perspective regarding the pros and cons of this OBOW exam and to note their objections, if any.

5.1 Focus Groups Results

While the students were well informed ahead of time about the OBOW exam that will be taken by the end of the semester, they expressed some anxiety and concerns at the beginning especially that the exam was supposed to be conducted individually and off campus. Their major concern was that in case they encounter any technical problem, they will be by themselves and could not complete the task on time which could result in a poor performance. Despite these worries, some others welcomed the idea and considered it as an opportunity and a new challenge to accomplish the required tasks (for a reason or another) and thought that it would be easier than the traditional method (see Table 3).

Table 3. Focus groups results concerning emotional tension/ anxiety

It was difficult for me to accept the idea. I had fears[1] and concerns (Female Student from group 1- school 1). I felt some tension[1], but it was ok. I like technology and don't have any problem dealing with it (Female Student from group 2- school 2). It isn't easy at all. There shouldn't be a problem. I personally didn't encounter[1] any problem at all.(Female Student from group 2- school 3).	**1-Emotional tension-anxiety**	**Baird, 2019; Hung et al. , 2014)**

Another factor emerged to be very important and in favor of OBOW: self-efficacy. When a student experiences anxiety during an exam, his mood activates the memories that are consistent with it. The negative mood provokes previous failures or negative experiences which could lead to a lower believe in their self-efficacy (Richardson et al., 2012). Therefore, when asked about their self-efficacy, during and before the exam, students described the feeling as excellent or as bad depending on their situation. Those who had negative feelings and expressed anxiety had resulted in lower self-esteem and believe in their self-efficacy sometimes and those who had high self-efficiency feeling, were less stressed and perceived well the ease of usefulness of such a method.

Table 4. Focus groups results concerning anxiety, self-efficacy, perceived ease of use, attitude towards using the system

When the online exam started, I was really confused[1]. I heard from other students that as a first time user, it wouldn't be easy for me[2]. I panicked for the first 15 mn. This was too complex for me.[1] I didn't even score as I anticipated. I really think this method is difficult[3] and not very useful[3] for me to use in the future… I would consider using[4] it in the future maybe if things get better (Female student from group 1- school 1).	1-Emotional tension-anxiety 2-Self-efficacy 3-Perceived ease of use. 4-Attitude towards using the system	Richardson et al., 2012;

The last topic that was discussed with them was the possible attitude towards using an online mean to conduct an exam based on their experience. Whether they would repeat the experience or not, and the antecedents that could affect their attitude whether negative or positive.

Table 5. Focus groups results concerning anxiety, self-efficacy, perceived ease of use, attitude towards using the system

The fact that the system is easy to use[3] is very encouraging, why not. Especially that based on my previous experiences that were successful[2], I feel that this could be encouraging[4] (Male student from group 1- school 2).	2-Self-efficacy 4-Attitude towards using the system	Richardson et al., 2012;

We have identified several factors and organized them randomly then sent them to a group of 307 students from the same sample. They were solicited by emails, and a set of 10 questions were asked and the students were expected to answer on a Likert scale from 1 to 5 (see table 6).

Table 6. Gender difference responses

	Male (n=101)	Female (n=110)
Emotional -tension- anxiety (ETANX)	3.1	4.2
Perceive Ease of Use (PEU)	4.2	2.88
Attitude towards e-learning (A)	3.9	2.4
Self-efficacy (SEF)	4.2	2.77

Note: 5-point Likert scale scoring system used: 5 = strongly agree,4= agree,3= neutral,2= disagree,1= strongly disagree.

6. SUMMARY AND CONCLUSION

Our main concern was investigating the experience and the factors that could affect the academic performance of OBOW exams by comparing them with the traditional closed book exams. Obviously, we were neither after harassing students nor filtering them. The progress in the teaching methods that appeared recently had driven many scholars to identify the best way to examine students and the OBOW was one of those methods (Baird et al, 2019). When observing the performance of the models (Tables 1 and 2), it is observed that there isn't much difference in the results. As for the cheating, we have suspected 4 cases in the OBOW based on the software results and tracking system compared to 5 cases in the traditional exam that were detected by the instructors. Comparing the results together, we can assert that the results of the exams in both methods were credible to investigate which could help us conclude, that the risk of cheating in the OBOW is about just the same as in traditional exams. The results in the second phase show an evident improvement with the OBOW model where the students had all the resources available in an exam that required a personal effort and was made at their convenience in a stress free environment. Based on the above stated results, we observe that the OBOW method is efficient if not more than the traditional method at least the same. Such method can pave the way for students to get ready for the real-world problems by giving them more motivation and confidence in a stress free environment and helping them in getting engaged with multi-media and depth in learning. Thus, and a result of the semi structured interviews and questionnaires that were sent, three important factors predicted the attitude towards OBOW exams: emotional tension- anxiety, self-efficacy, perceived ease of use and last but not least the gender difference as well. Thus, we propose the below model that should to be tested on a larger scale for more validity.

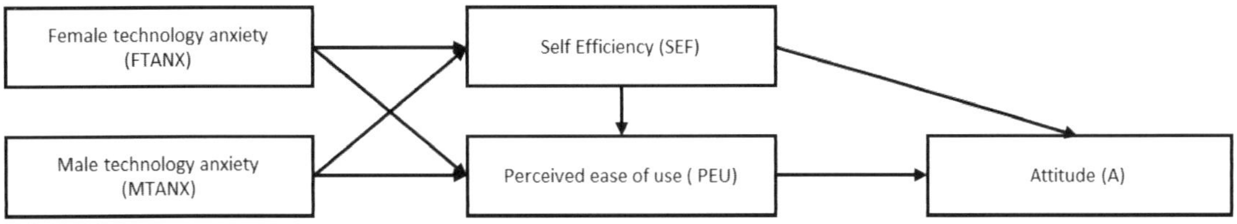

Figure 1. Proposed Model

7. LIMITATIONS

The current research had allowed us to shed the light on a topic that is still incomprehensible. An ongoing research concerning the Open Book Open Web exam method has given positive results concerning students' own perception and experience and was compared with the traditional examination method results. Furthermore, an attempt to compare test results as described earlier was done. Like any other research, this study has some limitations. The current study could be carried out on a larger sample to take into consideration different cases and analyze it with a quantitative method in order to have a more solid result.

REFERENCES

Baird, M., Sefcik, L., Steyn, S., & Price, C., 2019. Learning Analytics Leading to Remote Invigilation for eTests: A Case Study. In *Utilizing Learning Analytics to Support Study Success*. Springer, Cham. pp. 295-312.

Davis, F. D., 1989. Perceived Usefulness, Perceived Ease of Use, and User Acceptance of Information Technology. *MIS quarterly*, pp.319-340.

El Rassi, M. A. B., 2020. Why one e-business adoption model won't fit all firm sizes: The case of Lebanon's e-service industry. The Electronic Journal of Information Systems in Developing Countries, e12135.

El Rassi, M, 2018. Firm's Size Effect in the e-Service Industry: The Case of a Developing Country. *AIS electronic library (AISeL).*https://aisel.aisnet.org/cgi/view content.cgi?article=1013&context=ecis2018_rp

El Rassi, M. A. B., & Harfouche, A., 2016. E-Business Assimilation Levels in Lebanon. In Information and Communication Technologies in Organizations and Society. *Springer, Cham*. pp. 141-160.

Fishbein, M. & Ajzen,I.,1975 . Belief, Attitude, Intention and Behavior: An Introduction to Theory and Research, 181-202.

Guàrdia, L., Crisp, G., & Alsina, I., 2017. Trends and Challenges of E-Assessment to Enhance Student Learning in Higher Education. In *Innovative Practices for Higher Education Assessment and Measurement* IGI Global. pp. 36-56.

Howard, G. S., & Smith, R. D., 1986. Computer Anxiety in Management: Myth or Reality?. *Communications of the ACM*, 29(7), pp. 611-615.

Hung, C. M., Huang, I., & Hwang, G. J., 2014. Effects of Digital Game-Based Learning on Students' Self-Efficacy, Motivation, Anxiety, and Achievements in Learning Mathematics. *Journal of Computers in Education*, *1*(2-3), 151-166.

Joi,L.M., Camille,D.D.& Krista, G (2011). E-Learning, Online Learning and Distance Learning Environments: Are they the Same? *Internet High Educ*, 14,129-135.

Madorin, S., & Iwasiw, C.,1999. The Effects of Computer-Assisted Instruction on the Self-Efficacy of Baccalaureate Nursing Students. *Journal of nursing education*, 38(6), pp.282-285.

Miller, A., & Young-Jones, A. D., 2012. Academic Integrity: Online Classes Compared to Face-to-Face Classes. *Journal of Instructional Psychology*, *39*(3).

Ndubisi, N. O., 2004. Factors Influencing E-Learning Adoption Intention: Examining the Determinant Structure of the Decomposed Theory of Planned Behaviour Constructs. In *Proceedings of the 27th Annual Conference of HERDSA* (pp. 252-262).

Richardson, M., Abraham, C., & Bond, R., 2012. Psychological Correlates of University Students' Academic Performance: A Systematic Review and Meta-Analysis. *Psychological Bulletin*, *138* (2), 353.

Roca J.C, Chiu C-M. and Martinez F.J, 2006. Understanding e-Learning Continuance Intention: An Extension of the Technology Acceptance Model. *International Journal of Human-Computer Studies*, 64 (8), pp. 683-696.

Saadé, R. G., & Kira, D., 2006. The Emotional State of Technology Acceptance. *Issues in Informing Science & Information Technology,* 3.

Simonson, M. R., Maurer, M., Montag-Torardi, M., & Whitaker, M., 1987. Development of a Standardized Test of Computer Literacy and a Computer Anxiety Index. *Journal of educational computing research*, 3(2), pp. 231-247.

Steve, G., Ferrante, C. J., and Heppard, K.A., 2016. Using Open-Book Exams to Enhance Student Learning Performance, and Motivation.

Venkatesh, V., Morris, M. G., Davis, G. B., & Davis, F. D., 2003. User acceptance of Information Technology: Toward a Unified View. *MIS quarterly*, pp. 425-478.

ANALYSIS ITEMS TO ASSESS THE QUALITY OF OPEN ONLINE COURSES FOR HIGHER EDUCATION

Marina Marchisio[1] and Matteo Sacchet[2]
[1]*Department of Molecular Biotechnology and Health Sciences, University of Torino, Via Nizza, 52, 10126, Torino, Italy*
[2]*Department of Mathematics "G. Peano", University of Torino, Via Carlo Alberto, 10, 10123 Torino, Italy*

ABSTRACT

The quality of Massive Open Online Courses (MOOC) is an important topic to be addressed by different stakeholders: higher education institutions, MOOC providers, education companies, educational providers. National and international agencies are or will be deeply involved in preparing or attending common guidelines in order to fulfill quality of MOOCs. Some indicators that can help in analyzing quality are provided by the learner point of view, by pedagogy, by instructional design, by outcome measures. The latter has been the most widely adopted, since numerical data help in comparison between different platform or different educational experiences. But these data, such as completion and retention rates, were criticized when used to assess quality of MOOCs. In the literature, there are some checklists and framework that can help and guide the expert or novice designer in the process of MOOC developments. In the present work, we are going to address the experience of the start@unito project, an online platform developed at the University of Torino which offers 50 open online courses in order to facilitate the transition between secondary and tertiary education, making the students anticipate their career by attending a complete university module online prior to enrolment at the university. This could lead to an improvement in the number of ECTS credits acquired during the first year of university studies and to the drop-out rate. An analysis of the start@unito open online courses quality is provided according to the frameworks and checklists.

KEYWORDS

Instructional Quality, MOOC Quality, MOOC Quality Framework, MOOC Quality Checklist, Open Online Courses, Start@unito

1. INTRODUCTION

MOOCs, Massive Open Online Courses, can be defined by the following statement: "an online course designed for a large number of participants that can be accessed by anyone anywhere, as long as they have an internet connection, is open to everyone without entry qualifications and offers a full/complete course experience online for free" (Jansen et al., 2015). According to this definition, MOOC can potentially spread higher education and enhance the quality of life for millions of people. However, the basin of attraction of MOOCs contains mainly well-educated learners with a background in higher education and generally in possession of a qualification (Macleod et al. 2015). Another typical MOOC user is a learner already in employment. Moreover, by the definition stated above, it is not clear what is the threshold for an open online course to receive the M of "Massive", that is why in this work we will sometimes refer just to Open Online Courses (OOCs).

In the global education market, there are few platforms which contain thousands of MOOCs, created with the collaboration of universities and private companies. The growing trend of MOOCs raises issues about quality assurance. The first concern about quality regards the contents: MOOCs are courses consisting of different kind of educational resources, assessments, sometimes tutoring, usually peer-to-peer, rarely provided by academics. Higher education institutions usually outsource these components to third parties, for example, video recording of lectures, automatic grading programs, authentication services. The second concern about quality regards partnerships: for-profit education companies, educational publishers, global testing services collaborate with universities to provide MOOC, and this happens without internal academic capabilities. Thus, the focus on quality assurance is not only related to educational institutions. However, in (Ossiannilsson et al. 2015) note that partner organizations cannot easily be submitted to national higher education quality assurance standards and other regulatory instruments, since they were not designed to regulate such entities.

Apart from the ones listed above, MOOCs can serve different purposes. The main objective of the "Start@unito" project at University of Torino (Bruschi et al., 2018; Marchisio et al., 2019a), financed by Compagnia di San Paolo, is to improve the success rate of first year university students through the creation and dissemination of 50 OOCs available at https://start.unito.it, since a successful transition from secondary to higher education is a crucial challenge for both students and institutions (Barana et al., 2017). The project faced the major concerns about quality assurance. Since the project involves different kind of areas (sciences, humanities, economics, law, languages), there is a large difference in the typologies of contents and assessments according to the different need of the disciplines. Moreover, different kind of services collaborate to the various functionalities of the online platform: a Learning Management System (LMS), a Single-Sign On (SSO), an on-demand video service, an integrated Advanced Computing Environment (ACE) and integrated Automatic Assessment System (AAS).

This paper discusses issues related to the quality assurance of the OOCs provided by the project (not by single OOC), according to frameworks provided by the large literature.

2. STATE OF THE ART

In this section we will analyze the main aspects that emerge in the literature related to the quality assurance of MOOCs. First, we will focus on the importance of MOOC, while, secondly, we will analyze quality indicators and possible frameworks.

2.1 Importance of MOOC Quality

MOOCs are more subjected to external scrutiny than campus-based higher education, which usually receive internal or students' evaluation. This can affect the national higher education system. In the UK, the Quality Assurance Agency (QAA) stated that MOOC providers should "ensure that they reflect the established reputation of UK higher education" (QAA 2014). Therefore, it is highly probable that the quality of MOOCs will be influenced by the support of national governments, too. More in general, assuring the quality of MOOCs is a responsibility of MOOC providers, cross-institutional partnerships and institutions, with guidance from national quality agencies.

MOOCs have an important relation with both online and open education. Openness does not mean only "free". In general, open education should remove barriers (Bates 2015). Thus, quality indicators should consider accessibility and usability issues.

When choosing between different MOOCs, the learner should be assured of their quality, by means of reviews and recommendations of other learners. Despite the large numbers of MOOC users, there is no prominent MOOC rating website. The only indicators for the learner are given by the brand reputation or the originating institution, sometimes the course author. However, (Daniel, 2012) remark that university brand is a poor measure of quality in online teaching, because reputations of academic institutions derives from research than teaching.

2.2 MOOC Quality Indicators

The concept of quality in online education is quite complex. According to (Jansen et al., 2017), the quality of MOOCs can be considered from the following four perspectives.

1. Quality from the learner's point of view. Different kind of learners, with different motivations and different backgrounds, interact with a MOOCs. Thus, while designing MOOCs, goals, expectations, learning behaviors and abilities should be considered to facilitate learning.
2. Quality connected to the pedagogical framework of the MOOC. MOOCs should be scale to an unlimited number of learners, with the principle that the teaching effort must not increase proportionally. Researches examine the choice of pedagogical model according to qualitative indicators for dialogue and interaction.

3. Quality related to the input elements. The key role is played by instructional design (Margaryan et al., 2015). For example, (Costello et al., 2016) found flaws when analyzing multiple choice questions of several MOOCs.
4. Quality based on outcome measures. Data are going to play their part in this perspective. Possible indicators may include the number of learners completing a MOOC or achieving certification. However, not all learners want to follow till the end the path of a MOOC. Thus, completion rate has therefore been criticized (Aheran, 2018) when used to measure quality. Low values of generally used measures, such as retention and completion, may not indicate poor quality.

The quality assurance process involves different stakeholders. The first check is internally provided by the institution that is going to deliver the MOOC. The second step is provided by peer review, a person with experience in the topic and/or in online education. The third step is in the hands of the users, that should be entitled to leave feedback to the MOOC provider.

2.3 Frameworks and Checklists

Frameworks provide a useful tool for all the stakeholders involved in MOOC development. The QRF, Quality Reference Framework (Stracke et al., 2018), has been developed by the European Alliance for the Quality of Massive Open Online Courses (MOOCs), called MOOQ. It is a framework that analyze the needs and demands for MOOCs, in order to design, develop and implement new MOOCs and to evaluate and improve existing MOOCs. The framework is composed by 3 dimensions:

- Phases: Analysis, Design, Implementation, Realization, Evaluation.
- Perspectives: Pedagogical, Technological, Strategic.
- Roles: Designer, Facilitator, Provider.

Evaluation is a phase that surrounds all the other phases, it is the common background of every action in MOOC development.

National or international quality framework such as the OpenupEd Quality Label aims to supports institutions in the enhancement of MOOC quality, focusing on Quality Assurance processes in place (OpenupEd). OpenupEd developed some checklists that supports in self-assessing their MOOC development. One of these checklists concerns the quality of the design of MOOCs.

3. RESEARCH QUESTIONS

This research sourced as a necessity in order to understand the state of quality of the 50 OOCs provided in the framework of the start@unito project. The Research Questions (RQ) can be stated according to the following list items:

RQ1. How many are the quality indicators mentioned in the literature expressed in start@unito OOCs?

RQ2. What is the evaluation according to the OpenupEd checklist?

RQ3. How can be the evaluation phase improved according to the QRF with the focus on the Evaluation phase?

The three Research Questions highlight three main aspect that concerns MOOC quality. The individuation of general key aspects (RQ1), the need of a checklist to be used by universities designer and provider (RQ2), the meta-evaluation, i.e. the evaluation of the evaluation phase (RQ3).

The paper is not only devoted to the analysis of the quality of start@unito OOCs, but it will focus on a critical reflection around the various issues and topics connected to the RQs and the quality of MOOCs.

4. METHODOLOGY

This research, according to its questions, is divided into three parts. The first part addresses the presence of quality indicators (learners' point of view, pedagogy, input elements, outcome measures) inside the Start@unito experience, with reference to precise aspects of the project. The second part provides an evaluation of the quality of the OOCs according to a simplified version of the OpenupEd quality checklist.

The entries of the marking scheme are: Target group, Overall goal, Learning objectives, Learning activities, Feedback mechanism, Study-time, Workload, Assessment. These entries are graded according to the 4-point scale:

1. NA (Not achieved),
2. PA (Partially achieved),
3. LA (Largely achieved),
4. FA (Fully achieved).

The third part provides a reflection on the adopted evaluation, considering some main points of the QRF framework. The analysis regards the 50 courses overall because it considers transversal solutions and objectives. It is not part of this work, but with the same scheme it is also possible to make a single course analysis, which could be useful for teachers who intend to prepare online courses.

5. DISCUSSION

In this section, beyond the general reflection on quality of MOOCs, we will focus on the specific validation and critical analysis of the OOCs provided by the start@unito project, following the list provided by the research questions.

5.1 Start@unito OOCs: Quality Indicators

The first indicator is the learners' point of view. The main users that enters start@unito courses are high school students, or first year students. There is a percentage of teachers that logged in, since we carried out experimentations (Marchisio et al., 2019c), but we do not know the exact number of the different extractions, since the data required to access the OOCs are simply First name, Last name and Email. Further data are only required when the user wants to obtain the certification.

The second indicator is pedagogy. All the university professors and postgraduates involved attended a training course (Marchisio et al., 2020) in order to develop skills about the main aspects related to the development of OOCs. The topic of the first training session was exactly about pedagogy connected to Open Online Education and about the concept of learning object. The participation to the meetings was not mandatory, thus we cannot ensure that all professors were committed to the pedagogical criteria.

The third indicator concern input elements. The other training sessions of the course (Marchisio et al., 2020) faced other aspects, like the technological and the organizational point of view, since the platform allows very different kind of contents (videos, documents, assessment, external resources, etc.) that the teacher need to master. Besides all the training, many contents show instructional problems, since not all the teachers followed the exact recommendations. This is not to be intended as a critical problem, since many teachers were approaching online education for the first time.

The fourth indicators are outcome measures. As evidenced in Section 2, it is very difficult to find which measure to adopt, since the "standard ones" are not considered to be relevant. In the case of the start@unito OOCs it is even more difficult, since the project is quite young and more than half OOCs were opened in 2019, few of them at the beginning of 2020. Moreover, since the courses correspond to university module that, according to the different university courses, take pace in the first or in the second semester, the chance for student to sit the exam, which is compulsory to obtain the ECTS, may not have occurred. In our opinion, one year is the minimum amount of time in order to consider at least partially relevant the outcome measures. In fact, the data arising from the first 20 courses, completed in 2018, are very promising: even with this consideration and counting the newly opened courses, the average subscriptions to the courses is around 433 students and more than one thousand students already passed the exam, which is around the 5% of all enrollments. The examinations of the last two months, January and February 2020, whose records still have to be closed, are missing: this could bring to an increase in the percentage of completion between 10-15%, which is in line with the MOOC completion rates (Margaryan et al., 2015). There are of course students that uses the online contents, but do not take the examination.

5.2 Start@unito OOCs: Evaluation

We are going to follow the checklist provided by OpenupEd about "Quality of the design of MOOC". The median and average of the results arising from the various categories is LA, as depicted in Table 1 below.

5.2.1 Target Group

Start@unito OOCs are accessible to all people, but users of the various target groups, the needs, the challenges and prior knowledge cannot be identified in the description of the course. The target group of university students is supported by different references according to their study program, but there is no other differentiation for other kind of users (teachers, professionals, etc.). The overall judgment for this category is LA.

5.2.2 Overall Goal

The overall objective of start@unito OOCs is described in a short video, duration around 4 minutes, introducing the main topics and themes touched by the course program. Moreover, even if not necessary for learning purposes, the video shows the professors that created the course, providing the reference to "a person behind the machine". Usually but not in every course, short sentences provide a little more insight about course contents. The overall judgment for this category is FA.

5.2.3 Learning Objectives

Every course describes learning objectives, but usually there is no statement about learning outcomes, nor in the main description neither in the single learning objects. There is reasoned coherence between course contents, teaching strategy and assessment methods, but the prior knowledge of each learning objective is rarely described. The overall judgment for this category is PA.

5.2.4 Learning Activities

The online activities allow participants to construct their own learning, but few activities ask students to communicate their results to others or to the system. The activities contain just one level of difficulty and one learning pathway, while complexity is increasing together with the knowledge of students. Various activities are proposed with different formats, but there is no peer-to peer interaction, forum or video conferences with tutors. The courses contain enough interactivity learner-to-content. The overall judgment for this category is PA.

5.2.5 Feedback Mechanism

The only feedback provided from start@unito OOCs is the automatic feedback, there is no academic tutor and no monitoring, apart from the evaluation process. Despite this, the course provides learners with regular feedback through self-assessment activities and tests, the number of feedbacks can be improved. The overall judgment for this category is PA.

5.2.6 Study-time

The students learn autonomously and self-paced, so there is no timing, no periodic live session. The total study time of all learning activities is scaled on the number of ECTS, that lies for start@unito OOCs between 6 and 12 ECTS (1 ECTS equal around 25-30 hours of study). There was a lot of reflection about this topic in the design phase, it is a theme that professors care, thus the overall judgment for this category is FA.

5.2.7 Workload

The schedule of the course is such that the workload is suited for learners from the main target group. The start@unito OOCs are realistic in their pacing for the participant, accommodating to the personal rhythm, since the contents are always available, 24/7. The overall judgment for this category is FA.

5.2.8 Assessment

Some OOCs present a balance between formative and summative assessment. Automatic Formative assessment is essential for self-paced online courses. There are no measures appropriate to counter impersonation and plagiarism, however after completion students receive a certificate of completed learning activities that allows them to take the in-person exam at the university, thus the ECTS are obtained in a safe, reliable and valid way. The start@unito OOCs track score and progression. The overall judgment for this category is LA.

Table 1. Summary of the evaluation according to the OpenupEd checklist about "Quality of the design of MOOC" according to the scale: NA (Not achieved), PA (Partially achieved), LA (Largely achieved), FA (Fully achieved)

Category	Judgment	Value	Category	Judgment	Value
Target group	LA	3	Feedback mechanism	PA	2
Overall goal	FA	4	Study time	FA	4
Learning objectives	PA	2	Workload	FA	4
Learning activities	PA	2	Assessment	LA	3
Median	**LA**	**3**	**Average**	**LA**	**3**

5.3 Start@unito OOCs: Meta-Evaluation

The QRF (Stracke et al., 2018) focus on key Quality Criteria and Checklist for analyzing, designing, implementing, realizing and evaluating a MOOC. The quality criteria and checklist defined below are action items for activities in the evaluation phase. The QRF Quality Checklist asks questions intended for both novices and experts in MOOC design and development.

5.3.1 Evaluation Planning

In the design of the evaluation phase, the criteria or evaluation objectives must be set. In the case of the start@unito OOCs the measurable is given by improving the outcomes of the evaluation criteria of first year university students, which is given by the number of ECTS obtained, with many possible evaluation focus on learners engagement, with data mainly provided by their interaction with the online platform. The evaluation process still must start, and it will take place periodically, possibly once a year. A general overview of the trend is reported at the meetings of the Scientific Committee of the project. As a general approach, the design phase and the realization phase were evaluated.

5.3.2 Evaluation Realization

Among the various tools, we adopted questionnaires in order to gather precious feedback from students and high school teachers in order to assess the realization phase and from university professors in order to assess the design phase. Moreover, a first approach with learning analytics tools provided feedback on all learner activities (Marchisio et al., 2019b).

5.3.3 Evaluation Review

There is no precise protocol about data review, but all interested core stakeholders represented in the MOOC design team take part in the analysis and discussion of the results. The Scientific Committee concern about the overall progress, while the single university professor concern about its own specific OOC. The documentation about the data is strictly confidential and internal to the people involved in the project management, while documentation of findings, from learning analytics and other forms of data are published as open research items. Data collected provided recommendations for improvement.

5.3.4 Improvements and Optimization

Technical administrators of the platform and project managers are active in the experimentation of new kind of analytics and frameworks. It will be useful to consult an evaluation team to oversee the possible implementation of the recommendations obtained from the evaluation review process, bug fixing and operational improvements.

6. CONCLUSION

This research work provided an implementation of the analysis of MOOC quality with a marking scheme that evaluates 8 main points that addresses the quality of MOOCs according to studies and reflections provided by the rich literature. The points are marked with a 4-point scale. Moreover, a specific analysis in the local setting of the 50 start@unito OOCs at the University of Torino. Recalling the research questions, we can collect the ideas arose:

RQ1. Indicators are necessary as guidelines to MOOC designers and providers. Start@unito started its experience with a training program of academic staff and professors, giving emphasis to some of the listed indicators. Even trainers were exploring new strategies and ideas during the training course. Some university professors were quite new in the world of online education. The results from this point of view are different between courses, but even the ones in which the quality is lower are encouraging since academics have been positively engaged and admitted in a different way of teaching.

RQ2. The team of OpenupEd created useful checklists, which allows any MOOC designer and provider to assess himself. The reference table about quality seems to promote the start@unito OOCs. Not all the categories obtained a good mark according to the gridlines and the marking scheme over a 4-point scale, but the average between the various aspects is positive, and states that the quality objectives are largely achieved.

RQ3. Some of the criteria for a good evaluation phase are respected, since there is a literature of publications with results obtained from data arising from students, teachers, university professors and other users. It is needed more planning and review of results from all stakeholders, that may not be aware of the actual status of learner activity. Learning analytics are a promising way to go to explore new patterns in online learning processes.

Self-reflection on the quality of an experience provides an important insight and feedback. In this case it is even more important since there were many different actors involved in the design of the online courses. The marking scheme is quite basic in other to give a global overview on the quality of a MOOC, but it can be furtherly refined, with other entries or sub-entries. As a global view of the results and of the answers to the three research questions, start@unito appear as an important experience in the online education panorama. start@unito will continue to spread education for many years, trying to help students in their transition between secondary and higher education. Other evaluations could give more interesting results according to the maturity of the experience. As an example, future work will involve data analysis on user's activity in the online platform, students marks from the self-assessment system, outcomes arising from the exam board and the correlation between these data, in order to understand the usefulness of this experience from different point of views (students, teachers, professors, university).

REFERENCES

Aheran, A., 2018. Stop Asking About Completion Rates: Better Questions to Ask About MOOCs in 2019. Retrieved from https://www.edsurge.com/news/2018-11-28-stop-asking-about-completion-rates-better-questions-to-ask-about-moocs-in-2019

Barana, A., Bogino, A., Fioravera, M., Marchisio, M., Rabellino, S., 2017. Open platform of self-paced MOOCs for the continual improvement of academic guidance and knowledge strengthening in tertiary education. *Journal of e-Learning and Knowledge Society*, 13(3), pp. 109-119. https://doi.org/10.20368/1971-8829/1383

Bates, A. W., 2015. Teaching in a digital age. Guidelines for designing teaching and learning for a digital age. *Ed. Tony Bates Associates Ltd.* Retrieved from http://opentextbc.ca/teachinginadigitalage/, Last accessed March, 3rd 2020.

Bruschi, B., Cantino, V., Cavallo Perin, R., Culasso, F., Giors, B., Marchisio, M., Marello, C., Milani, M., Operti, L., Parola, A., Rabellino, S., Sacchet, M., Scomparin, L., 2018. Start@unito: a Supporting Model for High School Students Enrolling to University. *IADIS International Conference Cognition and Exploratory Learning in Digital Age* 2018, pp. 307–312.

Costello, E., Brown, M., and Holland, J., 2016. What Questions are MOOCs Asking? – An Evidence-Based Investigation. *Proceedings of the European Stakeholder Summit on experiences and best practices in and around MOOCs*, pp. 211–221.

Daniel, J., 2012. Making Sense of MOOCs: Musings in a Maze of Myth, Paradox and Possibility. Journal of Interactive Media in Education, 2012(3), p.Art. 18. http://doi.org/10.5334/2012-18

Jansen, D., Rosewell, J., and Kear, K., 2017. Quality Frameworks for MOOCs. *In: Jemni M., Kinshuk, Khribi M. (eds) Open Education: from OERs to MOOCs. Lecture Notes in Educational Technology. Springer, Berlin, Heidelberg.* https://doi.org/10.1007/978-3-662-52925-6_14

Jansen, D., Schuwer, R., Teixeira, A., and Aydin, C. H., 2015. Comparing MOOC Adoption Strategies in Europe: Results from the HOME Project Survey. *The International Review of Research in Open and Distributed Learning*, 16(6). https://doi.org/10.19173/irrodl.v16i6.2154

Macleod, H., Haywood, J., Woodgate, A., and Alkhatnai, M., 2015. Emerging patterns in MOOCs: Learners, course design and directions. *TechTrends*, 59(1), pp. 56–63. http://dx.doi.org/10.1007/s11528-014-0821-y

Marchisio, M., Operti, L., Rabellino, S. and Sacchet, M., 2019. Start@unito: Open Online Courses for Improving Access and for Enhancing Success in Higher Education. *In Proceedings of the 11th International Conference on Computer Supported Education - Volume 1: CSEDU*, ISBN 978-989-758-367-4, pp. 639-646. http://doi.org/10.5220/0007732006390646

Marchisio, M., Rabellino, S., Roman, F., Sacchet, M., and Salusso, D., 2019b. Boosting up Data Collection and Analysis to Learning Analytics in Open Online Contexts: an assessment Methodology. *Journal of E-Learning and Knowledge Society*, 15(3), pp. 49-59. https://doi.org/10.20368/1971-8829/1135048

Marchisio, M., Rabellino, S., Sacchet, M., and Salusso, D., 2020. From desk to desktop: the integration between classroom and online teaching from the teachers' perspective. Reports on E-Learning, Media and Education Meetings, 8(1), 43-48. Retrieved from https://www.je-lks.org/ojs/index.php/R-EMEM/article/view/1135104

Marchisio, M., Sacchet, M., and Salusso, D., 2019c. Instructional design to "train the trainers": The start@unito project at the university of turin ", *Multi Conference on Computer Science and Information Systems, MCCSIS 2019 - Proceedings of the International Conference on e-Learning 2019*, pp. 195-202, 2019. https://doi.org/10.33965/el2019_201909F025

Margaryan, A, Bianco, M., and Littlejohn, A., 2015. Instructional quality of massive open online courses (MOOCs). *Computers & Education* 80, pp 77–83. http://dx.doi.org/10.1016/j.compedu.2014.08.005

OpenupEd. Retrieved from https://www.openuped.eu/, Last accessed March, 3rd 2020.

Ossiannilsson, E., Williams, K., Camilleri, A. F., and Brown, M. L., 2015. Quality models in online and open education around the globe: State of the art and recommendations. Retrieved from https://www.pedocs.de/volltexte/2015/10879/pdf/Ossiannilsson_et_al_2015_Qualitymodels.pdf, Last accessed March, 3rd 2020.

QAA. (2014). Statement on massive open online courses. Retrieved from https://dera.ioe.ac.uk/19652/1/QAA-position-statement-MOOCs.pdf, Last accessed March, 3rd 2020.

Stracke, C. M., Tan, E., Texeira, A., Pinto, M., Vassiliadis, B., Kameas, A., Sgouropoulou, C., and Vidal, G., 2018. Quality Reference Framework (QRF) for the Quality of Massive Open Online Courses (MOOCs). Online available at www.mooc-quality.eu/QRF, Last accessed March, 3rd 2020.

ONLINE TUTORING THROUGH AN INTEGRATED PLATFORM TO SUPPORT LEARNING MATHEMATICS AT LOWER SECONDARY SCHOOL

Cecilia Fissore[1,*] Marina Marchisio[2,†] and Sergio Rabellino[3‡]
[1]*Department of Foreign Languages and Literatures and Modern Cultures, University of Turin, Via Giuseppe Verdi 10, 10124, Turin, Italy*
[2]*Department of Molecular Biotechnology and Health Sciences, University of Turin, Via Nizza 52, 10126, Turin, Italy*
[3]*Computer Science Department, University of Turin, Corso Svizzera, 185, 10149, Turin, Italy*

ABSTRACT

The technologies and online supports that can offer students study opportunities have increased a lot in recent years, but often students do not use computers or mobile devices in school and, in general, for educational purposes. The Action of the University of Turin, within the "Ragazzi Connessi" project, proposes strategies for school recovery in Mathematics which involve the introduction of an online service built around an integrated Moodle platform with an advanced computing environment, an automatic assessment system and a web conference service, which enable the use of innovative didactics methodologies. The project involved teachers and students from three different secondary schools in the city of Genoa. This paper shows the main aspects of the platform and the strategies for school recovery developed inside the Action, in particular mathematics recovery path for students, carried out entirely online.

KEYWORDS

Advanced Computing Environment, Innovative Teaching Methodologies, Integrated Moodle Platform, Mathematics, Online Tutoring, School Recovery

1. INTRODUCTION

In recent years, the use of e-learning platforms where students can always have access to school materials and have study support, has developed exponentially (Giuliani et al., 2015; Valle et al., 2010). Today's students are often referred to as digital natives and live in a world surrounded by technology (Prensky, 2001). However, the actual use of the technologies by students is still rather superficial and is mostly limited to play games, messaging or web browsing (Fini, 2011). Indeed, it is important that students can use technologies and mobile devices also in school or, more generally, for educational purposes, and it is important that students are instructed to use them correctly. Digital competence has been included by the European Union among the eight key skills for lifelong learning outlined by the Recommendation of the European Parliament and of the Council in 2018 (2018/C 189/01), confirming that educational institutions must have a significant role in this sector. It is therefore needful to train teachers on the use of digital resources through innovative and interactive teaching methodologies, in order to innovate their teaching practices. The project "Ragazzi Connessi - Online to develop talents and offer orientation opportunities" proposes the application of innovative learning techniques in the schools of Genoa, through integrated interventions. The main objectives of the project are to fight educational poverty and school failure improving cohesion between the school and social communities. Within the project, started in September 2018, several partners collaborate to propose different and complementary actions:

- coaching and peer education interventions for the enhancement of disciplinary and transversal skills;
- dialogue facilitation activities through narration and reflection methodology;
- virtual learning paths and online tutoring in the logical-mathematical field.

* [0000-0001-8398-265X]
† [0000-0003-1007-5404]
‡ [0000-0002-1757-2000]

The Action of the University of Turin "Virtual Learning Paths" exploits the skills gained by the School of Tasks project in the City of Turin (Barana et al., 2017; Cavagnero et al., 2015; Giraudo et. Al., 2014) proposing the teaching and learning of Mathematics through new technologies and innovative methodologies with the aim of counteracting school failure in Mathematics. All activities take place online through a Moodle platform, browsable with any mobile device, integrated with a web conference service, an Automatic Assessment System (AAS) and an Advanced Calculation Environment (ACE). An ACE is a software system which allows numerical and symbolic calculation, geometric visualization in two and three dimensions and the develop of interactive components that allows you to view how a result varies as the input data changes; this is a very powerful and flexible tool for learning math. This article presents the platform and strategies of the Action for contrasting school failure. The Action so far has involved 20 teachers and 50 students from 4 lower secondary schools of Genoa. In particular, the math recovery course for students will be presented, which took place entirely online.

2. ONLINE TEACHING STRATEGIES FOR THE RECOVERY OF SCHOOL FAILURE

Mathematics is undoubtedly one of the school disciplines in which students generally have the greatest difficulties, which in some cases may even compromise the relationship with this discipline. Often the student who finishes the lower secondary school already has a history of failures in this subject that lead him to face it with fear or disinterest. To recover the difficulties in Mathematics, teachers and schools, but also students and parents, devote a lot of resources in terms of time and actions taken. The University of Turin has designed, studied and developed innovative methodologies for the reduction of school failures, such as:

- the use of a Virtual Learning Environment for collaborative learning and online tutoring (Barana & Marchisio, 2016; Brancaccio et al., 2019; Fissore et al., 2019);
- the use of an ACE for interactive materials and for problem solving (Brancaccio et al., 2015);
- the use of an AAS for the construction of online tests with interactive feedback for recovery and enhancement (Barana et al., 2018a; Barana et al., 2018b).

The use of these new methodologies allows to propose a recovery intervention different from the traditional one with the use of new technologies (Turrentine and Macdonald, 2006; Ferrari, 2011). It also allows the development of digital skills in students, the enhancement of interest in the subject and confidence in the chance of success, as well as allowing the development of knowledge and skills related to learning Mathematics. The protagonists of the strategies and actions to be implemented are students with disciplinary deficiencies who need recovery. At the same time, however, their teachers are also involved: they are the first to intervene in student's recovery and they could use these methodologies for teaching with the whole class too. The strategies of the Action for the recovery of school failure are splitted in two main and complementary themes:

- the recovery path for students with the use of new methodologies;
- training of teachers on the use of new methodologies.

The training course for teachers, after a first 5-hour face-to-face training in presence, took place entirely online, while the recovery path took place entirely online. This was made possible by the integration of the platform with a web conference system, enabling remote interactions (audio, video, chat and PC screen sharing). The Action's Moodle platform, which can be visited at the link https://ragazziconnessi.i-learn.unito.it, was set up by the ICT Service of the Computer Science Department of the University of Turin. The integration of the platform with an ACE allows the distribution of interactive material and tests with various types of questions (not only multiple-choice questions but also open answers, questions with graphs and formulas, all of them particularly suitable for learning Mathematics) with automatic assessment and immediate feedback. The development of this platform allowed the design and implementation of educational activities based on the three methodologies mentioned above. The training course for teachers illustrated the innovative teaching methods for recovery and their possible use with students, to carry out online or face-to-face activities in blended modality using the platform. In the teacher training course, synchronous (five online one-hour meetings) and asynchronous training activities were provided (forums, questionnaires, database of available materials to consult and to use). A platform course has been created for each teacher in order to directly experience the methodologies proposed with their own classes. The teachers were also involved in organizing the student recovery path, which took place in parallel with their training course, to identify their students who needed a recovery in Mathematics. Students who had an insufficiency between 4 and a half and 5 and a half were chosen; students with very serious deficiencies have been referred to other interventions because they often require specific attention. The recovery path for these students, which in this first phase of the project was tested in a pilot version, took place entirely online. The duration of the recovery path was five weeks from the beginning of May, one and a half months before the summer break. Students were followed for one month by specially trained university tutors on the disciplinary topics reported by the teachers. The tutors were chosen specifically in the university environment to have greater effectiveness in the tutoring action since, for personal and school career issues, they are much closer to the students. All teachers had access to their students' recovery path and were able to check the activities they carried out, view all the materials made available by the tutor, if they wanted to use them with the whole class.

3. ONLINE TUTORING FOR THE RECOVERY PATH

The recovery path for students on the platform involved a total of: 7 teachers; 53 6th-grade or 7th-grade students from 12 sections of 4 lower secondary schools in the city of Genoa; 3 university tutors; 1 responsible for training and supporting tutors, organizing the path on the platform and keeping in contact with the teachers. Students were divided into 8 groups with the following criteria: no more than 5/6 students per group and possibly from the same teacher. In this way, the organization and supervision by the teacher himself was made easier and the participation of the students was stimulated by the presence of their classmates. Eight platform courses were designed and set up, one for each group. The respective course could be accessed at any time with personal credentials: the students, the tutor (one for each course) and the student teacher. Each recovery path included:

- 5 one-hour weekly meetings online where students were able to interact with the tutor exposing their doubts, difficulties and unclear topics;
- the exploration of interactive files and the execution of tests with automatic assessment for review, created by the tutor on the topics covered during the tutoring or reported by students.

The online meetings took place in the afternoon after school, on a day of the week established with the teacher, and the students connected with their computer or mobile device. During online meetings the tutor could share his screen with students, showing interactive materials or using the ACE to make calculations and show the resolution of an exercise on a problem. The tutor and students could communicate via audio and chat; webcams option usually do not add information to the meeting and could be a distraction from the main objective which is to learn something, so usually we asked tutors not to enable them. Figure 1 shows an example of an online meeting seen from the point of view of a participating student. Along the entire project the teachers gave fundamental support for the organization of the recovery process: for the collection of the names of the students with deficiencies in Mathematics; for the presentation of the recovery path to students; for the communication of the access credentials to the platform; and for the explanation of how to navigate it. The research question for this Action was whether this recovery model could work with young students exclusively online. A first unknown factor was the students' reaction to dealing with a tutor they had never seen and known in person but exclusively through online meetings without even using the webcam. A second unknown at an organizational level was whether the students would be able to access the platform independently, to view the recovery path and to navigate correctly between the various contents and to connect to the online meeting. In this regard, the design of the recovery path was focused on making the navigability of the platform as intuitive and clear as possible. In addition to the support of the teachers, the students had a Helpdesk service on the platform always available, in which they could open a ticket to request assistance for their personal problems. This Helpdesk service was essential to quickly resolve student access problems, communicated in some cases also with the support of parents, and to ensure that they participated in the platform activities without becoming discouraged or losing interest. Finally, week by week, a close monitoring of students' access to the platform and a report to the respective teachers was carried out in order to give any assistance to students who had not been able to access.

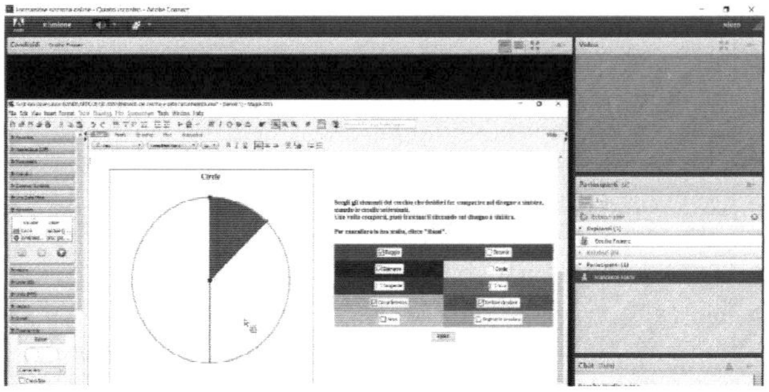

Figure 1. Example of online meeting from a student's perspective

At the beginning and end of the recovery process, students completed an initial and final questionnaire and the teachers filled out a final questionnaire on their students' recovery path. The structure and format of the platform course were the same for each course and are represented in the following figure (Figure 2).

Figure 2. Example of a platform course for the recovery path

In each path has been included: a forum for communications by the tutor (to remember online appointments or to report the availability of the material); a Forum for students' questions; the calendar of online meetings; the virtual room for online meeting; an initial and final questionnaire. Both forums have been set up as mandatory subscriptions, in this way all course participants receive an email with every intervention added to the forum, both as a reminder for online meetings and as an incentive to use this resource. In some cases, the students did not have a personal email address and provided that of the parents, involving them directly within the project. The use of the platform makes it possible to track all student activities within the course. For each resource or activity in the course, it is also possible to set a criterion for completing the activity, so that you can automatically check the activities completed by the students and set access criteria to other sections, providing guidance through the online materials. The course had 5 sections, one for each week. Within each section, the tutor included interactive materials and tests with automatic assessment on the topics covered during online meetings, for further review and consolidation of knowledge. During the online meetings, tutors reviewed the disciplinary topics indicated by the teacher and asked students if they had doubts about specific aspects or requests to review other topics, after which they created and made available to the students some material, which they could explore and carry out during the week before the next meeting. Students could also use the forum at any time to ask questions to the tutor, about theoretical topics, about the online materials or about the use of the platform. Figure 3 shows an example of interactive material created with the ACE, to review the equivalent fractions with the use of pie charts. The integration of the platform with the ACE allows students to view a material directly embedded the platform's pages without the needs of installing the program while maintaining the interactivity on educational resource. In this case, students can enter the numerator and denominator of two fractions in the boxes, represent them graphically and check whether the two fractions are equivalent by receiving immediate feedback. The exploration can be repeated as many times as the students wish and, in this way, they can also learn a procedure for studying the mathematical concept.

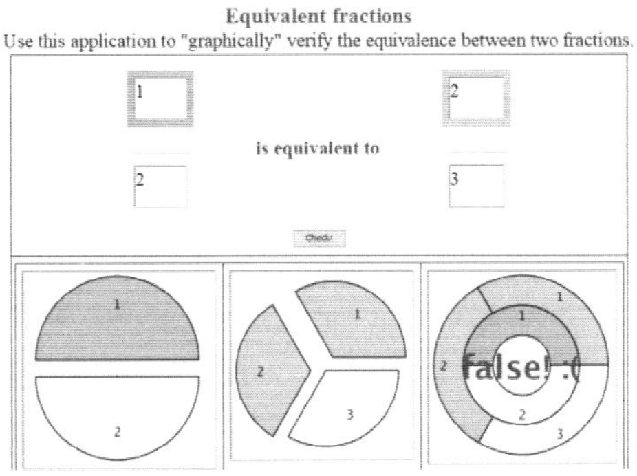

Figure 3. Example of interactive material created by tutors

The second type of material for recovery were tests with automatic assessment, very important for formative assessment (Barana et al., 2018a). Through them the students could carry out exercises with various types of questions having immediate and interactive feedback on the correctness of the answer and the possibility to try the question again, learning from his mistakes. Fig. 4 shows an example of question always inherent to equivalent fractions created with the AAS.

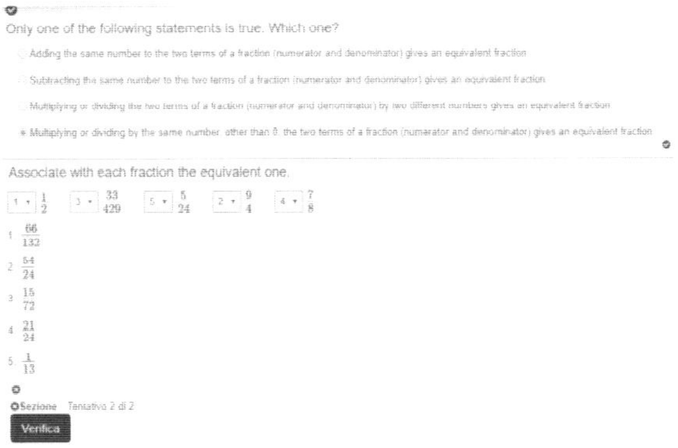

Figure 4. Example of question with automatic assessment and interactive and immediate feedback

In the first part of the question the student is asked to reflect on the theoretical definition of equivalent fractions choosing the correct answer among the four possible. In the second part, an application of the definition is proposed by associating the number of the equivalent fraction among those proposed to 5 fractions. The student in both sections of the question has the "Verifica" (which means "check" in italian language) button available to verify the correctness of the answer and it has 2 attempts to give the answer. In this way, if the student makes a mistake on the first attempt, he can rethink the reasoning and try to correct himself. The possibility to have multiple attempts available is very important for students' self-confidence.

4. ANALYSIS OF THE RESULTS

To understand the appreciation or otherwise of the students and their teachers on the recovery path and their considerations on the innovative methodologies proposed within it, we analyzed:

- the participation of students in online meetings;
- the activities carried out by the students on the platform;
- the collaboration through forums;
- students' answers to the initial and final questionnaires;
- teachers' answers to the satisfaction questionnaire on their students' progress.

From the initial questionnaire, to which only 22 students answered in total, we were able to get a general overview of the students in different aspects of Mathematics and their expectations at the beginning of the course. In the first question the students had to give themselves a score from "1=insufficient" to "5=excellent" in different aspects included in the following table.

Table 1. Student responses to different aspects of Mathematics

	Mean	Dev. Standard
Interest in the subject	2,96	1,27
Knowledge of the subject	2,60	0,91
Participation in the class lesson	3,72	1,06
Study at home	3,52	1,00
Confidence in the possibility of being able to recover	3,08	1,41

As can be seen from the mean and the standard deviation of the results, the initial situation was not very critical, and this is in line with the choice to direct the course to students with not too serious gaps. To the open question "Why are you having difficulties in this matter?" the students' most frequent answers were: "Because I am not passionate about the subject"; "Because I know things in theory, my difficulty is to put them into practice"; "I'm not good at math"; "Sometimes I'm not focused during the lesson"; "Because I have gaps"; "I don't really like it"; "I can't remember the formulas or all the rules by heart". These responses confirm what was said in the previous paragraph. Mathematics is seen as a difficult and uninteresting subject by students, very notional and mnemonic, in which it is only important to know how to do well the calculations. Finally, to the open question "What do you expect by participating in this project?" all students replied that they hope to improve and better understand the various topics; in two cases the " be more self-confident" was mentioned, in two others the "taking good marks" and only in one case "being able to have more interest". Out of 53 students, 30 students actively participated in the recovery path on the platform by participating in the online meetings, connecting to all or only some (frequencies shown in Figure 5).

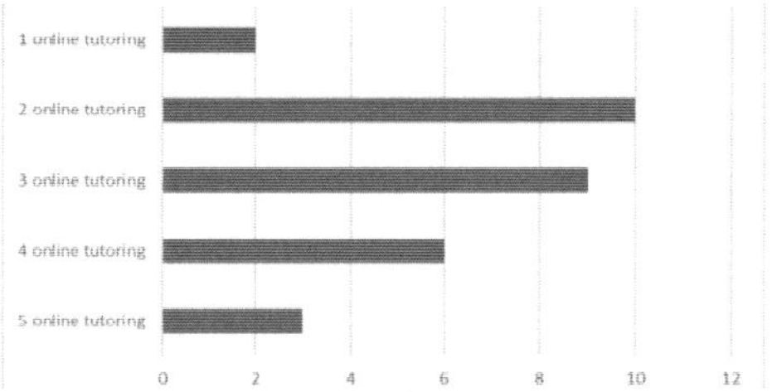

Figure 5. Frequency of students in online tutoring

The highest percentages concern participation in 2 or 3 online tutoring but the percentage on participation in 4 and 5 online tutoring is also good; the percentage of attendance to a single online tutoring is quite low. This data is encouraging because it means that after the first meeting the students were at least curious and interested enough to want to participate to the following ones. In some cases, the students did not participate to the online meetings but consulted the material and the activities on the platform, while 13 students never accessed the platform. Analyzing the completion of the activities in the assessment register, we found that 23 students completed at least one resource or one activity. Furthermore, there was no correlation between the number of people attending online meetings and the number of completed activities. There are, in fact, cases of students who participated in 3 online meetings or more and completed few or no activities; but there are also students who have completed many activities but attended few or no meetings. The only evidence in these results is that most of the students who did not attend any online meeting did not even complete the activities. This data shows that students need a guide to navigate the platform and discover its contents but also to interest and intrigue them and test themselves. The final questionnaire, which was answered by 15 students, revealed that 50% of the students mainly used the PC, 44% the smartphone and 6% the tablet to follow the recovery process. The data regarding the smartphone is a very positive result on the earlier talk about using mobile devices also for educational purposes. Table 2 shows a summary of the students' responses on the satisfaction of different aspects of the recovery process, including: the use of the platform, the web conference tool, the tutor's support, online collaboration and the proposed methodologies. The students had to answer by entering a value from "1 = not at all" to "5 = very much". The results are positive. Especially the students appreciated the relationship with the university tutors and their explanations and the fact of being able to follow the path in online mode and use the platform. The students also enjoyed the interactive material and the computer exercises and tests with the automatic assessment made available on the platform. 80% of students have chosen the "very much" answer to the question "Would you like to have a platform and be able to use the computer even in normal school lessons?".

Table 2. Summary of the students' answers to the final questionnaire on various aspects of the online course

	Mean	Dev.St.
Were the university tutor's explanations interesting?	4,5	0,64
Did you feel comfortable with the university tutor?	4,8	0,56
How much did you appreciate being able to take the online course?	4,7	0,49
Was it easy to use the platform?	3,5	1,30
How much did you appreciate having the interactive material made available on the platform?	4,4	0,91
How much did you appreciate being able to perform exercises and checks on the computer with automatic assessment?	4,1	1,06
How much did you appreciate being able to communicate with the tutor and classmates through the platform?	4,5	0,92
Do you think these platform resources have helped you improve?	4,3	0,90
Would you like to have a platform and be able to use the computer even in normal school lessons?	4,7	0,72

To also evaluate the impact of the course on the aspects of Mathematics required in the initial questionnaire (Table 1) we asked students the same question as the final questionnaire. The results are very good because in all aspects the scores have improved (Table 3).

Table 3. Comparison of students' answers on various aspects of Mathematics between initial and final questionnaires

	Mean before	Mean after	Dev.St. before	Dev.St. after
Interest in the subject	2,96	3,73	1,27	0,96
Knowledge of the subject	2,60	3,47	0,91	0,64
Participation in the class lesson	3,72	3,87	1,06	0,83
Study at home	3,52	3,67	1,00	0,62
Confidence in the possibility of being able to recover	3,08	3,53	1,41	1,46

For 73% of students grades in Mathematics improved after the course and recovered from the difficulties they had in this subject. To the open question "What did you like most by attending this recovery path?" the most significant responses were: "Helping each other both with the tutor and with friends"; "The help of the tutor"; "The possibility of being able to communicate through the platform"; "The fact that the computer was used"; "Studying in this way"; "That I could do math with a person I have never seen, but above all recover that it was my main goal"; "All"; "Share the explanations given with my classmates"; "Being able to talk and communicate my math doubts directly from home and to be able to recover"; "When the tutor helped us with our homework." Finally, we asked students if they had suggestions for improving the recovery path and everyone asked to make it last longer. All the teachers involved were very present and played a very active role within the student recovery process. In fact, they viewed many, if not all, the activities made available on the platform by the tutor and supervised the work done by their students. Their responses to the satisfaction questionnaire on the recovery path indicate that they have found a lot of satisfaction from the students and believe that the path was useful.

5. CONCLUSION

The recovery path for students within the Action of the University of Turin for the “Ragazzi Connessi” Project involved 7 teachers and 53 students from four lower secondary schools in the city of Genoa. The analysis carried out shows that the exclusively online method with which the path was provided has had good success.

The students had no difficulty in relating to a university tutor whom they did not see and know in person and greatly appreciated his help and explanations. Despite some initial difficulties, overcome with the help of teachers, parents and the Helpdesk service, students appreciated the use of the platform and would like it to be used during normal lessons. The students also appreciated the opportunity to participate in online meetings with the tutor and their classmates and appreciated the proposed methodologies (interactive files for recovery and tests with automatic assessment and interactive feedback). The course helped students to overcome difficulties in Mathematics and increase interest in the subject and in their self-confidence. The teachers' opinion on their students' recovery path is very positive. These results are encouraging in view of the second edition of the course currently underway, which will involve a greater number of students. The training course for teachers will also continue within the Action with the aim of using the innovative methodologies proposed in normal teaching with students. This online tutoring through an integrated online platform can support the normal teaching of teachers. It can also be essential in times of COVID-19 emergency, such as the one we are experiencing now, where face-to-face teaching activities are suspended.

REFERENCES

Barana, A., Conte, A., Fioravera, M., Marchisio, M., Rabellino, S., 2018a. A Model of Formative Automatic Assessment and Interactive Feedback for STEM. *Proceedings of 2018 IEEE 42nd Annual Computer Software and Applications Conference (COMPSAC)*, IEEE. Tokyo, Japan, pp. 1016–1025. https://doi.org/10.1109/COMPSAC.2018.00178.

Barana, A., Fioravera, M., Marchisio, M., Rabellino, S., 2017. Adaptive Teaching Supported by ICTs to Reduce the School Failure in the Project “Scuola Dei Compiti.”. *Proceedings of 2017 IEEE 41st Annual Computer Software and Applications Conference (COMPSAC)*. IEEE, pp. 432–437.

Barana, A., Marchisio, M., 2016. Dall’esperienza di Digital Mate Training all’attività di Alternanza Scuola Lavoro. *Mondo Digitale*, 15, 64, pp. 63-82.

Barana, A., Marchisio, M., & Sacchet, M., 2018b. Advantages of using automatic formative assessment for learning mathematics. *Proceedings of International Conference on Technology Enhanced Assessment, TEA 2018*. Amsterdam; Netherlands, pp. 180-198.

Brancaccio, A., Esposito, M., Marchisio, M., Sacchet, M., & Pardini, C., 2019. Open professional development of math teachers through an online course. *Proceedings of the International Conference on e-Learning 2019*. Porto, Portugal, pp. 131-138.

Brancaccio, A., Marchisio, M., Meneghini, C., and Pardini, C., 2015. Matematica e Scienze più SMART per l’Insegnamento e l’Apprendimento. *Mondo Digitale*, 14, 58, pp. 1-8.

Cavagnero, S., Gallina M. A., and Marchisio, M., 2015. Scuola dei compiti. Didattica digitale per il recupero dell'insuccesso scolastico. Mondo Digitale, 14, 58, pp. 834-843.

Ferrari, P.L., 2011. Le potenzialità dell’e-learning in educazione matematica e il ruolo della ricerca. *Tecnologie Didattiche*, 19, 3, pp. 136–141.

Fini, A., 2011. Nativi digitali. Un aggiornamento sulla discussione in rete. *Bricks*, 1, pp.136–142.

Fissore, C., Floris, F., Marchisio, M., & Rabellino, S., 2019. University tutoring actions using an integrated online platform. *Proceeding of 16th International Conference on Cognition and Exploratory Learning in Digital Age, CELDA 2019, IADIS Press*. Cagliari, Italy, pp. 69-76.

Giraudo, M. T., Marchisio, M., & Pardini, C., 2014. Tutoring con le nuove tecnologie per ridurre l’insuccesso scolastico e favorire l’apprendimento della matematica nella scuola secondaria. *Mondo Digitale*. 13, 51, pp. 834-843.

Giuliani, A., Moretti, G., Morini, A., 2015. Servizi di tutorato didattico e Obblighi Formativi Aggiuntivi, un’indagine empirica esplorativa: il caso del Dipartimento di Scienze della Formazione dell’Università Roma Tre. *Italian Journal of Educational Research*, 15, pp. 63-78.

Prensky, M., 2001. Digital Natives. Digital Immigrants. On the Horizon, 9, 5, pp. 1–6.

Raccomandazione 2018/C 189/01 del Parlamento Europeo e del Consiglio, 22 maggio 2018. Competenze chiave per l’apprendimento permanente.

Turrentine, P. and Macdonald, L., 2006. Tutoring Online: Increasing Effectiveness with Best Practices. *NADE Digest*. 2, 2, pp. 9–18.

Valle, V., Epifania, F., Folgieri, R., 2010. Un esperimento di didattica online per il recupero delle insufficienze scolastiche per studenti delle scuole superiori attraverso strumenti del web 2.0. *Proceedings of* Didamatica 2010. Roma, Italy, pp. 201-205.

ONLINE WRITTEN EXAMS DURING COVID-19 CRISIS

Goffredo Haus, Yuri Benvenuto Pasquinelli, Daniela Scaccia and Nello Scarabottolo
Università degli Studi di Milano, Milan, Italy[*]

ABSTRACT

The paper deals with the problem of carrying on online written exams in the University of Milan, suddenly closed due to the Covid-19 emergency. Main goal of the paper is to present and compare the different scenarios envisioned, depending on the number of students to be monitored in parallel to avoid cheating. For limited numbers, direct monitoring by the teacher has been suggested, with different supports depending on the type of exam proposed by the teacher (open vs. closed answer questions, presence of handwritten parts). For larger numbers, a proctoring system has been adopted, after some comparisons between two commercial solutions. Results show a very large adoption of a solution allowing teachers to monitor in real time students answering open questions on their home computers.

KEYWORDS

Universities, Written Exams, Closed Vs. Open Answer Exams, Online Student Monitoring, Proctoring

1. INTRODUCTION

The lockdown imposed by the Covid-19 pandemic around the end of February 2020 forced Italian Universities to suddenly transfer online all the teaching activities normally carried on with students physically present in classrooms in a traditional university.

To better understand the context, the University of Milan is constituted by height faculties: Agricultural and Food Sciences, Humanities, Law, Medicine, Pharmacy, Political, Economic and Social Sciences, Science and Technology, Veterinary Medicine, and 2 schools: Exercise and Sport Sciences, Language Mediation and Intercultural Communication. They offer 67 bachelor degrees (3 years, 180 ECTS – European Credit Transfer System – credits) 64 master degrees (2 years after bachelor, 120 ECTS credits) and 9 single-cycle master degrees (5 or 6 years, 300 or 360 ECTS credits). More than 3000 courses are taught by 2179 staff professors and almost 2000 contract professors, supported by 1960 support people (technical and administrative staff units).

Due to urgency requirements, the implementation of online lectures has been left to personal initiative of teachers, without the possibility of significant methodological guidelines. The support offered by the university personnel mainly consisted in a set of instructions published on the web portal helping teachers in registering audio and video lectures, in connecting with students through web conference platforms, in publishing didactical materials on the proprietary LMS (Learning Management Systems).

Similar approach has been followed to allow the thesis discussion of graduating students: the web conference platforms used for lectures have been adopted also to connect these students from home with the commission of teachers evaluating their final exam.

A third aspect of online learning required on the contrary some deeper considerations: the management of exams evaluating the knowledge and the competences acquired by students at the end of each single course present in their study curriculum.

Among the various references in literature regarding online exams, it is worth mentioning (Truszkowski 2019) (Weiner & Hurtz 2017) (Wibowo 2016) (Ardid et al. 2014) and (Hillier & Fluck 2013). In the first two, some comparisons between proctored and non-proctored tests are done, clearly showing that in absence of some form of proctoring the final grades are higher, due to usage of unauthorized supports and cheating. In the third one, a comparison between online and onsite proctored exams shows on the contrary no significant differences in final grades, allowing to state that the level of student behavior control can be satisfactory both online and onsite.

[*] *firstname.lastname@unimi.it*

To proctor exams online, the first suggestion coming from the University governance to all teachers has been to convert them in oral form, and to interact with students through the already mentioned web conference platforms to be able to evaluate and to grade them. However, this approach presents several limitations, among which the most critical one are:

- the impossibility in an oral exam to ask students to solve problems requiring (even a short) autonomous work, perhaps to be written by hand on a piece of paper;
- the difficulties in finding a set of equally difficult questions to several students (thus the difficulties in making a fair evaluation);
- the excessive time required for courses followed by hundreds of students.

For the above reasons, the authors of this paper:

- the Deputy Rector for Digital Innovation, ICT Services, Strategic and Special Projects;
- the Director of the ICT Division;
- the Director of CTU: the Teaching and Learning Innovation and Multimedia Technology Center of the University;
- the Rector Delegate to ICT infrastructures coordination;

have been charged with the task of studying possible ways to conduct online written exams, allowing teachers to avoid the limitations of oral exams while still guaranteeing a reasonable level of reliability in their evaluations. To this purpose, main aspects to be taken into account were:

- the possibility of submitting to students open answer tests as well as closed answer quizzes;
- the possibility of asking students to submit their work (partially or totally) written on paper, for example when mathematical formulas or graphical elements are required;
- the possibility for students to use some applications (e.g., compilers, statistical software, etc.) during their exam;
- the possibility of examining groups of students ranging from a few units to a few hundreds;
- the adoption of technological solutions enforcing teacher's control over students behavior (i.e., avoiding students to copy answers, to surf the web and to interact among each other during the exam).

The following section summarizes the impact of exams in our University, in terms of numbers of students and distribution over the year. Section 3 discusses the solutions identified to monitor student behavior during their exam, on the basis of the number of participating students. Section 4 presents three different scenarios identified by the authors and proposed around the end of April 2020 to the teachers of the university, letting them to adopt the most suitable one(s) for their needs. In section 5, the usage of these solutions up to beginning of June is considered in terms of numbers of exams, numbers of examined students, etc. Section 6 draws some concluding remarks and possible future developments of this aspect of online learning.

2. ANALYSIS OF EXAM SESSIONS

To better understand the different scenarios described in the following sections of this paper, it is worth knowing that in our University:

- each course must propose to students at least six different exam dates every academic year;
- a student can decide her/his first exam date after the end of the course lectures, but in case of failure or unsatisfying result, she/he can reapply for the same exam in a following date, without any penalty;
- there is no penalty for students that after application do not show up at the exam date: they are simply considered absent and they can reapply whenever they want.

Thus, each teacher has to plan for at least six exam sessions every year, with a number of participating students known only a few days before each session, i.e., after closing of the student application period for each exam date.

To evaluate the impact of exams both during the lockdown period and for the subsequent months – when we expect to be forced to ensure social distancing for a long time – data related to last complete "normal" year 2019 have been taken into account. The results are shown in Tables 1 and 2, letting to the following considerations:

- the largest number of exam sessions are located at the end of the winter and summer semesters, during breaks between lecture times (i.e., January-February and June-September, with August being the traditional vacation months in our country);

- the average number of students applying for each exam session is reasonably limited, and equal to 18.6 considering the overall year, but:
- there are exam sessions characterized by huge numbers of students, over 200 and arriving to more than 540 for a couple of exams;
- the largest number of exam sessions is organized by the faculty of Medicine, far above the faculty of Science and Technology which has the largest number of examined students;
- Humanities, i.e., the faculty where the highest number of students are enrolled, usually adopts oral exams, thus the number of written sessions is quite limited.

To propose to our colleagues suitable scenarios for conducting written exams online, we had to then consider such a wide variety of situations in terms of student numbers, always keeping in mind their uneven distribution over the year.

Table 1. Written exam sessions in 2019

Month	Exam sessions	Examined students	Average students per session	Max students per session
January	2'116	45'617	21.6	309
February	2'868	54'806	19.1	353
March	471	8'998	19.1	275
April	838	18'255	21.8	214
May	1'102	25'677	23.3	302
June	2'477	51'301	20.7	428
July	3'197	49'074	15.4	206
September	3'043	39'083	12.8	223
October	497	5'533	11.1	245
November	896	19'780	22.1	545
December	827	23'464	28.4	401
Total	**18'332**	**341'588**	**18.6**	**545**

Table 2. Distribution of students and sessions per faculties in 2019

Faculty/School	Enrollments in 2018/19	Exam sessions	Examined students
Agricultural and Food Sciences	3'431	1'613	27'462
Exercise and Sport Sciences	1'398	349	9'518
Humanities	14'878	1'037	32'633
Language Mediation and Intercultural Communication + Interfaculties	4'737	1'115	32'394
Law	6'748	397	10'696
Medicine	7'682	5'494	62'523
Pharmacy	3'075	1'161	24'286
Political, Economic and Social Sciences	7'708	2'614	53'776
Science and Technology	8'450	3'823	75'325
Veterinary Medicine	1'836	729	12'975
Total	**59'943**	**18'332**	**341'588**

3. MONITORING STUDENT BEHAVIOR DURING EXAMS

A first discriminating aspect considered in defining the different scenarios has been the possibility for the teacher to monitor in real time the behavior of the whole set of examined students or of a limited number of student groups through some web conference platforms.

After some tests, it has been seen that a reasonable number of students that can be monitored by a single person is in the range of 20-30, and that it was not worth to ask teachers to split students in more than 4 to 5 groups, to be monitored in parallel (with the help of some collaborators) or one after each other. Then, we decided to consider 100 students applying for the same exam date as the limit for exam sessions monitored under teacher's responsibility and exams sessions requiring external support.

Table 3 subdivides the number of sessions already given in Table 1 using this threshold to discriminate between sessions up to 99 applying students and sessions with 100 or more applying students. As it can be seen, the percentage of large sessions is definitely limited, even if they must deal with a number of applying students corresponding to 20% of the total number of students registered to exams in year 2019.

Table 3. Exam sessions in 2019 having less or at least 100 applying students

Month	Total # of sessions	Sessions with up to 99 students	Sessions with 100 or more students	% of large sessions	Total # of students in large sessions
January	2'116	2'043	73	3.45%	11'269
February	2'868	2'819	49	1.71%	7'299
March	471	458	13	2.76%	2'166
April	838	804	34	4.06%	5'056
May	1'102	1'056	46	4.17%	7'443
June	2'477	2'413	64	2.58%	9'865
July	3'197	3'163	34	1.06%	4'383
September	3'043	3'021	22	0.72%	2'995
October	497	494	3	0.60%	545
November	896	856	40	4.46%	7'752
December	827	768	59	7.13%	10'245
Total	**18'332**	**17'895**	**437**	**2.38%**	**69'018**

3.1 Direct Monitoring

Monitoring of a group of 20-30 students by means of a web conference platform (e.g., Microsoft Teams, Zoom, etc.) has been proposed in the following way:

- the web conference is established between the computer of the teacher and the smartphone of each student, who is requested to install the app of the web conference adopted by the teacher;
- students are admitted to the web conference planned by the teacher one after each other;
- after admission to the web conference, the student has to show an identity document to the teacher (to prove her/his right to participate to the exam;
- the teacher can ask the student to use her/his smartphone to show the room where she/he will take the exam, to demonstrate that no other people nor other support device (e.g., a second computer) is present;
- then, the student must position her/his smartphone – suitably powered to avoid battery exhaustion – as shown in Figure 1, in order to frame her/his work place (table and computer desktop).

Figure 1. Student smartphone framing student work place

Student monitoring through her/his smartphone instead of through her/his computer proved to have several advantages:

- the teacher can control that no forbidden material (e.g., books, written notes, other smartphone, etc.) is used by the student during the exam;
- by zooming on each student window in the web conference, the teacher can look at the desktop and see if the student is operating correctly (i.e., using only the allowed applications);

- the audio of the student smartphone is always kept on, allowing to immediately identify unexpected noises, other people's voices, etc.;
- students have no idea about what is the web conference window examined in each moment by the teacher, who can randomly browse among them. This has a psychological effect on student behavior, since they must expect to be deeply controlled in any moment.

Of course, this monitoring relies from one side on the reliability of the connection between student smartphone and web conference platform, and on the other side on the ability of the teacher to properly handle the web conference.

As regards the first aspect, the student may have a low quality internet connection (maybe due to the area where her/his home is located), her/his smartphone may have heating troubles after too much time of video and audio connection, or she/he may have other problem resulting in unexpected end of her/his presence in the web conference. In these cases, it is up to the teacher to decide how to proceed: our suggestion is to let the student to try recovering the connection quickly; in case of failure, she/he must have a second chance in the following days, either as part of a successive student group, or as a single examined student, perhaps in oral form.

As regards the second aspect, we published a set of guidelines on the University web portal to help teachers to train themselves before undergoing their exams. Up to now the only critical situation happened for a teacher not realizing in time that a group of students in a larger set was not monitored at all, and he decided to cancel the exams of that group, obviously raising student complaints that left the University governance to force the teacher to re-admit them.

3.2 Proctoring

When 100 or more students applied for a single exam session, it is not worth asking the teacher to monitor many student groups, either in parallel (too many collaborators needed) or in sequence (too much time required).

We then started considering different proctoring proposals available on the market, i.e., systems offering different kinds of monitoring supports having these general characteristics:

- no control in real time by the teacher or other collaborators is required: the systems record the behavior of the student during the exam through the webcam of her/his computer, and/or a second device like a smartphone;
- after the end of the exam, all recordings are processed by suitable Artificial Intelligence algorithms, that mark in red any "suspect" behavior of the student (e.g., eyes or head movements, noises, appearance of other people, etc.);
- the marked tracks are then sent to the teacher together with all recordings, to allow her/him to analyze the suspect behaviors and decide accordingly how to manage them.

Among the various offerings, we concentrated on two options – namely: Respondus and Proctorio – and we started some comparative tests in early May, first on simulated exams involving staff and then on real exams using volunteer teachers.

3.2.1 Respondus

As stated in (Respondus 2020) Respondus use its LockDown Browser to prevent cheating. With such a browser, assessments are displayed full-screen and cannot be minimized, almost all menu and toolbar options are removed, access to other applications including messaging, screen-sharing, virtual machines, and remote desktops is forbidden, as well as copying and pasting to or from an assessment.

Once activated, Lockdown Browser closes all other applications on the student computer, asks the student to show her/him identity document and her/his room and work place, tests audio and video devices on the student computer and finally let the student start accessing exam question on a suitably connected LMS.

Main pros and cons emerging from the testing phase were the following:

- Respondus has a very aggressive and attractive pricing policy for newcomers, especially related to the Covid-19 emergency, when all exams were to be planned online;
- setup of the student computer was not always straightforward, especially in MacOS environments, where the Lockdown Browser installation and/or activation required sometimes the intervention of a call center to let the student take the exam;

- sometimes, the system was not able to process the recording of some students, implying exam repetition;
- the AI algorithms revealed some limits in putting reds on the tracks: in some cases, the appearance of a second person during the exam was not spotted.

As a final result, the teacher had to examine in a different way around 10% of the students present at the session, either for setup or for post processing troubles.

3.2.2 Proctorio

As stated in (Proctorio 2020) Proctorio does not use a specific lockdown browser to prevent cheating, but a simple add-on for browsers like Chrome that creates a secure exam environment by restricting internet navigation and computer functionality. All internet browsing can be blocked or specific websites may be whitelisted to allow third-party quiz applications or blacklisted to prevent the use of unauthorized resources during exams.

Main pros and cons emerging from the testing phase where the following:

- Proctorio does not have any specific pricing policy related to the Covid-19 emergency, thus resulting in being far more expensive than Respondus especially when all exams have to be planned online; however:
- setup of the student computer was definitely simpler due to the absence of a pervasive tool like the Lockdown Browser;
- student behavior monitoring is more accurate, since Proctorio records the webcam stream and also the desktop of the student computer;
- the browser add-on sends only some video frames instead of a continuous streaming, thus significantly reducing the network bandwidth requirements (and facilitating monitoring of students with poor internet connections);
- AI algorithms can be tuned by the teacher in terms of sensitivity of the different kinds of suspected behaviors after receiving the recorded exams; this allows the teacher to emphasize the aspects considered most dangerous and/or more common.

As a conclusion, we decided to proceed for the coming summer period of exams, i.e., June-September 2020, using Proctorio for monitoring exam sessions with at least 100 students applying.

4. TYPES OF SUPPORTED EXAMS

Besides identifying the most suitable ways usable to monitor student behavior, we had to take into account the nature of the exam each teacher may decide to use; as already stated in the introduction, we had then to consider:

- the possibility of submitting to students open answer tests as well as closed answer quizzes;
- the possibility of asking students to submit their work (partially or totally) written on paper;
- the possibility for students to use some applications (e.g., compilers, statistical software, etc.) during their exam.

The resulting scenarios identified and proposed to our University teachers are described in the following subsections.

4.1 Open Answer Tests

For limited numbers of students – i.e., groups that can be monitored by the teacher – a proposed scenario is based on the exam.net platform (Exam.net 2020) implemented by the Swedish company Teachiq AB and free to use outside Sweden during 2020. Main characteristics of this platform are:

- a very easy teacher interface, greatly facilitating creation and test of exams;
- real time monitoring of student work, since the teacher can browse among students and see what each of them already wrote;
- chat support, allowing the teacher to interact with every student without disturbing the overall group;
- download of student work as a pdf file for correction and grading;
- possibility for students to include pictures of hand written work, taken through their smartphone in a controlled way (QR code generated by the platform to allow each student to take and submit her/his pictures).

Moreover, since the visibility of the student desktop through her/his smartphone (as described in section 3.1) can be limited by environment lighting, non ideal smartphone positioning, etc., the scenario adopts the safer approach proposed by exam.net and based on the usage of SEB (Safe Exam Browser). As stated in (SEB 2020) SEB is a software that turns any computer temporarily into a secure workstation. It controls access to resources like system functions, other websites and applications and prevents unauthorized resources being used during an exam. SEB cannot be considered totally safe: some ways to bypass it are claimed to exist, though not so easy to implement (usage of virtual machines, access through a second computer, etc.). However, the appearance of the student desktop when SEB is running and the back monitoring through student smartphone facilitate the teacher work in identifying such bypasses.

For larger numbers of students, requiring proctoring, Proctorio has been integrated with the Moodle LMS already adopted by CTU, where several types of exam questions can be defined and submitted to students. The only unavailable option is the possibility for students to submit handwritten contributions, since the activities students must scan and submit them and are not compatible with the AI monitoring approach of all proctoring systems.

4.2 Closed Answer Quizzes

The exam.net platform cannot be easily used for this kind of exams: it has no native support for quizzes and it does not integrate with an LMS like Moodle; it just gives the possibility to indicate some URLs accessible through SEB during the exam. However, there is no guarantee that from these URLs it is not possible to start surfing the web; moreover, we had several troubles in integrating exam.net with the Single Sign On feature of our University, used by students to authenticate themselves.

For the above reasons, closed answer quizzes for limited numbers of students (as well as any other types of exams that can be defined in Moodle) are implemented by directly integrating SEB with the Moodle LMS, without passing through exam.net.

For large numbers of students, quizzes are obviously handled through proctoring, as outlined at the end of section 4.2.

4.3 Exams Requiring Usage of External Applications

A reliable control of the actual usage of computer programs like compilers, spreadsheets, statistical software, and so forth, made by students during the exam cannot be easily ensured, especially for groups of students directly monitored by the teacher. In fact, even when the student desktop can be clearly seen by the teacher, it is almost impossible to ensure that no other unadmitted programs or websites are accessed during the exam.

The only possible approach, allowed e.g. by Proctorio, is the adoption of proctoring for student monitoring, but this would result in a far larger number of exam sessions requiring such a solution. In fact, since even for small student groups it would become necessary to set up a proctoring session, this would lead to extra costs but above all to unaffordable workload for the technicians managing them.

For these reasons, teachers have been requested to convert this kind of exams into an oral format.

5. FIRST EVALUATIONS

After the first month of application of the scenarios above described, we are able to show some very preliminary figures. As already stated, the hugest numbers of exam sessions just started beginning of June 2020, with the peak expected between the second part of June and the first part of July.

As it can be seen from Table 4, the scenario based on the exam.net platform (i.e., open answer questions or quizzes with few questions, for groups of students directly monitored by the teacher) shows a large number of sessions and a significant number of examined students, but a definitely smaller average number of students per session. Besides some bias due to session tests made by teachers (that we cannot evaluate), it is clear that such a way of examining students has been greatly appreciated. In fact, it allows teachers not familiar with Moodle to submit written exams also to very small groups of students, exploiting all the facilities and friendliness of that platform.

Moodle with SEB has been introduced a couple of weeks after exam.net, and Moodle is presently used only by few teachers of the University, thus numbers of sessions and students are definitely smaller. However, the average number of students per session is four times the one of exam.net. This is due from one side to the fact that teachers learn to use Moodle when useful, i.e., when they have to deal with larger classes. From the other side, to the adoption of Moodle for an exam evaluating the ability of students from several faculties in using basic computer utilities, monitored by several CTU staff technicians in parallel on large student groups.

Proctoring has been used initially – when testing Respondus and Proctorio – for smaller exam sessions. Then, once decided to adopt Proctorio, proctoring has been limited to exam sessions with at least 100 applied students, as said before. This explains why in Table 4 the average number of students per proctored session is very low for Respondus (used almost only during test) while for Proctorio it is rapidly increasing towards 100 and more.

Table 4. Summary of first month of online written exams

Scenario	# of sessions	% of sessions	Average # of students per session	# of examined students	% of examined students
Exam.net	1'333	93.7%	9.5	12'673	74.0%
Moodle with SEB	55	3.9%	32.6	1'793	10.5%
Proctoring using Respondus	9	0.6%	39.3	354	2.1%
Proctoring using Proctorio	26	1.8%	89.0	2'314	13.5%
Total	**1'423**	**100.0%**	**12.0**	**17'134**	**100.0%**

6. CONCLUSIONS

After evaluation, and interaction with other Universities facing similar problems, three different scenarios have been identified for carrying on written exams online during the Covid-19 emergency period.

Cost and setup complexity of proctored exam sessions forced to limit this last scenario to very large groups of students (≥100) to be evaluated in parallel: of course, this limitation has been considered excessive by some teachers, reluctant to perform by themselves a direct monitoring.

However, the identification of two scenarios allowing reasonably affordable handling of groups of 20-30 students by a single teacher or collaborator allowed the implementation of a lot of written exams, definitely less time consuming than the oral exams initially proposed as the only possible solution. However, further studies are required to assess the efficacy of online exams on much larger cohort of students. Also, the results of this study may not be replicable to other institutions as this was based on one case study. Hence, other universities can assess the exams systems this study explored.

REFERENCES

Ardid, M, Gómez-Tejedor, JA, Meseguer-Dueñas, JM, Riera, J & Vidaurre, A 2014, 'Online exams for blended assessment. Study of different application methodologies', Computers and Education, vol. 81, pp. 296-303.

Exam.net 2020, A robust, easy-to-use and secure exam platform, viewed June 10th 2020, < https://exam.net/>.

Hillier, M & Fluck, A 2013, 'Arguing again for e-exams in high stakes examinations', 30th ascilite Conference 2013 Proceedings, pp. 385-396.

Proctorio 2020, A Comprehensive Learning Integrity Platform, viewed June 10th 2020, < https://web.proctorio.com/>.

Respondus 2020, Assessment Tools for Learning Systems, viewed June 10th 2020, < https://web.respondus.com/>.

SEB 2020, Safe Exam Browser, viewed June 10th 2020, < https://safeexambrowser.org/>.

Truszkowski, D 2019, 'Proctored Versus Non-Proctored Testing: A Study for Online Classes', Dissertation of the Doctoral Program of the American College of Education.

Weiner, JA & Hurtz, GM 2017, 'A Comparative Study of Online Remote Proctored versus Onsite Proctored High-Stakes Exams', Journal of Applied Testing Technology, vol. 18, no. 1, pp. 13-20.

Wibowo, S, Grandhi, S, Chugh, R & Sawir, E 2016, 'A Pilot Study of an Electronic Exam System at an Australian University', Journal of Educational Technology Systems, Vol 45, Issue 1, 2016.

DELIVERING AN ONLINE COURSE ON 'HEALTH EMERGENCY FROM SARS-COV-2, THE NOVEL CORONAVIRUS: PREPARATION AND CONTRAST' FOR HEALTH PROFESSIONS STUDENTS AT ITALIAN UNIVERSITIES

Giovanni Galeoto[1], Anna Berardi[2], Marco Tofani[1], Luisa Saiani[3], Alvisa Palese[4] and Donatella Valente[2]

[1]*Department of Public Health and Infection disease, Sapienza University of Rome, Piazzale Aldo Moro,5, 00185, Rome, Italy*

[2]*Department of Human Neurosciences, Sapienza University of Rome, Viale dell'Università 30, 00185, Rome, Italy*

[3]*Department of Diagnostics and Public Health, University of Verona, Via S. Francesco, 22, 37129 Verona*

[4]*Department of Medical Sciences, University of Udine, Via delle Scienze, 206, 33100 Udine, Italy*

ABSTRACT

Many Italian universities had numerous students attending hospital wards during the coronavirus disease 2019 (COVID-19) pandemic. The training of healthcare professionals and students was necessary to facilitate good practices, disseminate knowledge about COVID-19, and minimize contagion among students who were completing internships. On 28 February 2020, the Italian National Institute of Health (NIH) created a course that aimed to guide healthcare personnel so that they can appropriately address the health emergency due to severe acute respiratory syndrome coronavirus 2 (SARS-CoV-2), making use of the available scientific evidence and official sources of information and updates. The purpose of this paper was to describe the method used by the Sapienza University of Rome in delivering the Italian NIH course for health professions students at Italian universities. The research group in charge of delivering the course decided to use the Google Classroom platform. Since 1 April, 80 classes have been created, and currently, 15000 students from 28 health professions bachelor's and master's degree programs and 43 universities around Italy are attending the course. A total of 13000 students have completed the final test. This paper represents a clear advantage in the field of e-learning, not only because it describes an effective method for delivering a course to many students but also because it demonstrates how health professions students can be protected while allowing them to continue or restart internships in health facilities more safely and with more awareness.

KEYWORDS

COVID-19, e-Learning, Health Professions Students, Prevention

1. INTRODUCTION

Severe acute respiratory syndrome coronavirus 2 (SARS-CoV-2) is a major pathogen that primarily targets the human respiratory system. Previous outbreaks of coronaviruses (CoVs) include severe acute respiratory syndrome (SARS)-CoV and Middle East respiratory syndrome (MERS)-CoV, which have previously been characterized as agents that greatly threaten public health (Bogoch, 2020; Lu, 2020). Extensive measures to reduce person-to-person transmission of SARS-CoV-2 have been required to control the current outbreak. Special attention and efforts to protect or reduce transmission should be applied in susceptible populations, including children, healthcare providers, and elderly people. A guideline was published for medical staff, healthcare providers, and public health workers and researchers who are interested in SARS-CoV-2 (Jin, 2020). On 11 March 2020, the WHO Director General officially declared the outbreak of coronavirus disease 2019 (COVID-19) a pandemic. (World Health Organisation, 2020) Many Italian universities had numerous students attending hospital wards during the COVID-19 pandemic. The training of healthcare professionals and students was necessary to facilitate good practices, disseminate knowledge about COVID-19, and minimize contagion among students who were completing internships.

Since 2004, the e-learning working group of the Italian National Institute of Health (NIH) (Barrows, 1980; Barbina, 2011; Barbina, 2014) has been delivering e-learning courses on the EduISS platform (https://www.eduiss.it), assessing the quality of e-learning programs and paying attention to several key factors, such as navigability, a multimedia approach, and the degree of interactivity. Specific e-learning methodologies developed and mainly adopted by EduISS, which were originally developed for classroom learning, are innovative ways to reproduce problem-based learning (PBL) in the e-learning context using the best available web tools (Barrows, 1980; Barbina, 2011; Barbina, 2014).

On 28 February 2020, the Italian NIH created a course that aimed to guide healthcare personnel so that they can appropriately address the health emergency due to SARS CoV-2, making use of the scientific evidence currently available and official sources of information and updates (https://www.eduiss.it/course/index.php?categoryid=51).

Experts with different backgrounds developed the course, namely, experts who provided the scientific content (Italian NIH) and experts on e-learning methods and technological aspects (Training Office of the Italian NIH). The learning method selected to develop the e-learning course was based on the integration of PBL, an active learning methodology.

The course was developed within the continuing medical education Italian regulation and delivered through the e-learning platform of the Italian NIH, EduISS (https://www.eduiss.it).

During the bachelor's degree curriculum, the student is required to acquire professional specifications by completing internships in facilities identified by the degree course council (CCL) and in the defined periods. The curriculum for healthcare professions degrees provides theoretical and practical training.

The purpose of this paper was to describe the method used by Sapienza University of Rome for delivering the Italian NIH "Health Emergency from New SARS CoV-2 Coronavirus: Preparation and Contrast" course for health professions students at Italian universities.

2. BODY OF THE PAPER

On 10 March 2020, the Italian NIH officially entrusted the Sapienza University of Rome with delivering the 'Health Emergency from SARS-COV-2, The Novel Coronavirus: Preparation and Contrast'' course, which was already available for Italian healthcare professionals, to health professions students enrolled in Italian universities.

2.1 Course Development

The research group in charge of delivering the course, who was already experienced in managing online courses (Farina, 2019; Paterniani, 2019; Galeoto, 2019a; Galeoto, 2019b), decided to use the Google Classroom platform. First, a specific email address was created (corsonuovocoronavirus@gmail.com) to administer the courses and serve as a reference contact to provide support to students. Currently, 80 twin-classes with the same content of the original Italian NIH course have been created with the reference contact, and guidelines for student registration were shared with all Italian universities. Specifically, the research group sent the guidelines to the commission of the permanent conference of the health professions, and each manager sent them to the students in the courses for which they were responsible.

2.2 Guidelines for Students

To register for the course on the Google Classroom platform, students need an internet connection and a browser on their personal computer (PC) (e.g. Chrome, Firefox, Internet Explorer, or Safari). In general, the platform is supported by the main versions of browsers on an ongoing basis. To use the tool, students need to access their Gmail e-mail inbox, and then they must access the Google menu and click on Classroom (Figure 1).

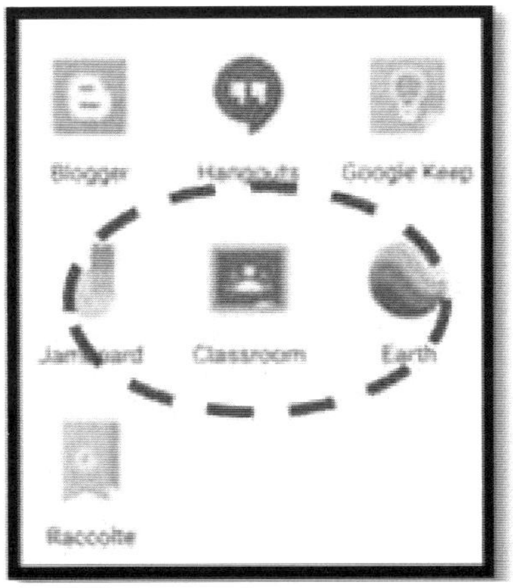

Figure 1. Classroom Icon

Alternatively, after logging in with their email credentials, they can access the Classroom application directly from the following link: https://classroom.google.com/. For participants who do not have a Gmail account, the creation of an account is required to register for the course. It is not possible to register with the institutional email; this feature is why students and teachers (corsonuovocoronavirus@gmail.com) must have the same email domain. Google Classroom does not currently support multiple domains. At the first authentication, simply click on the + symbol at the top right ('Create your first course or Register') by selecting the subscribe to the course icon (Figure 2).

Figure 2. Create a course

Once the subscribe to the course item has been selected, simply enter the course code from the guidelines. Codes are constantly updated at http://www.associazioneroma.org/covid19-Over-students /. All the course material is immediately visible in the Stream section of the course (Figure 3).

Figure 3. STREAM section

All students are required to complete the entrance test and the final test, which are found at the beginning and end of the course materials in the Stream section. To obtain the certificate of participation, it is mandatory to complete the two evaluation tests. At the end of the test, simply click on delivery, and the certificate of participation in the course will be sent to the participants at the email with which they enrolled. Only upon successfully completing all the course activities is an attendance certificate provided for each participant. The tutors are available by email to resolve any doubts regarding the course content, methodological aspects, and technological issues.

2.3 The e-Learning Course Characteristics

The course was structured in three learning units, all reproducing an entire PBL cycle. The general objectives of the e-learning course were to update the participants about the main concepts of COVID-19 and to guide healthcare professionals and students on clinical practice with COVID-19 (Figure 4).

Figure 4. Example of a course

The three units and the related specific learning objectives were as follows:

1. Characteristics of the international and national situation of the health emergency due to SARS CoV-2;

2. Surveillance, detection, and management of suspected cases;

3. Information for healthcare professionals for prevention, identification, and control in clinical settings.

Participants were expected to spend 16 hours to complete the course. They could access the course at any time; however, they were required to complete the course within four weeks. Participation in the course was voluntary for universities, courses, and students, and at the time of recruitment, the participants were informed about the modalities and objectives of the project. The results of the tests were communicated individually to the participating students and did not affect the evaluation in progress or the final evaluation, while the aggregated data were transmitted to the coordinators of the courses involved and to the university referents. A group of experts screened all these elements, establishing the number and type of questions required. Once the number and type of questions were established, the working group followed four steps: (1) development of multiple choice questions with four possible answers, one of which is correct; (2) choice of the maximum time to answer each question (approximately one minute and a half); (3) choice of the scores to give to the items (one point for each correct answer); and (4) choice of the randomization and administration methods. Randomization was considered necessary to standardize the attention levels to all questions. From this analysis, 31 questions were obtained and divided into three units in the course.

3. RESULTS

Since 1 April, 80 classes have been created. Each class allows a maximum of 250 participants (Figure 5).

Figure 5. Courses

Currently, 25479 students from universities around Italy are attending the course, and 20000 have completed the final test. A total of 43 universities have been involved. Students from all the 28 health professions bachelor and master's degrees (e.g. healthcare, physiotherapy, nursing, speech therapy, medicine, odontology, biomedical laboratory techniques, medical radiology techniques, and occupational therapy) have attended the course.

4. CONCLUSION

COVID-19 has significantly affected all of our lives. It is challenging our ability to adapt and be resilient, and people are facing major challenges worldwide. The education sector is responding to quarantines with a sudden shift to online learning (Electronic Platform for Adult Learning in Europe, 2020). The present study represents an important element for the emergency that the world is experiencing. Experts in the academic world must be encouraged to spread and share strategies used to face difficulties. The advantage of international communication lies in the sharing that allows ever-higher standards in education. This paper illustrates clear advantages of e-learning, not only as an effective method to deliver a course to many students but also because as a method by which health professions students can be protected while allowing them to continue or restart internships in health facilities more safely and with more awareness.

ACKNOWLEDGMENTS

Authors express their thanks to Dr. Alfonso Mazzaccara, for allowing such study to be performed, by offering direct assistance for the develop of the course.

REFERENCES

Barbina D. et al, 2011. Case study - National Health Institute, Italy. In: *Moodle 2.0 for business: Beginner's guide. Implement Moodle in your business to streamline your interview, training, and internal communication processes.* Packt Publishing Birmingham, England, pp. 161-4.

Barbina D. et al, 2014. *Study of the effectiveness of an e-learning course to high interactivity*. Mondo Digitale; Rome.

Barrows H.S. et al, 1980. *Problem-based Learning: an approach to medical education*. Springer Publishing Company; New York.

Bogoch I. et al, 2020. Pneumonia of Unknown Aetiology in Wuhan, China: Potential for International Spread via Commercial Air Travel. *J Travel Med*, Vol. 27, No. 2, pp taaa008.

Electronic Platform for Adult Learning in Europe. COVID-19 is reviving the need to explore online teaching and learning opportunities. 24 March 2020. Available at: https://epale.ec.europa.eu/en/blog/covid-19-reviving-need-explore-online-teaching-and-learning-opportunities (Accessed: 29 April 2020) World Health Organization, Coronavirus disease 2019 (COVID-19) Situation Report 46, 2020.

Farina I. et al, 2019. High-Fidelity Simulation Type Technique Efficient for Learning Nursing Disciplines in the Courses of Study: An Integrative Review. In: *Methodologies and Intelligent Systems for Technology Enhanced Learning, 9th International Conference, Workshops*. Avila, Spain

Galeoto G. et al, 2019 a. The Use of a Dedicated Platform to Evaluate Health-Professions University Courses. *In book: Methodologies and Intelligent Systems for Technology Enhanced Learning, 8th International Conference.* Toledo, Spain.

Galeoto G. et al, 2019 b. Evaluation of the Disciplinary Competences of the Students of the Bachelor's Degree in Physiotherapy at "Sapienza" University of Rome Through the TECO: A Cross-Sectional Study. *In book: Learning Technology for Education Challenges.* Zamora, Spain.

Jin Y.H. et al, 2020. A rapid advice guideline for the diagnosis and treatment of 2019 novel coronavirus (2019-nCoV) infected pneumonia (standard version). *Military Medical Research,* Vol.7, No 4.

Lu H. et al, 2020. Outbreak of Pneumonia of Unknown Etiology in Wuhan, China: The Mystery and the Miracle. *J Med Virol,* Vol.92, No. 4, pp 401-402.

Paterniani A. et al, 2019. Electronic Test of Competence Administration: Qualitative Evaluation of Students' Satisfaction on Telematic Platform a Cross Sectional Study. In: *Methodologies and Intelligent Systems for Technology Enhanced Learning, 9th International Conference, Workshops*. Avila, Spain

World Health Organisation, Coronavirus disease 2019 (COVID-19) Situation Report 46, 2020

THE EFFECT OF GENDER ON UNIVERSITY TEACHERS' ICT USE

Manica Danko, Mitja Dečman, Damijana Keržič and Vida Zorko
University of Ljubljana, Slovenia

ABSTRACT

Information communication technology (ICT) that is used in instruction has attracted the attention of researchers with many studies having looked at the factors affecting how university instructors apply it in their teaching. Yet little is known about whether the gender of university teachers can impact their ICT use. This research relies on quantitative data from a survey of 428 teachers at the University of Ljubljana in Slovenia to explore differences in pedagogical ICT use in terms of gender. The results show that gender positively correlates with ICT use and that particular ICT tools and their pedagogical uses are more frequent among female teachers whereas males scored higher for certain ICT-related attitudes. This implies that gender may be viewed as a predictor of certain types of and attitudes to ICT use in university instruction.

KEYWORDS

Higher Education, Instructional ICT Use, Gender

1. INTRODUCTION

Information communication technology (ICT) has made its way into the area of instruction within higher education (HE), with studies revealing that it is commonly used to enhance teaching practices (Collis and van der Wende, 2002, p. 29; Gaebel et al., 2014, pp. 24, 71). A large number of factors may affect teachers' use of ICT in the HE context and many are well explored. For instance, Al-Busaidi and Al-Shihi (2012) identify intention, attitude, perceived usefulness, ease of use, perceived risk, perceived behavioural control, social influence and facilitating conditions as factors that determine how satisfied academics will be with ICT and, more specifically, with learning management systems (LMSs). Their level of satisfaction will thus impact their intention to adopt and use LMSs. Similarly, Motaghian et al. (2013) claim that perceived usefulness, perceived ease of use and system quality affect university teachers' use of online learning systems, with perceived usefulness being the most decisive factor. Wang and Wang (2009) point out that the quality of the system and service together with self-efficacy are strongly associated with university teachers' use of online learning systems. Kocaleva et al. (2015) highlight effort expectancy and facilitating conditions, social influence and facilitating conditions as determinants of university teachers' intention to use new ICT.

However, this paper focuses on university teachers' gender given that much less literature on this factor can be found. Thus, the following research question guided the research: Is there any correlation between university teachers' gender and their self-reported educational use of ICT?

To answer the question, this study relies on quantitative data obtained from a survey conducted by the University of Ljubljana (UL) as part of the project "Digital UL – with innovative use of ICT towards excellence – DiUL" that aims to enhance and support flexible ICT-supported teaching approaches within the university. The DiUL survey explored pedagogical, technical and organisational aspects of ICT use at the UL. Its objective was to identify how ICT is being promoted in UL study programmes, which ICT-supported teaching methods and practices are in use, which ICT tools are adopted, and what the university's needs are with regard to technical, technological and organisational support. Findings of the DiUL survey will inform the development of innovative learning environments, the introduction of ICT-supported methods and pedagogical practices in the UL's study programmes.

This paper first reviews relevant literature on the effects of gender on instructional ICT use in HE. It then outlines the methodology employed in the research and presents the results. A discussion of the findings and their implications follows in the final section.

2. LITERATURE REVIEW

Considerable research exists on the effect of teachers' demographic variables like gender, age and teaching experience on their ICT adoption (Rahimi and Yadollahi, 2011, p. 18). However, it primarily focuses on teachers in general. Much less literature is available on how these factors affect the ICT use of teachers in HE.

Research into the impact of gender on ICT use in modern society shows differences between males and females. For example, Broos (2005) reveals significant gender differences with regard to attitudes to ICT. Men hold positive attitudes to computers and the Internet whereas women display higher levels of computer anxiety. Moreover, men have greater computer experience and, compared to women, consider themselves as being ahead of others concerning computer or Internet use.

With respect to teachers, in the early 2000s Ilomäki (2011, p. 336) found differences between males and females who self-assessed their use of ICT. In most applications, male teachers evaluated their skills as being higher than their female colleagues. Yet, a more recent study of the digital competence of 2,477 upper secondary school teachers indicates a different trend. It shows that in this regard women have a higher mean score than men (Krumsvik et al., 2016, p. 157).

As for academic staff, the literature reveals differences between males and females, although the research is inconclusive. On one hand, certain studies conclude that gender differences do not exist. For example, while exploring how academic staff perceive the use of ICT at a university in Saudi Arabia, Alkhasawneh and Alanazy (2015, p. 494) find no significant gender-based differences among the staff. They believe that this is due to ICT use having become normalised in today's world. This is in line with the findings of a survey in India by Bhat and Bashir (2017) that reveals no significant differences between male and female university teachers with respect to gender, and that males and females have a similar attitude to ICT use. Similarly, Soydal et al. (2012, p. 287) analysed academic staff at a Turkish university and reveal that gender is mostly not a factor in e-learning readiness.

On the other hand, Soydal et al. note one exception, namely, confidence in using computers. Their research shows that males are more confident (2012, p. 287). Consistent with this finding, Agboola (2006, p. 5) finds a significant connection between gender and e-learning confidence: male lecturers have greater confidence than their female colleagues. Other gender differences are identified by Tena et al. (2016) who studied how e-learning has been adopted by various universities in Andalusia, Spain. They find that male lecturers have better ICT skills and knowledge of certain tools than their female counterparts. However, they also reveal that females use these tools more often in their teaching than males (2016, p. 33). Further differences between male and female university teachers were uncovered by Okazaki and Renda dos Santos (2012, p. 101). They carried out a study that included three Brazilian universities to explore how faculty members adopt e-learning tools. The results show that males and females differ with regard to certain causal relationships. For the male faculty members, perceived usefulness more strongly shapes their attitude to e-learning and, similarly, their feeling of ease of use more strongly impacts their perceived usefulness of e-learning.

Thus, it could be tentatively concluded that gender does not often play a role in HE ICT use. When it does, however, confidence, better ICT skills, along with the causal relationships "perceived usefulness → positive attitude" and "ease of use → perceived usefulness" can more often be ascribed to males. Frequent instructional use of ICT tools is more likely to be associated with female HE teachers.

3. METHODOLOGY AND DATA

The purpose of this study was to explore the effects of gender on teachers' ICT use. To realise this research objective, we relied on data collected in a survey conducted at the UL as part of the DiUL project in 2017. Participants were academic staff from 23 faculties and 3 academies. The invitation to participate in the survey was sent by email. All 2,682 teachers were invited to participate. The survey comprised 64 questions in the form of individual statements measured with ordinal scales using a 5-point Likert-type scale. The responses were scaled as follows: from 1 – "disagree very strongly" to 5 – "agree very strongly" (to express agreement), from 1 – "never" to 5 – "very often" (to describe how often they use ICT in teaching), and from 1 – "once a year/never" to 5 – "every day" (to describe how often they use ICT at home).

The survey was responded to by 960 teachers; 53 records where more than seven values (half the total) were missing were removed. In the pre-processed dataset, some values (<1%) were still missing. We replaced them with the default parameters used in the Expectation-Maximisation (EM) algorithm in SPSS. The final sample comprised 428 complete responses, representing a 16% response rate. To achieve a confidence level of 95% indicating that the true value is within ±5% of the measured value, 337 responses are required, meaning this condition was met.

Teachers were also asked about certain demographic data such as gender, age, educational qualification, classification of their educational field, academic title and the faculty they work at. Among all of the academic staff, 40% were female and 60% were male. However, the valid and complete records in our possession were for an equal number of male and female respondents (Table 1).

Table 1. Demographic profile of 428 respondents

	N	Percentage
Gender		
Female	214	50%
Male	214	50%
Age		
21 – 40	91	22.7%
41 – 50	166	41.3%
51 – 55	73	18.2%
55+	71	17.7%

To detect any gender differences considering different survey indicators, a Mann-Whitney U rank-based nonparametric test was applied. The Mann-Whitney U test or Wilcoxon-Mann-Whitney test is a rank-based nonparametric test used to determine differences between two groups on a continuous or ordinal dependent variable. This test was feasible since we have ordinal dependent variables, the independent variable is categorical with two groups (gender) and the observations are independent of each other (Field, 2007, p. 542). In the next step the feature selection method was used. This method is usually applied in machine learning to reduce the number of input variables. The method calculates the relationship between each input variable and the target value in a predictive or classification model. In our case, the target value was gender, therefore binary classification was the task. We used Naïve Bayes which can achieve relatively good results with classification problems despite the assumption of independent predictors (Novaković et al., 2011). Completely independent variables are very rarely obtained in real life.

4. EMPIRICAL RESULTS

Using the Mann-Whitney U rank test, we detected statistically significant differences between the means of values for males and females for certain indicators shown in Table 2. Significant differences in median values and mean rank values are found in the rows where the p-value is below 0.05 (marked in bold).

Table 2. Indicators with statistically significant differences between males and females

Indicator	MrM	MrF	MdnM	MdnF	p	U	z
Use of presentation slides	149.72	230.61	5	5	**<0.001**	26,274	3.770
Use of online video lectures	189.76	229.24	2	3	**0.001**	25,967	3.420
Use of online resources (books, articles etc.)	195.62	226.60	4	4	**0.007**	25,415	2.719
Use of LMSs	201.10	215.00	4	4	0.220	22,970	1.227
Use of online bibliographic databases	181.82	239.45	3	4	**<0.001**	28,101	5.026
Use of online communication tools (email, forums etc.)	191.95	231.22	5	5	**<0.001**	26,401	3.928
Use of online social networking services (Facebook, Twitter etc.)	202.30	215.86	1	1	0.198	23,146	1.288
Use of collaboration tools (wikis, Google Drive etc.)	204.98	224.02	4	4	0.086	24,934	1.717
Personal use of ICT for entertainment (music, movies, etc.)	206.54	215.29	5	5	0.456	23,064	0.746
Personal use of ICT to obtain information, news	218.89	205.08	5	5	0.194	20,905	-1.299
Personal use of ICT for communication (email, chat, videocalls etc.)	209.03	214.00	5	5	0.474	22,784	0.716
Personal use of ICT for social networking	189.08	209.92	2	3	0.061	21,873	1.870

MrM - Mean rank (male), MrF - Mean rank (female), MdnM - Median (male); MdnF - Median (female);
p - asymptotic p-value; U - Mann-Whitney U; z - Standardised Test Statistic

To further examine gender differences in the teachers' responses to the survey questions, feature selection methods were employed. These methods are commonly used in data pre-processing to reduce the number of features by selecting a subset of variables which efficiently describes the data according to a certain criterion. In feature selection methods it is considered that the features describing the data are independent. These methods allow us to rank features regarding their relevance for a predicted (class) variable. Different indices may be used to calculate the dependency between the variable and the predicted variable (class), and to then rank variables by their relevance (Chandrashekar and Sahin, 2014; Jović et al., 2015).

In our case, each unit (a teacher) is described with 64 ordinal variables (from 1 to 5) – responses to the questionnaire statements and gender as the target binary class. The investigation proceeded using Orange, an open source machine learning and data visualization platform (Demšar et al., 2013). We calculated different indices, namely information gain, gain ration and Gini decrease, compared the obtained ranks and combined them to create a new rank of features. Different results subsets of the highest-ranking features were then tested with a Naïve Bayes classifier. The performance of different variants of the subset was measured using a 10-fold stratified cross-validation (Novaković et al., 2011). Figure 1 presents the classification accuracy of various numbers of the selected ranked features. The classification for the best subset of features is presented as a confusion matrix that shows the percentage classification. The final set of 13 relevant variables, in order of their significance, contains:

- Use of online bibliographic databases
- Use of ICT in lectures
- I can become a promoter of innovative ICT use in my department/chair/faculty
- Use of ICT in seminar work, problem-based or project-based learning
- Use of online communication tools (e-mail, online forums ...)
- Use of ICT for revising knowledge
- Use of presentation slides
- Use of ICT for designing the study process
- I am able to improve my ICT skills for use in the study process
- I can use ICT in my academic research (e.g. conducting research, report writing, presenting findings)
- Applying ICT in the study process requires more time for planning and preparation
- Use of online social networking services (Facebook, Twitter ...)
- Use of online video lectures

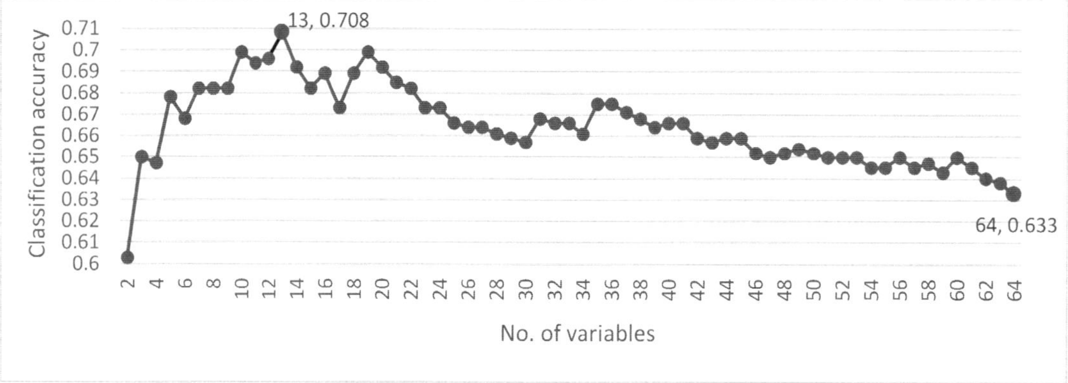

		Predicted		
		Male	Female	Total
Actual	Male	69.7%	30.9%	214
	Female	30.3%	69.1%	214
	Total	211	217	428

AC = 0.708

		Predicted		
		Male	Female	Total
Actual	Male	63.1%	36.5%	214
	Female	36.9%	63.5%	214
	Total	211	217	428

AC = 0.633

Figure 1. Classification accuracy (AC) depending on the number of ranked values selected. Confusion matrices of the performance of the classification Nave Bayes model based on the chosen subset features (left) and on the entire set features (right)

The median, mean and results of the Mann-Whitney U test for the best subset of variables is presented in Table 3. Indicators where the mean for females is greater than for males are shown in bold. Only one of the indicators (Use of online social networking services (Facebook, Twitter ...)) reveals no significance in the median values and mean rank values ($p < 0.05$).

Table 3. Median, mean and Mann-Whitney test for indicators from the best subset

Indicator	Median M	Median F	Median Total	Mean M	Mean F	Mean Dif. (M - F)	Mann-Whitney Sig.*
Use of online bibliographic databases	3	4	3	3.3	3.9	- 0.6	0.000
Use of ICT in lectures	4	4	4	3.8	4.2	- 0.4	0.000
I can become a promoter of innovative ICT use in my department/chair/faculty	3	2	3	3.0	2.5	0.5	0.000
Use of ICT in seminar work, problem-based or project-based learning	4	4	4	3.3	3.6	- 0.3	0.001
Use of online communication tools (e-mail, online forums ...)	5	5	5	4.3	4.6	- 0.3	0.000
Use of ICT for revising knowledge	3	4	3	3.2	3.6	- 0.4	0.000
Use of presentation slides	5	5	5	4.2	4.6	- 0.4	0.000
Use of ICT for designing the study process	4	4	4	3.7	4.0	- 0.3	0.000
I am able to improve my ICT skills for use in the study process	4	4	4	3.9	3.6	0.3	0.000
I can use ICT in my academic research (e.g. conducting research, report writing, presenting findings)	4	4	4	4.3	4.1	0.2	0.001
Applying ICT in the study process requires more time for planning and preparation	3	3	3	3.0	2.7	0.3	0.013
Use of online social networking services (Facebook, Twitter ...)	1	1	1	1.8	2.0	- 0.2	**0.198**
Use of online video lectures	2	3	3	2.4	2.8	- 0.4	0.001

M - Male, F - Female
*Statistically significant difference in median values and mean rank values at $p < 0.05$

5. DISCUSSION AND CONCLUSION

The main objective of this study was to examine UL teachers' use of ICT instructional tools in terms of gender. Our analysis of their responses is conclusive: female instructors use ICT more often than their male colleagues whereas males showed higher self-reported ICT skills and confidence in instructional use. This agrees with the findings of Tena et al. (2016).

Female UL teachers more often use presentation slides, online video lectures, resources, bibliographic databases, communication tools and social networking services to support and enhance their teaching. There are also some pedagogical activities in which female UL teachers more often apply ICT. These include lectures, problem presentation in problem-based or project-based learning, revising knowledge, and designing the study process. In sum, female teachers scored higher in a number of instructional ICT uses. These findings may suggest that female UL teachers are more diligent because applying ICT in the study process generally requires greater time for instructional design and preparation.

However, the male respondents scored higher than the females in their attitudes to ICT use. They seem to be more digitally savvy than the females since more of them feel they could become promoters of innovative ICT use in their institutions. More of them are reportedly able to improve their ICT skills for use in the study process. This is in line with the findings of Agboola (2006, p. 5) and Soydal et al. (2012, p. 287) who also identified higher confidence levels among male academic staff. Moreover, our findings suggest that more males believe they can use ICT in their academic research. These findings may mean that male teachers feel confident in their ICT skills but are more reluctant to use ICT in their teaching.

One area where we did not find gender differences is personal ICT use. Here, our results agree with the findings of Alkhasawneh and Alanazy (2015, p. 494) and Bhat and Bashir (2017) who did not identify any important gender differences among academic staff. We may therefore conclude that personal use of digital technology has become normalised for both genders.

We believe that these findings can assist by informing the planning and implementation of pedagogical support at the UL, for which gender differences must be considered. To help increase the confidence levels of female teachers, we suggest that staff development and training provide forms of recognition such as e.g. teaching excellence awards for those adopters of ICT with a significant positive impact on teaching and learning experience and results. To increase motivation among males to adopt ICT, incentives could be provided to share good teaching practices where ICT is found to enhance the teaching quality. Further, training to encourage ICT use by males and females must be provided in the workplace. Such training should be based on a needs analysis to provide for the specific requirements of individual teachers so that they can better meet the criteria.

This research has a few limitations. One is that other demographic data were not included in the analysis, e.g. age, educational attainment level, and years of service. Another is the problem of generalisation as the sample is from a single university. As the research formed part of a UL project, data from other universities were not available. The data set should be broader and incorporate additional universities in the analysis. Future research on university teachers' ICT use could entail a larger sample that includes more universities and explore the correlation between gender and other demographic data. Another interesting research area could involve comparing instructional ICT use across different disciplines, study programmes and courses.

ACKNOWLEDGEMENT

The research was supported by the University of Ljubljana within the project "Digital UL – with innovative use of ICT towards excellence – DiUL" (Digitalna UL – z inovativno uporabo IKT do odličnosti). The project was financed by the Republic of Slovenia and the European Union under the European Social Fund.

REFERENCES

Agboola, A. K., 2006. Assessing the awareness and perceptions of academic staff in using e-learning tools for instructional delivery in a post-secondary institution: A case study. *The Public Sector Innovation Journal*, Vol. 11, No. 3, article 4.

Al-Busaidi, K. and Al-Shihi, H., 2012. Key factors to instructors' satisfaction of learning management systems in blended learning. *Journal of Computing in Higher Education*, Vol. 24, pp. 18–39.

Alkhasawneh, S. and Alanazy, S., 2015. Adopt ICT among Academic Staff in Aljouf University: Using UTAUT Model. *Mediterranean Journal of Social Sciences*, Vol. 6, No. 1, pp. 490–494.

Bhat, S. A. and Bashir, M., 2018. Measuring ICT orientation: Scale development & validation. *Education and Information Technologies*, Vol. 23, No. 3, pp. 1123–1143. DOI:10.1007/s10639-017-9656-4

Broos, A. M. A., 2005. Gender and Information and Communication Technologies (ICT) Anxiety: Male Self-Assurance and Female Hesitation, *CyberPsychology & Behavior,* Vol. 8, No. 1, pp. 21-31.

Chandrashekar, G. and Sahin, F., 2014. A survey on feature selection methods. *Computers and Electrical Engineering*, Vol. 40, pp. 16–28.

Collis, B. and van der Wende, M., 2002. *Models of Technology and Change in Higher Education.* Center for Higher Education Policy Studies (CHEPS), Enschede. http://www.utwente.nl/cheps/documenten/ictrapport.pdf

Demšar, J., Curk, T., Erjavec, A., Gorup, Č., Hočevar, T., Milutinovič, M., Možina, M., Polajnar, P., Toplak, M., Starič, A., Štajdohar, M., Umek, L.,Žagar, L., Žbontar, J., Žitnik, M. and Zupan, B., 2013. Orange: Data Mining Toolbox in Python, *Journal of Machine Learning Research*, Vol. 4, pp. 2349−2353.

Field, A., 2009. *Discovering Statistics Using SPSS* (3rd edition). SAGE Publications Ltd.

Gaebel, M., Kupriyanova, V., Morais, R., Colucci, E., 2014. *E-learning in European higher education institutions: Results of a mapping survey conducted in October-December 2013.* European University Association, Brussels. http://old.eua.eu/Libraries/publication/e-learning_survey

Ilomäki, L., 2011. Does Gender Have a Role in ICT Among Finnish Teachers and Students? *Scandinavian Journal of Educational Research,* Vol. 55, pp. 325–340.

Jović, A., Brkic, K. and Bogunovic, N., 2015. A review of feature selection methods with applications. *MIPRO 2015*, 25-29 May 2015, Opatija: Croatia, pp. 1200–1205. DOI:10.1109/MIPRO.2015.7160458

Kocaleva, M., Stojanovic, I. and Zdravev, Z., 2015. Model of e-Learning Acceptance and Use for Teaching Staff in Higher Education Institutions. *International Journal of Modern Education and Computer Science*, Vol. 7, No. 4, pp. 23–31.

Krumsvik, R. J, Jones, L. Ø., Øfstegaard, M. and Eikeland, O. J., 2016. Upper secondary school teachers' digital competence: Analysed by demographic, personal and professional characteristics. *Nordic Journal of Digital Literacy*, Vol. 11, No. 3, pp. 143–164.

Novaković, J., Strbac, P. and Bulatović, D., 2011. Toward optimal feature selection using ranking methods and classification algorithms. *Yugoslav Journal of Operations Research*, Vol. 21, No. 1, pp. 119–135.

Motaghian, H., Hassanzadeh, A. and Moghadam, D. K., 2013. Factors affecting university instructors' adoption of web-based learning systems: Case study of Iran. *Computers & Education*, Vol. 61, pp. 158–167.

Okazaki, S. and Renda dos Santos, L.M., 2012. Understanding E-Learning Adoption in Brazil: Major Determinants and Gender Effects. *International Review of Research in Open and Distributed Learning*, Vol. 13, pp. 91–106.

Rahimi, M. and Yadollahi, S., 2011. ICT use in EFL classes: A focus on EFL teachers' characteristics. *World Journal of English Language*, Vol. 1, No. 2, pp. 17–29.

Soydal, İ., Alır, G. and Ünal, Y., 2011. Are Turkish Universities Ready for E-learning: A Case of Hacettepe University Faculty of Letters. *Information Services & Use*, Vol. 31, pp. 281–291.

Tena, R., Almenara, J. C. and Osuna, J. B., 2016. E-learning of Andalusian University's lecturers. *Turkish Online Journal of Educational Technology*, Vol. 15, No. 2, pp. 25–37.

Wang, W. and Wang, C., 2009. An empirical study of instructor adoption of web-based learning systems. *Computers & Education*, Vol. 53, No. 3, pp. 761–774.

DEVELOPMENT OF A MEASUREMENT TOOL TO EVALUATE THE LEARNING EXPERIENCE IN AN E-LEARNING SYSTEM

Yassine Safsouf [1,3], Khalifa Mansouri[2] and Franck Poirier[1]
[1]*Lab-STICC, University Bretagne Sud, France*
[2]*Laboratory SSDIA, ENSET of Mohammedia, University Hassan II of Casablanca, Morocco*
[3]*LIMIE Laboratory, ISGA Group, Centre Marrakech, Morocco*

ABSTRACT

The purpose of this study is to find ways to monitor and evaluate the user experience of learners as they use an e-learning system. To do this, we have identified several factors that allow us to measure this experience. We have designed an online measurement scale, presented as a self-administered questionnaire, specifically dedicated to e-learning platforms. With this tool, we can quickly isolate aspects that are perceived as critical, and that often require improvement actions. Finally, we tested our measurement tool over two sessions of an online course. The results of statistical analysis are very encouraging, showing that the learning platform used is considered simple by learners, flexible, secure and encouraging autonomy. The results also show that the platform has a deficit of social interaction (interactions between learners and their teachers, as well as between pairs), which should be remedied in order to improve learners' experience.

KEYWORDS

User Experience, Learning Management System, UX Scales, Learning Experience, FASER LX Test

1. INTRODUCTION

User experience (UX) refers to the lived or anticipated user experience in all its dimensions. This has been much confused with usability, which is described by the International Organization for Standardization (ISO) as the extent to which a product can be used by specified users to achieve specified goals with effectiveness, efficiency and satisfaction in a specified context of use (ISO9241-11, 1998), while UX deals with all aspects of the user experience before, during and after interaction with a product, service, environment or company (ISO9241-210, 2010). These two aspects are inseparable from each other in order to have a positive user experience. In the field of e-learning, the use of a digital learning platform is indispensable. These learning platforms, often called LMS (Learning Management System) platforms, allow managers to design, deploy and share online learning resources to make them accessible any time and from anywhere. In addition to sharing and exchanging resources, these platforms allow the efficient monitoring of e-learning actions (individually and in groups) through advanced analyses and integrated course reports. This makes it possible to identify points in the course that do not correspond to learners' expectations. However, even though the use of LMSs probably has an added value for the learner, the absence of commitment and motivation can leave the learner unsatisfied and lead him/her to stop his online training.

The term learning experience (LX), refers to the overall experience that a learner has in a setting where learning takes place, in a traditional academic environment (such as a school, classrooms), or in a non-traditional environment (outside-of-school locations, online training). An LMS that has a poor LX may diminish the sense of quality of the overall programmes, leaving the learner frustrated and not very engaged in his or her training. In this regard, this article is intended to clarify the following issues:

- What factors measure the learning experience?
- How can the LX be evaluated?

This article is divided into 5 sections: following this introduction, in the next section, we review the literature to determine the factors that will be used to measure LX. Section 3, presents our measurement tool, designed for LMS, to evaluate and monitor the improvement of the learning experience in an online course. Section 4, describes the methodology adopted to collect and analyze the study data, followed by a discussion of the results obtained. Finally, a conclusion with some limitations of this study is discussed in section 5.

2. UX MEASUREMENT FACTORS

The term UX was originally coined in the 1990s by the American cognitive psychologist Donald Norman. His books have made the term very popular in the scientific community specializing in human-computer interaction (HCI). In his book "The Design of Everyday Things", Donald Norman states that the term UX encompasses all aspects of interaction with a product or service, including factors related to emotional and hedonic aspects (Norman, 2004). In 1991, the User Experience Professional Association (UXPA) was created to present and defend user experience as a new discipline. This association defines (www.uxpa.org) UX as every aspect of user interaction with a product, service or company that constitutes the user's perception of practical aspects such as utility, usability and system efficiency, as well as the emotional aspects of a person using a particular product, system or service. In the UX literature, many definitions are proposed, according to Jakob Nielsen, UX brings all aspects of the end-user's interaction with the company, its services and products (Nielsen, 1999). He added that the concept of usability of a system is based on 5 criteria, namely: efficiency (the ease with which the user achieves his/her objective), satisfaction, ease of learning, memorability, and safety (low error rate). Another definition, proposed by Leena Arhippainen and Marika Tähti of the University of Oulu, Finland, presents UX as, the experience a person may obtain when interacting with a product under particular conditions (Arhippainen and Tähti, 2003). They also explain that UX is the result of the interaction of five categories of factors: user-related factors, social factors, cultural factors, contextual user factors and product factors. Marc Hassenzahl & Noam Tractinsky, two researchers in the field of HCI and interaction design, argue that the term UX is associated with a wide variety of meanings, ranging from traditional usability (pragmatic aspects), to beauty, hedonic, affective or experiential aspects of technology use (Hassenzahl and Tractinsky, 2011). Based on these qualities, Hassenzahl created a UX measurement tool called AttrakDiff (Hassenzahl, Burmester and Koller, 2003). The latter includes 28 questions (normal version) or 10 questions (shortened version), divided into 4 sub-scales (pragmatic, hedonic-stimulation, hedonic-identity and overall attractiveness).

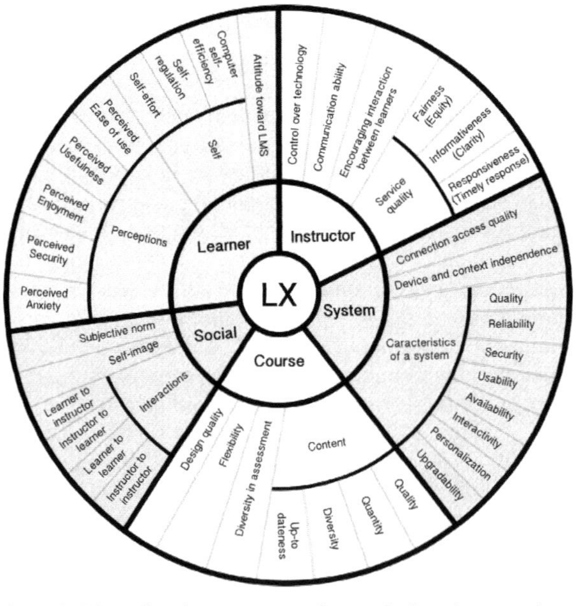

Figure 1. Dimensional measurement factors for learning experience

An empirical study in which Kasper Hornbæk and Morten Hertzum, investigate the relationship between the TAM (Technology Acceptance Model) (Venkatesh and Davis, 2000) and UX (Hornbæk and Hertzum, 2017). The factors selected were classified into three categories: experiential and utilitarian aspects (anxiety, design aesthetics, cost, perceived usefulness, actual usage, behavioural intention), individual and social aspects (attitude towards use, curiosity, perceived critical mass, trust, system quality, subjective norm) and perceptual and objective aspects (excitement, intention to use, satisfaction, age, gender, mode of use, facilitating conditions, unplanned purchases).

In our previous research (Safsouf, Mansouri and Poirier, 2018, 2019, 2020), we identified and classified several factors, which allowed us to explain satisfaction, self-regulation, intention to continue using and success in an LMS. These factors were derived from several models: the TAM3 model (Venkatesh and Bala, 2008), the Expectation Confirmation Model (ECM) (Bhattacherjee, 2001), the DeLone and McLean Information Success Systems Model (D&M ISS) (Delone and Mclean, 2003) and the Self-Regulated Learning Theory (SRL) (Zimmerman, 2013), (Panadero, 2017). Figure 1 presents our research framework.

Five dimensions were proposed for an initial classification, which are: learner factors (characteristics of learners that influence the adoption of the LMS), system factors (characteristics of the LMS platform), instructor factors (characteristics of instructors that play an important role in the perception of the effectiveness of the system), course factors and social factors (characteristics of the social environment in which learning activities take place). A second classification was done to highlight the pragmatic and hedonic aspects of these factors. Five qualities were proposed: pragmatic qualities (the system's manageability and how it enables users to achieve their objectives), "hedonic-stimulation" qualities (stimulation of the learner initiated by the system), "hedonic-satisfaction" qualities (feeling of satisfaction provided by the system), quality of effort (effort deployed when using the system), and finally, quality of social interaction (a user's social interactions with the actors of the LMS). Table 1 presents the factors for measuring UX in relation to the use of LMS and summarizes our proposed classification.

Table 1. Factors to measure the learning experience

	Pragmatic	**Hedonic**		**Effort**	**Social**
		Stimulation	**Satisfaction**		
Learner	Computer self-efficiency, Self-regulation	Perceived usefulness	Perceived enjoyment, Self-security	Self-effort, perceived anxiety	
Instructor		Responsiveness		Informativeness	Communication ability, Fairness
System	Connection access quality, Efficiency, reliability, Perceived ease-of-use, Usability, Availability, Personalization	Interactivity		device and context independence	
Course	Diversity in assessments	Content diversity, Up-to-dateness.	Design quality and system quality	Course quality, course flexibility	
Social			Self-image		Subjective norm, Learner-learner interaction, Learner-instructor interaction and Instructor-instructor interaction.

3. LX MEASURING SCALE

The main objective of this study is to improve the learning experience of our learners during their training, but it is still necessary to know how to evaluate it. UX scales are among the most widely used instruments for evaluating UX. These measurement tools, often self-administered questionnaires, either paper or online, provide a quick indication of whether your system is perceived as innovative, effective, reliable or challenging.

The AttrakDiff survey (Hassenzahl, Burmester and Koller, 2003), is one of the most widely used tools. Initially developed in German, translated and validated in French (Lallemand *et al.*, 2015), it presents the items in the form of semantic differentiators to be assessed using 7-point Likert scales ranging from -3 to +3.

In this article, we propose a measurement tool for LMS platforms to evaluate and monitor the improvement of the learning experience in an online course. We have chosen to call it "FASER LX Test" for "Formation, Apprenant, Système, Enseignant, Relation Learning eXperience" from the French acronym (Course, Learner, System, Teacher, Relationship). Table 2 shows the items chosen by factor.

Table 2. The 30 items of the FASER LX scale

SUCCESS FACTORS	ANTONYM PAIRS		
Computer self-efficiency	Autonomous	-	Non-autonomous
Self-enjoyment	Unpleasant	-	Pleasant
Perceived usefulness	Boring	-	Captivating
Self-effort	Undemanding	-	Demanding
Self-regulation	Free use	-	Compulsory use
Self-security	Confident	-	Distrustful
Perceived anxiety	Calming	-	Stressing
Communication ability	Easy communication	-	Difficult communication
Responsiveness	High reactivity	-	Low reactivity
Informativeness	Not comprehensible	-	Comprehensible
Fairness	Unfair	-	Highly fair
Connection access quality	Slow	-	Fast
Device and context independence	Device dependent	-	Device independent
Efficiency	Tedious	-	Efficient
Reliability	Unreliable	-	Very reliable
Perceived Ease-of-use	Difficult learning	-	Easy learning
Availability	Not available	-	Very available
Interactivity	Not interactive	-	Very interactive
Personalization	Customizable	-	Not customizable
Course Quality	Confused	-	Clear
Content diversity	Not diversified	-	Very divided
Course Flexibility	Rigid	-	Flexible
Design and system quality	Pleasant	-	Unpleasant
Up-to-dateness	Static	-	Dynamic
Diversity in assessments	Diversified assessment	-	Not diversified assessment
Subjective norm	Recommendable	-	Not recommendable
Self-image	Valuable	-	Non-valuable
Learner-learner interaction	Gets closer to learners	-	Separates me from learners
Learner-instructor interaction	Get closer to teachers	-	Separate me from teachers
Instructor-instructor interaction	Bring teachers together	-	Separate teachers

Like AttrakDiff, FASER LX is composed of questions in the form of opposite adjectives, each representing factors presented above (see Table 1). FASER LX is self-administered and available online in two languages: in French (www.safsouf.net/fr/faserlx/) and in English (www.safsouf.net/en/faserlx/). The items do not have the same valence (sometimes the word on the left is positive and sometimes it is negative). Before calculating a score, it is therefore necessary to make sure that the items are scored in the same direction.

4. RESEARCH METHOD

4.1 Data Collection

In this article, we chose to evaluate the learning experience provided by the Moodle platform, in an online course entitled "Object-Oriented Programming", over a six-week period.

The participants are all students of the 1st year of the computer engineering cycle, from a private higher education institution (ISGA Campus of Marrakesh). The target class is composed of 25 students (32% female and 68% male), aged between 18 and 35 years (76% between 18 and 25 years and 24% between 26 and 35 years). In terms of computer usage time per day, 8% reported using the computer one to two hours per day, 16% between two and five hours, 68% between five and ten hours, and 8% more than ten hours per day. Regarding their computer skills levels, 8% expressed being novice, 52% intermediate, 32% advanced and 8% expert.

4.2 Data Analysis

In order to evaluate and monitor the improvement of our students' online learning experience, we tested the FASER LX Test in two periods. The first was during the second week of the course. The second was during the final week of the course. The data collected was analyzed using SPSS v. 23. New variables representing the dimensions and qualities (see Table 1) were created and calculated as the average (Avg) of the different associated factors. We also calculated the standard deviation (SD) of these new variables, in order to see the homogeneity of our participants' responses. Table 3 detail the results obtained with the percentage of improvement noted.

Table 3. Summary of the results obtained by dimensions and qualities

		2nd week		6th week		Progress %
		μ	σ	μ	σ	
Dimensions	Learner	3.868	0.542	4.468	0.653	+8.57 %
	Instructor	4.660	0.831	4.678	0.798	+0.25 %
	System	4.365	0.675	4.605	0.674	+3.42 %
	Course	4.520	0.567	4.733	0.783	+3.04 %
	Social	4.656	0.596	4.528	0.752	-1.82 %
Qualities	Pragmatic	4.205	0.543	4.845	0.625	+9.14 %
	Hedonic-stimulation	4.120	0.612	4.780	0.617	+9.42 %
	Hedonic-satisfaction	3.744	0.932	4.104	0.910	+5.14 %
	Effort	4.840	0.902	5.106	0.844	+3.80 %
	Social interaction	4.566	0.666	4.606	0.898	+0.57 %

The FASER LX Test measurement tool, offers a visualization of the results obtained in the form of a radar chart for the whole class. As shown in figures 2 and 3, two radar diagrams are generated. The first one shows the average of the percentage factors grouped by dimension. The second diagram represents the average of the percentage factors grouped by grade. The FASER LX also offers an individual visualization of the results obtained. The graphs obtained are the same as for the whole class, but this visualization is not discussed in this article.

This method of representation has the advantage of quickly distinguishing aspects (of the learner, the instructor, the system, the course or the social environment) which are perceived as critical, and which may or may not call for short or long-term improvement actions.

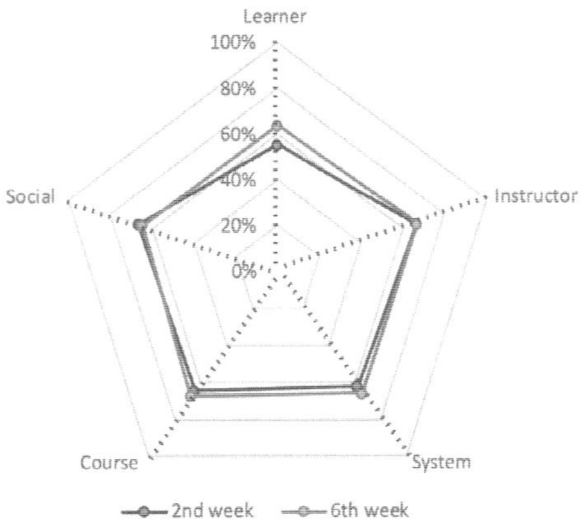

Figure 2. Result of the FASER LX Test by dimensions

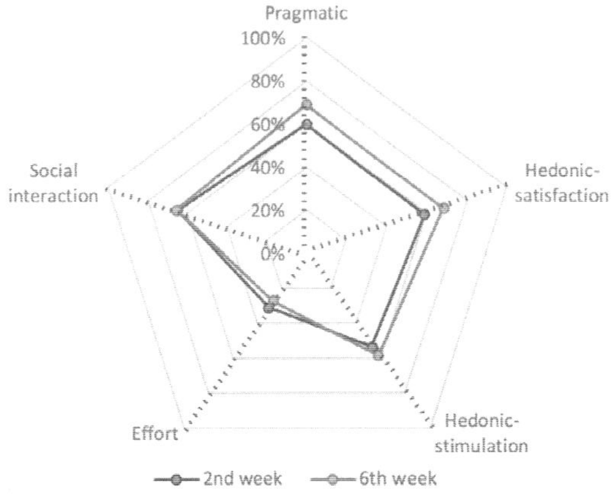

Figure 3. Result of the FASER LX Test by qualities

4.3 Discussion of Results

Based on the results of the statistical analysis presented in Table 3, as well as the ranking of the factors measuring the learning experience (Table 1 and Figure 1), we note an improvement of 8.57% for the factors composing the "learner" dimension with an increase of 9.14%, 9.42% and 5.14% respectively for the pragmatic, hedonic-satisfaction and hedonic-stimulating qualities. This means that the factors affected by this improvement are, computer self-efficiency, self-regulation, perceived usefulness, self-enjoyment and self-security. In other words, towards the end of the course, learners understood the usefulness of online training, and they claim to feel increasingly secure and autonomous using the platform. There was also an improvement in effort (3.80%), indicating that learners now put in less effort and are less stressed.

The " Instructor" dimension showed almost no improvement (0.25%), which means that learners didn't perceive any change in the level of the instructor. The results also indicate a small improvement in both dimensions "System" (3.42%) and "Course" (3.04%). This means that the factors affected by the improvement are, perceived efficiency, perceived ease-of-use, availability, course flexibility and diversity of content and assessments.

Finally, for the "Social" dimension, we noted a slight decrease (-1.82%), explained by the fact that no interaction was recorded in the online course, neither with the teacher nor with peers. This confirms that collaborative learning is essential and should be encouraged in an online course.

5. CONCLUSION AND LIMITATIONS

The objective of this research is to identify factors that can be used to measure the learning experience of online learners in order to improve it. We have identified several factors, grouped according to five dimensions (learner, instructor, system, course and social). On the basis of these factors, an online measurement tool was created to evaluate this experience. Named FASER LX Test, it is composed of five sub-scales (pragmatic qualities, hedonic-satisfaction qualities, hedonic-stimulation qualities, qualities of effort and social qualities). The results of a study conducted during two periods of an online course show that learners found the platform rather easy to use, functional, reliable, flexible, and encouraging self-regulation.

Although this study identifies a few factors that can be used to measure the e-learning experience, several limitations should be noted. The first is that the sample is limited to a single class. Conducting the study in multiple classrooms would require greater resources. Due to the small number of participants, more detailed statistical analyses were not conducted. Finally, this study is limited to e-learning in the private education sector in Morocco and did not include the public education sector. These limitations may constitute an obstacle to the generalization of the results obtained. Future studies should also be conducted in the public sector.

REFERENCES

Arhippainen, L. and Tähti, M. (2003) 'Empirical evaluation of user experience in two adaptive mobile application prototypes', Proceedings of the 2nd international conference ..., pp. 27–34. Available at: http://www.ep.liu.se/ecp/011/007/ecp011007.pdf.

Bhattacherjee, A. (2001) 'Understanding Information Systems Continuance: An Expectation-Confirmation Model', MIS Quarterly, 25(3), p. 351. doi: 10.2307/3250921.

Delone, W. . and Mclean, E. r. (2003) 'the Delone and Mclean model of information sys- tems success: A ten-year update', Journal of Management Information Systems. 19th, 4th edn, pp. 9–30.

Hassenzahl, M., Burmester, M. and Koller, F. (2003) 'AttrakDiff: Ein Fragebogen zur Messung wahrgenommener hedonischer und pragmatischer Qualität', J.Ziegler & G. Szwillus (Eds.), Mensch & Computer, pp. 187–196.

Hassenzahl, M. and Tractinsky, N. (2011) 'Behaviour & Information Technology User experience-a research agenda User experience-a research agenda'. doi: 10.1080/01449290500330331.

Hornbæk, K. and Hertzum, M. (2017) 'Technology acceptance and user experience: A review of the experiential component in HCI', ACM Transactions on Computer-Human Interaction, 24(5). doi: 10.1145/3127358.

ISO9241-11 (1998) Ergonomic requirements for office work with visual display terminals (VDTs), Part 11: Guidance on usability. Available at: https://www.iso.org/fr/standard/16883.html.

ISO9241-210 (2010) Ergonomics of human-system interaction, Part 210: Human-centred design for interactive systems. Available at: https://www.iso.org/standard/52075.html.

Lallemand, C. et al. (2015) 'Création et validation d'une version française du questionnaire AttrakDiff pour l'évaluation de l'expérience utilisateur des systèmes interactifs', Revue Europeenne de Psychologie Appliquee. Elsevier Masson SAS, 65(5), pp. 239–252. doi: 10.1016/j.erap.2015.08.002.

Nielsen, J. (1999) Designing Web Usability: The Practice of Simplicity. New Riders PublishingPost Office Box 4846 Thousand Oaks, CAUnited States.

Norman, D. A. (2004) Designers and Users: Two Perspectives On Emotion and Design. doi: 10.1007/BF02065545.

Panadero, E. (2017) 'A Review of Self-regulated Learning: Six Models and Four Directions for Research.', Frontiers in psychology, 8(April), p. 422. doi: 10.3389/fpsyg.2017.00422.

Safsouf, Y., Mansouri, K. and Poirier, F. (2018) 'A New Model of Learner Experience in Online Learning Environments', Information Systems and Technologies to Support Learning. Springer International Publishing, 111(Lx), pp. 29–38. doi: 10.1007/978-3-030-03577-8.

Safsouf, Y., Mansouri, K. and Poirier, F. (2019) 'Design of a new scale to measure the learner experience in e-learning systems', Multi Conference on Computer Science and Information Systems, MCCSIS 2019 - Proceedings of the International Conference on e-Learning 2019, pp. 301–304. doi: 10.33965/el2019_201909c042.

Safsouf, Y., Mansouri, K. and Poirier, F. (2020) 'AN ANALYSIS TO UNDERSTAND THE ONLINE LEARNERS' SUCCESS IN PUBLIC HIGHER EDUCATION IN MOROCCO', Journal of Information Technology Education: Research, 19(2020), pp. 87–112. doi: https://doi.org/10.28945/4518.

Venkatesh, V. and Bala, H. (2008) 'Technology Acceptance Model 3 and a Research Agenda on Interventions', Decision Sciences, 39(2), pp. 273–315.

Venkatesh, V. and Davis, F. D. (2000) 'A Theoretical Extension of the Technology Acceptance Model: Four Longitudinal Field Studies', Management Science, 46(2), pp. 186–204. Available at: http://pubsonline.informs.org/doi/abs/10.1287/mnsc.46.2.186.11926 (Accessed: 16 January 2018).

Zimmerman, B. J. (2013) 'From Cognitive Modeling to Self-Regulation: A Social Cognitive Career Path', Educational Psychologist, 48(3), pp. 135–147.

USING SOCIAL MEDIA FOR PEER INTERACTION IN HIGHER EDUCATION: STUDENTS' PERCEPTION OF USING FACEBOOK TO SUPPORT PEER LEARNING

Marie Claire Ukwishaka[1] and Naghmeh Aghaee[2]
Department of informatics, Linnaeus Universiy, Växjö/Kalmar, Sweden
[1]MSc
[2]PhD

ABSTRACT

Facebook is growing fast in various fields including education field. Most studies showed that today students in higher education use Facebook to communicate, cooperating and finding solutions. The main purpose of this study is to investigate and reflect on students' perspectives regarding the use of Facebook and its influence on students' collaborative learning, motivation of communication, and peer connection, in higher education. Concerning to the purpose of the study, how students perceive using Facebook to support peer interaction and educational learning. In addition, students' perspective on the benefits and limitations of using Facebook in educational learning were investigated. A qualitative interpretative research study was conducted and data was collected through interviews. The main results showed both benefits and limitations of using Facebook followed by a set of strategic suggestions that would be beneficial for students, universities, and this research area to associate with a set of standards for Facebook usage in higher education.

KEYWORDS

Facebook, Higher Education, Social Media, Peer Interaction, Educational Technology, Collaborative Learning

1. INTRODUCTION

Popularity and growth of the online social networks has created a new way of interaction, communication and collaboration in the field of education (Cheung, 2011). Social media platforms such as Facebook provide unlimited means for the Internet users to update themselves, interact, express, share, and create content (Muntinga, Moorman & Smith, 2011; Lin, Huarui & Tang, 2012). Social networks such as Facebook have the capability to connect learners for collaborative learning that are both social and academic (Selwyn, 2007). Social media, as a collection of applications, are based on internet and web 2.0 technologies, which facilitate access to the contents and information exchange alongside face-to-face communications and using the formal learning management systems (Kaplan & Haenlein, 2010; Hrastinski & Aghaee, 2010). Using social media such as Facebook for retrieving content or initiating contacts makes students seeing social media as one of key means of the educational experience and coordinate group work and collaborative learning (Hrastinski & Aghaee, 2010; Keles, 2018).

Social media spread information fast, which could be very useful in education (Dogruer, Eyyamb & Menevisab, 2011). Studies (such as Selwyn, 2007; Muntinga, Moorman & Smith, 2011; O'Keeffe & Clarke-Pearson, 2011; Boulos, Maramba, & Wheeler, 2006) reflect on the use of social media for collaborative learning with general purposes or as a part of informal learning. Other studies (such as Arnold & Paulus, 2010; Hrastinski & Aghaee, 2010; Dogruer, Eyyamb & Menevisab, 2011; Esteves, 2012; Mourad et al., 2015) demonstrate that social media, such as Facebook, are becoming more of a communication and collaboration medium for educational learning; or as a part of the teaching/learning strategy in supporting students in coordination of sharing information and group work organization and collaboration. The integration of technology and social media in the cognitive process of acquiring knowledge has made teaching and learning activities more efficient and effective (Woo & Reeves, 2008). Social media offers social interaction and provides opportunities for students to reconnect with peers for learning purposes in formal educational settings (Mourad et al., 2015, pp.35).

Studies show how social media and Facebook increase students' performance, advantages and disadvantages, or teachers and/or students' experiences, by using social media or specifically Facebook for educational purposes (Cain & Katherine, 2013; Pardo, 2013; O'Keeffe & Clarke-Pearson, 2011; Subrahmanyam & Greenfield, 2008; Arnold & Paulus, 2010; Kirschner & Karpinski, 2010; Kuppuswamy & Shankar, 2010; Lin, Huarui & Tang, 2012; Lin, 2018). However, research on how student-student (peer-to-peer) interaction can be improved or facilitated by social media as a standard, is still needed in the educational technology research area. Investigating students' perceptions of using Facebook to support peer interaction and collaborative learning is important for the academic society, as this social media based communication method shows significant positive influence on students' motivation, classroom environment, and affective learning (Mazer, Murphy & Simonds, 2007).

Additionally, providing suggestions on using Facebook for educational learning purposes that students can follow may enhance peer's interactions and collaborative learning. This study hence addresses this gap in the literature about using Facebook to facilitate collaborative learning activities among peers. The aim was to investigate and reflect on students' perspectives regarding the use of Facebook and its influence on students' collaborative learning, motivation of communication, and peer connection, in higher education. The guiding research question is: how social media such as Facebook can facilitate peer interaction and support formal learning in higher education. The study was based on the perceptions and practices of students enrolled at Linnaeus University in Sweden.

In order to establish a basis for this study, it was necessary to study the current usage of social media (Facebook) in higher education. This was done as part of the study, primarily by defining the concept of social media and reviewing how Facebook supports peer interaction in educational learning. In the second phase, the study focuses on investigation of students' perceptions of using Facebook to support peer interaction and educational learning. The result shows both benefits and limitations of using Facebook. Based on the first two phases, the contribution of study followed by a set of strategic suggestions, for students to benefit using social media, specifically Facebook, in higher education. The suggestions are based on the current stage of using social media in education and students' reflections, which would be beneficial for other students, other universities, and this research area to associate with structured use of Facebook in higher education. Since technology use and social media is increasingly being deployed within educational settings, specially with the current situation of COVID-19 pandemic, structured use of Facebook would facilitate collaboration and learning and add educational values to the digital age of the 21st century.

2. METHODOLOGY

The data for this research was collected through literature review and individual interviews in order to investigate students' perceptions and opinions in their own words (Creswell, 2009). The purpose of this study was intentionally to choose students from different discipline, educational level, gender and age, to fulfill the criteria of diversity (Creswell, 2009). The target group of the study was students at Linnaeus University, and sampling selection was random voluntary selection to cover a broad range of students with no specific direction of study or discipline, or any educational level.

2.1 Interview

The main empirical data collection method in this study was interview. The interviews were conducted in a semi-structured way, face-to-face, audio recorded in the university library, at Linnaeus University, in Växjö, Sweden. The interview sample was purposely selected broadly, in order to get a broad perspective, but sufficient amount of data, which got to the saturation level, very early in the data collection process after the fifth interview. Fusch and Ness (2015: p 1408) note "failure to reach saturation has an impact on the quality of the research conducted". According to Morse (2015: p 587), the saturation aspect is "present in all qualitative research" and it is generally considered as the gold standard in qualitative research for identifying sample size.

The interviews were contacted and new respondents were requested in person to be involved in this research after analyzing the collected data and hence the number of respondents were gradually increased until no new information came up any longer. The interviews were continued until saturation was met, in order to make meaningful and valid conclusion and develop the strategic suggestions (presented at the end of the paper), which were based on the literature review in connections to the theoretical and empirical aspects, collected specifically for this study.

The participants were represented by codes as SP (Student Participant), as shown in table 1. The interviewees in this study were seven students, including three male and four female, two studying in bachelor level and five in master level. All interviewees were voluntarily participated, with no given bonus or present. The demographical factors such as interviewees' codes, study discipline (department), level of study, and interview dates, were shown in the table 1.Figures should de numbered consecutively as they appear in the text.

Table 1. Demographic factors of interview participants (interviewees)

Student	**Department**	**Level of study**	**Date**	**Duration**
SPI	Informatics	Masters	12/04/19	35min
SP2	Design	Bachelors	12/04/19	40min
SP3	Organization and Entrepreneurship	Bachelors	13/04/19	38min
SP4	Informatics	Masters	13/04/19	41min
SP5	Social studies	Masters	15/04/19	35min
SP6	Building Technology	Masters	15/04/19	37min
SP7	Informatics	Masters	17/04/19	40min

The interview begun with a presentation about the research topic, purpose and methodology used, and then the consent form was given to participants to aid them to carefully view all the terms of this research study to sign it. Participants were informed about their rights, to get ensured that their privacy and personal information were confidential in order to provide trust and openness. During the interviews, it was discussed about the benefits and limitations of using Facebook to support peer interaction, collaborative and educational learning in higher education settings. At the end of the interviews, the interviewees were also asked for further suggestions and how using Facebook or in general social media could be part of the formal educational settings in higher education.

2.2 Data Analysis

The data gathered from interviews were audio-recorded, transcribed verbatim, and analyzed thematically, then categorized into themes and sub-themes, in which, each theme and sub-theme were part of the strategic suggestions, developed and presented as the contribution of this study, at the end of the paper. Concerning validity, multiple techniques have been tried in this research in order to assure the internal validity of research findings and to generate a specific and acceptable result. The two researchers checked the accuracy of the data collection, data analysis, and the developed reflections, in order to enhance the trustworthiness of the data presented in this paper. The following tactics elaborated by Creswell (2009) have been applied:

• Using various data sources like interviews with participants and other sources like the electronic database provided the feasibility of research study; it also enabled the evaluation and comparison of the results which are essential for validity.

• After conducting interview, data collected was transcribed verbatim and some re- examination were done to ensure that whether the written form is similar with what the participants have expressed with no bias or modifications in context.

This research study followed these six phases during the analysis of data collected through interview as follows (Braun & Clarke, 2006: p. 87-93): "1. Becoming familiar with the data; 2.Generation of the initial codes; 3.Evolvement of themes; 4.Review of potential themes; 5.Establishment of themes; 6.Write-up of report". The data collected from interviews were hence examined and re-examined to discover reappearing patterns of meaning as recommended by Braun and Clarke (2006). This procedure allowed the derivation of themes that were used in data analysis.

3. RESULT AND DISCUSSION

In regards to the derivation of themes from the existing literatures, four main theoretical aspects were used as the fundamental parts of developing the six following themes in this study. The four aspects were Facebook as a social media, peer interaction and collaborative learning, connectivism as a learning theory (for the digital age), synchronous versus asynchronous communication in edication. Data collected from interviews were analyzed using thematic analysis based on these main aspects, which let to identifying the six main themes, based on the findings of this study. The developed themes were presented in table 2, as the main result of the empirical data based on the theoretical aspects. Each theme is presented in detail (in table 2), with the description of the theme, and contains some reflections on the students' perceptions on each aspect.

Table 2. Summary of interview findings per theme

Themes	Description	Findings
Theme 1: Facebook platform as a means for learning	Facebook social networking site as platform for both formal and informal learning.	■ All student participants have been on Facebook for at least 5 years and they believed that Facebook usage support them for formal learning, students participants explained Facebook as helpful platform which support their formal learning however on the other hand student stated that Facebook homepage distracts students' attention to other things. ■ Facebook also enables students to learn other things that are not related to their courses (Informal Learning). like cooking. ■ Facebook provides additional tools for learning that support students. ■ Most of students use groups, likes, post, chat, messenger in general. Both posts and chat through messenger are the most ones used for formal learning. ■ Students share different kind of learning materials like videos, documents and books with other peers and as a result students are able to perform well.
Theme 2: Facebook platform as a means of interaction and collaboration	Facebook as a facilitator of peers 'interaction and connections establishment.	■ Facebook platform offers useful functionalities that allow users to organize meeting, event, party, and group discussions. ■ The internet accessibility and bandwidth speed of all participants is either average or excellent; all student participants check their Facebook accounts at least 3 times per day and these enhance student peers' interactions. ■ Facebook creates good relations among peers. ■ Students on Facebook help each other towards good performance ■ Facebook functionalities enable collaboration among peers. ■ Collaboration on Facebook are helpful If peers are active and collaborate with each other.
Theme 3: Facebook platform as a means for information and knowledge exchange	Facebook as a communication (both synchronous and asynchronous) medium for sharing information, ideas and knowledge	■ Sharing picture/video which is not related to courses does not affect some students. In contrast, there students who become angry or loose motivation when such picture or video is shared on student peers' group. ■ Student peers use Facebook functionalities such as: messenger, posts, groups, pages to share ideas, information and experience easier.

Themes	Description	Findings
Theme 4: Benefits of Facebook platform usage	Advantages of Facebook for supporting peers' interaction and educational learning.	■ Sharing useful information and making more friends. ■ Communication with peer students is easier, not only with peers but also with teachers. ■ Facebook is a friendly environment where peers help each other. ■ Facebook enables group discussions and performing task together like assignment. ■ It enables student peers to conduct their research studies (e.g. conducting survey).
Theme 5: Difficulties of Facebook platform usage	Limitations associated to Facebook usage for supporting peers' interaction and educational learning.	■ Peers who are not active/responsible. ■ Inaccessibility of Facebook in some countries. ■ Peers who like to post useless picture, video and chats. ■ Lack of facial expression. ■ Misunderstanding during discussions since peers can send messages at the same time and this may create confusions among student peers. ■ Technical issues that occur while she is interacting with peers. For instance connection issue during video/audio call. ■ Privacy and security on Facebook are limited. ■ Limited knowledge, consequently, all questions posted on the group are not well answered by peers.
Theme 6: Ideas for improvement	Suggestions for enhancing peers' interaction and educational learning on Facebook platform	■ Respecting group peers and the purpose of group may improve educational learning through Facebook platform. ■ Collaboration on Facebook is needed in order to improve educational learning ■ Students who use Facebook have to be more active, disciplined and responsible. ■ Students also expressed that it may be better if there are some groups on Facebook that both peers and lectures can join. ■ Limitation of connection during audio/video call, privacy and security, accessibility issue should be eliminated.

Technology and social media are increasingly being deployed within educational settings (Cain & Katherine, 2013; Pardo, 2013; O'Keeffe & Clarke-Pearson, 2011; Subrahmanyam & Greenfield, 2008; Arnold & Paulus, 2010; Kirschner & Karpinski, 2010; Kuppuswamy & Shankar, 2010). The empirical results of this study were truly in line with the previous studies (such as Selwyn, 2007; Muntinga, Moorman & Smith, 2011; O'Keeffe & Clarke-Pearson, 2011) regarding the social media for general learning purposes, and in line with some other studies (such as Keles, 2018; Arnold & Paulus, 2010; Dogruer, Eyyamb & Menevisab, 2011; Esteves, 2012; Mourad et al., 2015) regarding the usefulness of social media to facilitate collaborative learning.

3.1 Reflections and Strategic Suggestions

Based on the findings above, following are the four developed categories of the strategic suggestions, which Facebook can be part of the learning process in higher education. The following strategic suggestions presented below were developed based on the themes (showed in table 2), as the current stage of using social media in education and students' reflections and perceptions about the use of Facebook as a useful standard to facilitate peer interaction and learning in higher education. The categories of strategic suggestions below clarify the benefits and challenges associated with Facebook usage for collaborative learning.

3.1.1 Facebook Platform as a Means for Educational Learning

The functionalities of Facebook as a platform for learning were appreciated by all participants. All respondents in this study reflected that they have been on Facebook for at least five years. Students pointed out that Facebook is a helpful platform that has supported their formal and informal learning in different study levels. Facebook platform supports students' formal learning (Selwyn, 2007; Muntinga, Moorman & Smith, 2011; O'Keeffe & Clarke-Pearson, 2011; Arnold & Paulus, 2010; Hrastinski & Aghaee, 2010; Lin, Huarui & Tang, 2012). In line with this, students praised the fact that Facebook is an easy and fast way to share ideas and learn from each other. At this point, students explain Facebook functionalities as a helpful platform that facilitate the learning process. In general, all participants in this study used Facebook groups, likes, post, chat, and messenger for learning purposes.

This is while, on the other hand, one respondent claimed that Facebook platform might distract students and draw attention to other things, if not structured teacher/learner guided with specific purposes, as also mentioned by earlier studies such as Hrastinski and Aghaee (2010). However, the other respondents did not mentioned and saw Facebook more toward a help both generally and specifically for their studies. Hence, as the result, the study reflects that posts and chat through messenger and the Facebook platform are the most used functions for sharing information and supporting the formal learning.

3.1.2 Facebook Platform as a Means of Interaction and Collaboration

Interaction and collaboration through Facebook platform can be done through pages, groups and messenger. During the interviews, it was noted that the internet accessibility and bandwidth speed of all participants is either average or excellent. The students (interviewees) check their Facebook accounts often, at least three times per day. Therefore, peers are able to stay in touch and make group discussions very constantly. Peers can get the latest updates about their meetings, group works organizing, planning and any other updates faster than through other learning platforms, as also discussed by previous studies such as Dogruer, Eyyamb and Menevisab (2011).

Most of the participants agreed that Facebook platform helps peer interaction in educational learning process, for instance student peers could organize group meetings and events through Facebook, as also discussed by earlier studies (Hrastinski & Aghaee, 2010; Esteves, 2012; Mourad et al., 2015). Although, students believed that collaboration on online platforms such as Facebook would facilitate their formal learning, still among students, some peers are not always taking responsibilities as they should and do not do their task and take it more informal. However, Facebook functionalities such as pages, groups and messenger facilitate interaction and collaboration among peers, group connections and sharing file, drafts, and information, which support collaborative learning in the formal educational settings.

3.1.3 Facebook Platform as a Means for Gaining Information and Knowledge Exchange

Facebook platform offers several functionalities that facilitate communication from students to students (peer-to-peer) and supports both formal and informal learning (Selwyn, 2007; Muntinga, Moorman & Smith, 2011; O'Keeffe & Clarke-Pearson, 2011; Arnold & Paulus, 2010), for educational purposes. For instance, it was observed that student use both synchronous (or direct communication such as chatting) versus asynchronous communication (indirect communications such as posting comments or questions on Facebook wall, Rovai, 2002), to share information related to their courses such as course results, lectures cancelled, or if the official Learning Management System (LMS) link does not work.

Base on the respondents, there are students who post questions on both formal platforms (learning management systems) and informal platforms (such as Facebook) and wait for the answers. It seems that peers directly chat or call them through informal platforms such as social media (Facebook), which makes the communication faster and more convenient. However, there was a mixed perceptions among the students, when one student shares a video or picture which is not related to courses for instance in an educational group or through messages. Some stated that It does not affect them and the others mentioned that it may have negative influences and cause distractions or in some cases misleading them. Hence, even though it is proved that the communication through Facebook platform is helpful to share information and exchange knowledge synchronously and asynchronously, and it allows peers to communicate easier and faster, still it may causes distractions and negative effects in some cases. However, if the groups are more structured and specifically designed for formal learning, such problems might would be reduced.

3.1.4 Facebook for Peer/Collaborative Learning

Facebook platform is widely used to enable collaboration and connectivity at massive levels, and it was adapted in the classroom for educational purposes (Shaw, 2017; Chugh, & Ruhi, 2018). Similarly, all students participated in this study believed that Facebook has different advantages when they interact with peers since communication on Facebook creates enjoyable environment, and facilitate the peer interaction even though the platform was not created for that purpose (Keles, 2018, p. 204). Facebook platform is a friendly environment where peers have the possibility to help each other. It allows peers to share useful information and making more friends with their classmates, program-mates, or university peers. Additionally, Facebook enables group discussions and performing task together like assignment or other formal activities. Facebook can connect students in different years of the same program.

As mentioned by O'Keeffe and Clarke-Pearson (2011), Learner to learner engagement is associated with risks such as: online harassment, cyberbullying and there are negative effects of social media like, accessing irrelevant content and privacy issue. In the same way, students mentioned that there are difficulties associated with Facebook usage, when it comes to privacy and security. Others challenges are slow connection that occurs in audio/video calls, which makes the communication challenging, peers who are not active/responsible. The limitations that were identified, besides the lack of connection during audio/video call, group members who are not active or responsible, and security and privacy issue, there is a lack of face to face communication, and inaccessibility of Facebook in some countries where it has been blocked/filtered. Furthermore, participants of this research study pointed out that students who use Facebook for learning purpose should be more attentive in order to enhance educational learning. They added that privacy and group objectives should also be respected by peers.

4. CONCLUSION

This research study shows that there are different benefits and limitations of using Facebook for peer interaction by students. Students that were interviewed show that Facebook is a useful platform for student peer interaction and peer learning, since it provides an easy way of communication among peers for both formal and informal learning. Most of the participants expressed that social network platform such as Facebook is useful for students and it improves educational learning if peers communication become more responsible (standard) and avoid distracting posts and chats. Students also expressed that it may be better if there are some groups on Facebook that both peers and lectures can join to support peer-to-peer and student-teacher interactions. Additionally, it was noted that limitation of privacy and security, connection issue, inaccessibility of Facebook should also be eliminated.

Furthermore, the four categories of strategic suggestions were discussed as; Facebook platform as a means for educational learning; Facebook platform as a means of interaction and collaboration; Facebook platform as a means for information and knowledge exchange, and Facebook for peer learning. These suggestions would be beneficial for students, universities, and this research area to associate with a set of standards for Facebook usage in higher education.

REFERENCES

Arnold, N., and Paulus, T. (2010). Using a Social Networking Site for Experiential Learning: Appropriating, Lurking, Modeling and Community Building. *Internet and Higher Education, 13*(4), 188-196.

Boulos, M. N. K., Maramba, I., and Wheeler, S. (2006). Wikis, Blogs and Podcasts: A New Generation of Web-Based Tools for Virtual Collaborative Clinical Practice and Education. *BMC medical education, 6*(1), 1-8.

Braun, V, and Clarke,V. (2006). Using Thematic Analysis in Psychology. *Qualitative Research in Psychology,3* (2), 77-101.

Cain, J., & Katherine, C. (2013). Exploring Social Media's Potential in Interprofessional Education. Journal of Research in Interprofessional Practice and Education, 3(2), 1-7.

Chen, W., & Hirschheim, R. (2004). A Paradigmatic and Methodological Examination of Information Systems Research from 1991 To 2001. *Information systems journal, 14*(3), 197-235.

Cheung, C. M., Chiu, P. Y. and Lee, M. K. (2011). Online Social Networks: Why Do Students Use Facebook?. *Computers in Human Behavior, 27*(4), 1337-1343.

Chugh, R., & Ruhi, U. (2018). Social Media in Higher Education: A Literature Review of Facebook. *Education and Information Technologies, 23*(2), 605-616.

Creswell, W. J. (2009). *Research Design: Qualitative, Quantitative and mixed method approaches.* London: SAGE Publications.

Dogruer, N., Eyyam, R. and Menevis, I. (2011). The Use of the Internet for Educational Purposes. *Procedia-Social and Behavioral Sciences, 28*, 606-611.

Esteves, K. K. (2012). Exploring Facebook to Enhance Learning and Student Engagement: A Case from the University of Philippines (UP) Open University. *Malaysian Journal of Distance Education, 14*(1), 1-15.

Fusch, P.I. and Ness, L.R. (2015). Are We There Yet? Data Saturation in Qualitative Research. *The qualitative report, 20*(9), 1408–1416.

Hrastinski, S., & Aghaee, N. M. (2012). How Are Campus Students Using Social Media to Support Their Studies? An Explorative Interview Study. *Education and Information Technologies, 17*(4), 451-464.

Kaplan, A. M. and Haenlein, M. (2010). Users of The World, Unite! The Challenges and Opportunities of Social Media. *Business Horizons, 53*(1), 59-68.

Keles, E. (2018). Use of Facebook for The Community Services Practices Course: Community of Inquiry as a Theoretical Framework. *Computers and Education, 116,* 203–224.

Kirschner, P. and Karpinski, A. (2010). Facebook® and Academic Performance. *Computers in Human Behavior, 26*(6), 1237-245.

Lin, G. Y. (2018). Anonymous Versus Identified Peer Assessment via a Facebook-Based Learning Application: Effects On Quality of Peer Feedback, Perceived Learning, Perceived Fairness, And Attitude Toward The System. *Computers and Education, 116*, 81–92.

Lin, M. U., Huarui, C. A. O., and Tang, Y. A. O. (2012). Why Consumers Like Sharing on the Internet? *Journal of Chinese Marketing, 5*(2), 55-59.

Mazer, J. P., Murphy, R. E. and Simonds, C. J. (2007). I'll See You on "Facebook": The Effects of Computer-Mediated Teacher Self-Disclosure on Student Motivation, Affective Learning, and Classroom Climate. *Communication Education, 56*(1), 1–17.

Morse, J. M. (2015). Data Were Saturated.... *Health Research. 25*(5), 587–588.

Mourad, B., Tarik, A., Karim, A., and Pascal, E. (2015). System Interactive Cyber Presence for ELearning to Break Down Learner Isolation. *International Journal of Computer Application, 111*(16), 35-40.

Muntinga, D. G., Moorman, M. and Smith, E. G. (2011). Introducing Cobras: Exploring Motivations for Brand-Related Social Media Use. *International Journal of Advertising, 30*(1), 13- 46.

O'Keeffe, G. and Kathleen, C. (2011). The Impact of Social Media on Children, Adolescents, and Families. *Pediatrics, 127*(4), 799-805.

Pardo, A. (2013). Social Learning Graphs: Combining Social Network Graphs and Analytics to Represent Learning Experiences. *Int. J. Social Media and Interactive Learning Environments, 1*(1), 43-58.

Rovai, A. P. (2002). Sense of Community, Perceived Cognitive Learning, And Persistence In Asynchronous Learning Networks. *Internet and Higher Education, 5*, 319-332.

Selwyn, N. (2007). *Web 2.0 Applications as Alternative Environments For Informal Learning - A Critical Review.* OCEDKERIS International expert meeting on ICT and educational performance. Cheju Island, South Korea: Organization for Economic Co-Operation and Development.

Shaw, C. M. (2015). Using Facebook as an Educational Resource in the Classroom. *In Oxford Research Encyclopedia of International Studies, 1,* 1-14.

Smith, J. W. (2006). A Marketplace of Social Engagement. *Marketing Management, 52.*

Subrahmanyam, K., and Patricia, G. (2008). Online Communication and Adolescent Relationships. *The Future of Children, 18*(1), 119-46.

Woo, Y. and Reeves, T. C. (2008). Interaction in Asynchronous Web-Based Learning Environments. *Journal of Asynchronous Learning Networks, 12,* 179-194.

SHORT-TERM LEARNERS' MOTIVATION MODELING IN WEB BASED EDUCATION SYSTEM

Shahzad Shabbir[1], Muhammad Adnan Ayub[1], Farman Ali Khan[1] and Jeffrey Davis[2]
[1]*Comsats University Islamabad, Attock Campus, Pakistan*
[2]*American Realty Academy, Phoenix, Arizona, USA*

ABSTRACT

Recent research regarding personalized web based educational systems demonstrate learners' motivation to be an essential component of the learning model. This is due to the fact that low motivation results in either students' less engagement or complete drop out from the learning activities. A learner motivation model is considered to be a set of perceptions and beliefs that the system has developed about a learner. This includes both short-term and long-term motivation of learners. Short-term motivation encompasses specific, challenging and attainable goals that develop in the limited timespan. On the other hand, long-term motivation indicates a sort of continuing commitment that is required to complete assigned task. Since, short-term motivational problems span for a limited period of time such as a session, therefore, needs to be addressed in real-time to keep the learner engaged in the learning process. This paper proposes the framework of a domain independent short-term learner motivation model based on Keller ARCS motivation theory and Social Cognitive Theory. The proposed motivation identification framework consists of two modules. The primary module deals with real time identification of motivation, and the secondary module maintains the profile of learners associated with the short-term motivation.

KEYWORDS

E-learning, Motivation Model, Adaptation, Real Time Learner Modeling, Web-Based Education Systems

1. INTRODUCTION

Web based learning is getting prevalent in the present era. This make the learners to learn anywhere and anytime. Moreover, it allows learner to learn at their own pace (Acadamic Resources., 2017). There are two modes of delivering information in web-based learning that is synchronous and asynchronous (Ramaha and Ismail, 2012; Lim, 2017). Asynchronous mode let the students to take courses at own pace. Similarly, they have the choice to learn at different times according to their own schedule. This mode includes some common features such as message boards, discussion forums and self-paced courses. Real-time communication between students and instructors is a limitation in this method. On the other hand, synchronous methods let the students to enroll in a class that is paced at a particular interval. Student and teachers can interact in real time via video conferencing and web chat. Hrastinski (2008) describes that learners are more motivated in synchronous mode compare to asynchronous mode, due to its resemblance with the face-to-face communication. Keller and Suzuki (2004) indicated drop out as an important challenge in asynchronous mode. This is because learners feel lonely and isolated.

Abas (2003) illustrated that the success of web-based education system mainly depended on how well the system keeps the students motivated, energized and excited to learn. Therefore, identification of learner motivation is a vital research issue both in traditional class room environment as well as in web-based education systems. Research about incorporating motivational aspects in adaptive learning systems is reported as a critical research issue (Weld *et al.*, 2012; Fryer and Bovee, 2016).

Due to the rapid technological advancements, e-learning has been changed from the simple ways of delivering content to the complex learning environments such as recommender systems (Abas, 2003). This change arises the need to consider motivation in a more personalized way and to build adequate interventional strategies for learners' motivation (Ramaha and Ismail, 2012). Therefore, many researchers emphasize on providing personalized interventional strategies based on a firm learners' motivation model (Keller and Suzuki, 2004; Hrastinski, 2008). Although, there are several studies available which tries to analyses and identify learners' motivation both in traditional classroom environment and web-based e-learning systems. However, there is a very little research that has been conducted to identify learners' motivation in real time. Therefore, the need of motivational diagnosis and including short-term motivation model in web-based education system arises, that can assess and resolve learners' motivation issues in real time.

Cocea (2006) indicated that motivation model of learners must be based on a firm and well-established learning motivation theory. Therefore, this research takes Keller's ARCS Motivational Model and Social Cognitive Theory (Self- Regulation) as the basis for the framework of short-term motivation model. The framework consists of two modules. The primary module deals with real time identification of motivation, and the secondary module maintains the profile of learners associated with the short-term learners' motivation. The research is structured as follows: Section two describes the related work. Section three explains the framework for identification and modelling of short-term learners' motivation. Section four conclude the research work. Finally, section five presents the future work.

2. RELATED WORK

Initially, motivation has been perceived as a matter of design in web-based education systems. Specifically, learner can be engaged in learning through information presentation and providing efficient and effective instruction (Cocea and Weibelzahl, 2006b). Matsuo et al. (2008) used learners' study history, encourage function, etc. to implement / stimulate motivational design. Similarly, Burguillo (2010) describe introduction of friendly competitions among students. This enables students to increase their performance and results. Designing an e-learning curriculum that keep learner motivated during the complete learning program is one of the major issues in web-based education systems (Ghergulescu and Muntean, 2010). However, Cocea (2006) indicated that design approach does not take into account the personalized characteristics of the learners. Therefore, design strategy does not play an active role to enhance learners' motivation. As far as traditional class room environment is concerned, expert instructors generally deduce motivation of the learner from observational cues such as attitude, posture, gesture, conversation etc. which are challenging to be processed by computer (Cocea, 2006). Consequently, studies in the field of web-based education systems are mostly directed towards finding a way for the assessment of motivation utilizing cues. These cues must be easily processed by the e-learning systems such as learners' actions, learners' opinion about their level of motivation, and time spent on a given task.

This led the research to another strategy based on the log file analysis. Unobtrusiveness of the evaluation method is the key advantage of this approach. It is similar to the traditional classroom scenario where an instructor can perceive learners' motivation without interfering his/ her activities (Cocea, 2006). Zhang et al. (2003) used factorial analysis approach to identify motivation of the learner in a programming course. Two motivational traits of ARCS model (Keller and Suzuki, 2004) attention and confidence were taken into account. Results of their research work indicated that by means of factorial analysis user's action can be grouped, to differentiate between related actions that predict attention and confidence.

For log analysis, a rule-based methodology is developed by De Vicente and Pain (2002) to detect the motivational states of the learner using motivational characteristics. Qu, Wang and Johnson (2005) targeted aspects of learners' motivation such as effort, confidence, and confusion. Many cues related to the learners' actions were considered. This includes time to read the paragraph related to the task, time to perform the task, and the time when the learner starts/ finishes the task. Moreover, it considers, the time for the learner to decide how to perform the task, the number of tasks the learner has finished with respect to the current plan, number of questions asking for help, and the number of unexpected tasks performed by the learner (Qu, Wang and Johnson, 2005; Cocea, 2006). A dynamic mixture model was proposed by Johns and Woolf (2006). This model relates a hidden Markov model with IRT (Item Response Theory). Learners' skill, motivation, signs of motivation, and learners' reaction to a problem are the traits used in model to incorporate motivational aspect of the learner.

Nevertheless, motivational characteristics are not always evident and therefore invisible by observation (Cocea, 2006). This led the research to another strategy known as self-assessment that would also guarantee the accurate information. Learners' self-assessment has been proved to be reliable, helpful and precise source of motivational information (Beal, Qu and Lee, 2006). This research therefore uses both log file analysis and learners' self-assessment. Log file analysis would provide the benefit of unobtrusiveness and the learners' feedback/ self-assessment would provide the accurate information about learners' motivation.

3. FRAMEWORK FOR SHORT-TERM LEARNERS' MOTIVATION MODELING

This methodology is built on Keller's ARCS motivational model and Social Cognitive Theory. This framework includes characteristics such as Attention, Relevance, Confidence, and Satisfaction from Keller model and Self- Regulation from Social Cognitive Theory. Real time motivational status of the learner is stored in short-term motivation model. This method is shown in Figure 1.

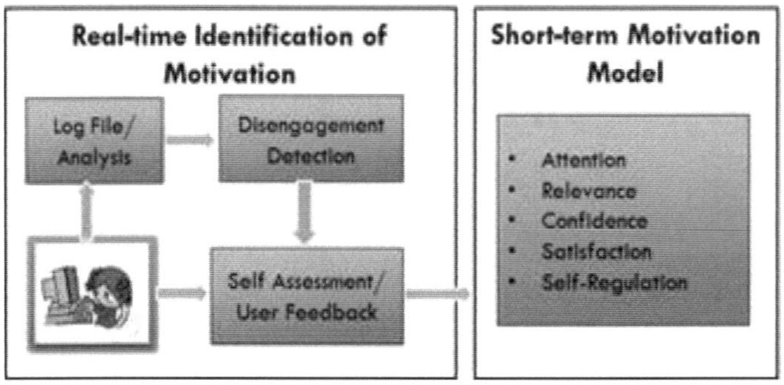

Figure 1. Short Term Learners' Motivation Modeling Framework

First step for short term motivation model is eliciting most appropriate motivational problems in web-based learning. For this, a generic list of motivational problem was drawn based on the research and commendations discussed in the related work (Cocea, 2006; ChanLin, 2009). The primary list included 28 motivational problems that were faced in web-based learning (See Appendix). All the motivational problems are assigned with a unique problem ID for example A1 for Attention problem no 1.

An online survey was conducted to rate the most frequent motivational problems on the Likert scale, involving expert from the Moodle research community and undergraduate online learners of Virtual University of Pakistan. There were three reasons for seeking the views of experts and online learners:

(a) To elicit motivational problems that are best suited for the different characteristics outlined in the list.
(b) To rate most frequent motivational problems; and
(c) To validate the motivational problems contained in the list.

The survey was conducted using Google Forms. The online learners were given the list of motivational problems with the characteristics and were asked to rate the motivational problems on the Likert scale (where 1 represent rarely and 5 represent mostly) from each of the four domains of Keller motivational model and one from each of three domains of self-regulation. The learners were asked to suggest any further motivational problem that they faced during interaction with online learning environment. This question was asked in order to elicit any motivational problem that may have been overlooked when the list was being compiled.

The results show that mean value of the motivational problems ranges from 2.3 to 3.5 (see Figure 2). The motivational problems were then arranged according to the rating of the participants and would be presented to the learner in a dialogue to report their motivational state.

For the next step, input of the learner from the dialogue would be feed to short-term learner model with problem ID, time, date, and course ID (see Fig 3). Moreover, recommended strategies for intervention would be provided to instructor along with problem ID, to keep the learner motivated in learning process. Instructor would be allowed to mark the motivational problem as resolved when the intervention is provided to the learner. The short-term motivation model would be updated, and the time, date, and course ID fields would be assigned with null value.

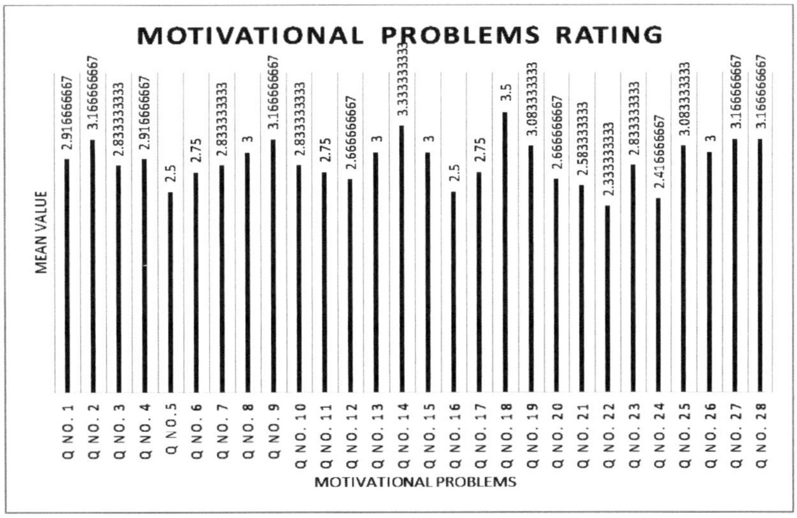

Figure 2. Results of online survey

3.1 Log File Analysis/ Disengagement Detection

As discussed earlier, the key benefit of log file analysis is the unobtrusiveness of the motivational assessment process. However motivational characteristics are not always evident and therefore untraceable by observation. For example, a general indicator of engagement or disengagement is time spend on a topic (Cocea and Weibelzahl, 2006a). Time spend (too short or too long) on a topic or task may specify disengagement. Obviously, both could be due to some other reasons, for example one can explain a short time duration spent on a topic might be due to fair or prior knowledge of the topic. On the other hand, a too long time could be advocated by causes such as deep thought breaks. This would recommend the use of self-assessment/ learner feedback that would also confirm the accurateness of information. However, obtrusiveness of the process is limitation in self-assessment.

Similar to Cocea and Weibelzahl (2006) research, this paper proposes an approach that combines the log file analysis and learner feedback. This balances the benefit of unobtrusiveness offered by Log file with the significance of accuracy of information provided by Learner Self-assessment. So, the proposed approach is divided in two phases that is log file analysis and learners' self-assessment. The initial phase is disengagement detection using log file analysis. This would guarantee that a learner would be interrupted only when identified as disengaged by the system. Similarly, in second phase, as soon as disengagement is identified, the system would ask the learner about their motivational state. If the learner approves system diagnosis, a dialog would be initiated by system and asks the student to provide information about their motivational state.

As discussed earlier, there are some behavioral cues which indicates disengagement of the learner. For example, non-systematic progression, skipping sections, browsing fast rather than reading, and quickly answering the questions, that is even in less time that is essential to read the questions. This paper considered reading time, mouse movement and correct / wrong answers of the question at the end of each topic as the indicators of motivation. An average man can read with the speed of 200 to 250 words per minute assuming user did not skim the words nor fail to understand the meaning of what was read (Speed Reading Facts., 2018). So, we can calculate minimum average time of a page by the following formula.

$$\text{minTimeReq(Seconds)} = \frac{\text{No of words on the page}}{\text{maximum Average Speed (250 words/minute)}} \times 60$$

Similarly, maximum average time of a page can be calculated as follows.

$$\text{maxTimeReq(Seconds)} = \frac{\text{No of words on the page}}{\text{minimum Average Speed (200 words/minute)}} \times 60$$

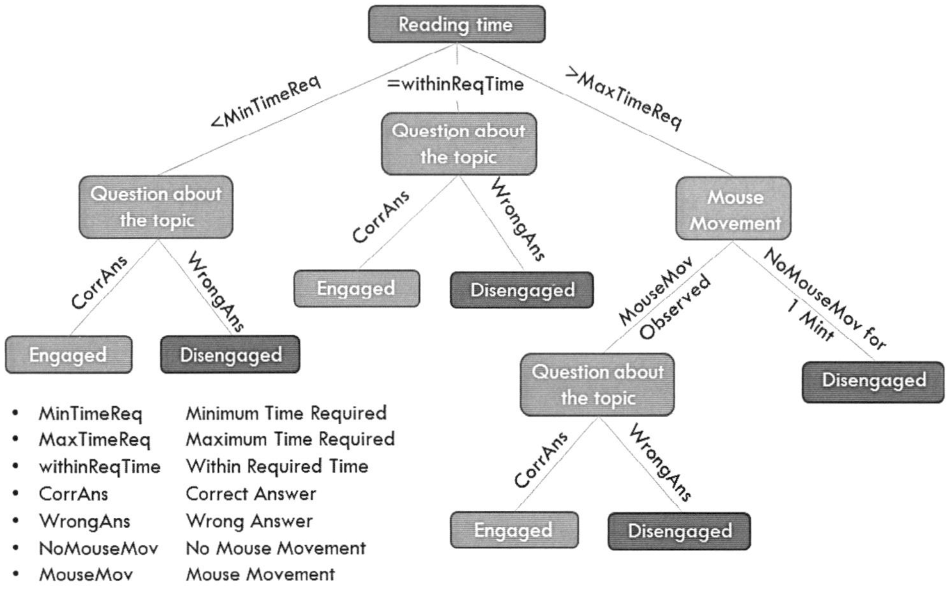

Figure 3. Process to identify real time engagement/disengagement of the learner

The Figure 3 shows the process to identify real time motivation of the learner. A good level of motivation is termed as engaged and low level of motivation is termed as disengaged in Fig 3. In case the learners' reading time is less than the minimum time required to read and understand the topic, the system would ask a question at the end of the topic. If the learner correctly answers the question, system would consider learner as engaged and allow the learner to proceed to the next topic. On the other hand, if the learner fails to answer the question correctly, the system would inform the learner that it has detected disengagement. If the learner approves system diagnosis, the system would initiate a dialog. The questions could be MCQs and fill in the blanks or both. A fill in the blank question would be a good idea so the blind guess can be avoided.

In the same context, if the learner read the page within required time and answer the question correctly, would be identified as engaged by the system. On the other hand, if a learner spends too much time on a page i.e. greater then maximum time required to read the page, the system would observe the mouse movement for a minute. If no mouse movement is observed by the system for one minute, it would ask the learner about his/her motivational state. The system would expire the session time if the learner doesn't response for a while and update his/her user model. Conversely, if the system observes the mouse movement, it would wait until the learner answer the question at the end of the page. The system would classify the learner as engaged if the answer is correct otherwise disengaged and asked for the motivational state.

3.2 Self-Assessment / Learners' Feedback

The purpose of the learner feedback is to involve a learner in a dialogue process with the system reported as disengaged. This would enable the system to identify some motivational traits that would further be used to update learners' motivational model.

The conversation would be initiated by notifying the learner that they are detected as disengaged by the system, followed by a question intended to confirm whether the student agrees with the diagnosis of the system or not. The dialogue is presented with mostly occur motivational problem at the top followed by less occurred motivational problems as categorized using google survey discussed earlier. Knowing the fact that the learner providing the information would already be disengaged, only first ten problems would be presented on the first page to elicit motivational problems. Learner can select one or more option in the following dialogue to report their motivational problems. In case the specific motivational problem is not presented, the learner would be provided with next ten problems on second page and so on. The selected motivational problem would be feed to short-term motivational model.

3.3 Short-Term Motivation Model

The short-term learners' motivation model would receive information from the disengagement detection section and learner feedback. The reported motivational problem would provide values for the motivational characteristics i.e. Attention, Relevance, Confidence, Satisfaction, and Self-Regulation. Similarly, the motivational problem would be registered in short-term motivational model of the learner with Problem ID, Course ID, Time and Date (see Fig 4).

The disengagement detection would provide real-time information about learners' motivation state. At the bottom of short-term motivation model, recommended strategies would be provided to instructor to resolve each motivational problem. This would enable instructor to provide personalized intervention to the learner.

	Problem ID	Time	Date	Course ID	
Attention	A1	-	-	-	
	A2	1545	20160107	WP1	Resolve
	A3	-	-	-	
	A4	-	-	-	
Relevance	R1	-	-	-	
	R2	-	-	-	
	R3	-	-	-	
	R4	-	-	-	
Confidence	C1	-	-	-	
	C2	-	-	-	
	C3	-	-	-	
	C4	1134	20160108	WP1	Resolve
	C5	-	-	-	
Satisfaction	S1	-	-	-	
	S2	-	-	-	
	S3	-	-	-	
Self Regulation	SR1	-	-	-	
	SR2	-	-	-	
	SR3	-	-	-	
	SR4	-	-	-	
	SR5	-	-	-	
	SR6	-	-	-	
	SR7	-	-	-	
	SR8	-	-	-	
	SR9	-	-	-	
	SR10	-	-	-	
	SR11	-	-	-	
	SR12	-	-	-	

Recommended Strategies

A2: Post reminding of learning activities.
C4: Encourage the learner to recognize the content and understand what they learnt.

Figure 4. Short-term Learners' Motivational Model

4. CONCLUSION

Motivational diagnosis is important for both traditional class room and web-based education systems. It is one of the major elements that contribute in the success of the learning process. However, dropout rate among online students is very high which lead to incorporate motivational elements in more personalized way. Because motivated students will retain the course until they successfully complete it. Hence, identifying learners' motivation and providing personalized intervention is key for the success of web-based education systems.

This paper presented a framework for real-time identification of the learners' motivation. Log file analysis was proposed to detect the real-time learners' motivation. Reading speed, mouse movement and correct answer to question at the end of the page were attributes considered for motivational diagnosis. Learners' self-assessment was used to ensure the accuracy of the motivation identification process as user feedback is proved as a helpful, reliable and precise source of learners' motivational information. The presented framework is based on widely recognized and firmed research methodologies. So, it is believed that the presented model would enhance the learning process by motivational diagnosis of the learner and assisting instructors to provide personalized intervention based on system diagnosis.

5. FUTURE WORK

Future work deals with the development of learner motivational model incorporating both long-term and short-term motivational characteristics. Moreover, an experiment would be conducted to know the impact of motivational model over the dropout rate of learners.

REFERENCES

Abas, Z. W. (2003) 'Incorporating motivational elements in a Web-based learning environment for distance students: A Malaysian experience', in *International Conference on Web-Based Learning*, pp. 396–410.

Acadamic Resources. (2017). Available at: http://www.dso.iastate.edu/asc/academic/elearner/advantage.html (Accessed: 17 May 2017).

Beal, C. R., Qu, L. and Lee, H. (2006) 'Classifying learner engagement through integration of multiple data sources', in *Proceedings of the National Conference on Artificial Intelligence*, p. 151.

Burguillo, J. C. (2010) 'Using game theory and competition-based learning to stimulate student motivation and performance', *Computers & Education*. Elsevier, 55(2), pp. 566–575.

ChanLin, L.-J. (2009) 'Applying motivational analysis in a Web-based course', *Innovations in Education and Teaching International*. Routledge, 46(1), pp. 91–103.

Cocea, M. (2006) 'Assessment of motivation in online learning environments', in *International Conference on Adaptive Hypermedia and Adaptive Web-Based Systems*, pp. 414–418.

Cocea, M. and Weibelzahl, S. (2006a) 'Can log files analysis estimate learners' level of motivation?', in *LWA*.

Cocea, M. and Weibelzahl, S. (2006b) 'Motivation: included or excluded from E-learning', in *Cognition and exploratory learning in digital age, CELDA 2006 proceedings*. IADIS Press.

Fryer, L. K. and Bovee, H. N. (2016) 'Supporting students' motivation for e-learning: Teachers matter on and offline', *The Internet and Higher Education*. Elsevier, 30, pp. 21–29.

Ghergulescu, I. and Muntean, C. H. (2010) 'Assessment of motivation in gaming based e-learning', in *Proceedings of the IADIS International Conference on WWW/Internet*, p. 71.

Hrastinski, S. (2008) 'Asynchronous and synchronous e-learning', *Educause quarterly*, 31(4), pp. 51–55.

Johns, J. and Woolf, B. (2006) 'A dynamic mixture model to detect student motivation and proficiency', in *Proceedings of the National Conference on Artificial Intelligence*, p. 163.

Keller, J. and Suzuki, K. (2004) 'Learner motivation and e-learning design: A multinationally validated process', *Journal of educational Media*. Taylor & Francis, 29(3), pp. 229–239.

Lim, F. P. (2017) 'An Analysis of Synchronous and Asynchronous Communication Tools in e-Learning'.

Matsuo, K. *et al.* (2008) 'Implementation and Design of New Functions for a Web-Based E-learning System to Stimulate Learners Motivation', in *Complex, Intelligent and Software Intensive Systems, 2008. CISIS 2008. International Conference on*, pp. 513–518.

Qu, L., Wang, N. and Johnson, W. L. (2005) 'Using learner focus of attention to detect learner motivation factors', in *International Conference on User Modeling*, pp. 70–73.

Ramaha, N. T. and Ismail, W. (2012) 'Assessment of learner's motivation in web based e-learning', *International Journal of Scientific and Engineering Research*, 3(8), p. 11.

Speed Reading Facts. (2018). Available at: http://www.execuread.com/facts/ (Accessed: 11 April 2018).

De Vicente, A. and Pain, H. (2002) 'Informing the detection of the students' motivational state: an empirical study', in *International Conference on Intelligent Tutoring Systems*, pp. 933–943.

Weld, D. S. *et al.* (2012) 'Personalized online education—a crowdsourcing challenge', in *Workshops at the Twenty-Sixth AAAI Conference on Artificial Intelligence*, pp. 1–31.

Zhang, G. *et al.* (2003) 'A WWW-based learner's learning motivation detecting system', in *Proceedings of International Workshop on" Research Directions and Challenge Problems in Advanced Information Systems Engineering", Honjo City, Japan.*

APPENDIX

Initial List of Motivational Problems

Problem ID	Motivational Characteristics	Motivational Problems
A1	Attention	The content area was not interesting as expected.
A2		Online class attendance did not concern me.
A3		Unlike face-to-face meeting, I had problems in attending to each learning task.
A4		Knowing that we have plenty of time to learn in a Web-based class, we paid less attention to the specific learning time.
R1	Relevance	A lot of unfamiliar materials were involved in the lesson.
R2		Inappropriate experiences, such as weak theoretical-grounded folk prescriptions were related to the course due to uncertainty about the content.
R3		Use of discussion forum was found irrelevant to learning content.
R4		I am not accustomed to chat for course related content.
C1	Confidence	Knowledge we explored was so extensive that I had problems preparing for the exam' websites.
C2		I believe, I cannot understand it.
C3		Learning from the foreign websites do not provide desired results.
C4		The content is too hard to understand.
C5		There is always an uncertainty about the use of Web-based resources for assignments and research projects.
S1	Satisfaction	'Too much work!' 'Lack of time!'.
S2		'Not seeing class members made me feel insecure about the course'.
S3		I often fail to participate in course activities and fail to submit assignments regularly.
SR1	Self-Regulation	In a tough situation I cannot stick to the schedule I have made for myself.
SR2		I cannot stick to a certain timetable when I'm studying.
SR3		I have used the time that I have reserved for studying.
SR4		I never stick to the study schedule that I have made.
SR5		Requirements of this course did not match with my own style of studying.
SR6		Before a study activity, I often go through its different steps in my mind. These steps are not provided in the beginning of the activity.
SR7		I set learning goals to be able to direct my studies, but I am unable to meet them.
SR8		I think I performed badly in this study activity and I cannot improve my performance.
SR9		I often feel so lazy or bored studying course literature that I quit before finishing.
SR10		I often give up when I'm studying difficult issues and focus on the easier ones.
SR11		I often feel difficulties in motivating myself to complete the study tasks if they are not particularly interesting to me.
SR12		I often give up if I don't like all the tasks or the material I am reading.

INTERNOVA E-LEARNING PLATFORM IN AN ENTREPRENEURIAL CONTEXT

Isabel Araújo[1,2], Rita Pinheiro[1,3,4], Pedro Miguel Faria[1], João Nuno Azevedo[1], Sónia Faria[1] and Manuela Vaz Velho[1,4]

[1]Instituto Politécnico de Viana do Castelo, Viana do Castelo, Portugal
[2]Centre for Studies in Education and Innovation (CI&DEI), Instituto Politécnico de Viseu, Portugal
[3]Centro de Engenharia Biológica (CEB), Universidade do Minho, Portugal
[4]Centro de Investigação e Desenvolvimento em Sistemas Agroalimentares e Sustentabilidade (CISAS), Instituto Politécnico de Viana do Castelo, Portugal

ABSTRACT

Currently, there is still an opposition of teachers to the implementation of new technologies in an educational context. Although several studies point out the relevance of the use of information and communication technologies in pedagogical practices, providing educational contexts more focused on learning practices and fostering more active and autonomous professionals. In this context, this article emphasizes the purpose of using Information and Communication Technologies (ICT), as well as virtual learning environments, in the higher education system, to support the teaching-learning processes. In this article, a state of the art was carried out, in order to demonstrate some advantages of the teaching-learning process, the teacher's and student behaviour profiles and its role in relation to the use of new technologies. The objective of this study was to analyse the impact of using a digital platform on the teaching-learning process in an educational context. An e-learning digital platform, *INTERNOVA*, developed within the scope of the INTERNOVAMARKET-FOOD project (0437_internovamarket-food_1_E - Internovamarket accelerator program to increase the competitiveness of the food sector in Galicia-Northern), within the curricular unit of Food Safety and Certification of the Master in Food Engineering's curriculum. In order to assess the impact of the training course on the students' learning outcomes, a survey was applied to master's students and Food Engineering research fellows (participants). The same survey was applied before the training and after it in order to compare both results. At the end of each training course, another survey was addressed to all the participants asking about the organization, quality and the easiness of the platform. The results obtained show that the students had no difficulties in using the platform, having revealed that they would like to continue using it more frequently. The data obtained are an evidence of the participants' learning improvement and their involvement in the learning process through the *INTERNOVA* platform. With this work, it can be concluded that the ICT applied to a curricular program can be a very important support in the teaching-learning process. In this context, it is important to recommend well-designed curricular programs so that teachers can improve their teaching practices, enhancing students' digital skills, and thus contributing to the development of more active and autonomous professionals.

KEYWORDS

E-learning Digital Platform, ICT, LMS, Virtual Learning Environments, Higher Education, Engineering Teaching

1. INTRODUCTION

As a result of technological developments, namely in higher education system, the use of Information and Communication Technologies (ICT) in the educational context has constantly increasing (Daniela et al, 2019), which has led to changes in teaching and learning processes. The evolution of ICT facilitates the access of information by the majority of the population, promoting deep changes in several areas of knowledge, mainly in the academic field, where it is discussed and built knowledge. However, the teaching and learning processes in higher education system have not been able to keep up with the fast-technological development.

In his work, Moran (2007) stated that many conventional classes were outdated, in which the method adopted was only expository and the student was merely a receiver of knowledge. Furthermore, he warned that the fundamental issue in education does not depend only on technologies. In this sense, several studies were carried out in order to try to understand the impact of ICT in the teaching and learning processes (Nortvig et al, 2018, Araújo & Faria, 2019).

Current students, born in the digital generation, show more technological skills, compared to their teachers, who are still somewhat reluctant to use ICT in an educational context, particularly in the use of learning platforms.

In this article, it was demonstrated the experience and the results obtained by implementing an e-learning platform in a higher educational context, within the curricular unit of Food Safety and Certification of the Master in Food Engineering. The e-learning platform was developed as part of the Internovamarket-food project for training of employees of companies in the agri-food sector.

2. ICT IN THE TEACHING-LEARNING PROCESS

Several studies point out the advantages of using ICT in an educational context (Al-Samarraie et al, 2018; Nortvig et al, 2018, Cidral et al, 2018; Araújo & Faria, 2019). These technologies, in addition to enabling access to information, are valuable tools in the development of new methods of learning and support new contexts for the corresponding learnings (Dias, 2004). Furthermore, citing Daniela, Strods & Kalniņa (2019: 12), "On the one hand, there is the conviction that technologies are indispensable, both for improving learning and for making learning process more effective, both in terms of learning outcomes and in terms of costs. Additionally, technology and technological solutions can provide sustainability of knowledge because students develop the competences that they will need in their future professional work".

Such technologies facilitate the development of virtual learning environments, enhancing spaces for the construction of knowledge, and thus are an asset for the teaching and learning processes (Junior & Coutinho, 2010). Consequently, they can change the way students acquire, use and build knowledge (Trinder et al, 2008), promoting new forms of learning. In this context, the traditional teacher, who transmits knowledge, starts to have the role of advisor and facilitator of learning (Araújo, 2014), playing a crucial role in creating and sustaining conditions for the (co) construction of knowledge. The passive student, the recipient of knowledge, takes on a more active role in the construction of knowledge, self-managing his learning process.

In fact, ICT provide diversified access to information, and students can interact with digital subjects and also communicate synchronously or asynchronously with other users. However, it is not technologies themselves that improve teaching or students' learning, ICT allows that teachers and students can work together in a way that traditional teaching methods did not permit, bringing substantial advantages for teachers and students (Dias & Diniz, 2010).

Several studies reflect the impact of ICT on learning environments, concluding that these environments can be a space full of meaning, where human beings and technical objects interact, enhancing the construction of knowledge (Ribeiro, 2010).

The adoption of learning environments, supported by platforms to support face-to-face, distance or mixed educational processes is growing. According to Coutinho & Bottentuit (2007), in terms of functionalities, e-learning platforms should allow the availability and access to pedagogical content, communication/interaction between teachers and students and mechanisms for the evaluation and management of teaching/learning processes.

According to the literature, in these environments the students stop being so dependent on the teacher, assuming greater responsibility for his own learning, becoming more active, more autonomous and having greater freedom to plan his learning activities.

However, according to Marchiori et al. (2011) the performance of higher education students depends on the attention they dedicate to their studies, which consequently has implications to learning success. The use of technologies in higher education system facilitates access to information, but it is necessary for the teacher to teach students to turn this information into knowledge (O'Donnell & Sharp, 2012).

3. THE *INTERNOVA* PLATFORM

The *INTERNOVA* platform (Figure 1) was developed within the Internovamarket-food project (0437_internovamarket-food_1_E - Internovamarket accelerator program to increase the competitiveness of the agro-food sector in Galicia-Northern Portugal (Financial support: Portugal Interreg V-A Spain-Portugal (POCTEP) 2014-2020, in axis 2 "Integration of growth through cross-border cooperation in favour of business competitiveness"), with the primary objective of providing training to employees of agri-food companies in the North of Portugal and Spain.

This platform offers two training courses: a) International Featured Standard (IFS) Food & BRC Global Standard for Food Safety, b) ISO 22000:2018 - Food Safety Management System (ISO22000) (Figure 1). The contents of each of the two training courses were divided into several modules. Each module has a learning component and a component for assessing what was learned by the students/trainees. The evaluation component consists of a set of questions related to the respective modules' contents. The students/trainees can only access the next module after obtaining approval (success) on the previous one.

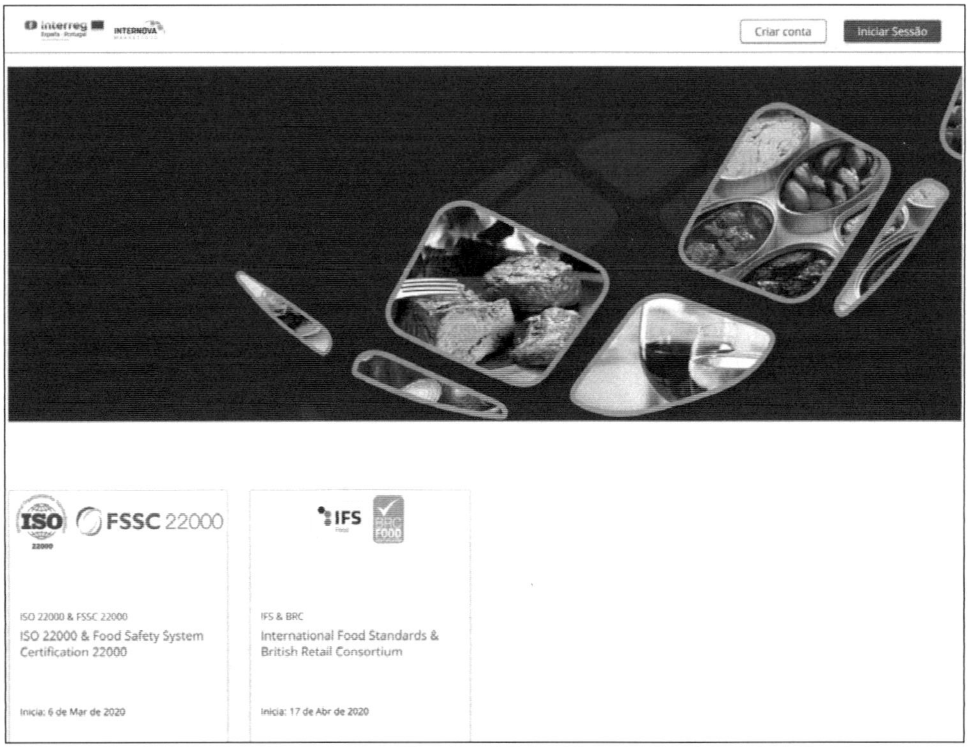

Figure 1. The *INTERNOVA* platform

For a student/trainee to be able to attend the course it is mandatory to make the registration in the platform (account creation). The contents of the modules are available in an audio-visual format. The training videos available provide trainees with all the information necessary to carry out the assessment tests. The trainees, after having successfully completed all modules, are automatically given a Certificate of achievement, by the platform.

4. METHOLOGY

The Food Safety and Certification curricular unit is part of the 1st year of the Master in Food Engineering's curriculum at the Higher School of Technology and Management of the Polytechnic Institute of Viana do Castelo (ESTG-IPVC).

The *INTERNOVA* platform offers two training courses: a) International Featured Standard (IFS) Food & BRC Global Standard for Food Safety, b) ISO 22000:2018 - Food Safety Management System (ISO22000). These two training courses contain the contents that are part of the Food Safety and Certification's curriculum. The study took place at the beginning of the 2nd semester of the academic year of 2019/2020. This study was attended by 11 master students (MEA1 to MEA11) and 6 food engineering research fellows (Scholarship1 to Scholarship6) from the Food Engineering Group of ESTG-IPVC. In order to study the use of the *INTERNOVA* platform in an educational context, the students and the research fellows were asked to register in the platform (create an account). Then the participants were requested to take the course on a non-face-to-face basis, that is, online. The period available for each training course was 30 days.

In order to assess the impact of the training course on the students' learning outcomes a survey was applied to students/research fellows. The same survey was applied before the training and after it in order to compare both results. At the end of each training course, another survey was addressed to all the participants asking about the organization and the easiness of the platform and the training course. A link with the survey was send through email. The survey had 10 questions related to the easiness of the platform, two questions related to the tasks available and two other questions related to the global assessment of the platform and its contents, in order to assess the satisfaction degree of the trainees.

The System Usability Scale (SUS) is an evaluation model used by Brooke (1986), as it is considered one of the most accepted for its reliability and validity. It contains a simple scale of ten items related to usability, allowing the assessment of subjective perceptions. It uses the Likert scale with values ranging from 1 (strongly disagree) to 5 (strongly agree), with 3 meaning neutral. In addition, the survey contains 4 extra questions to better assess the platform's purpose in an educational context. The survey was made available on an online platform and subsequently a descriptive statistical analysis was carried out and also a SUS analysis which encompasses five quality components: ease of learning, efficiency, ease of memorization, minimization of errors and satisfaction (Nielsen, 2012).

5. RESULTS AND DISCUSSION

Graphic 1 shows the results obtained in the pre-test, applied before training, and in the post-test applied after training. The scale used was from 0 points (lowest grade) to 20 points (highest grade). Of the 17 trainees who participated in this study, the majority was female, with only 18% male, aged between 21 and 38 years old, with mode being 22 years old (corresponding to 35% of the graduates) and 23 years old being the median. As shown in Graphic 1, all students scored a better result in the post-test. In all cases, there was an increase in the grades when comparing pre- with post-test. Regarding the IFS/BRC and ISO2200 courses, respectively, the highest absolute improvement was 12 points (MEA7) and 10 points (MEA2).

The lowest increase was, respectively, 4 points (Scholarship5 and Scholarship6) and 2 points (all scholarship holders except Scholarship4). The average of the increases obtained scored 7.6 points and 5.1 points. It was observed a higher increase in the score obtained by the group of master students than by the group of research fellows, for both course trainings. It should also be referred that in the post-test of the ISO22000 training, all trainees scored 20 points.

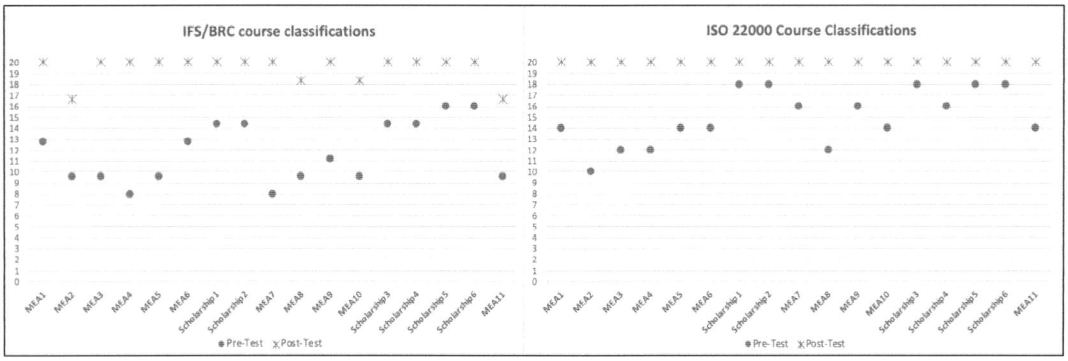

Graphic 1. Ratings of evaluations in training courses

Concerning both tests moments (pre- and post-), for the two training courses (Graphic 1), results show that the average rates of evaluations increased, 11.8 points to 19.4 points, for pre- and post-test, respectively, in the IFS/BRC course, and 14.9 points to 20 points, for pre- and post-test respectively, in the ISO22000 course. The data obtained are an evidence of the participants' learning improvement and their involvement in the learning process through the *INTERNOVA* platform.

At the end of the IFS/BRC training course, all the trainees who attended both tests (pre- and post-test) answered the other survey. Analysing the results obtained (Graphic 2), on a scale from 1 - Totally Disagree to 5 - Totally Agree, regarding the easiness of using the *INTERNOVA* platform, 94% of the trainees scored 5 (56%) or 4 (39%) that "the platform was easy to use". As well as the same percentage, 94%, scored between 1 (72%) and 2 (22%) that "the platform was very complicated to use" (Graphic 2) which reinforces that for most users, this platform is easy to use. Thus, the same percentages showed students "had to learn a lot before being able to deal with this e-learning platform" and, accordingly, the majority (89%) scored between 1 (61%) and 2 (28%) "needing help from a technician to be able to use it". Furthermore, 83% scored between 5 (50%) and 4 (33%) that "most people would learn to use this e-learning platform quickly".

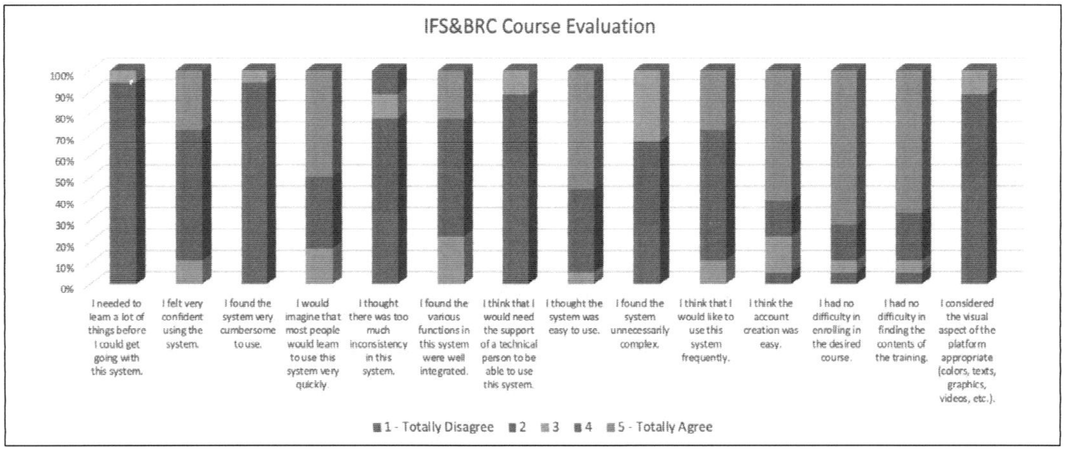

Graphic 2. Evaluation results of IFS/BRC training satisfaction survey

Concerning the question about "the visual aspect is adequate" the majority of participants scored it 1 (50%) and 2 (39%). Regarding the question about "who liked to use it frequently", the majority scored it 5 (28%) and 4 (61%). Furthermore, most of the participants (67%) disagreed, having scored 1 (28%) or 2 (39%), about "the platform is unnecessarily complex", as well as 78% disagreed, having indicated 1 (33%) and 2 (44%), for "the platform has many inconsistencies". About "the ease of access to training", namely the creation of an account and enrolment in training, there was no significant disagreement. Finally, regarding the IFS/BRC training course, a large majority of the participants (89%) scored between 4 (22%) and 5 (67%) "who had no difficulty in finding the training content" and 78% scored between 4 (56%) and 5 (22%) that "the various functionalities of this e-learning platform are well integrated".

Regarding ISO22000 course training (Graphic 3), only 59% of the students who attended the course answered the second survey. It should be noticed that after the implementation of the previous course (IFS/BRC), some adjustments were made to the platform, taking into account the feedback obtained from the trainees. All participants scored between 4 and 5, that they "would like to use the platform more often", found the platform easy to use, that creating the account was easy, that most people would learn to use it quickly and did not experience difficulties in find training content. Most of the participants (90%) scored "felt very confident using this e-learning platform" between 4 and 5 (Graphic 3).

In addition, all participants scored 1 and 2 to several questions, namely: "the need for help from a technician to be able to use this e-learning platform", " e-learning platform is very complicated to use", "having to learn a lot before being able to deal with this e-learning platform" and "visual aspect of the platform is adequate (colors, text, graphics, videos, etc.)". Although the trainees considered the visual aspect to be inadequate, they would like to use the platform frequently and felt confident in using it, which reveals some incongruity that may have resulted from the interpretation of the questions.

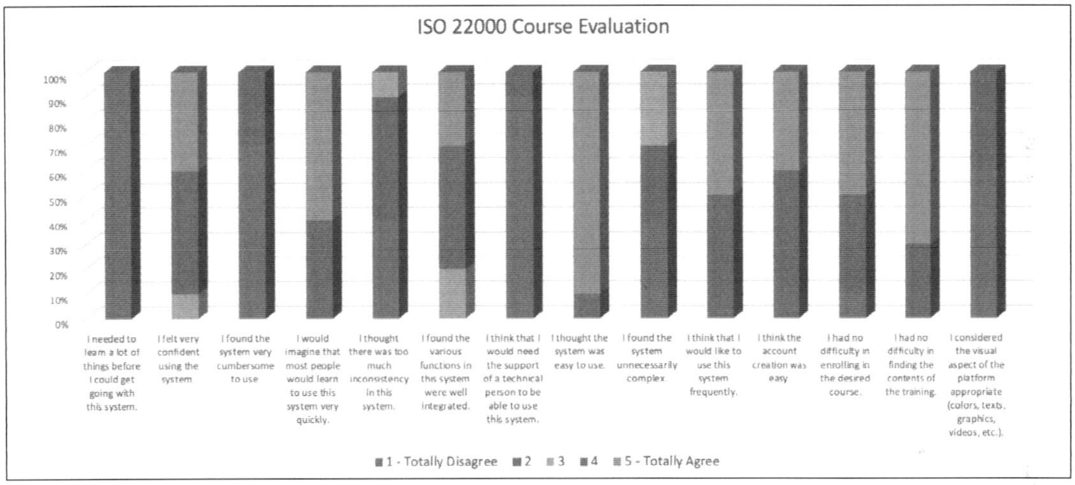

Graphic 3. Evaluation results of ISO22000 training satisfaction survey

In Graphic 4, it is possible to observe the results obtained from the usability analysis through the application of the SUS method considering the average of the normalized scores of the first 10 questions of the survey. From the results of the surveys carried out concerning both training courses, IFS&BRC and ISO22000, were scored at 82.4 and 88.5 respectively. From the results of the questionnaires conducted in the context of the IFS&BRC and ISO22000 training courses, a score of 82.4 and 88.5 respectively was obtained. In both training courses it was obtained a SUS value higher than 80.3, scored as "A", which corresponds to an excellent evaluation. With the results, it was concluded that the *INTERNOVA* platform, in both training courses, has an excellent usability (Bangor et al, 2009).

Specifically, considering the quality components indicated by Nielsen (2012), it appears that regarding both training courses, IFS&BRC and ISO22000, the following values were obtained, respectively:

- Learning easiness - the average result of questions 3, 4, 7 and 10 from SUS are 85.4 and 96.3;
- Efficiency of the system - the average result of questions 5, 6 and 8 of SUS are 79.2 and 84.2;
- Ease of memorization - result of question 2 whose score are 79.2 and 77.5;
- System inconsistency - result of question 6 whose score are 75.0 and 82.5;
- Satisfaction - the average result of questions 1, 4 and 9 of SUS are 82.9 and 89.2.

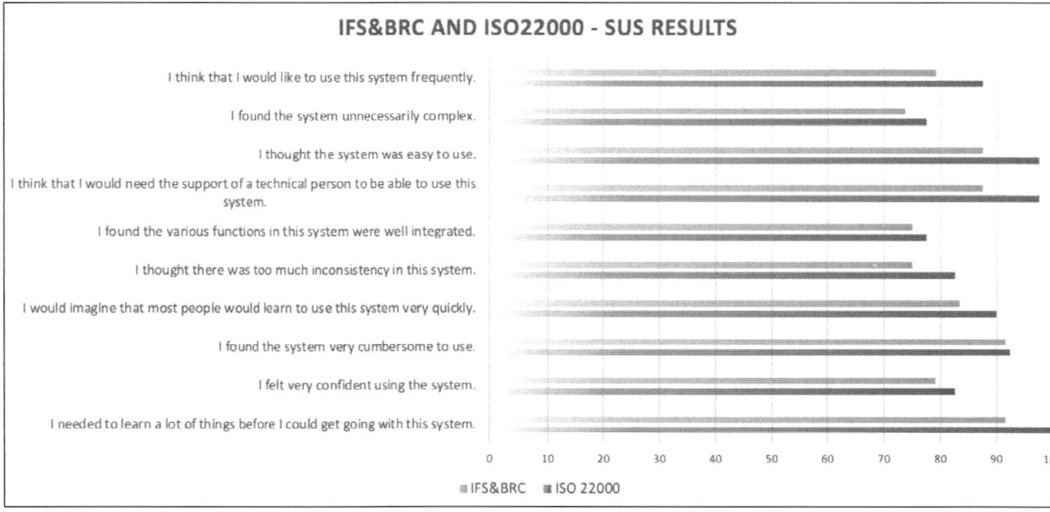

Graphic 4. SUS results of *INTERNOVA* platform survey

Regarding quality components of the platform, from the results obtained it was concluded that users have demonstrated easiness in learning how to use it, considering it efficient and easy to memorize, with low-level inconsistencies and a high degree of satisfaction.

6. CONCLUSION

The SUS score obtained for the *INTERNOVA* platform shows that this e-learning platform meets the usability requirements of the trainees who used it in an educational context. Approximately 90% of the participants involved in this study indicated that they liked using the *INTERNOVA* platform, considering it easiness and did not experienced difficulties in finding the training contents. These results lead to the conclusion that the students in the teaching-learning context used the platform as an online teaching tool.

Furthermore, through the online courses training available on the *INTERNOVA* platform it was concluded that all trainees acquired knowledge. From the data presented, it is believed that the use of a e-learning platform in an educational context is favourable to the construction of knowledge, that is, it was a driving force in the progress of teaching-learning process.

Thus, the present article reinforces the relevance of the development and use of LMS platforms in the educational context, corroborating with O'Donnell & Sharp (2012) on the use of technology as facilitating tools in higher education seems to bring some advantages. Thus, it is the responsibility of higher education institutions to recommend well-designed curriculums, promoting teaching methodologies less focused on the teacher. In this way, teachers can improve their teaching practices, making them more appealing and attractive for students, to them to be more interested and more active in acquiring knowledge (Lobo & Maia, 2015). On the other hand, the study here presented leads us to reflect on the relevance of using e-learning platforms in entrepreneurial context, enhancing a more flexible and more learner-centered learning environment.

ACKNOWLEDGMENTS

This work was supported by INTERREG V-A Espanha-Portugal (POCTEP) 2014-2020 (0437_INTERNOVAMARKET-FOOD_1_E) under the development of the project entitled "INTERNOVAMARKET-FOOD – Programa acelerador para aumentar a competitividade do sector alimentar da Galiza-Norte de Portugal".

REFERENCES

Al-Samarraie, H., Teng, B., Alzahrani,A. & Alalwan, N., 2018. E-learning continuance satisfaction in higher education: a unified perspective from instructors and students. *Studies in Higher Education*, Vol 43, Nº 11, pp 2003-2019

Araújo, I., 2014, *Aprendizagem matemática no ensino superior: a influência da plataforma M@t-educar com sucesso.* Tese de doutoramento. Aveiro: Universidade de Aveiro

Araújo, I. & Faria, P. M., 2019. Potentialities of Using an Online Platform to Learn Mathematics in Engineering. *In Proceedings of International Symposium on Project Approaches in Engineering Education: Preparing Teachers and Students for Challenging Times in Engineering Education / 16th Active Learning in Engineering Education Workshop - PAEE/ALE'2019*, pp 268-275.

Bangor A, Kortum P, Miller, J., 2009. Determining what individual SUS scores mean: adding an adjective rating scale. Journal of Usability Studies, Vol l4, Nº 3, pp 114-123.

Brooke J., 1986. *SUS - A quick and dirty usability scale.* 1986. Disponível em https://hell.meiert.org/core/pdf/sus.pdf

Cidral, W., Oliveira, T., Felice, M. & Aparicio, M., 2018. E-learning success determinants: Brazilian empirical study. Computers & Education, Vol 122, pp 271-290.

Coutinho, C., & Bottentuit Junior, J., 2007. Utilização da Plataforma Blackboard num Curso de Pós-Graduação da Universidade do Minho. In Dias, P., Freitas, C.V., Silva, B., Osósio, A., & Ramos, A. (orgs.), *Actas da V Conferência Internacional de Tecnologias de Informação e Comunicação na Educação: Desafios 2007/ Challenges 2007.* pp. 305-313.

Daniela, L., Strods, R. & Kalniņa, D., 2019. Technology-Enhanced Learning (TEL) in Higher Education: Where Are We Now? In M. Lytras, L. Daniela, A. Visvizi (Eds.), *Knowledge-Intensive Economies and Opportunities for Social, Organizational, and Technological Growth*, pp 12-24.

Dias, P., 2004. Processos de Aprendizagem Colaborativa nas Comunidades Online. In Dias, A., & Gomes, M. (2004), *E-Learning para E-formadores*. TecMinho/Gabinete de Formação Contínua da Universidade do Minho, 19-31.

Dias, S., & Diniz, J., 2010. Um estudo de caso no ensino superior – Avaliação de uma plataforma Moodle. *Sistemas, Cibernética e Informática: CISCI 2010.* Florida. Disponível em https://www.iiis.org/CDs2010/CD2010CSC/CISCI_2010/PapersPdf/CA267FV.pdf

Junior, B., & Coutinho, C., 2010. Recomendações para Produção de Podcasts e vantagens na utilização em Ambientes Virtuais de Aprendizagem. *Revista Prisma.com*. Vol. 6, 125-140.

Lbo, A. & Maia, L., 2015. O uso das TICs como ferramenta de ensino-aprendizagem no Ensino Superior. *Caderno de Geografia*, Vol 25, Nº 44, pp 16-26.

MARCHIORI, L., MELO, W. & MELO, J., 2011. Avaliação docente em relação às novas tecnologias para a didática e atenção no ensino superior. Avaliação: Revista da Avaliação da Educação Superior, Vol. 16, Nº 2, pp 433-443.

Moran, J., Masetto, M., Behrens, M., 2007. *Novas tecnologias e mediações pedagógicas*. 13ª. ed. São Paulo: Papirus.

Nielsen, J., 2012. *Usability 101: Introduction to usability*. Disponível em https://www.nngroup.com/articles/usability-101-introduction-to-usability/

Nortvig, A., Petersen, A. & Balle, S., 2018, A Literature Review of the Factors Influencing E-Learning and Blended Learning in Relation to Learning Outcome, Student Satisfaction and Engagement. *Electronic Journal of e-Learning*, Vol 16, Nº 1, pp 46-55.

O,Donnell, E. & Sharp, M., 2012, Students' Views of E-Learning: The Impact of Technologies on Learning in Higher Education in Ireland. In Moyle, K. & Wijngaards, G., *Student Reactions to Learning with Technologies: Perceptions and Outcomes*, pp 204-225.

Ribeiro, J., 2010. *Ambientes Virtuais de Aprendizagem no ensino superior: um estudo de caso sobre a utilização da plataforma Moodle*. Disponível em http://www.fatecjp.com.br/revista/art-ed02-009.pdf

Ribeiro, N., 2012. *Multimédia e tecnologias interativas* (5ª ed.). Lisboa, Portugal: FCA

Trinder, K., Guiller, J., Margaryn, A., Littlejohn, A. & Nicol, D., 2008. *Learning from digital natives: Bridging formal and informal learning*. Higher Education Academy.

DIGITAL LITERACY ASSESSMENT OF UNDERGRADUATE STUDENTS FROM PHYSICAL EDUCATION PROGRAM OF THAILAND NATIONAL SPORTS UNIVERSITY

Narumon Rodniam
Faculty of Education, Thailand National Sports University, Chumphon Campus, Thailand

ABSTRACT

The purposes of this research were to 1) assess levels of digital literacy of undergraduate students from Physical Education Program of Thailand National Sports University (TNSU); and 2) compare digital literacy levels of the students with consideration on the variables of sex and class level. Using a quantitative research method, the sample of this study consisted of 400 undergraduate students from Physical Education Program, Faculty of Education, TNSU, who were studying in their first semester of the academic year 2019. It was obtained via a multistage random sampling technique. The data collection tool was the Digital Literacy Assessment for Undergraduate Students of Wawta Techataweewan and Ujsara Prasertsin (2016), which contains four components for a total of 54 questions. The data analysis was relied on descriptive statistics and multiple techniques, including independent-samples t-test, one-way ANOVA, and post-hoc comparison with Scheffe's method. The results revealed that: 1) the undergraduate students from the Physical Education Program of TNSU had a high level of overall digital literacy, 2) the female students had significantly higher digital literacy than males, and 3) the students in the 5th class level had higher digital literacy than those in the first-class level significantly at the significance level of .05. However, no significant differences among other class levels were discovered.

KEYWORDS

Digital Literacy, Undergraduates, Thailand National Sports University

1. INTRODUCTION

At present, the Internet and digital technology have become an infrastructure for daily living of many people. Therefore, it is necessary for people in society to have skills and knowledge in digital technology in order to gain access to contents, communications, and data processing in various forms via critical and moral thinking to enhance the capacity of individuals in using media and digital technology for utmost benefits. As a result, digital literacy has been specified as an essential learning skill of citizens in the 21st century.

Newman. (2012) has defined that digital literacy refers to abilities in terms of awareness and technical skills in using information and communication technologies for retrieving, assessing, creating, and communicating information as intended. Similarly, Cornell University (2009) defines digital literacy as an ability to retrieve, assess, utilize, share, and create content based on information technology and the Internet. In their case, students of Cornell University had to be able to write a report, create and make presentation with multimedia, and post information related to oneself or others on the Internet. All of these requirements involve common activities that the students practice daily. Bawden (2008) defined that digital literacy refers to literacy in computer and Information and Communication Technology (ICT) that enables the person to read, understand, create, communicate, assess, and recreate knowledge from digital information based on good attitudes toward learning and using digital media morally and responsibly. It can therefore be seen that digital literacy does not involve only with ICT skills, but also other aspects of skills namely: 1) cognitive skills, which require knowledge and understanding; 2) motor skills, which are important when doing operations related directly and indirectly to technologies; 3) social skills, which guide good practices such as being a good citizen of the society who always regard impact on the community and overall people; and

4) emotion skills, which enable the person to manage one's own emotion and be aware of effects on interpersonal relationship. (Stepić, Gordana, 2013).

The fast-growing number of digital learning media leads to an enormous learning source being closest to the learners. (Simpson&Obdalova, Olga, 2014). Consequently, digital technology has played a more significant role in education. Students in education programs and young-generation teachers should acquire skills and capacities in digital literacy to promote learners to learn better within the digital environment and to manage digital classrooms more smoothly and efficiently. (Krumsvik, 2008, Maderick, Zhang, Hartley, & Marchand, 2015).

From investigating literature related to the digital literacy of Thai students within the past five years, researches on this topic are quite limited. In the case of Thailand National Sports University (TNSU), no research has been found so far to conduct on assessing the digital literacy of students. However, as research from Asri Saidi, Sittisak Boonhan, and Jitratda Thamathes (2019) found that keeping media, information, and digital literacy is one of the competencies of physical education teachers in the 21st century. For this reason, to prepare physical education teachers in the 21st century, the researcher finds that it is essential to study and assess the digital literacy levels as a whole and also for each component of the digital literacy of Physical Education students inTNSU. The digital literacy levels should also be assessed to compare between students of different sexes, and class levels, which had hypotheses were students of different sexes (No.1), and class levels (No.2) have different levels of digital literacy—this study to reveal strengths and weaknesses in the digital literacy skills of the students. The findings are expected to provide useful information for planning, supporting, promoting, and developing learners in response to the ongoing progress of digital technology.

2. METHODOLOGY

A quantitative research method was employed for this study. The sample consisted of 400 undergraduate students of Physical Education Program of TNSU who were studying in their first semester of academic year 2019. Applying a multi-stage sampling technique, the sample was acquired through 2 stages.

Stage 1: the randomization was made according to regions (Northern, North-eastern, Central, and Southern regions) so that two campuses were selected for each region. The derived 8 campuses consisted of Sukhothai Campus, Lampang Campus, Bangkok Campus, Samutsakhon Campus, Udonthani Campus, Mahasarakham Campus, Chumphon Campus, and Krabi Campus.

Stage 2: stratified random sampling was applied to obtain samples throughout all 5 class levels. This stage yielded 93 students from class level 1, 89 students from class level 2, 76 students from class level 3, 71 students from class level 4, and 70 students from class level 5. After that, the proportion of students from each of the eight campuses as determined in Stage 1 was specified.

The tool used for assessing the digital literacy of Thai undergraduate students in this study is the assessment developed by Wawta Techataweewan and Ujsara Prasertsi. (2016). (This 5-level rating scale assessment contains 54 questions that cover 4 components of digital literacy, namely operation skills, thinking skills, collaboration skills, and awareness skills. It is showed at https://forms.gle/YjybFRnhJnCPy38E7) The reliability value of the whole questionnaire was determined using Cronbach's Alpha coefficient, and was found to be equal to 0.91.

The data were collected by allowing the sample to complete the questionnaire either in the campus's computer laboratory or via their smartphones during July 22nd to August 22nd, 2019. After finishing the data collection process, the research checked for accuracy and completeness of answers in all questionnaires. Data analyses were then conducted by initially finding descriptive statistics, namely means and standard deviations. Next, the difference in the mean values of the digital literacy of students with different sexes was tested by means of Independent-samples t-test at the significance level of .05. Digital literacy levels of students in different class levels were then analyzed using an F-test in One-Way ANOVA, followed by post-hoc comparison with Scheffe's method. Subsequently, the results were interpreted by relying on the mean-value criteria according to the concept of Best (Best. 1970) as follows: 4.50 - 5.00 = highest, 3.50 - 4.49 = high, 2.50 - 3.49 = moderate, 1.50 - 2.49 = low, and 1.00 - 1.49 = lowest levels.

3. RESULTS

This research received answers from a total of 400 students who are mostly males (68.25%). Categorized by class levels, most of the responders were first-year students (23.30%), followed by second-year students (22.50%), and third-year students (19.00%). The research results were obtained as follows.

3.1 Results of the Analysis on Digital Literacy Level of the Undergraduate Students

The undergraduate students from Physical Education Program of TNSU had overall digital literacy at a high level. Considering at each component, there was only one aspect that their digital literacy was at a moderate level, which is the operation skills aspect. The remaining aspects were at a high level. Ranked by their mean values, these aspects are awareness skills, collaboration skills, and thinking skills, respectively. Detailed results for each component can be described below.

1) For the awareness skills, all indicators were found to be at a high level, with 'Self-defense' having the highest mean, followed by 'Morality.' 'Law awareness' was the indicator that received the lowest mean value.

2) For the collaboration skills, two indicators were found to be at a high level. 'Teamwork' was the indicator with the highest mean, followed by 'Networking.' The indicator 'Sharing' was at a moderate level.

3) For the thinking skills, all indicators were at a high level. 'Creative thinking' had the highest mean, followed by 'Assessment ability,' while 'Analysis ability' had the lowest mean.

4) For the operation skills, only one indicator, i.e., 'Cognitive domain,' was at a high level. All other indicators were at a moderate level. Ranked by mean values, they are 'Presentation' and 'Invention,' respectively. As shown in Table 1.

3.2 The Results from Comparing Digital Literacy Levels of the Undergraduate Students by Considering Sex and Class Level as Variables

1) For the variable of sex, it was found that the undergraduate students from Physical Education Program of TNSU with different sexes had significantly different levels of digital literacy. This finding corresponds with the Research Hypothesis No. 1, as female students had significantly higher digital literacy than males. Considering at each component, the comparison tests revealed that the undergraduate students from Physical Education Program of TNSU with different sexes had different levels of digital literacy in two components namely the collaboration skills and the awareness skills, with the female students having higher digital literacy levels than the males at the significance level of .05. However, for the operation skills and the thinking skills, both sexes did not have significant difference in their literacy. As shown in Table 2

2) For the variable of class level, it was found that the undergraduate students from Physical Education Program of TNSU who studied in different class levels had different levels of digital literacy, which is in according with the Research Hypothesis No.2. Based on the post-hoc comparison between each pair, the fifth-year students had higher digital literacy than the first-year students, at the significance level of 0.5, while other pairs expressed no significant differences. Considering at each component, the analysis results revealed that the undergraduate students from Physical Education Program of TNSU of different class levels had different digital literacy levels in two components namely the operation skills and the thinking skills. For the operation skills, the fourth-year students had higher skills than the first-year students, at the significance level of .05. In case of the thinking skills, the fifth-year students had higher thinking skills than the first-year students, at the significance level of .01. However, for the collaboration skills and the awareness skills, students of all class levels showed no differences in their literacy.

4. DISSCUSSION

1. The undergraduate students from Physical Education Program of TNSU had overall digital literacy in a high level. This is likely to be because the sampled students were born during the years 1996-2000, which makes them be considered as the new generation or Gen Z citizens. Being born in the digital era, they are

naturally accustomed and have expertise in using digital technology. (Greedisgoods, 2018; Sarunjade, 2016) That explains why their overall digital literacy is at a high level. Simultaneously, digital technology has been utilized widely, with communication infrastructure being expanded to cover the whole country. The subsequent higher stability and cheaper price of high-speed broadband communication promotes higher use of the internet. (Ministry of Information and Communication Technology, 2015). In addition, the policy to develop quality and standard of education as specified in the National Education Act, B.E. 2542, and its revision B.E. 2545 requires that all universities must manage education according to the Thai Qualifications Framework for Higher Education, The standard No. 5 concerning the digital analysis, communication, and IT skills (Wicharn Panich, 2009), specifies that there must be utilization of information technology and integrated communication skills in education. Moreover, TNSU has supported education in a form of integrated learning by establishing online education and using multimedia in the teaching with integration of digital technology into various courses. The research result is in agreement with the result of Wawta Techataweewan and Ujsara Prasertsin (2016) whose study revealed that the undergraduate students in Bangkok and vicinity had a high level of digital literacy. Similarly, Ng. (2012) and Shopova. (2014) also found that the sampled students had a high level ofdigital literacy. However, the result is incompatible with those of Bullen; Morgan;& Qayyum. (2011), Dornaleteche-Ruiz; Buitrago-Alonso; & Moreno-Cardenal. (2015) and Ting. (2015) whose studies were conducted with students in multiple countries and found the levels of digital literacy to range from a moderate level to a basic level. This contrary might be due to differences in the applied assessments and the technological environments of each country.

2. The undergraduate students from Physical Education Program of TNSU had the highest mean value of digital literacy in the awareness skills aspect. This is possibly because the government pays attention to and supports digital technology, leading to origination of campaigns to distribute information and examples of wrong doings against the Computer-related Crime Act B.E. 2550 widely via popular social media such as Facebook, Line, Twitter, etc. In addition, the studied group of students belongs to the Physical Education Program, which is a program for professional teacher education and its curriculum demands learning in information technology and morality in using information technology. Therefore, the students are aware of appropriate practices regarding information technology and digital technology. This result also corresponds with the study of Skonwan Paruang (2011) who found that the students of professional teacher education had the highest capacity in the Affective domain. A research of Ozdamar-eskin; Ozata; & Banar (2015) also revealed that the students had the highest levels of digital literacy in 'Safety' and 'Morality', as compared to other aspects.

3. This study found that the undergraduate students from Physical Education Program of TNSU had a moderate level of digital literacy in the aspect of operation skills. This is probably because most of the students used digital technology in a role of end users rather than as an inventor or a presenter. It can be seen from the mean score for each indicator in the operation skills component that the students had a high mean score for the 'Cognitive domain' indicator, but their scores for the 'Invention' and 'Presentation' indicators were at a moderate level. Inventing something from digital technology requires higher knowledge and skills than regular usage of the technology. Presentation also requires application of techniques and designs to attract attention from the audience. Hence, presenters have to know how to use online media properly for their presentation, especially when using multimedia for stimulating interest and enhancing understanding of audience more than using merely text. This research finding is in agreement with the study of Wawta Techataweewan and Ujsara Prasertsin (2016), which found that the undergraduate students in Bangkok and vicinity had a moderate level of digital literacy in terms of operation skills. The research of Ting (2015) also revealed that most students used multimedia technology only at a basic level, and they lacked technical knowledge of advanced multimedia usage. However, this finding disagrees with the studies of Ng. (2012) and Shopova. (2014), which showed that most students had a high level of digital literacy in the technical aspect or ICT aspect. The disagreement could be due to differences in the study areas and the technological environments.

4. The undergraduate students from Physical Education Program of TNSU with different sexes had different levels of digital literacy. Female students were found to have higher digital literacy than males. This finding could be attributed to difference learning between males and females. Likewise, the research of Dornaleteche-Ruiz; Buitrago Alonso; &Moreno-Cardenal. (2015) conducted with Spanish population found that people of different sexes had different levels of digital literacy. The research of Li; & Ranieri. (2010) also revealed that the female Chinese teenagers had higher capacity in digital technology than the male

counterpart. On a contrary, the research of Hall; Nix; & Baker. (2013), conducted with United Kingdom students, found that the male students paid more attention to digital literacy than the females.

5. The undergraduate students from Physical Education Program of TNSU who studied in different class levels were found to have different levels of digital literacy, with the fifth-year students had higher digital literacy than the first-year students, although there was no significant differences between other class levels. This should be because the fifth-year students have learned almost all course contents in the curriculum and are about to perform teaching in an academy outside the university. This makes them have greater maturity and experience for overall digital literacy than the first-year students who have just entered the university and never learned required courses for teacher production. This finding corresponds to those of Li &Ranieri. (2010) who found individuals of different ages to have different levels of digital literacy. However, they found the younger teenagers to have higher digital capacity than the older ones. This is possibly because of difference in the studied populations and the assessments. The digital literacy assessment tool in this study has been designed not only for assessing operation skills but also for awareness skills, thinking skills, and collaboration skills

5. CONCLUSION

As this research found that the undergraduate students from Physical Education Program of TNSU had just a moderate level of digital literacy in the operation skills, strategies should be implemented to improve digital literacy of students in terms of operation skills. The learning management should allow students to play a role of an innovative inventor and/or a presenter based on application of various forms of digital technology. The learning environment should be managed to facilitate digital media usage of all students together. Besides that, the team responsible for developing students in Physical Education Program of TNSU should assess digital literacy skills of first-year students in order to know weaknesses and strengths that are useful for planning to develop them. Teachers and technical supporting personnel of the Faculty or persons responsible for developing students in Physical Education Program of TNSU should receive training to acquire knowledge on digital literacy so that they can understand and apply the knowledge to their teaching and their technical supports. For recommendations for future research, we hope study in factors or requirements for promoting digital literacy to students of Physical Education Program or other programs with similar learning environments should be studied further in order to obtain guidelines for developing appropriate digital literacy to that specific group of students.

ACKNOWLEDGEMENT

I would like to express my gratitude to an anonymous reviewer for their helpful comments. In addition, this research would not be conducted successfully without moral supports from my family and friends. Finally, I would like to send many sincere thanks to the Thailand National Sports University, Chumphon Campus for the research support towards this opportunity.

REFERENCES

Asri Saidi, Sittisak Boonhan, and Jitratda Thamathes, 2019. Competency of PE Teachers in the 21st Century *e-Journal of Education Studies, Burapha University.* (In Thai), Vol.1 No.4, pp. 14-24.

Bawden, D. Origins and Concepts of Digital Literacy, 2008. *In Digital Literacies: Concepts, Policies and Practices.* Ed. C. Lankshear & M. Knobe. Peter Lang, New York, pp. 17-32.

Bullen, Mark; Morgan, Tannis; & Qayyum, Adnan, 2011. Digital Learners in Higher Education: Generation is Not the Issue. *Journal of Learning and Technology.* Vol. 37, No.1, pp. 1-24.

Cornell University. 2009. *What is Digital Literacy?.* [Online]. Available: http://digitalliteracy.cornell.edu/

Dornaleteche-Ruiz, Jon; Buitrago-Alonso, Alejandro; & Moreno-Cardenal, Luisa, 2015. Categorization, Item Selection and Implementation of an Online Digital Literacy Test as Media Literacy Indicator. *Comunicar.* (In Spanish). Vol. 22, No.44, pp.177-185.

Greedisgoods, 2018. *Who is Gen-Z.* (In Thai).[Online]. Available: https://greedisgoods.com/

Hall, Marion; Nix, Ingrid; & Baker, Kirsty, 2013. Student Experiences and Perceptions of Digital Literacy Skills Development: Engaging Learners by Design?. *The Electronic Journal of e-Learning.* Vol. 11, No.3, pp.168-272.

Krumsvik, R. J., 2008. Situated learning and teachers' digital competence. *Education and Information Technologies.* Vol. 13, No. 4, pp. 279-290.

Li, Y., & Ranieri, M, 2010. Are 'digital natives' really digitally competent? A study on Chinese teenagers. *British Journal of Educational Technology*. Vol. 41, No.6, pp.1029-1042.

Maderick, Zhang, Hartley, & Marchand, 2015. Preservice Teachers and Self-Assessing Digital Competence. *Journal of Educational Computing Research*. Vol. 54, No. 3, pp. 4-38.

Ministry of Information and Communication Technology, 2015. *Report of the internet user behavior survey in Thailand.* Bangkok.

Newman B.L, 2012. *Defining Digital Literacy.*Available:http://www.districtdispatch.org/2012/04/defining-digital-literacy.

Ng, Wan, 2012. Can We Teach Digital Natives Digital Literacy?. *Computers & Education*. Vol.59, pp. 65-1078.

Ozdamar-Keskin, Nilgun; Ozata, Fatma Zeynep; & Banar, Kerim, 2015. Examining Digital Literacy Competences and Learning Habits of Open and Distance Learners. *Contemporary Educational Technology.* Vol.6, No.1, pp.74-90.

Sarunjade, 2016. *3 behaviors of "Generation Z"* (In Thai) [Online]. Available: https://www.marketingoops.com/news/-tech-update/3-behaviors

Simpson&Obdalova, Olga, 2014. New Techno-logies in Higher Education-ICT Skills of Digital Literacy? *Procedia-Social and Behavioral Sciences*. Vol.154, pp.104-111.

Skonwan Paruang, 2011. *Development of competency in information and communication technology of students in education education*. Thesis in Political Science Bangkok: Chulalongkorn University. (In Thai)

Shopova, Tatiana, 2014. Digital Literacy of Students and Its Improvement at the University. *Journal on Efficiency and Responsibility in Education and Science*. Vol. 7, No.2, pp. 26-35. Doi: 10.7160/eriesj.2014.070201.

Stepić, Gordana, 2013. Possibilities for the Development of Digital Literacy of the Junior Grades Students of Primary School. *Proceedings of eLearning and Software for Education*, pp.368-375.

Ting, Yu-Liang, 2015. Tapping into Students' Digital Literacy and Designing Negotiated Learning to Promote Learner Autonomy. *Internet and Higher Education.* Vol. 26, pp.25-32.

Wawta Techataweewan, & ujsara Prasertsin, 2016. *Development of digital literacy test for undergraduate students.* (In Thai). Department of Library and Information Science Faculty of Humanities Srinakharinwirot University.

Wawta Techataweewan, & Ujsara Prasertsin, 2016. Digital Literacy Skills For Developing Learning Ability of Undergraduate Students: A Qualitative Interview Approach. *Proceedings of 53rd ISERD International Conference.* Zurich, Switzerland, 30th-31st October 2016.

Wicharn Panich, 2009. *TQF* [Online]. Available: http://www.academic.nu.ac.th/

APPENDIX

Table 1. Digital literacy levels of the undergraduate students from Physical Education Program of TNSU

Components of DL	$\bar{X}$	SD	sk	kt	Interpret
Overview DL level	**3.621**	**0.622**	**-0.508**	**0.273**	**High**
1.Operation skills	**3.312**	**0.732**	**-0.225**	**-0.285**	**moderate**
Cognitive domain	3.586	0.686	-0.424	0.288	High
Invention	2.955	0.946	-0.154	-0.632	moderate
Presentation	3.396	0.835	-0.270	-0.414	moderate
2.Thinking skills	**3.677**	**0.695**	**-0.506**	**0.328**	**High**
Analysis ability	3.553	0.822	-0.351	-0.010	High
Assessment ability	3.731	0.776	-0.453	0.249	High
Creative thinking	3.748	0.766	-0.492	0.061	High
3.Collaboration skills	**3.575**	**0.729**	**-0.432**	**0.109**	**High**
Teamwork	3.688	0.747	-0.517	0.298	High
Networking	3.658	0.879	-0.491	-0.035	High
Sharing	3.378	0.873	-0.335	-0.284	moderate

Components of DL	$\bar{X}$	SD	sk	kt	Interpret
Overview	3.575	0.729	-0.432	0.109	High
4.Awareness skills	**3.919**	**0.788**	**-0.778**	**0.141**	**High**
Morality	3.903	0.818	-0.730	0.141	High
Law awareness	3.895	0.927	-1.021	0.669	High
Self-defense	3.960	0.854	-0.743	0.273	High

Table 2. Comparison on digital literacy levels of the undergraduate students from Physical Education Program of TNSU based on the variable of sex, as a whole and separated for each component

DL	Sex	n	$\bar{X}$	SD	df	t
Overview of DL level	Male	273	3.578	0.627	398	-2.020*
	Female	127	3.713	0.604		
1.Operation skills	Male	273	3.289	0.734	398	-0.932
	Female	127	3.362	0.728		
2.Thinking skills	Male	273	3.652	0.696	398	-1.064
	Female	127	3.731	0.691		
3.Collaboration skills	Male	273	3.518	0.727	398	-2.314*
	Female	127	3.698	0.722		
4. Awareness skills	Male	273	3.854	0.787	398	-2.435*
	Female	127	4.059	0.776		

*p<.05

PERSONALIZED FEEDBACKS BASED ON LEARNING ANALYTICS TO ENHANCE THE LEARNING OF PROGRAMMING

Zahi Hodeib and Yvan Peter
Université de Lille, CNRS, UMR 9189, CRIStAL, F-59000 Lille, France

ABSTRACT

This paper presents a new learning environment called Codeclick. The purpose of the environment is to provide personalized feedbacks and recommendations to novices in order to improve their learning of programming. Codeclick uses a Learning Analytics statistical approach based on the learners' digital traces. It also provides visualizations to allow learners to monitor their performance levels and identify their errors. These visualizations also allow the teacher to identify blocking problems and intervene at the appropriate moment. Preliminary results of the design and the use of Codeclick show an improvement in the learners' performance, in terms of the number of errors made, as well as the time spent per activity.

KEYWORDS

Programming, Learning Analytics, Feedbacks, Visualizations, Higher Education

1. INTRODUCTION

Recently, programming courses has become essential in the curriculum of several academic fields. However, their practical learning represents a difficulty for the majority of students, and particularly for novices (Lahtinen et al., 2005). This explains the high failure and dropout rates in introductory to programming courses (Bennedsen and Caspersen, 2007). Among the main reasons, we can mention the large number of learners who are enrolled to these practical activities and the differences in terms of pedagogical capacities and skills between them, which considerably increases the workload of the teachers to ensure a good follow-up (Gulwani et al., 2014). Consequently, these teachers will be unable to support learners by providing personalized feedbacks and recommendations, during these practical activities. However, several studies consider that providing an appropriate feedback to learners at the right moment could be among the best contributors to improving the learning process (Hattie and Timperley, 2007).

On the other hand, several programming learning platforms have been developed in recent years. Some of these educational systems provide the learners with practical programming activities supported by certain forms of feedbacks. However, the quality of the feedbacks delivered by the majority of these systems remains unsatisfactory for the learners (Ferguson, 2011). Actually, these feedbacks suffer from a poor relevance, since they are based on static information about the learning process. Consequently, these feedbacks do not clearly reflect the performance level really achieved by the learners. In addition, they are mainly focused on displaying the errors committed by the learner, in the manner of traditional compilers, whose messages are incomprehensible and do not provide solutions on how to overcome these problems (Keuning et al., 2019). Moreover, the huge amount of information, also called learners' digital traces, resulting from the interaction of the latter with the educational platforms, paved the way for the development of the Learning Analytics (LA) field. LA mainly aims to effectively use these digital traces to improve the learning experience (Pardo et al., 2015). The following section presents an overview of the main works carried out to exploit the learners' digital traces with the aim to support practical learning of programming.

2. RELATED WORK

According to the first international conference on Learning Analytics and Knowledge (LAK11), LA was defined as the measurement, collection, analysis and reporting of data about learners and their contexts, for purposes of understanding and optimizing learning and the environment in which it occurs (Siemens and Long, 2011). In other words, LA aims to use the learners' digital traces to provide teachers and institutions with capabilities allowing them to follow the progress of their students, identify the main causes of failure, intervene with personalized feedbacks and making decisions to adapt their teaching methods (Villamañe et al., 2018). Referring to the literature, the main approaches used by LA, namely, prediction, visualizations via Learning Analytics Dashboards (LAD) and statistical techniques, to assess learners' performance and consequently provide feedbacks and recommendations to assist them (Nunn et al., 2016). Several Intelligent Tutoring Systems (ITS), Intelligent Laboratories, tools and web applications have been developed to assist learners or teachers. Table 1 presents and compares some of these technologies, by focusing mainly on the types of feedbacks and recommendations delivered and the kind of data collected and used to generate them.

Table 1. Works offering feedbacks based on learners' digital traces

Technologies	Publications	Feedbacks and Recommendations	Digital Traces
Web Applications	WebToTeach (Arnow and Barshay, 1999)	Alerts and Messages	Code
	Data2U (Khan and Pardo, 2016)	Dashboards	Interactions
Tools	Retina (Murphy et al., 2009)	Recommendations Reports	Time and Errors
	Ontask (Pardo et al., 2018)	Personalized Messages	Interactions
	Course Signal (Arnold and Pistilli, 2012)	Personalized Emails	Histories, Grades, Interactions
Intelligent Laboratories	Smart Lab (Alammary et al., 2012)	Personalized Visualizations	Interactions
	Lab4CE (Broisin et al., 2017)	Messages, Visualizations	Code, Interactions

Generally, these systems collect different information and traces about the learners (Code, Interactions, Number of clicks, Screenshots and Time spent per task). However, numerous of these systems provide inadequate feedbacks and do not take into account the real and personalized needs of each learner, especially their current profile and knowledge. Therefore, the learner finds himself overwhelmed by the enormous amount of inconsistent and incomprehensible feedbacks received and remains blocked in his activity. Moreover, some researchers have noticed that many learners cannot even understand certain feedbacks, or even the results provided by the LAD, therefore these latter will have no impact on the learners' performance. Rather, they could have negative psychological effects on some of them (Corrin and de Barba, 2015). In this paper, we present a new learning environment called Codeclick, relying on a LA approach, to allow novices to practice programming, supported by personalized feedbacks and recommendations, but also visualizations illustrating their performance levels and errors.

3. CONTRIBUTION

Codeclick is a programming learning environment offering practical activities intended for novices and their teachers. It was developed on the WAMP server using PHP with JavaScript and uses a MySQL database. Codeclick allows the learners to practice programming activities in two modes: Feedback mode (F) or Without Feedback mode (WF). The F mode provides personalized feedback to learner on code errors and recommendations on how to overcome them. Codeclick collects and analyzes the learners' digital traces (Codes, Number of clicks, Time spent by activity), classifies and stores them in a database. These digital traces are then used as indicators within a statistical analysis phase, to calculate the performance of each learner according to equation (1) and consequently generate feedbacks and visualizations illustrating this level of performance and the problems encountered during these activities. These visualizations allow the learner to understand the reasons of his weakness and compare himself to his colleagues. Also, they allow the teacher to identify the main causes of errors and the level of performance of each learner, which allows him to intervene and support the latter at the appropriate moment.

$$P = 100 - 2.5 * NC - 3 * NE - T \qquad (1)$$

Given
NC: Number of clicks
NE: Number of Errors
T: Time in minutes/Activity

In this equation, the performance of each learner is directly associated to three dynamic indicators collected from the activity done by the learner, namely the Number of Errors (NE), Number of Clicks (NC) and the time spent per activity (T). We affected a weight to each indicator according to its significance in the completion of the activity. Therefore, the NE is assigned the highest weight since it is the most significant indicator followed by NC and finally the time per activity. Each user login to Codeclick using a username and a password and accesses his own session, which records the date and time of the access. Different forms of activities have been integrated (fill the gaps, puzzles, select list). Codeclick was inspired from the works of (Alammary et al., 2012), (Arnold and Pistilli, 2012) and (Murphy et al., 2009). The Figure 1 shows the architecture of Codeclick.

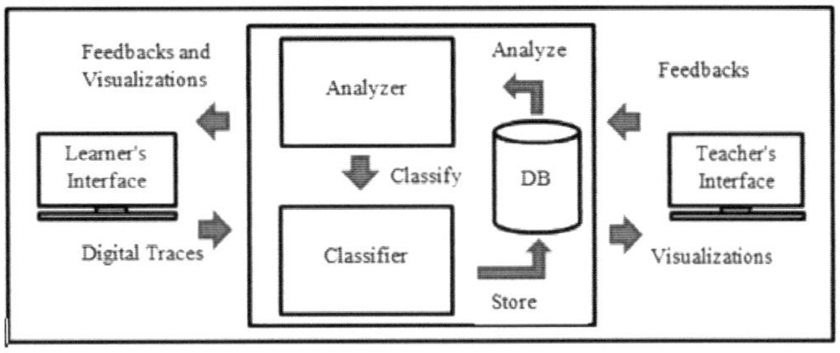

Figure 1. Codeclick architecture

4. EXPERIMENT AND PRELIMINARY RESULTS

In order to evaluate Codeclick, we conducted a preliminary experiment on two groups composed each by seven learners and for the same activity (the variables in Java). The learners were only boys with an average age of 19 years. The first group G1 used the F mode and the group G2 used the WF mode. Our goal was to assess the learners' performance level, to do this we relied on statistics based on the digital traces collected and recorded, more precisely indicators like the time spent per exercise, the number of clicks on the button validation (represent the number of errors), but also the number of clicks on the help button. These statistics are then used to generate personalized feedbacks and visualizations. Preliminary results of the experiment show that learners of the G1 achieved more satisfactory performance levels than those of the G2 in terms of errors made and time spent per exercise, thanks to the formative feedbacks and recommendations generated (see Fig. 2 and Fig.3). Furthermore, we noticed a correlation between the time spent per exercise, the number of errors made and the number of clicks on the help button. The Fig.4 depicts a feedback generated on error detection.

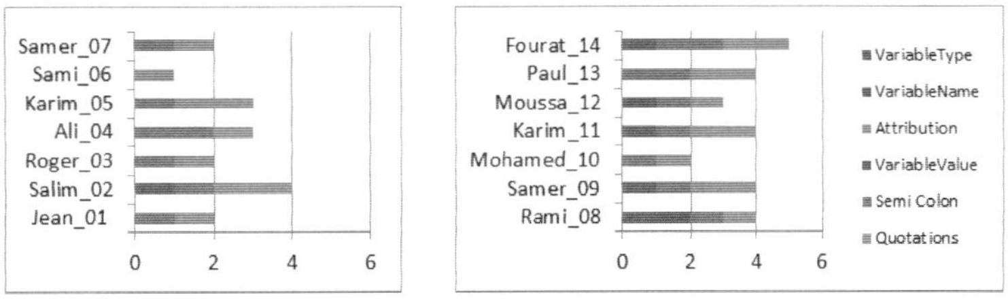

Figure 2. Visualizations representing the number and types of errors within groups G1 and G2 respectively in the activity the variables

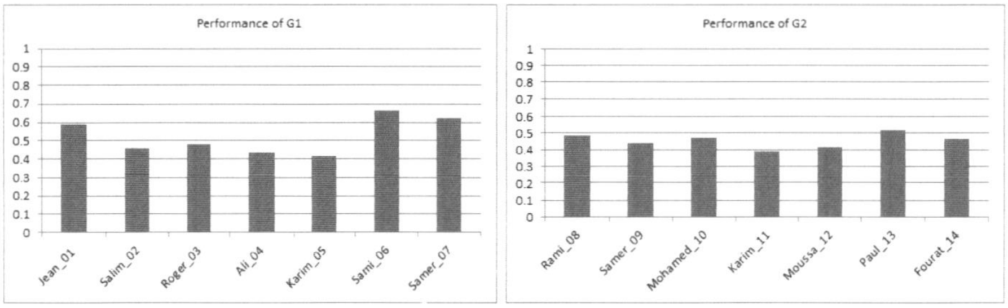

Figure 3. Visualizations representing the performance of G1 and G2 according to equation (1)

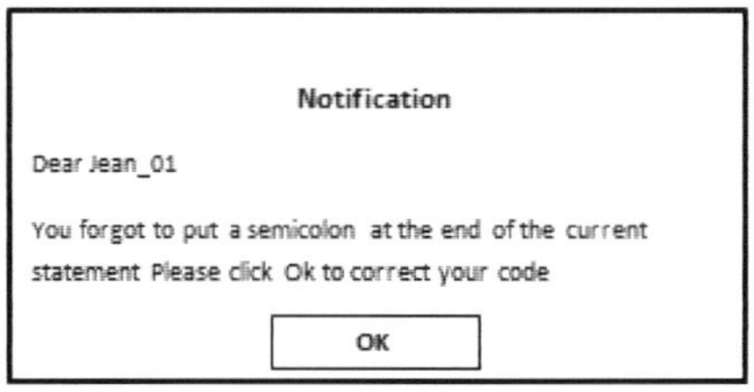

Figure 4. Example of feedback delivered on error detection

5. CONCLUSION

Practical learning of programming can be improved by performing appropriate activities, supported by a personalized feedback mechanism based on the learners' digital traces. In this article, we introduce a new programming learning environment called Codeclick, capable to analyze the learners' digital traces and provide personalized feedbacks and recommendations to support them. Codeclick uses a LA statistical approach based on indicators to assess the learners' performance level and provides feedbacks and visualizations to both learners and teachers. We have evaluated and compared the learners' performance levels within two groups that used Codeclick in both F and WF modes. Preliminary result shows that the learners within G1 privileged by feedbacks achieve more satisfactory performance levels in terms of number of errors and spend less time on exercises. Moreover they rarely use the help button. In future work we aim to validate the results on large scale groups and improve the analysis phase of Codeclick to support more complex programming activities while exploring other performance indicators.

REFERENCES

Alammary, A., Carbone, A., Sheard, J., 2012. Implementation of a Smart Lab for Teachers of Novice Programmers 123, 10.

Arnold, K.E., Pistilli, M.D., 2012. Course signals at Purdue: using learning analytics to increase student success, in: Proceedings of the 2nd International Conference on Learning Analytics and Knowledge - LAK '12. Presented at the the 2nd International Conference, ACM Press, Vancouver, British Columbia, Canada, p. 267.

Arnow, D., Barshay, O., 1999. WebToTeach: an interactive focused programming exercise system, in: FIE'99 Frontiers in Education. 29th Annual Frontiers in Education Conference. Designing the Future of Science and Engineering Education. Conference Proceedings

Bennedsen, J., Caspersen, M.E., 2007. Failure Rates in Introductory Programming. SIGCSE Bull. 39, 32–36.

Broisin, J., Venant, R., Vidal, P., 2017. Lab4CE: A Remote Laboratory for Computer Education. International Journal of Artificial Intelligence in Education 27, 154–180.

Corrin, L., de Barba, P., 2015. How Do Students Interpret Feedback Delivered via Dashboards?, in: Proceedings of the Fifth International Conference on Learning Analytics And Knowledge, LAK '15. ACM, New York, NY, USA, pp. 430–431.

Ferguson, P., 2011. Student perceptions of quality feedback in teacher education. Assessment & Evaluation in Higher Education 36, 51–62.

Gulwani, S., Radiček, I., Zuleger, F., 2014. Feedback Generation for Performance Problems in Introductory Programming Assignments, in: Proceedings of the 22Nd ACM SIGSOFT International Symposium on Foundations of Software Engineering, FSE 2014. ACM, New York, NY, USA, pp. 41–51.

Hattie, J., Timperley, H., 2007. The Power of Feedback. Review of Educational Research 77, 81–112.

Keuning, H., Jeuring, J., Heeren, B., 2019. A systematic literature review of automated feedback generation for programming exercises. ACM Transactions on Computing Education (TOCE) 19, 3.

Khan, I., Pardo, A., 2016. Data2U: scalable real time student feedback in active learning environments. pp. 249–253.

Lahtinen, E., Ala-Mutka, K., Järvinen, H.-M., 2005. A Study of the Difficulties of Novice Programmers, in: Proceedings of the 10th Annual SIGCSE Conference on Innovation and Technology in Computer Science Education, ITiCSE '05. ACM, New York, NY, USA, pp. 14–18.

Murphy, C., Kaiser, G., Loveland, K., Hasan, S., 2009. Retina: Helping students and instructors based on observed programming activities. Presented at the ACM Sigcse Bulletin, pp. 178–182.

Nunn, S., Avella, J.T., Kanai, T., Kebritchi, M., 2016. Learning Analytics Methods, Benefits, and Challenges in Higher Education: A Systematic Literature Review. OLJ 20.

Pardo, A., Bartimote-Aufflick, K., Buckingham Shum, S., Dawson, S., Gao, J., Gašević, D., Leichtweis, S., Liu, D., Martinez-Maldonaldo, R., Mirriahi, N., Moskal, A.C.M., Schulte, J., Siemens, G., Vigentini, L., 2018. OnTask: Delivering Data-Informed, Personalized Learning Support Actions. JLA 5, 235–249.

Pardo, A., Dawson, S., Dawson, S., 2015. Learning Analytics: How Can Data Be Used to Improve Learning Practice? [WWW Document]. Measuring and Visualizing Learning in the Information-Rich Classroom.

Siemens, G., Long, P., 2011. Penetrating the Fog: Analytics in Learning and Education. EDUCAUSE Review 5, 30–32.

Villamañe, M., Alvarez, A., Larrañaga, M., 2018. Supporting competence-based learning with visual learning analytics and recommendations, in: 2018 IEEE Global Engineering Education Conference (EDUCON). Presented at the 2018 IEEE Global Engineering Education Conference (EDUCON), pp. 1572–1575.

COMPUTER SIMULATION WITH ARGUMENTATION SCAFFOLDING FOR ELEMENTARY STUDENTS' COLLABORATIVE SCIENTIFIC EXPLANATION

Fan-Jun Yang and Chien-Yuan Su
College of Education, Zhejiang University, Hangzhou, China

ABSTRACT

In elementary science education, it has many potential benefits to engage students in scientific explanations through evaluating claims, evidence and reasonings. This study intends to develop a web-based platform that integrates such functions as science simulation and synchronous online discussion, embedded with argumentation scaffolding, so that elementary students could conduct simulated scientific experiments and construct scientific explanations collaboratively in an interactive online science learning environment. A modified argumentation scaffolding is designed based on Toulmin's framework and applied in this platform, which consists of six components: claim, evidence, reasoning, agreement, query, and rebuttal. Each component contains several semi-structured or structured text templates to provide guidelines for students' online practices in argumentation and explanation. An investigation will be made on whether this platform is useful in supporting students' collaborative construction of scientific explanations in simulated scientific experiments.

KEYWORDS

Scientific Explanation, Scaffolding, Science Simulation, Elementary Students

1. INTRODUCTION

With the speed-up advancement of digital technologies, computer-based simulations have been used as essential learning resources in science education, while abstract concepts or non-observable scientific phenomena could be visualized through simulation, thus rendering science learning more adaptable to learners at diverse cognition levels (Heradio et al., 2016). Moreover, by using simulations for scientific learning, students could enhance their learning engagements, gain a deeper understanding of scientific knowledge, facilitate conceptual conversions, and develop inquiry skills (Chang et al., 2020; Verstege et al., 2019; Wen et al., 2020).

The construction of scientific explanations by students is considered an essential practice that can not only strengthen their understanding of science content, but can also improve their critical thinking and logical reasoning (Beyer and Davis, 2008; McNeill and Krajcik, 2012). As some researchers have argued, however, constructing scientific explanations is a challenging task for younger students, because it entails an intensive integration of claims and evidence in an authentic context, such as argumentation, to make their explanations persuasive to others (Sandoval and Millwood, 2005). In order to enhance students' skills in constructing scientific explanations, certain argumentation frameworks developed from Toulmin's model have been used to facilitate students to make explanations by taking such approaches as sentence openers, graphic organizers or prompts in science writing, oral presentations, and classroom discussions (McNeill and Krajcik, 2012).

Although several studies have been recently made to integrate argumentation scaffoldings with computerized contexts, such as virtual chatrooms or forums, to make students more actively engaged in online argumentation and explanation, these studies usually used general materials in the forms of text, images and videos to develop interactive context and present scientific issues that could stimulate further debate. Further, few studies have attempted to use computer simulations to provide students with scientific learning as well as allow students to perform scientific explanations on specific content. This study will develop an elementary science learning environment integrated with computer-based simulation and design an argumentation scaffolding derived from Toulmin's model, so that elementary students could conduct virtual scientific experiments and carry out collaborative construction of scientific explanations with online peers synchronously in virtual scientific experiments.

2. ARGUMENTATION AND EXPLANATION IN SCIENCE

Explanations are a central artifact of science, and their construction and evaluation entail core scientific practices of argumentation (Sandoval and Millwood, 2005). In scientific communities, in fact, explanations are often questioned, evaluated, and revised through argumentation (Berland and Reiser, 2008). Some researchers have therefore proposed that both opportunities of argumentation and appropriate pedagogical strategies are needed to assist students in constructing scientific explanations and make them more deeply engaged in scientific inquiry (Hsu et al., 2015). One of the widely used pedagogical strategies is to design and apply argumentation scaffoldings derived from Toulmin's Argumentation Pattern (TAP), which holds that an entire argument can be divided into six components: claim, data, warrant, backing, rebuttal, and qualifier. TAP provides guidelines for how to coordinate and organize a scientific explanation (Zembal-Saul, 2009). Based on TAP, McNeill and Krajcik (2012) present a simplified framework for scientific explanation, covering four components: claim, evidence, reasoning, and rebuttal. As shown in Figure 1, the first three components form the content of a complete scientific explanation, so students ought to generate appropriate and sufficient evidence to support their claims and use logical reasoning to strengthen the connections between their claims and evidence. The last component is rebuttals, which connect the other three components to indicate why an alternative explanation cannot appropriately explain the problem.

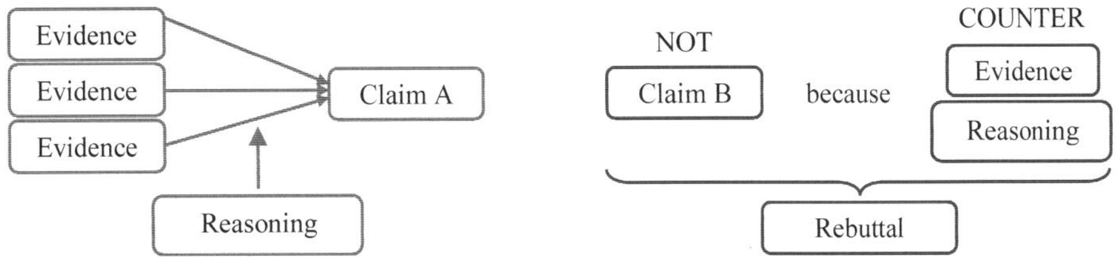

Figure 1. The instructional framework for the scientific explanation (McNeill and Krajcik, 2012)

Numerous studies have applied Toulmin's argument framework in computer-supported learning environments to help students construct arguments or explanations. For instance, Yeh and She (2010) have developed an online synchronous scientific argumentation program, which presents five components of TAP on the webpage, with 3-4 writing frames provided for each component to support students' arguments. Similarly, Yang et al. (2015) have built an Online Synchronous Scientific Inquiry and Argumentation Learning (OSSIAL) environment and designed several scripts or templates to help students compose arguments. Hsu et al. (2015) have also developed an Argumentative Scientific Inquiry System (ASIS) with structured argumentation scaffolding to improve students' skills in constructing scientific explanations. Several prompts and sentence openers are designed and integrated into ASIS by following a framework presented by McNeill and Krajcik (2012). Weng et al. (2017) have designed an online argumentation learning program (OALP) for collaborative group argumentation and provided students with a learning scaffolding consisting of four types of arguments and several writing templates. In general, most of these studies have set up certain forms of argumentation scaffoldings, such as sentence templates, prompts or hints, as an effective way to promote scientific explanation or argumentation in online learning environments.

3. A LEARNING PLATFORM THAT COMBINES SCIENCE SIMULATIONS AND SCIENTIFIC EXPLANATIONS

By employing several mature web technologies, including JavaScript, Socket and AJAX, this study creates an online collaborative learning environment, which can facilitate elementary students' scientific explanation by integrating science simulation and group discussion. As shown in Figure 2, the interface of this platform contains three modules: virtual science simulation, synchronous group discussion, and user-interactive information. Embedded in the first module is one of the Physics Education Technology Project (PhET) simulations, called *Balancing Act*, to support students to conduct virtual physical experiments. By dragging and dropping objects, such as bricks and packages with different weights, students are able to place them on the sides of the rocker and further observe the balance of the rocker, so as to understand the principle of leverage.

Moreover, some questions are set on this subject situation to trigger students to think deeply and encourage them to link up with the scientific explanations. In the module of the synchronous group discussion, students can conduct group scientific explanations after performing individual operations on scientific simulation subjects. A modified argumentation scaffolding is designed to help students construct scientific explanations effectively. When students work with others to construct scientific explanations, the argumentation scaffolding can help students construct claims, evidence and reasonings with various sentence templates. Additionally, students could make different types of responses, such as agreement, query and rebuttal, to any individual message in this discussion context. At the right side of the interface is a user-interactive information module, which shows a list of all online participants and an immediate-updating social network. All interactive actions, such as sending messages or replying to peers, will be visualized in this social network.

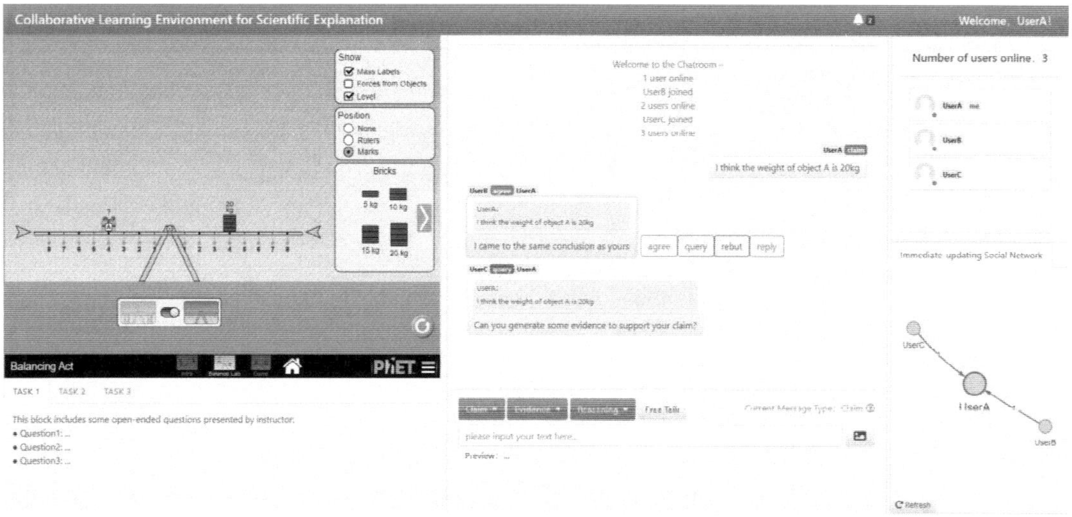

Figure 2. Collaborative learning environment for scientific explanation

4. SCAFFOLDING DESIGN FOR SCIENTIFIC EXPLANATION

In order to help elementary school students construct scientific explanations more effectively, a modified argumentation scaffolding is built into the synchronous group discussion module, which may improve students' interactions by facilitating the explanation construction in synchronous group discussions. As shown in Table 1, the framework of the argumentation scaffolding is divided into two categories according to the users' statements/replies. Students can actively send messages to present their claims, evidence and reasonings in the whole-group interactive context, or they can reply (agree, query and rebut) to specific students' messages.

Table 1. The framework of the modified argumentation scaffolding

Categories	Types	Description
Statement	Claim	A statement or conclusion that answers the original question/problem
	Evidence	Scientific data (such as observations and measurements from experiments) that supports the claim
	Reasoning	A justification that connects the evidence to the claim in scientific principles
Reply	Agreement	A consensus on others' statements
	Query	A question, especially expressing doubts or requesting information
	Rebuttal	A description of views or facts about why an alternative explanation is not appropriate

Figure 3 presents two different ways of using argumentation scaffolding in the platform interface that could facilitate students to interact with other online participants. When making a statement, students can use some dropdown buttons above the input box to designate the claims, evidence or reasonings. Several semi-structured text templates related to each component of scientific explanation are presented to assist students in performing scientific explanation construction. As an alternative, they can just use a blank box to be free to comment. When making a reply, students should first select a message bubble and choose a reply type (agreement/query/rebuttal) before selecting a corresponding text template and sending out a reply to a specific peer's comment. Any message constructed with argumentation scaffolding will be tagged with its type.

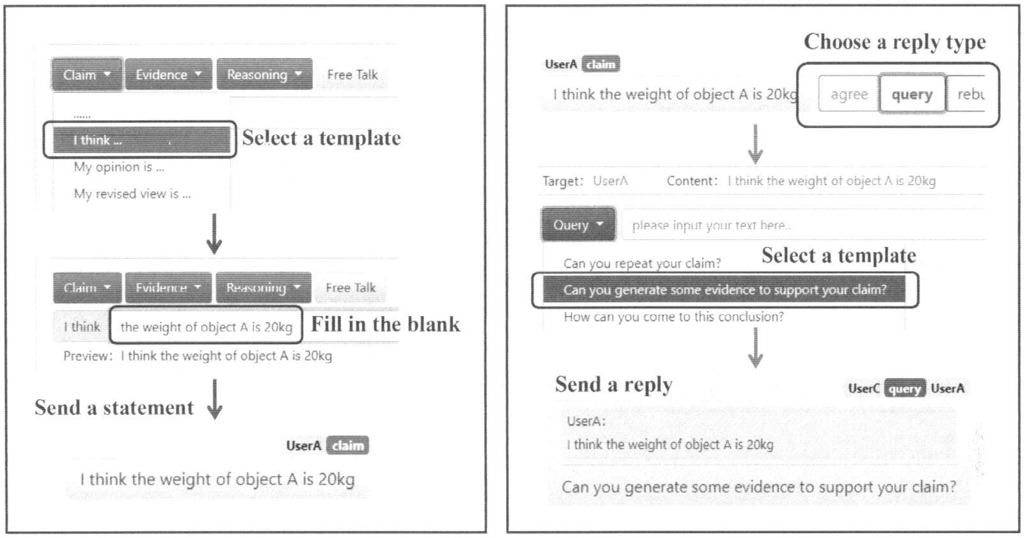

Figure 3. Use the scaffolding to make a statement (left) or reply (right)

In order to promote students' interactions in synchronous group discussions, such as exchanging views through replies, an immediate-updating social network is developed in the user-interactive information module. In JavaScript, the process of interactions is visualized to present a directed network graph, which could be updated whenever a new message is sent to the chatroom, so as to provide an instant overview of the interactions happening in the current group discussion. In the immediate-updating social network, all participants online are initialized as nodes with the same size and color. As the discussion proceeds, the active students, i.e., those who have contributed more replies to exchange views with peers, will be represented with larger pink nodes, indicating that they have actively participated in argumentation and explanation. Moreover, all replies are converted to connections between nodes with frequency tags. Thus, students could get detailed information about the interactions between peers, while reflecting on their self-participation, so as to adjust strategies for the follow-up discussion. This process may promote self-engagement and encourage students to elaborate on their explanations through argumentation.

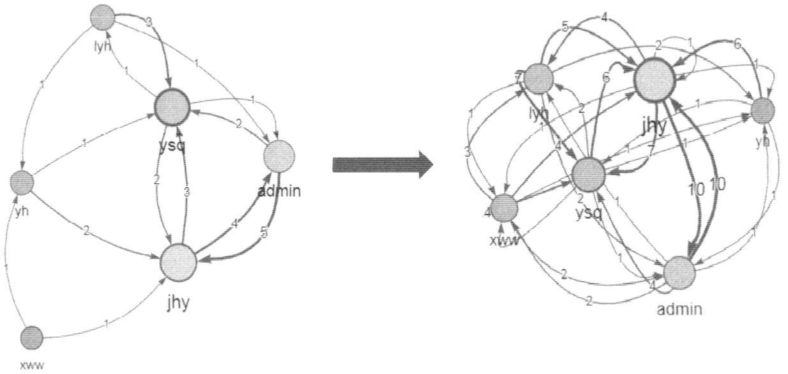

Figure 4. Changes during group discussion in the social network

5. CONCLUSION

This study establishes an online learning environment, in which elementary school students can perform a computer-based simulation to understand science concepts (such as leverage, force and etc.) as well as construct scientific explanations on certain topics in computer simulations together with online peers. This learning platform can deliver the following potential benefits:

Collaborative learning environment: The online platform incorporates computer-based simulations and synchronous group discussions to enhance collaborative science learning, so that students are able to implement a series of science activities in a virtual environment.

Modified argumentation scaffolding: The modified argumentation scaffolding adapted from TAP can boost the ability of the elementary school students to construct scientific explanations.

Immediate-updating social network: The directed network is designed and deployed in our platform to provide a visual presentation of the group interaction process.

Further research is needed to explore the effectiveness of this platform in promoting elementary school students' science learning, and in particular, to test and prove the function of the argumentation scaffolding to support students' collaborative construction of scientific explanations.

REFERENCES

Berland, L. K. and Reiser, B. J., 2008. Making sense of argumentation and explanation. *Science education*, Vol. 93, No. 1, pp. 26-55.

Beyer, C. J. and Davis, E. A., 2008. Fostering Second Graders' Scientific Explanations: A Beginning Elementary Teacher's Knowledge, Beliefs, and Practice. *Journal of the Learning Sciences*, Vol. 17, No. 3, pp. 381-414.

Chang, C. et al, 2020. The impact of light-weight inquiry with computer simulations on science learning in classrooms. *Computers & Education*, Vol. 146, 103770.

Heradio, R. et al, 2016. Virtual and remote labs in education: A bibliometric analysis. *Computers & Education*, Vol. 98, pp. 14-38.

Hsu, C. et al, 2015. Enhancing skill in constructing scientific explanations using a structured argumentation scaffold in scientific inquiry. *Computers & Education*, Vol. 91, pp. 46-59.

McNeill, K. L. and Krajcik, J. S., 2012. *Supporting Grade 5-8 Students in Constructing Explanations in Science: The Claim, Evidence, and Reasoning Framework for Talk and Writing*. Pearson Education, Boston, MA.

Sandoval, W. A. and Millwood, K. A., 2005. The Quality of Students' Use of Evidence in Written Scientific Explanations. *Cognition and Instruction*, Vol. 23, No. 1, pp. 23-55.

Verstege, S. et al, 2019. Relations between students' perceived levels of self-regulation and their corresponding learning behavior and outcomes in a virtual experiment environment. *Computers in Human Behavior*, Vol. 100, pp. 325-334.

Wen, C. et al, 2020. Students' guided inquiry with simulation and its relation to school science achievement and scientific literacy. *Computers & Education*, Vol. 149, 103830.

Weng, W. et al, 2017. Scaffolding for argumentation in hypothetical and theoretical biology concepts. *International Journal of Science Education*, Vol. 39, No. 7, pp. 877-897.

Yang, W. et al, 2015. The Effects of Prior-knowledge and Online Learning Approaches on Students' Inquiry and Argumentation Abilities. *International Journal of Science Education*, Vol. 37, No. 10, pp. 1564-1589.

Yeh, K. H. and She, H. C., 2010. On-line synchronous scientific argumentation learning: Nurturing students' argumentation ability and conceptual change in science context. *Computers & Education*, Vol. 55, No. 2, pp. 586-602.

Zembal-Saul, C., 2009. Learning to teach elementary school science as argument. *Science education*, Vol. 93, No. 4, pp. 687-719.

TEACHING PROGRAMMING SKILLS TO GIRLS

Nataša Hoić-Božić, Martina Holenko Dlab, Ivona Franković, Marina Ivašić-Kos
University of Rijeka, Department of Informatics, Rijeka, Croatia

ABSTRACT

Educational digital games have the potential to motivate students and make complex and abstract topics like programming more appealing. This paper presents an innovative game based learning (GBL) approach, developed within the project Coding4Girls, that aims to prepare and motivate girls for building programming skills. It is based on playing games related to programming concepts, as well as on providing the students with skills and knowledge to design and develop their own games in Snap! visual programming interface.

KEYWORDS

GBL, Coding4Girls Project, Digital Games Project, Visual Programming, Snap!

1. INTRODUCTION

Women represent only the 17% of ICT specialists and the 34% of STEM graduates while UNESCO affirms that less than 30% of researchers worldwide are women (European Commission, 2019). According to the National Center for Education Statistics in the US (Cunningham, Hoyer, & Sparks, 2015), women make up only 18% of university graduates in computer science so it is necessary to try to make computer science and related fields attractive to girls from early age using appropriate approaches such as GBL.

According to (Carmichael, 2008), learning computer science concepts combined with video games is useful, specifically for younger female target group. A conceptual model for gender-based engagement in educational games has been developed (Alserri, Zin, & Wook, 2018), consisting of five elements:

- Learning elements that distinguish entertainment games from educational games;
- Female preferences for digital games that consist of exploration, character customization, storyline, social interaction, collaboration, challenges, fun, control and feedback;
- Flow state theory elements: challenges, fun, control, feedback, concentration, clear goals, skill and immersion;
- Female game types and genres: fantasy and role-playing games;
- Social gender factors: parental, peers and teacher influence.

Computer games can be used to teach coding not only by allowing the students to play serious games that include learning outcomes related to programming, but also by teaching students to develop and create their own basic games through visual programming languages or block-based environments for teaching programming (Kazimoglu et al., 2012). Examples of some popular visual programming languages are: Scratch ("Scratch," 2020), Snap! ("Snap!," 2020), and Alice ("Alice," 2020).

This paper presents an innovative approach for building programming skills, developed within the project Coding4Girls, that aims to prepare and motivate girls and boys to enter computer science careers by pointing out the possible application of programming knowledge in solving real-life problems.

2. CODING4GIRLS PROJECT

The Coding4Girls (C4G) project (www.coding4girls.eu) is an ongoing project funded by the Erasmus+ Programme that aims to address the gap between male and female participation in computer science education and careers by introducing early methodological learning interventions that make computer science attractive to all, girls and boys. The main goal is to attract girls by raising their awareness on the wide array of possibilities for professional and personal growth that computer science offers. The project started in September 2018 and lasts until August 2020. The project coordinator is the University of Ljubljana (Slovenia) and partners are universities and institutions from Portugal, Greece, Bulgaria, Italy, Turkey, and Croatia ("Coding4Girls web site", 2018).

Coding4Girls aims to develop innovative methodological learning framework for building programming skills and introduces innovation in several different aspects: into a pedagogical approach, into the field of technology use, and at the level of learning interventions. In terms of pedagogical approach, the project will introduce design thinking that encourages students to think entrepreneurially about how computer science and ICT can solve real-world problems (Wrigley & Straker, 2017). At the technology-based learning level, Coding4Girls will validate the proposed design thinking pedagogical approach through the development and implementation of didactic games (Backlund & Hendrix, 2013). At the learning intervention level, Coding4Girls will promote active learning through game-based learning (GBL) and link specific learning objectives to scenarios that promote critical thinking as an integral part of programming.

3. APPROACH TO TEACHING PROGRAMMING TO GIRLS USING GBL

The C4G approach to teaching programming is based on the GBL. It is not just about playing games related to programming concepts, but also providing the girls with skills and knowledge to design and develop their own games taking a constructive approach to learning.

In the context of C4G project, playing video games is combined with games development in order to develop a GBL methodological framework for building programming skills among young people in primary and secondary education. The methodology encourages participation in programming activities through a "low entry high ceiling approach" that has low knowledge requirements in the beginning while not limiting problem-solving challenges for more advanced students. Students are provided with "half baked" scenarios of simple games in block-based visual programming environment Snap! and encouraged to finish partially completed solutions by building blocks of code. Snap! scenarios are included in the Coding4Girls adventure game for learning basic programming concepts. This game is a part of C4G software designed for the learners. The second part of the software is the teacher's platform.

3.1 Coding4Girls Software

C4G software for the learning environment consists of two interconnected parts or platforms, one for teachers and one for students.

The platform for students includes a 3D single player first person adventure game. The game is developed in Unity and includes various logical games or mini-games such as puzzles, mazes and other problem-solving mini-games that are chosen to be attractive to girls.

Teachers are using web-based platform for creating the courses implemented into the C4G game. Those courses are functioning as a grouping space for connected activities called "challenges" or chapters of the game which are related to programming concepts such as variables, loops, conditionals, etc. At the beginning of each "challenge", a task related to a concept is displayed to students. Students play different types of mini-games to reach the final challenge where they need to solve the Snap! assignment. The goal of mini-games is to entertain and motivate the players, but also to introduce new programming concepts more easily. It is expected that Snap! coding environment will help students to use and apply these concepts (Franković, Hoić-Božić, Holenko Dlab, & Ivašić-Kos, 2019).

3.2 Design of Coding4Girls GBL Scenarios for Teachers

In order to help teachers integrating the C4G approach into the courses for the game as well as to include Snap! activities in their teaching practices, learning scenarios have been prepared and adapted to the design thinking approach and the structure of the C4G software. The focus is on the identified characteristics of games preferred by girls but also on the activities related to the real-world problems. In that way the games are suitable for building programming skills for both girls and boys.

The prepared learning scenarios present in concise manner the following information:

- Learning scenario title
- Required programming experience
- Expected learning outcomes
- Aim, tasks and short description of activities
- Duration of activities
- Learning and teaching strategies and methods
- Teaching forms
- Step-by-step description of all Coding4Girls game design based learning activities
- Questions for initiating discussion among learners in the context of class collaboration
- Assessment methods for evaluating the knowledge and skills
- Tools and resources for the teacher and students.

A total of 21 learning scenarios have been prepared and divided into two groups: the first group is related to the "basic learning scenarios" (with some simple programming concepts) while the second one is referred to the "advanced ones" (with multiple programming concepts). All learning scenarios contain activities for developing games in Snap! that include real-life problems. For example, in the basic learning scenario "Picking up trash and cleaning the park" students learn how to use variables and how to duplicate a block of code or a whole Sprite (Figure 1). In an advanced scenario "Buying food for a picnic" students learn how to work with variables: setting different starting values, using conditionals to compare variables' value, changing variables' value, using variables for counting (un)healthy food (Figure 2). Teachers can use the scenarios in the proposed sequence or can select them freely according to their preferences and needs.

Figure 1. Game "Picking up trash and cleaning the park"

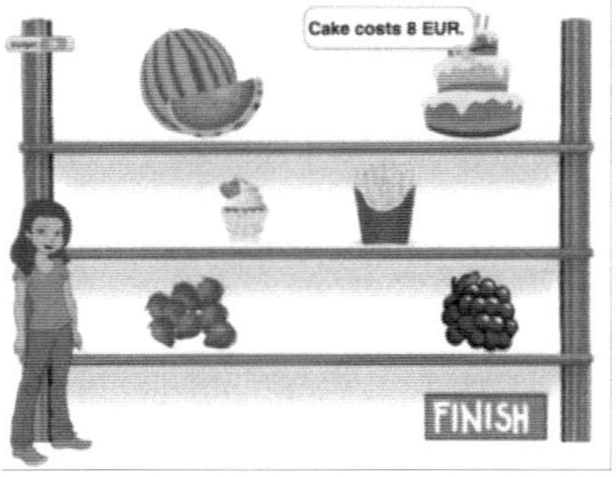

Figure 2. Game "Buying food for a picnic"

The learning scenarios are available in English as well as the national languages of project partners – Bulgarian, Croatian, Greek, Italian, Portuguese, Slovenian and Turkish (Coding4Girls project documentation and results, 2020).

4. CONCLUSIONS AND FUTURE WORK

Currently, the project team is engaged in testing the C4G methodology for building programming skills in the project partner countries. Teachers from primary and secondary schools were selected to apply developed learning scenarios for teaching programming using GBL with their students. This represents the first iteration of the Design Based Research (DBR) approach (Wang & Hannafin, 2005) that was chosen to evaluate the proposed framework.

Teachers were advised to choose a subset of the prepared learning scenarios according to their needs, and to try to achieve learning objectives related to programming concepts presented in the chosen scenarios. Just before the start of the implementation, schools were closed due to COVID-19 pandemic so activities were adjusted for online teaching in virtual learning environments like Microsoft Teams, Edmodo and similar. Additional instructions for teachers and students were prepared in written and video form, to enhance teaching and learning in virtual classrooms.

Upon completion of implementation, students and teachers were asked to fill questionnaires and give their feedback about the C4G methodology and the implementation that will be used to make improvements in the following DBR iterations. Preliminary results show that both teachers and students accepted the C4G approach for building programming skills. Students like to learn programing by creating games, especially those related to real-life problems, and teachers find the approach effective for achieving learning objectives.

Research will be continued within the project Digital Games. In the next DBR cycle, teaching programming in Snap! will be combined with the use of the C4G game. To familiarize students with the environment of the 3D adventure, the game will be at first used to explain just one programming concept. Subsequently, the game will be improved based on the obtained results and feedback and more concepts will be added. In the last DBR iteration, the entire framework will be tested. During the Digital Games project, additional learning scenarios for the use of the abovementioned game will be developed.

ACKNOWLEDGEMENT

The research has been co-funded by the Erasmus+ Programme of the European Union under the project „Coding4Girls" (2018-1-SI01-KA201-047013) and by University of Rijeka under the project "Digital games in the context of learning, teaching, and promoting inclusive education" (uniri-drustv-18-130).

REFERENCES

Alice, 2020. Retrieved May 25, 2020, from http://www.alice.org/

Alserri, S. A., Zin, N. A. M., & Wook, T. S. M. T., 2018. *Gender-based Engagement Model for Serious Games*. International Journal on Advanced Science, Engineering and Information Technology, 8(4), 1350–1357.

Backlund, P., & Hendrix, M., 2013. *Educational games - Are they worth the effort? A literature survey of the effectiveness of serious games.* 5th International Conference on Games and Virtual Worlds for Serious Applications (VS-GAMES), 1–8. https://doi.org/10.1109/VS-GAMES.2013.6624226

Carmichael, G., 2008. *Girls, computer science, and games*. ACM SIGCSE Bulletin, 40(4), 107–110. https://doi.org/10.1145/1473195.1473233

Coding4Girls web site, 2018. Retrieved May 26, 2020, from https://www.coding4girls.eu/

Coding4Girls project documentation and results, 2020.

Cunningham, B. C., Hoyer, K. M., & Sparks, D., 2015. *Gender Differences in Science, Technology, Engineering, and Mathematics (STEM) Interest, Credits Earned, and NAEP Performance in the 12th Grade*. In Stats in Brief. Retrieved from https://eric.ed.gov/?id=ED554303

European Commission, 2019. *Shaping Europe's digital future - Women in Digital*. Retrieved May 25, 2020, from https://ec.europa.eu/digital-single-market/en/women-ict

Franković, I., Hoić-Božić, N., & Holenko Dlab, Martina Ivašić-Kos, M., 2019. *Supporting Learning Programming Using Educational Digital Games*. Proceedings of the 13th European Conference on Game Based Learning, 999–1003. Denmark.

Kazimoglu, C., Kiernan, M., Bacon, L., & Mackinnon, L., 2012. A *Serious Game for Developing Computational Thinking and Learning Introductory Computer Programming*. Procedia - Social and Behavioral Sciences, 47, 1991–1999. https://doi.org/10.1016/j.sbspro.2012.06.938

Scratch, 2020. Retrieved May 25, 2020, from https://scratch.mit.edu

Snap!, 2020. Retrieved May 25, 2020, from https://snap.berkeley.edu

Wang, F., & Hannafin, M. J., 2005. *Design-based research and technology-enhanced learning environments*. Educational Technology Research and Development, 53(4), 5–23. https://doi.org/10.1007/BF02504682

Wrigley, C., & Straker, K., 2017. *Design Thinking pedagogy: the Educational Design Ladder*. Innovations in Education and Teaching International, 54(4), 374–385. https://doi.org/10.1080/14703297.2015.1108214

E-LEARNING COURSE IN SMART TEXTILES

Ion Razvan Radulescu[1], Luis Almeida[2], Benny Malengier[3], Zoran Stjepanovic[4], Mirela Blaga[5] and Petra Dufkova[6]

[1]INCDTP – Bucharest, Str. L. Patrascanu 16, Bucharest, Romania
[2]University of Minho / TecMinho, Campus de Azurem, Guimaraes, Portugal
[3]Ghent University, Technologiepark-Zwijnaarde 70A, Ghent, Belgium
[4]University of Maribor, Smetanova 17, Maribor, Slovenia
[5]Technical University of Iasi, Str. D. Mangeron 29, Iași, Romania
[6]Textile Testing Institute – TZU, Cejl 480/12, Brno, Czech Republic

ABSTRACT

E-learning offers multiple benefits for learners and is especially compatible with STEM fields. Smart textiles are a modern trend of the textile domain and represents a multi-disciplinary field. Smart textiles are used to showcase an end-application of STEM fields for VET students, within the Erasmus+ project Skills4Smartex. A course of 28 theoretical (STEM to Smart) modules and 28 practical modules (Smart to STEM) was achieved, by combining seven chapters of textile technology with each of the four modules of basic STEM disciplines: Mathematics, Physics, Material science – Chemistry and Electrotechnics. A Moodle e-learning course in weekly format was created for each national language of the project – Czech, Dutch, Portuguese, Romanian, Slovenian and English. The e-learning course includes an embedded SWF presentation of each of the theoretical modules in national language, a Book resource and a Quiz activity of each of the theoretical modules in English, as well as a Chat activity of communication between tutor and trainee. Blended courses are envisaged for the ongoing Skills4Smartex project during autumn 2020. For the pandemic restrictions period (March-May 2020), educational resources achieved in previous Erasmus+ projects were offered with Guest access for students and 214 access sessions were registered. The proposed educational approach combines smart textiles prototypes construction and related educational modules from theory to practice and from prototypes to theory, available as Open Educational Resources in e-learning format.

KEYWORDS

Vocational Education and Training, Basic Disciplines, Smart Textiles

1. INTRODUCTION

E-learning may be introduced in various fields of education (Grosseck G., Malita, L, 2015). It may serve as instrument for primary school teaching, humanistic sciences, creative and show arts and STEM (Science, Technology, Engineering and Mathematics) fields (Radulescu, I. R., Almeida, L., Stjepanovic, Z. et al, 2017). E-learning is especially applicable with STEM fields, due to rigorous structuring of content, compatibility with informatics instruments and possibility to show multimedia content on technologies (Radulescu, I. R, Ghituleasa, C.; Visileanu, E. at al, 2018). Textile technology is a multi-disciplinary field, combining several STEM fields, such as: material science and chemistry, mathematics, physics, electronics, informatics, mechanics and mechatronics etc (Dodu A, 2005). Smart textiles represent a modern trend in the textile field, consisting of textile materials that are able to sense stimuli from the environment, to react to them and adapt to them by integration of functionalities in the textile structure (Van Langenhove L., 2013). Moreover, smart textiles may include for these functionalities components such as: sensors, data processing, actuators, energy storage and communication (Malengier B., Tseghai G.B., Van Langenhove L. et al., 2019).

The preparation of technical VET (Vocational Education and Training) students in the last two years of high school and in first two years of college means acquiring of a high amount of theoretical basic disciplines, such as: mathematics, physics, chemistry-material science, electrotechnics. Mathematical relations such as integrals or derivative for physics and engineering remain often theory without an end-application horizon for the students. The link between theory and praxis for the future technician and engineer has to be made by showcasing end applications of basic disciplines. Smart textiles is a suitable topic for this purpose: they combine various basic disciplines and they represent applications of the acquired knowledge.

Thus, VET is needed to complete the current learning curricula in high schools and colleges. By providing smart textiles prototypes examples, both in a do-it-yourself (DIY) approach and in an explanatory approach (by means of educational modules), students may integrate acquired knowledge in a broader view of end-applications. Current educational approaches are oriented either practical or theoretical, either in classroom or e-learning format.

Main aim of this study is to provide a comprehensive educational approach, with smart textiles prototypes construction and related educational modules from theory to practice and from prototypes to theory, available as Open Educational Resources in e-learning format.

2. THE SKILLS4SMARTEX PROJECT

The Erasmus+ VET project "Smart textiles for STEM training" tackles this rationale. It is an ongoing project with the duration of two years (2018-2020), involving a prestigious consortium of educational providers in textiles: The National R&D Institute for Textiles and Leather – Bucharest, TecMinho / University of Minho – Portugal, Ghent University – Belgium, University of Maribor – Slovenia, Technical University of Iasi and the Textile Testing Institute of Czech Republic. More info on the project's website: www.skills4smartex.eu.

The project's partners have developed educational modules in the field of smart textiles in relation to the basic disciplines, such as: mathematics, physics, material science - chemistry and electrotechnics. The educational modules are divided mainly in two directions: from theory to praxis (STEM to Smart) and from practice to theory (Smart to STEM). The modules of Smart to STEM direction present achieved smart textile prototypes (Figure 1).

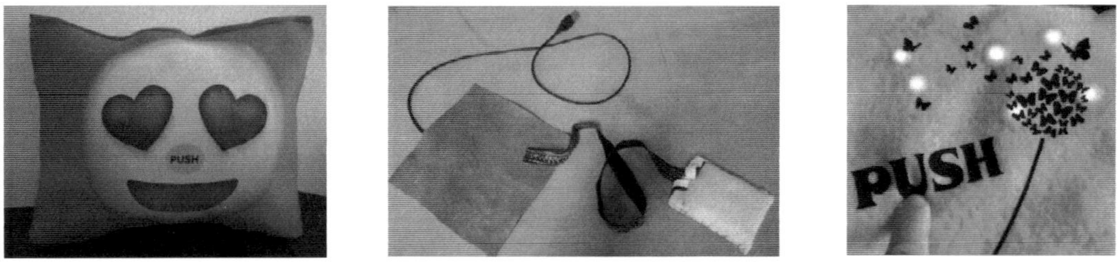

Figure 1. Manufactured smart textiles prototypes for educational purposes

This approach is meant to highlight for the VET students in technical disciplines, some end-application of basic disciplines they are learning. Further on, the modules are divided on seven chapters of textile technology, meant to follow the production chain of smart textiles: Novel fibers and yarns, materials and methods, virtual prototyping for sensors on smart textiles, smart textile design, smart textile prototypes, data processing and new methods for testing smart textiles. As such, it results in a total number of 56 modules: two directions (relation between STEM and Smart) multiplied with seven chapters of textile technology and with the four basic disciplines. A dedicated e-learning instrument was programmed in PHP in order to access all these modules via a filter, freely accessible online via the URL address: www.skills4smartex.eu/instrument.php. (Radulescu I R, Ghituleasa C, Visileanu E., et al, 2020) However, this paper focuses on the Skills4Smartex Moodle e-learning course developed on the project's e-learning platform www.advan2tex.eu/portal/. Since due to pandemic restrictions no face-to-face valorization of the achieved educational modules could be performed yet, the project was prolonged with three months and organization of blended courses is planned for autumn 2020. However, existing e-learning resources were provided with free access (Guest access).

3. THE E-LEARNING COURSE

The Moodle e-learning platform was configured within a first Erasmus+ VET project Advan2Tex, www.advan2tex.eu . The e-learning platform includes the Open Educational Resources (OER) of three Erasmus+ VET projects: Advan2Tex (2014-2016), TexMatrix (2016-2018) and the ongoing project Skills4Smartex (2018-2020). The courses of the first two projects are available online with Guest access (Figure 2).

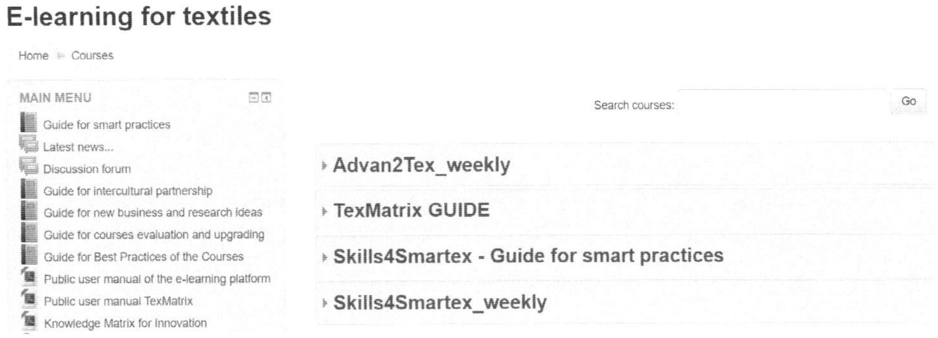

Figure 2. The e-learning courses of the three projects (www.advan2tex.eu/portal/)

The Moodle e-learning course of Skills4Smartex is meant for blended courses training of VET students of high schools and colleges of technical domains. Blended courses are a mixed form of classroom and e-learning courses according to the Erasmus+ Programme Guide (Erasmus+, 2020). Classroom courses are expected to train students with smart textiles prototypes do-it-yourself methods, while the e-learning courses will support the trainees with the needed online resources. This blended type of course has multiple benefits, for it combines face-to-face explanations of tutors and offers the OER in a modern format for distance access.

The Skills4Smartex e-learning course category includes six courses in national languages of the partner's countries organizations – Czech, Dutch, Portuguese, Romanian, Slovenian - and English. Each course is conceived in weekly format: the seven chapters are divided over three weeks of lesson plans. The first week includes the chapters: Novel fibers and yarns and Materials and methods; the second week includes: Virtual prototyping for sensors on smart textiles, Smart textile design and Smart textile prototypes, while the third week includes: Data processing and New methods for testing smart textiles. Each chapter includes the 4 modules of basic technical disciplines: Mathematics, Physics, Material science and chemistry and Electrotechnics. The following Moodle activities and resources were created for each module:

- One Presentation in national language
- One Book resource with the module in English
- One Quiz activity with 15-20 multiple choice questions on the module in English
- One Chat activity for synchronous communication between tutor and trainee per week

As such, a print screen of the course in English is presented in Figure 3.

Figure 3. Print screen of the e-learning course structure

The presentation is originally a PPT file, which was transformed into SWF file and implemented within the course page as Moodle Label resource, by modifying the HTML code. This solution provides interactive and quick access to the resources in national language. Table 1 presents the applied e-learning implementation solutions for adapting the educational content to the target group, in an attractive and practical manner.

Table 1. Solutions to implement the educational content into e-learning resources

Educational content	E-learning solution	Technical data
Asynchronous communication	Forum for general questions and answers	Forum is meant for questions of trainees for tutors regarding content of the course
Synchronous communication	Chat sessions lecturers - trainees	Once per week on Thursday for one hour for on spot clarifications regarding the course
Module content in national language	Embedded SWF presentation	The PPT of the module was transformed into SWF and implemented as label in the course
Module content in English	Moodle Book resource	The content of the module (text, images) was implemented as Book (navigation bars, table of contents)
Multiple choice questions in English	Moodle Quiz activity	The 15-20 questions per module were implemented via Aiken format (total of 420 questions)

These e-learning resources are meant for the blended courses to be organized by the project's partners in autumn 2020. Some of the OERs provided by the e-learning platform were used during pandemic restrictions in the time interval March-May 2020 too. As such, 8 trainees from the Technical University "Gh. Asachi" from Iasi – Faculty of Industrial Design and Management, were assigned to the e-learning course of Advan2Tex project, which includes following modules: advanced knitting technology; virtual prototyping of garments; textile testing; standardization; sustainability, LCA and eco-labelling; entrepreneurship and innovation management. The interest of the trainees was focused on advanced textile technologies. Moreover, the e-learning courses were provided with Guest access for the University of Oradea – Faculty of Energy Engineering and Industrial Management - Department of Textiles, Leather and Industrial Management and University "Aurel Vlaicu" of Arad – Faculty of Engineering – Department of Spinning and Weaving. During the pandemic a total number of 214 accesses sessions of the course were registered.

4. CONCLUSION

This paper presents an e-learning implementation contribution for a course of STEM fields' application by means of smart textiles. The multi-disciplinarily of smart textile manufacturing showcases end-applications for Mathematics, Physics, Material science - Chemistry and Electrotechnics. A total number of 56 modules were accomplished on two directions (from theory to practice and vice-versus). The implemented solutions envisage an embedded SWF presentation, a Book resource and a Quiz activity for each of the 28 theoretical modules (STEM to Smart direction). Presentations are in national languages (CZ, DU, PT, RO, SI), while Book resources and Quiz activities are in English language. This concept of the e-learning course is tailored with the educational content achieved and sets the premises of attractive and useful blended courses, to be organized in autumn 2020. During the pandemic restrictions (March-May 2020), the available OER courses on the e-learning platform (www.advan2tex.eu/portal/) were offered with Guest access. A total number of 214 access sessions were registered during this period, with focus on the Advan2Tex (2014-2016) course on innovative textile fields.

ACKNOWLEDGEMENT

This project has been funded with support of the European Commission. The European Commission's support for the production of this publication does not constitute an endorsement of the contents, which reflect the views only of the authors, and the Commission cannot be held responsible for any use which may be made of the information contained therein. Publishing has been funded by Ministry of Research and Innovation, by Program 1 – Development of the national system for R&D, Subprogram 1.2 – Institutional performance – projects for funding excellence in R&D&I, contract no. 6PFE from 16.10.2018.

REFERENCES

Dodu A. (coordinator), 2005, Handbook of the Textile Engineer, AGIR Publishing, Bucharest, Romania

Erasmus+ Programme Guide, online resource: https://ec.europa.eu/programmes/erasmus-plus/resources/programme-guide_en , accessed May, 2020

Grosseck G., Malita, L, 2015. *Guide for best practices E-learning,* West University Publishing, Timisoara, Romania.

Malengier B., Tseghai G.B., Van Langenhove L. et al., 2019, Functional Shoe for the Detection of Walking Pattern Anomalies, *ITMC 2019 International Conference on Intelligent Textiles and Mass Customisation*, Marrakech, Morocco

Radulescu, I. R., Almeida, L., Stjepanovic, Z. et al, 2017, E-learning in advanced textiles, *Industria textila scientific magazine*, vol. 68, no. 3, pp. 226-231

Radulescu, I. R, Ghituleasa, C.; Visileanu, E. at al, 2018, Benchmarking evaluation of innovation in textile enterprises, *ELSE 2018 international scientific conference e-learning and software for education*, Bucharest, Romania, pp. 194-199

Radulescu I R, Ghituleasa C, Visileanu E., et al, 2020, Dedicated e-learning instrument to support STEM knowledge by means of smart textiles, *ELSE 2020 international scientific conference e-learning and software for education*, Bucharest, Romania, pp. 339-345

Van Langenhove L., 2013, *Smart textiles for protection – Part 1 – An Overview*, Woodhead Publishing Limited, Cambridge, UK

DESCRIPTION OF METHOD USED BY SAPIENZA UNIVERSITY IN ROME TO DELIVER REHABILITATION PROGRAM E-COURSES TO STUDENTS FOLLOWING THE COVID-19 EMERGENCY

Anna Berardi[1], Marco Tofani[2], Giovanni Galeoto[2], Maria Auxiliadora Marquez[3] and Donatella Valente[1]

[1]*Department of Human Neurosciences, Sapienza University of Rome, Viale dell'Università 30, 00185, Rome, Italy*
[2]*Department of Public Health and Infection disease, Sapienza University of Rome, Piazzale Aldo Moro,5, 00185, Rome, Italy*
[3]*Paraplegic Center of Ostia, Rome, Italy, Viale Vega, 3, 00122 Lido di Ostia, Rome, Italy*

ABSTRACT

Most governments around the world have temporarily closed educational institutions in an attempt to contain the spread of the coronavirus disease 2019 (COVID-19). In Italy, teaching activities were suspended on March 5, 2020 based on provisions from competent authorities. Sapienza University in Rome has addressed the COVID-19 emergency by putting available tools in place to support remote teaching. The purpose of this paper is to describe and share the method used for the degree courses in the rehabilitation health program at Sapienza University in Rome to deliver courses to their students. The provision of distance learning was divided into three phases: (1) Activation of the teacher-student work environment (virtual class) using Google Classroom; (2) Publication on the teacher's webpage; (3) Teaching provision using Google Classroom or Google Meet. By March 11, 2020, all courses were created and access codes were communicated to the students, and to date several students are successfully attending the courses. In the academic world, sharing experiences is extremely important and necessary to achieve higher standards in education.

KEYWORDS

COVID-19, e-Learning, Examination, Universities

1. INTRODUCTION

Since March 11, 2020, when the World Health Organization (WHO) declared the coronavirus disease 2019 (COVID-19) to be a pandemic, most governments around the world have temporarily closed educational institutions in an attempt to contain the spread of COVID-19 (WHO, 2020). These nationwide closures are impacting over 90% of the world's student population (UNESCO, 2020a).

Normally, March is one of the busiest months in the academic calendar; even with buildings in lockdown and staff barred from their offices, learning goes on, displaced, but not discontinued. This year, COVID-19 is challenging the ability of the academic world to adapt and be resilient, and the education sector is responding to quarantine with a sudden shift to online learning (Electronic Platform for Adult Learning in Europe, 2020). In many respects, COVID-19 is drawing out the best from staff, who are committed to ensuring the education and wellbeing of all students is maintained. (Jones S., 2020)

In Italy, teaching activities were suspended on March 5, 2020 based on provisions of competent authorities (Decree of the President of the Council of Ministers, March 4, 2020) in response to the COVID-19 emergency. Sapienza, like all Italian universities, adopted the provisions of the government to confront the COVID-19 emergency. In this context, everything that followed was done with the dual objective of protecting the health of the country's citizens and guaranteeing the continuity of the university's activities. Sapienza faced the COVID-19 emergency by putting available tools in place to support educating by teachers and learning by students. In particular, in the unique circumstances caused by the pandemic, the university has begun delivering distance lessons by using the tools and training aids already available to the university community. The map of all useful tools and information for teachers and students accessible on the university website is available in the United Nations Educational (UNESCO) document (UNESCO, 2020b). The reorganization of remote activities for degree courses is under the coordination and control of the Presidents of the courses, to ensure proper planning of the lessons, clear communication to the students, and full monitoring of the process. The purpose of this paper is to describe and share the method used to deliver degree courses for the health profession's rehabilitation program at Sapienza University in Rome to its students.

2. BODY OF PAPER

Administrators of the degree courses for occupational therapy, speech therapy, physiotherapy, podiatry, orthoptics and ophthalmological assistance, psychiatric rehabilitation technique and therapy of neuro-psychomotricity of developmental age followed a common line to face the emergency. The courses were created by professionals who was already experienced in managing online courses (Farina, 2019; Paterniani, 2019; Galeoto, 2019a; Galeoto, 2019b). The provision of distance learning was divided into three phases:

Phase 1 - Activation of the teacher-student work environment (virtual class)

The course director activated the teacher-student work environment to deliver lessons remotely by using the functionality of Google Classroom for creating a virtual classroom, sharing teaching materials, and engaging in direct communication (chat/forum) with students. It was necessary to access the mailbox with @uniroma1 university credentials and to access Classroom through the square icon in the icon menu (Figure 1). Each course in Google Classroom corresponds to a single teaching unit from the teacher. At the first authentication, it is necessary to click on the + symbol at the top right (Create your first course or Register) by selecting the Create Class item (Figure 2).

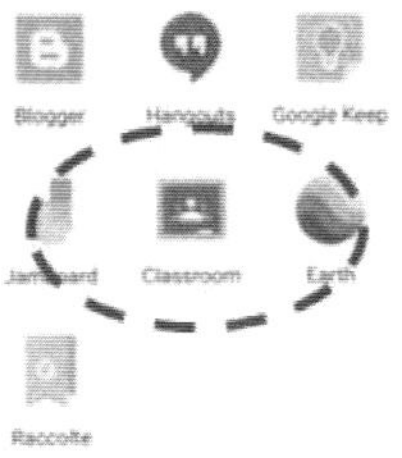

Figure 1. Classroom icon on Google

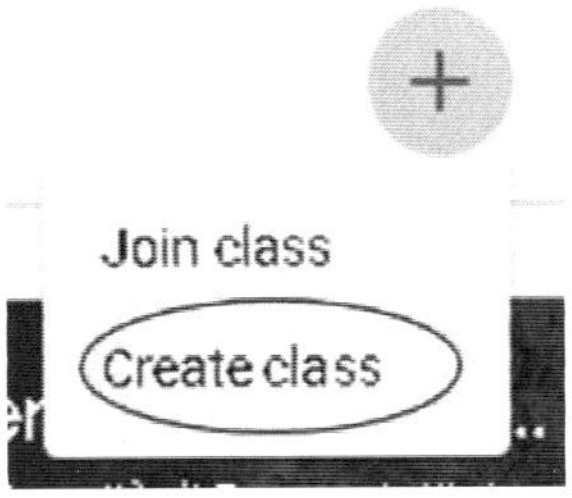

Figure 2. To create a class, click on the + symbol at the top right

Once the course is created, it will appear as shown in Figure 3. At this time, the teacher can share material with students in the Stream section, assign tasks and quizzes in the Classwork section, and view the list of enrolled students in the People section. Selecting the icon with three horizontal lines at the top left allows students to return to the initial page showing all courses available (Figure 4).

Figure 3. Classroom interface for course work

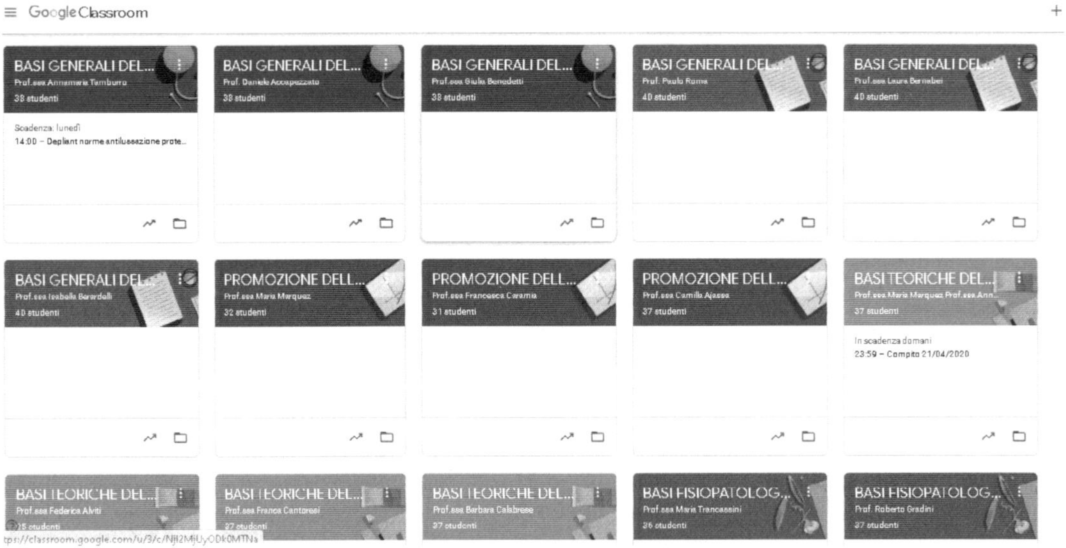

Figure 4. Classroom homepage listing all courses

Phase 2 - Publication on the teacher's webpage

Once the virtual classroom has been activated, the teacher must notify the students on the notice board of the teacher card in the Study Program Catalog, and then specify the platform used and the link or code of the online course.

Phase 3 - Teaching provision

To provide distance teaching, the teacher can use one of the methods described below.

1) Off-line mode: The teacher prepares and loads the lesson with recorded audio using the IT tools made available by the university or other options of the teacher's choice. The recording of the lesson must contain the explanation by the teacher in audio format. In the event that the teacher has difficulty in realizing a lesson with recorded audio, text must be made available that completely replaces the content from and the duration of the audio recording.

2) Online mode: The teacher delivers the lesson via streaming or video conferencing at a time agreed upon by the students. The communication of the timetable and methods to students is facilitated through the virtual classroom. Upon starting the online delivery of the lesson, the teacher activates the video call recording mode to record the lesson.

The Meet functionality of Google was chosen by Sapienza University's degree courses in the rehabilitation sciences program as the software for the realization of remote lessons, receptions and webinars. This tool allows several people to connect remotely through video lessons, receptions and meetings. It facilitates communication via chat and video conference capabilities with useful accessibility tools, such as automatic subtitles. To cope with the COVID-19 emergency, until 1 July 2020, Google has made available to all schools that use G Suite for Education some advanced Meet features, such as making video calls with up to 250 participants and the possibility of saving recorded meetings on Google Drive (live streaming).

To use the Meet tool, it is necessary to first access the @uniroma1 university mailbox, and then select the square Meet icon from the icon menu in the mailbox. The main screen of the application is presented (as shown in Figure 5) and the user can select 'Join a meeting' to begin. At the end of the lesson, the teacher loads the registration inside the activated teacher-student work environment.

Figure 5. Google Meet Homepage

3. CONCLUSION

By March 11, 2020, all courses were created and access codes communicated to students. To date, several students are successfully attending the courses. From preliminary opinions collected, students have already expressed positive feedback regarding the quality of the content and the methods of lesson delivery. It would be beneficial to confirm this response by conducting an in-depth investigation in the coming months. Although the data available was minimal by coming from one program at the university, the results are positive, effective and worthy of being shared with other disciplines. The authors of this study believe that sharing their experiences is extremely important and necessary given the challenging and incredible circumstances of emergency response that universities are facing. It is the wish of the authors that academic experts will be encouraged to share strategies being used to address the challenges that threaten the high educational standards of universities around the world.

REFERENCES

Decree of the President of the Council of Ministers of March 4, 2020. Available at: http://www.governo.it/sites/new.governo.it/files/DPCM4MARZO2020.pdf (Accessed: 29 April 2020).

Electronic Platform for Adult Learning in Europe. COVID-19 is reviving the need to explore online teaching and learning opportunities. 24 March 2020. Available at: https://epale.ec.europa.eu/en/blog/covid-19-reviving-need-explore-online-teaching-and-learning-opportunities (Accessed: 29 April 2020) World Health Organization, Coronavirus disease 2019 (COVID-19) Situation Report 46, 2020.

Jones S. Covid-19 is our best chance to change universities for good. The Guardian. 31 Mar 2020. Available at: https://www.theguardian.com/education/2020/mar/31/covid-19-is-our-best-chance-to-change-universities-for-good. (Accessed: 29 April 2020).

Farina I. et al, 2019. High-Fidelity Simulation Type Technique Efficient for Learning Nursing Disciplines in the Courses of Study: An Integrative Review. In: Methodologies and Intelligent Systems for Technology Enhanced Learning, 9th International Conference, Workshops. Avila, Spain

Galeoto G. et al, 2019 a. The Use of a Dedicated Platform to Evaluate Health-Professions University Courses. In book: Methodologies and Intelligent Systems for Technology Enhanced Learning, 8th International Conference. Toledo, Spain.

Galeoto G. et al, 2019 b. Evaluation of the Disciplinary Competences of the Students of the Bachelor's Degree in Physiotherapy at "Sapienza" University of Rome Through the TECO: A Cross-Sectional Study. In book: Learning Technology for Education Challenges. Zamora, Spain.

Paterniani A. et al, 2019. Electronic Test of Competence Administration: Qualitative Evaluation of Students' Satisfaction on Telematic Platform a Cross Sectional Study. In: Methodologies and Intelligent Systems for Technology Enhanced Learning, 9th International Conference, Workshops. Avila, Spain

The United Nations Educational, Scientific and Cultural Organization (UNESCO) a. COVID-19 Educational Disruption and Response. Available at: https://en.unesco.org/covid19/educationresponse (Accessed: 29 April 2020).

The United Nations Educational, Scientific and Cultural Organization (UNESCO) b. Distance learning solutions. 2020. Available at: https://en.unesco.org/covid19/educationresponse/solutions (Accessed: 29 April 2020)

DESCRIPTION OF THE METHOD USED BY TOR VERGATA UNIVERSITY OF ROME FOR THE ELECTRONIC FINAL EXAM OF THE DEGREE COURSE IN PHYSIOTHERAPY

Annamaria Servadio[1], Anna Berardi[2], Marco Tramontano[3], Marco Tofani[4], Rosaria Alvaro[5], Pasquale Farsetti[6] and Giovanni Galeoto[7]

[1]*Director of the degree course in physiotherapy, Tor Vergata University of Rome, Tor Vergata Hospital, Viale Oxford, 81, 00133, Rome, Italy*

[2]*Sapienza University of Rome, Piazzale Aldo Moro 5, 00185, Rome, Italy*

[3]*Director of the degree course in physiotherapy, Tor Vergata University of Rome, Santa Lucia Foundation IRCCS Via Ardeatina, 306/354, 00179 Rome, Italy*

[4]*Department of Public Health and Infectious Diseases, Sapienza University, Rome, Italy, Piazzale Aldo Moro 5, 00185, Rome, Italy*

[5]*Full professor of nursing sciences, coordinator of Bachelor's degrees in the health area, Viale Oxford, 81, 00133, Rome, Italy*

[6]*Full professor President of the degree course in physiotherapy, Tor Vergata University of Rome, Tor Vergata Hospital, Viale Oxford, 81, 00133, Rome, Italy*

[7]*Teacher of the degree course in physiotherapy, department of Public Health and Infectious Diseases, Sapienza University, Rome, Italy, Piazzale Aldo Moro 5, 00185, Rome, Italy*

ABSTRACT

On 11 March 2020, the Director General of the World Health Organisation (WHO) officially declared the outbreak of the coronavirus (COVID-19) as a pandemic. Much of the global higher-education community has been thrust into an unplanned, unwanted and fraught experiment in online learning. Experts in the academic world must be encouraged to spread and share the strategies they are using to face these challenges. This extraordinary health emergency, which is being experienced in our country and all over the world, has forced Italian universities to modify the organisation of the final tests of their degree courses, including those of the health professions, with the effect of transforming them into online tests. The objective pursued is to not interrupt the completion of university courses by ensuring that students can complete the qualifying exams for these professions. This paper describes the method used at an Italian university to carry out the final exam of the degree course in physiotherapy in electronic form. Final exams have been organised on the basis of the guidance provided at a national level. The technical tool chosen by this university to allow participation in remote exams is the Microsoft Teams platform. The Exam Commission will start the exam, after verifying the environmental requirements in which each candidate wishes to take the exam. At the end of the exam, the President of the Exam Commission will transcribe the names and marks of the student, as well as the names of the members of the Commission on the minutes, and he or she will sign them. This paper represents a first step in the dissemination and sharing, at an academic level, of how one university is dealing with the current situation. It is an important element in helping academics and academia to manage this emergency.

KEYWORDS

COVID-19, e-Learning, Examination, Universities

1. INTRODUCTION

On 30 January 2020, the World Health Organisation (WHO) declared the outbreak of the coronavirus (COVID-19) as a Public Health Emergency of International Concern. On 11 March 2020, the WHO's Director General officially declared the outbreak a pandemic and called on "all countries to continue efforts that have been effective in limiting the number of cases and slowing the spread of the virus." (World Health Organisation, 2020) Countries around the world are currently implementing measures to slow the spread of the coronavirus, from national quarantines to school closures. Several countries, such as Italy, have imposed restrictions, and the virus has thrust much of the global higher-education community into an unplanned, unwanted and fraught experiment in online learning. For most faculty members and students this is not what they want, but it is what they are being forced to deal with until the end of this academic year.

In Italy, the study path of students enrolled in the degree course in physiotherapy ends with a final exam, the professional qualifying state exam. The exam is organised into two sessions and consists of the following tests:

1. A practical test, during which students must demonstrate that they have acquired a physiotherapist's knowledge and theoretical-practical and operational skills.
2. The preparation of a thesis paper and its dissertation.

The legislation governing the final test defines that, in the practical test, the following skills set out by the Dublin descriptors 2, 3 and 4, built into the Bologna Process, are assessed (European Commission/EACEA/Eurydice, 2018):

- Descriptor 2. Applying knowledge and understanding.
- Descriptor 3. Making judgements.
- Descriptor 4. Communication skills, and, in particular, the ability to identify problems; make decisions on professional problems; identify priorities for individual patients, groups or work processes; plan and decide on interventions on the basis of available evidence and organisational conditions; act safely; consider the ethical, deontological and legal dimensions of their actions; demonstrate an orientation to inter-professional practice and evaluate the outcomes on patients.

The regulatory document also provides that the procedures for carrying out the practical test may include one or more of the following methods (Guidelines for the final test of the Degree Courses belonging to the classes of Health Professions):

- A structured, semi-structured or open-ended written test on paradigmatic cases/situations of professional practice.
- An oral interview with discussion of cases or a project.
- Observation of professional skills (e.g. technical, relational, diagnostic and design) in real clinical contexts, simulated laboratory contexts or with video support – a structured examination of clinical skills.

The health emergency that is being experienced in our country, and all over the world, has forced Italian universities to modify the organisation of the final tests of their degree courses, including those of the health professions, with the effect of enabling the profession to transform its tests into online tests, both for the practical test and for the thesis. The objective is to not interrupt the completion of university courses by ensuring that students can complete the qualifying exams for their profession. This paper describes the method used at an Italian university to carry out the final exam of the degree course in physiotherapy in electronic form.

2. BODY OF PAPER

The exams were organized by professionals who was already experienced in managing online courses (Farina, 2019; Paterniani, 2019; Galeoto, 2019a; Galeoto, 2019b). Based on the guidance provided jointly by the Ministry of University and Research (MIUR) and the Italian Ministry of Health (ministerial circular of 30 September 2016) (Directorial Decree n.3478 of 14 April 2020), the final exam, based on the selection of core competencies, can take place following one of the three methods provided. Alternatively, an oral test can be taken involving the discussion and classification of clinical cases or paradigmatic situations of professional practice, with questions by the Commission based on real and/or simulated situations. This choice is in line with what is stated in the standard and can be adapted in a telematic context. Following the above, online tests for the degree in physiotherapy course were organised.

Digital learning management systems, communication tools and e-learning platforms are playing a crucial role during this pandemic. Software and apps can help learning providers to manage, plan, deliver and track the learning process. The United Nations Educational, Scientific and Cultural Organization (UNESCO) has recently published a list of useful tools for this purpose (UNESCO, 2020). The technical tool chosen by the Tor Vergata University of Rome, to allow participation in remote exams, is the Microsoft TEAMS platform.

To participate, in university email account is required. However, for a better user experience, students are advised to download and install the desktop version of Microsoft Teams, available on different devices or from https://teams.microsoft.com/downloads. Ideally, effective use of the platform requires a personal computer equipped with a video camera and microphone. If access is through the web, it is advisable to use Google Chrome or Microsoft Edge.

For a good-quality video call, the minimum network requirements are 500kbs (upload)/1Mbps (download). On the day of the exam, an invitation containing a link will be sent via email (to the email address provided to the University during the enrolment phase) to students so they can access the exam's virtual classroom on Microsoft Teams.

Candidates must connect at least 30 minutes before the exam start time, taking care to check that the technical requirements (previously reported) are respected and that they have a valid identity document with them. The Exam Commission, composed by two members designated by the professional college, the MIUR and the Ministry of Health, supervise the regularity of the exam and verifies the candidates' documents.

After verifying the environmental requirements in which the candidates wish to take the exam, the Exam Commission proceeds to the examination. The practical test is conducted through the discussion of a clinical case and related questions from the Commission. The Commission will prepare a number of clinical cases equal to the number of candidates present plus a number of five. On the day of the exam, a clinic case will be drawn for each student and with a Simple Randomization, based on a single sequence of random assignments, the clinical case will be assigned to each student, the cases not extracted must be opened and described at the end of the test. At the end of the exam, the President of the Exam Commission will transcribe the names and marks of the student, as well as the names of the members of the Commission on the minutes, and he or she will sign them. The President of the Exam Commission records the students' marks for the exam.

When conducting remote examinations, several precautions must be taken. The environment in which the exam takes place must be silent and sufficiently illuminated to allow recognition of the candidate, and no other people must be present. Students are asked to position their video camera so that it is framed in "half length," with their hands in the frame so it is easy to verify that they do not have a cell phone or notes from which they can read. Furthermore, candidates must not wear hats and must have their ears uncovered to check for earphones or the like. During their oral presentation, candidates are asked to keep their gaze fixed on the video camera to verify that they do not read from unseen sources. If the connection is lost during the interview, the question is cancelled, and the interview resumes with a new application. In the event that candidates have to write something to answer an exam question (e.g. a formula, chemical reaction or graphic scheme), the video shot must include the support on which the candidates will write, for example, a sheet of white paper. It is advisable to ask candidates to bring the paper closer to the video camera once completed and to also read its contents out loud.

If Microsoft Teams is installed on your PC just click on Open Microsoft Teams (Figure 1). If Microsoft Teams is NOT installed on your PC click on Join the Web (Figure 1). The following screen will appear, where you will be asked to enter your name and then, by clicking on Join now, you will enter the meeting (Figure 2).

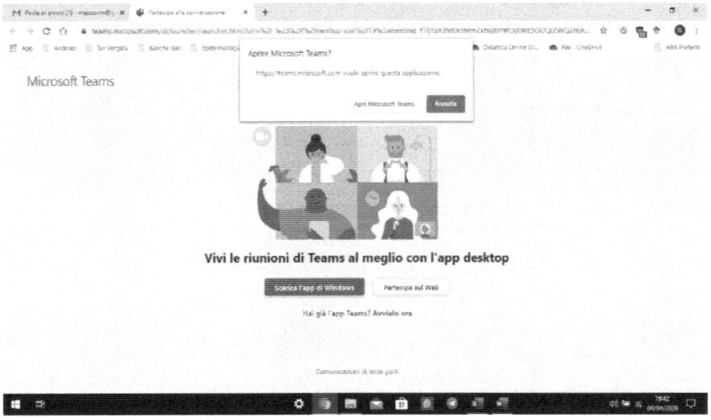

Figure 1. Microsoft Teams, front page

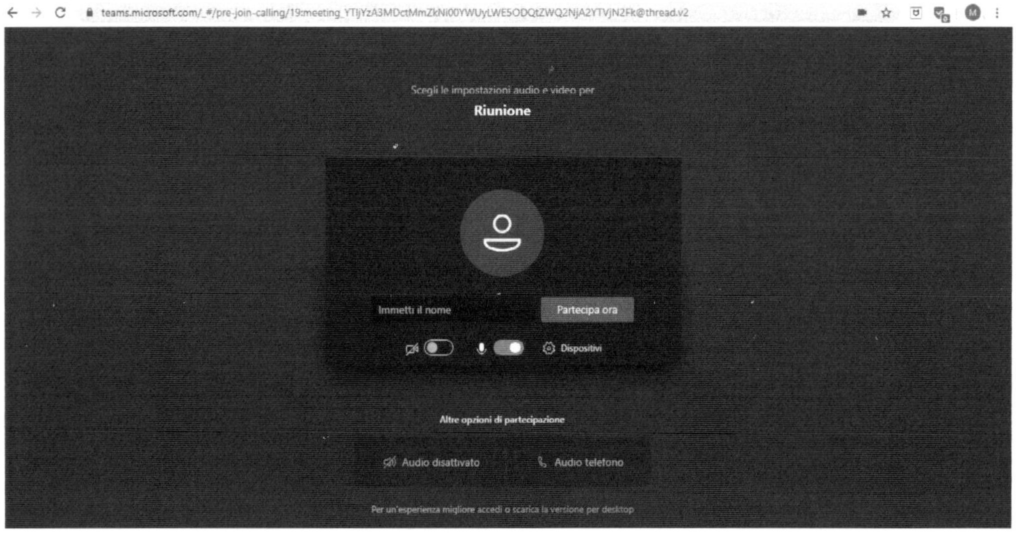

Figure 2. Microsoft Teams, how to enter the meeting

3. CONCLUSION

Most governments around the world have temporarily closed educational institutions in an attempt to contain the spread of the COVID-19 pandemic. COVID-19 has significantly affected all of our lives, but it is also challenging our ability to adapt and be resilient. The education sector is responding to quarantine with a sudden shift to online learning (Electronic Platform for Adult Learning in Europe). The present study, conducted by Tor Vergata University of Rome, represents an important insight for the emergency that the world is experiencing. Experts in the academic world must be encouraged to spread and share the strategies they are using to face these challenges. The advantage of international communication lies in the sharing that allows ever-higher standards in education. Authors found a lack of evidences in literature, especially related for the Italian context, which would have guided the structuring the online testing. Given the emergency we are facing, the authors believe that it is most important to inform the international-academic community about the strategies their university has chosen. Despite the lack of comments from the learners and a case study that records the effectiveness of online-testing methods, this paper only intended to describe the methodologies used by Tor Vergata University of Rome. In conclusion, this paper represents a first step in the dissemination and sharing, at an academic level, of how to face the current challenges in teaching. Further studies suggested by the authors of this paper include the organization of consensus workshops or consensus conferences especially on the topic of internship exams at national and international level. Intraprofessional consensus meeting, world cafè and qualitative analysis could represent an excellent way to identify and appraise experts' relevant consensus statements according to health professionals Core Curriculum and Core Competence.

REFERENCES

Directorial Decree n.3478 of April 14, 2020. Document of the Minister of University and Research Gaetano Manfredi on post lockdown. Available at: https://miur.gov.it/web/guest/-/decreto-direttoriale-n-3478-del-14-aprile-2020 (Accessed: 26 April 2020)

Electronic Platform for Adult Learning in Europe. COVID-19 is reviving the need to explore online teaching and learning opportunities. 24/ March 2020. Available at: https://epale.ec.europa.eu/en/blog/covid-19-reviving-need-explore-online-teaching-and-learning-opportunities (Accessed: 26 April 2020)

European Commission/EACEA/Eurydice, 2018. The European Higher Education Area in 2018: Bologna Process Implementation Report. Luxembourg: Publications Office of the European Union. Available at https://eacea.ec.europa.eu/national-policies/eurydice/sites/eurydice/files/bologna_internet_0.pdf (Accessed: 26 April 2020)

Farina I. et al, 2019. High-Fidelity Simulation Type Technique Efficient for Learning Nursing Disciplines in the Courses of Study: An Integrative Review. In: *Methodologies and Intelligent Systems for Technology Enhanced Learning, 9th International Conference, Workshops*. Avila, Spain

Galeoto G. et al, 2019 a. The Use of a Dedicated Platform to Evaluate Health-Professions University Courses. *In book: Methodologies and Intelligent Systems for Technology Enhanced Learning, 8th International Conference.* Toledo, Spain.

Galeoto G. et al, 2019 b. Evaluation of the Disciplinary Competences of the Students of the Bachelor's Degree in Physiotherapy at "Sapienza" University of Rome Through the TECO: A Cross-Sectional Study. *In book: Learning Technology for Education Challenges.* Zamora, Spain.

Guidelines for the final test of the Degree Courses belonging to the classes of Health Professions. Ministerial Decree 19 February 2009 Official Journal 25 May 2009, n.119. Available at https://www.fnopi.it/wp-content/uploads/DM190209.pdf (Accessed: 26 April 2020)

Ministerial circular of 30 September 2016. operational indications about the final test of the courses related to the degree classes for the health professions. Available at https://translate.google.com/#view=home&op=translate&sl=it&tl=en&text=indicazioni%20operative%20circa%20la%20prova%20finale%20dei%20corsi%20afferenti%20alle%20classi%20di%20laurea%20per%20le%20professioni%20sanitarie (Accessed: 26 April 2020)

Paterniani A. et al, 2019. Electronic Test of Competence Administration: Qualitative Evaluation of Students' Satisfaction on Telematic Platform a Cross Sectional Study. In: *Methodologies and Intelligent Systems for Technology Enhanced Learning, 9th International Conference, Workshops*. Avila, Spain

The United Nations Educational, Scientific and Cultural Organization (UNESCO). Distance learning solutions. 2020. Available at: https://en.unesco.org/covid19/educationresponse/solutions (Accessed: 26 April 2020)

World Health Organisation, Coronavirus disease 2019 (COVID-19) Situation Report 46, 2020

REMOTE TEACHING FOR DEAF PUPILS DURING THE COVID-19 EMERGENCY

Federica Baroni and Marco Lazzari*
University of Bergamo
Department of Human and Social Sciences, Piazzale Sant'Agostino 2 – I-24129 Bergamo, Italy

ABSTRACT

The coronavirus emergency has accelerated the digitization processes of Italian schools, bringing new challenges to inclusive teaching. We present the remote teaching experience that is still in progress at the Scuola Audiofonetica in Brescia, and describe actions taken and initial results achieved. The families appreciated the school's educational choices, and from this positive experience, some good practices can be derived and shared at technological, methodological and organizational levels.

KEYWORDS

School Inclusion, Remote Teaching, Distance Learning, Covid-19 Emergency, Deafness, Accessibility, Educational Technology

1. INTRODUCTION

The evolution of digital technologies is a major turning point for deaf people—for example, for accessing public administration services, e-commerce and interpersonal relationships, especially through text chat and video chat (Barak and Sadowsky, 2008; Keating et al., 2008). The introduction of information and communication technologies (ICT) in schools is a significant step towards the personalization of learning paths and the application of active teaching methodologies. ICTs may help in offering differentiated stimuli through multimedia, providing modular and flexible contents, and supporting new teaching approaches (Hwang et al., 2015; Ibáñez and Delgado-Kloos, 2018). For deaf students, this means accessing teaching methods other than frontal lessons, even in the spirit of the Universal Design for Learning (UDL; Rose and Meyer, 2002). However, up until now, the technologies were mainly exploited either in the classroom or in a blended mode, and possible disadvantages of distance teaching were kept to a minimum.

The COVID-19 emergency in Italy led the government to cease face-to-face teaching activities from 26 February 2020 and forced schools to start totally remote educational activities. To date, the scientific literature on emergencies, with a focus on schools, is limited to organizational and health management aspects (Viner, 2020), whereas there are many experiences documented by teachers and experts in newspapers, on the Internet, and social networks.

At all levels, the debate focused on the concern of including the most fragile pupils, that is, those who belong to families lacking either adequate technological devices (digital divide), or digital skills (cultural divide), or those with learning impairments (due to disabilities or other causes). For deaf pupils, in addition, there is the risk of exclusion due to a lack of accessibility to synchronous lessons on e-learning platforms, which is already described in the literature (Martins et al., 2015).

According to the Italian Institute of Statistics (Istat, 2019), in Italy the issue of the diffusion of the technological equipment is still open: only 74.7% of households have a broadband connection, and 41.6% of Internet users exhibit low digital skills, with a significant gap between generations (only 34% of people over 65 have a broadband connection). During the emergency, many Italian children and young people lived with their grandparents because their parents were sick or busy working to face the emergency (for example, in hospitals), or teleworking; others had to share their connections and devices with many family members, meaning that their access to tools and services was limited. The emergency clearly highlighted the country's limits in terms of technological innovation and digitalization of schools.

*Both the authors contributed to the final version of the manuscript. F.B. is the inclusion coordinator of the project

2. THE EXPERIENCE

The Scuola Audiofonetica is a private school that for the academic year 2019/20 enrolled a total of 540 pupils aged from 1 to 13 (from nursery school to first grade secondary school), of whom 87 had disabilities (57 deaf). Furthermore, 26% of deaf pupils have other associated disabilities, and 37% come from families of non-Italian origin, and therefore they have a double source of language and learning difficulties. All pupils with disabilities attend ordinary classes, with hearing classmates, according to a model that in 1974 transformed a special institute (born in 1856) into an experiment of school inclusion. The school is located in Brescia, one of the Italian towns most affected by the COVID-19 emergency.

The Audiofonetica implements its model by integrating educational and rehabilitation services (which is not common in Italy), with a psychologist, an education expert, an audiologist, an audiometrist, an inclusion coordinator, specialized teachers, communication assistants, sign language interpreters, educators, and speech therapists. The staff works to customize teaching in classes made up of 18-24 pupils, including 2 to 4 children with deafness. The laboratories (music, cognitive-operational, artistic), as well as flexible and small-group teaching methods, enable the inclusion.

Deaf people are proven to be different from each other in their cognitive styles (Marschark and Hauser, 2008): their variability depends on the degree of deafness, the language competence in the mother tongue, the prevalent type of communication (verbal language or signs), and on many other contextual factors. At the Audiofonetica, there are deaf pupils with different characteristics, from well-compensated deafness to sensory multidisability with serious language impairment: moving away from an exclusively oral approach and a ban on sign language (still a vital idea in Italy), today, the school adopts the Total Communication Approach (Jordan et al., 1976), exploiting various communication methods, such as Italian, Italian Sign Language (LIS), and non-verbal communication systems.

In such a complex context, the lockdown and the closure of schools have posed new challenges in terms of remote teaching accessibility. The Audiofonetica did not have any major projects to exploit educational technology, except for the use of a computer lab during curricular hours and the introduction (Sept. 2019) of interactive whiteboards at the first year of primary and middle school. Therefore, the teachers were not all ready for the transition to remote teaching, as in most Italian schools.

During the first weeks of the lockdown, materials and tasks were sent through the school electronic register (asynchronous mode), and individualized meetings (1:1) were started for deaf pupils, taking advantage of video call services that guarantee security, privacy, and functions such as two-way chat, screen sharing, and file exchange. In this way, it was possible to provide educational, logopedic, and psychological support to pupils and families. The teachers were invited – with training, guides, and tutorials – to produce accessible and high-quality multimedia content based on shared principles:

- exploitation of all communication channels, according to the principles of multimedia learning (Mayer, 2005);
- short audio-video lessons (maximum 8 minutes), which were modular, complete, coherent, and with adequate communication style, according to guidelines on the quality of podcasts in education (Lazzari and Betella, 2007) and to recent recommendations to plan distance learning solutions by UNESCO (2020);
- personal presence of the teachers on video to explain the sense of a task and introduce or synthesize a difficult concept, avoiding the reproduction of the typical face-to-face teaching;
- accessibility through subtitles and sign language translations, avoiding separate solutions for deaf pupils according to the UDL approach, which requires: (1) multiple means of representation of content by teachers; (2) multiple modes of expression by students; and (3) multiple stimuli to engage students (Rose and Meyer, 2002);
- use of repositories that do not ask for log-in or for the sending of data by minors.

From March, a communication and collaboration platform (Microsoft Teams) was gradually introduced (from secondary to primary schools) for the synchronous participation of students and the exchange of materials in virtual classes. For nursery and kindergarten families, the educational path continued with the publication (on the school site and social networks) of stories accessible to all children and by sending various proposals, activities, and materials to parents for educational and recreational purposes.

In May, the school provided a total of 85 curricular and 150 individualized weekly hours in primary education (on 13 classes) through remote teaching in synchronous mode; 126 curricular and 65 individualized weekly hours in secondary school (on 7 classes); 14 weekly hours of contact with pupils with disabilities and their families in kindergarten/nursery (on 6 sections of kindergarten and 1 section of nursery); and approximately 60 weekly hours of remote speech therapy for deaf pupils.

3. RESULTS AND DISCUSSION

Due to the choices made and the actions undertaken, all the pupils were reached by distance teaching, and none were excluded. Before extending remote teaching to the primary school, an online questionnaire was administrated to parents in order to assess their technological equipment, with respect to the emergency situation (children hosted by grandparents, devices occupied by siblings and parents in telework): 223 out of 254 answered (response rate: 87.8%), showing a high rate of availability of digital devices (85.7% have a PC, 60.5% have a tablet, 67.3% have a printer) and connections (85.2% having a landline and 39% having mobile networks). However, the emergency situation reduced the availability of devices among family members (PCs drop to 68.2%, tablets to 56.1%, and printers to 46.6%, with 4.9% having no tools at all because they are used by others) and compressed the adults' time to support the children (only 30% can guarantee assistance without limits).

While the starting situation is pretty good for most hearing students, who come from medium-high socio-economic contexts, several families of deaf pupils have disadvantaged economic backgrounds and have received support from local authorities to attend the Scuola Audiofonetica; the school provided them with PCs, tablets, and Internet connections. Experts gave technical assistance to families with poor digital skills to limit their cultural gap. Continuous contact with families enabled them to monitor every difficulty and to find solutions and adaptations. Some parents were able to directly perceive their children's efforts and difficulties in the classroom, and this generated a need for support, closeness, and strategisation; others have been able to directly experience sign language and learn certain signs from online teachers to use in the family (in Italy, there are no courses for hearing parents who want to learn sign language for communicating with their deaf children).

The situation has been continuously monitored through colloquia and interviews with the families, meetings and focus groups with the teachers, and by means of a survey among parents—the preliminary results of which show that the actions undertaken by the school have been highly appreciated by the families. As an example, among the families of secondary school pupils (63 out of 139 answers, response rate 45%), the level of satisfaction is on average 9.13/10 vs. 8.89 in 2019 (9.44 among families with children with disabilities); with reference to the lockdown period, they feel that their children received appropriate stimuli (8.83 avg; 9.44 children with disabilities) and think that the school staff has paid appropriate attention to pupils and families (8.89; 9.38). Tests to measure the impact on learning are under development and will be administered as soon as the school re-opens.

On the ground of this experience, we can conceive of remote teaching with deaf pupils on three levels: (1) technological; (2) methodological; and (3) organizational.

On a *technological level* (1), in terms of accessibility it is necessary that the digital materials (self-produced or found on the Internet) present adequate speech with clear audio and without background music, that they be subtitled and/or translated into LIS (based on the age of the pupils and the use of sign language), and that they have a correct framing of the face (eyes and mouth always clearly visible in the foreground to facilitate reading of lips and expressions) or of the signing space (that is, the area from head to waist where signs are articulated; Klima and Bellugi, 1979).

It is important that contents are accompanied by self-explanatory images (one must be able to grasp the meaning even without speech), coherent and cleaned of unnecessary decorative details, which are likely to result in high levels of extraneous cognitive load (Chandler and Sweller, 1991). Such products are useful for anticipating a topic to be treated in class or for making an effective summary (Lazzari, 2016), perhaps in a video that can be reviewed several times by the student. One of the greatest efforts for deaf pupils in the classroom comes from the simultaneous and long-term management of different sensory stimuli (e.g. listening while taking notes, looking at the blackboard or the screen). Diversifying channels and languages is also a good solution to respond to the variability of their communication needs: for some pupils, in fact, auditory information is sufficient with minimal guidance, whereas for others, constant eye contact is mandatory. For some students, writing represents a stimulating alternative. If the poor quality of the Internet connection makes it difficult to read lips or see a translation in signs, one can take advantage of the chat function as an accessible and practical tool for the written language.

On a *methodological level* (2), it was necessary to propose activities with few variables and micro-objectives, considering the efforts to participate in a virtual classroom lesson (feel, understand, speak). Operational tasks and flipped learning, with the use of technologies, increase attention, motivation, and a sense of self-efficacy. Eventually, remote teaching requires teachers to produce multimedia with greater content customization.

On an *organizational level* (3), the importance of teamwork between teachers and assistants is evident, even more so for remote teaching, for a correct balance between generality and specificity of the educational intervention. Coordination and monitoring are fundamental both in traditional, in-person teaching and in remote teaching.

4. CONCLUSIONS

During the COVID-19 emergency, technologies are building a bridge of continuity among teachers, pupils, and families. Despite some difficulties, our experience shows that remote teaching with deaf pupils is possible if the school accepts the challenge and the community of practice affirms itself (Wenger, 1998), finding technical, methodological, and organizational solutions to achieve inclusion through learning.

Remote teaching during lockdown forced experimentation with different ways of conducting schooling, focusing attention on accessibility and generating new expertise among teachers and on the use of technologies. It is known that technologies alone do not improve learning processes (Hattie, 2008; Halverson and Smith, 2009): their effectiveness, even in deaf pupils' schooling, is mediated by methodological aspects, such as balancing specificity and universality, and requires strong investments in teacher training. After the first months of emergency distance teaching, the Scuola Audiofonetica appears to have exploited digital technologies to implement its educational offering, guaranteeing continuity to its educational project centred on inclusion.

After the hoped-for exit from the health emergency, this wealth of multimedia materials (more than 1500 resources generated in two months), knowledge, and good practices on technologies, accessibility, and inclusive teaching for deaf pupils must not be lost, but must be made available to the entire school community, in a perspective of networking between schools.

ACKNOWLEDGEMENT

We would like to thank the management, teachers, specialists, pupils, and families of the Scuola Audiofonetica for their passion in ordinary and extraordinary challenges.

REFERENCES

Barak, A. and Sadowsky, Y., 2008. Internet use and personal empowerment of hearing-impaired adolescents. *Computers in Human Behavior*, Vol. 24, No. 5, pp. 1802-1815.

Chandler, P. and Sweller, J., 1991. Cognitive load theory and the format of instruction. *Cognition and Instruction*, Vol. 8, No. 4, pp. 293–332.

Halverson R. and Smith, A., 2009. How new technologies have and have not changed teaching and learning in schools. *Journal of Computing in Teacher Education*, Vol. 26, No. 2, pp. 49-54.

Hattie, J., 2008. *Visible learning: a synthesis of over 800 meta-analyses relating to achievement*. Routledge, London, UK.

Hwang, G. et al., 2015. Seamless flipped learning: a mobile technology-enhanced flipped classroom with effective learning strategies. *Journal of Computers in Education*, Vol. 2, No. 4, pp. 449–473.

Ibáñez, M.-B. and Delgado-Kloos, C., 2018. Augmented reality for STEM learning: A systematic review. *Computers & Education*, Vol. 123, pp. 109-123.

ISTAT, 2019. *Report Cittadini e ICT – anno 2019*. Istituto Nazionale di Statistica, Roma, Italy, https://www.istat.it/it/files/2019/12/Cittadini-e-ICT-2019.pdf

Jordan, I. et al., 1976. Current communication trends at programs for the deaf. *American Annals of the Deaf*, Vol. 121, No. 6, pp. 527-532.

Keating, E. et al., 2008. Cybersign and new proximities: Impacts of new communication technologies on space and language. *Journal of Pragmatics*, Vol. 40, No. 6, pp. 1067-1081.

Klima, E.S. and Bellugi, U., 1979. *The signs of language*. Harvard University Press, Cambridge, USA.

Lazzari, M., 2016. Digital storytelling for inclusive education: an experience in initial teacher training. In M.B. Nunes and M. McPherson (eds.), *Proceedings of the 10th International Conference on e-Learning*, Funchal, Portugal, 1-4 July 2016, pp. 199-203.

Lazzari, M. and Betella, A., 2007. Towards guidelines on educational podcasting quality. In Michael J. Smith, Gavriel Salvendy (eds.), *Human interface and the management of information*, Springer, Berlin, Germany, pp. 404-412.

Marschark, M. and Hauser, P., 2008. *Deaf cognition: foundations and outcomes*. Oxford University Press, New York, USA.

Martins, P. et al., 2015. Accessible options for deaf people in e-Learning platforms: technology solutions for Sign Language translation. *Procedia Computer Science,* Vol. 67, pp. 263-272.

Mayer R., 2005. *The Cambridge handbook of multimedia learning*. Cambridge University Press, New York, USA.

Rose, D. and Meyer, A., 2002. *Teaching every student in the digital age: Universal Design for Learning*. Association for Supervision and Curriculum Development, Alexandria, USA.

UNESCO, 2020. *COVID-19: 10 Recommendations to plan distance learning solutions.* Retrieved at https://en.unesco.org/news/covid-19-10-recommendations-plan-distance-learning-solutions

Viner, R. et al., 2020. School closure and management practices during coronavirus outbreaks including COVID-19: a rapid systematic review. *The Lancet Child & Adolescent Health,* Vol. 4, No. 5, pp. 397-404.

Wenger E., 1998. *Communities of practice: Learning, meaning, and identity*. Cambridge University Press, Cambridge, UK.

STUDENT'S SOCIAL VULNERABILITY IN DISTANCE LEARNING IN COVID-19 TIMES

Bertil P. Marques[1], Rui Marques[2] and Rosa Reis[1]
*GILT/ISEP/IPP [1], DEI/ISEP [2], Portugal**

ABSTRACT

This work aims to analyze the social vulnerability of students in the disciplines taught in distance education in the context of the COVID-19 pandemic. This is a theoretical study, reflective analysis on the various issues of social vulnerability, focusing on how students experience distance learning within the social isolation obligation context. The following points are based on literature review with discussion: Distance learning as a realistic response on the fight against social isolation and social vulnerability, on higher education students, while aiming to avoid losing any semester topics. As a result, it is important to highlight the student's requirements in terms of preparation with information and communication technologies and, especially, those in a situation of social vulnerability who do not have all the necessary resources to access contents taught in this teaching modality, at a distance. There must be a perception of diversity, accessibility and the principles of inclusion so that the demands of students in situations of social vulnerability can be met in an equitable way.

KEYWORDS

Distance Education, Educational Technology, Social Equity, Educational Equity, Distance Learning, Coronavirus, COVID-19, Pandemic

1. INTRODUCTION

In the world scenario, the respiratory disease called COVID-19 was named as a pandemic on March 11, 2020, by the World Health Organization (WHO, 2020). In several countries, including Portugal, social isolation measures were taken to prevent and mitigate the spread of COVID-19. Among these measures, it was verified that many educational institutions had to close their classes and presential activities (Camacho *et al*, 2020).

Taking into account the measures of social isolation, the Presidency of the council of ministers establishes Decree-Law 10-A/2020, of March 13, 2020, which provides for the substitution of face-to-face classes with classes in digital media, while the pandemic of the New Coronavirus (COVID-19) lasts. In this compliance, article 1 states that the authorization period for substituting presential classes with classes in digital media for the duration of the pandemic situation, is up to thirty days, extendable. Such authorization depends on guidance from the Ministry of Health and regional, municipal and district health agencies. Still in the second article, it is emphasized that, is the institutions' responsibility to define the subjects that can be replaced, the array of tools available to students that allow monitoring of the disposed contents, as well as the performance of evaluations during the authorization period (PCM, 2020).

Given this new reality, it appears that this information and communication technology used for Education at a Distance (E@D), represents a way of thinking about its viability, while also bringing challenges. The term accessibility, present in several areas of activity, places a great burden on computing, a great responsibility, of important relevance. It represents, for the user, not only the right to access the information network, but also the right to eliminate architectural barriers, availability of communication, physical access, appropriate equipment and programs, content and presentation of information in suitable formats and so on. In addition to this, there are other principles of great importance, that also need to be taken into account: the profile of students and their requirements (it must be taken into account that there may be cases in which the

*{bpm rfm,rmr}@isep.ipp.pt

equipment foreseen to be used by teachers, has to be adapted to a potential group of students); the objectives for which they are intended; the contents necessary for the effective activities execution (Ramos, 2009), were placed in a E@D environment in record time by teachers, thus to minimizing time without classes and also preventing course calendar lagging.

In this perspective, a movement was transformed from the face-to-face reality to the E@D present, so that it was possible to revert courses, without excluding students in the conversion/adaptation process, for whatever reason. The biggest challenge for teachers today is to keep the school/course/institution where, students with different degrees, levels and learning conditions, stay together and motivated. Teachers are also facing these situations all over the world whatever course, school or institution.

A relevant aspect is the difficulty that not all students are on an equal ground regarding technology access, while some still struggle to maintain some kind of access: those who are from lower social classes and live in areas where access to internet is inexistent or its speed is below minimum requirements. Many are at home, unable to go out due to the lack of accessibility, some located in difficult access places. There are also those cases that do not have enough financial resources to have access to technological facilities (people without financial resources to buy a higher end computer, faster Internet, or simply having a suitable space to study and work) and now also unable to find these assets outside their home, due to social isolation.

In a day-to-day, traditional teaching face-to-face interaction, common sense and tact on the part of teachers have granted a way of analyzing, discussing and identifying such cases (students' right of access to E@D but, who's in a situation of social vulnerability). E@D requires didactic computer resources, with preparation and planning of activities that form the key moments of active learning, having greater meaning for both the student and teacher (Camacho *et al.*, 2020).

Thus, in the context of the current scenario, it aims to analyze the social vulnerability of students in E@D disciplines in times of COVID-19.

2. METHODOLOGY

Reflection study on students in social vulnerability in E@D disciplines in times of COVID-19. The use of the analysis of the different types of reflection, in formative experiences, can favor a greater understanding of the student and the teacher, about the reasons for their actions; enable the questioning of these actions; raise awareness of how theoretical frameworks are present in practice; expand the possibilities for reflection when the professional is faced with situations of uncertainty and conflict of interests, and also serve as a source of evidence for improving the practice (Marcolino & Mizukami, 2008).

This work is a review of narrative literature by discussing the following points: E@D as a proposal due to social isolation and E@D students in social vulnerability.

Thus, the review of narrative literature is characterized by broad publications, appropriate to describe and discuss the development of a given subject, from a theoretical or contextual point of view. The narrative reviews do not inform the sources of information used, the methodology to search for references, nor the criteria used in the evaluation and selection of works. They basically consist of an analysis of literature published in books, articles from printed and / or electronic magazines in the interpretation and personal critical analysis of the author (Rother, 2007).

3. RESULTS AND DISCUSSION

In Portugal, social isolation measures were implemented to prevent and mitigate the spread of COVID-19. The closure of educational institutions was determined by the competent authorities in the country, as well as other situations in which only classes and presential activities were suspended, making E@D via videoconferencing, video classes, synchronous and/or asynchronous classes a requirement.

3.1 E@D as a Proposal Due to Social Isolation

According to the General Directorate of Health (DGS, 2020) it's important to combine two strategies: first, to stop virus transmission, with every social distance measure that can be adopted into the country reality. Second and foremost, to prepare all National Health Service (SNS,2020) services, so that in case of need, at any time and in any place, assistance capacity can be increased.

Therefore, the isolation period brought immense challenges, new forms of relationship, skills for teleworking and the redefinition of "daily routine". Social isolation generates the preservation and contribution to the common good to prevent the number of cases of COVID-19 from rising in an uncontrolled fashion and, specially, due to a shortage of Intensive Care Units (UCI) available for the treatment of critically ill patients.

In the case of E@D brings to light some considerations. Is absolutely necessary that educational institutions, teachers and their students are prepared and to, pedagogically, socially and technologically, fulfilling their tasks. The situations, terms and conditions, were different between different courses and institutions, but at the level of higher education it was found that adaptation period varied from 3 days to 2 weeks.

Especially for students in a social vulnerability situation, who do not have all the resources to access the content taught in the E@D modality, in this case, it's particularly important to meet student's needs, in terms of information access and communication technologies.

It is fundamental for teachers and students the existence of computers with the right software, to be used in the subject of the discipline, while still having access to the course information necessary for the semester's classes, so that, with the help of colleagues, this strategy can provide the production of works, monitoring of classes, synchronous and asynchronous, performance of generic tasks, everything that is defined by the course, for all intents and purposes, helping the students in their progress, while mitigating the potential negative impact.

According to Carmo & Franco (2019), one of the challenges in teaching via web, is the lack of physicality of the student, a factor that influences the teaching work both from the point of view of building knowledge and interpersonal relationships. In search of university education for professional and human training, students' reading and writing are means by which tutors/teachers are guided to determine who these students are, what their learning needs are and what teaching strategies to direct the they in the face of the difficulties of distance learning.

We must also not forget that the teacher/tutor who works must master this whole set of information and communication technologies (software, virtual learning environment and the available content) with perfection. This makes this teacher a person with highly specialized educational competence and with a solid background in operating computer equipment.

3.2 Distance Learning Higher Education Students in Social Vulnerability

The concept of social vulnerability is a concept that presents itself with a multifaceted character and can encompass several dimensions. Being aware of such dimensions, it is possible to identify situations of difficulty for individuals, families or communities. Such dimensions relate to elements linking characteristics of individuals and families, such as their assets and socio demographic characteristics, or even those related to the social media where they are inserted. What is perceived is that, for scholars who deal with the theme, there is an essential character of vulnerability, that is, an attribute related to the ability to respond to situations of risk or constraints (Cunha *et al.*, 2016).

In such context, the understanding of legislation, as a reality and not a utopia, needs to be taken into account. E@D needs to be seen as a continuous orientation work in our inclusion-oriented society. Inclusion alternatives are in our daily lives. Respect and application of inclusive legislation to people must be a reality. Technologies must be at the service of everyone and not just a few. Hence other constraints arise: the opportunity to integrate knowledge with reality.

Therefore, there is an urgent need to implement Public Policies aimed at youth, such as offering internships and jobs, aimed at insertion in the labor market, and also, keeping their studies up-to-date, so that one can access job opportunities. It should be noted that digital inclusion has become a fundamental element to tackle socioeconomic inequalities, even for students who do not want to pursue academic studies, it is essential to guarantee the well-being of citizens, regardless of the level of education, the use of information and communication technologies, where today, still represents a strong disparity when analyzed in a socio demographic way (Dambros, 2018).

Facing the inequality in education that takes place in contexts of social vulnerability in large cities, would require profound changes and great efforts in new educational policies implementation. Given the difficulty of general discussion between educational institutions and political bodies, in country education direction and intent. Reflections on the challenges ahead, for increasing the equality and quality of Portuguese education, are thoroughly necessary (Ribeiro & Vóvio, 2017).

Fortunately, every day we witness an undeniable change in posture, preconceptions and attitudes on behalf of teachers, researchers, opinion makers and general public. The integration of differences as natural attribute of humanity, in the recognition and affirmation of human rights, in the openness for innovation in the theoretical-practical field, and in the assimilation of values, principles and goals to be achieved.

Social inclusion is way for equalize opportunities for all students, and in this case of E@D, it can be a very powerful tool. It is intended that this new way of teaching, continues to demonstrate an array of possibilities and advances for all, allowing the democratization of education for citizens of different levels, places and timezones (Maia and Bokums, 2018).

All this streamlining generated needs for flexible schedules, recording of online transmissions of classes so that students can have access to content at other timezones (asynchronous). This also allows greater opportunity for flexibility in controlling students' attendance, through their access to virtual learning environments (Moodle and others) and Videoconferencing Tools (MSTeams, ZOOM, GoogleClassRoom, etc ...). The teachers are committed to offering quality services, reducing stress, avoiding an increase in social vulnerability, defending the democratic process and promoting social emancipation. The commitment to students' autonomy is emphasized, strengthening their potential in order to break the exclusion process, providing assisting through local school or parent institution, in order to maintaining their protagonism, in their own stories of realization of their student rights (Dambros, 2018).

Thus, it is essential to assert a constitutional right of every citizen, the right of access to knowledge so that, from there, with training and commitment, it can be independent of assistance policies, breaking the cycle of social vulnerability, which is sometimes passed down from generation to generation in low-income families (Dambros, 2018).

These findings help us understand that for E@D to be effective, in COVID-19 context, has to be considered as multi-part process that includes: planning, organization, information technology and open communication between teachers and students within the established class schedule. In addition, students in a situation of social vulnerability and with low accessibility to information and communication technologies would become invisible, because they do not have all the technological resources to access the content taught in the E@D modality, but as we have already said, once identified, they can be supported, allowing them not to miss the courses in which they were enrolled.

It was necessary to outline action plans, that should be put into practice, when democratic solutions, based on participatory democracy oriented towards solidarity and cooperation were needed, and not towards entrepreneurship and competitiveness at all costs (Santos, 2020).

The understanding of diversity, accessibility and the principles of inclusion must always be taken into account, so that the demands of students in situations of social vulnerability can always be met in an equitable manner, especially when a situation arises that makes them leave their comfort zone, while imposing rules, at a national level, in an exceptional situation, as it was the case of COVID-19.

4. FINAL CONSIDERATIONS

In order to analyze the social vulnerability of students in E@D disciplines in times of COVID-19, it was needed to attend inclusive practices, allowing visibility into the difficulties of students, in terms of organization, dealing with information, communication technologies and, especially, those in situations of social vulnerability who do not have all the resources to access the content taught in the E@D modality.

As a limitation, it is highlighted that the difficulty of access to information and communication technologies, by students in times of Pandemic COVID-19, arises (into the education authorities) new reflections on the reality of the population when we move to the National panorama.

As a recommendation, it is suggested an increased attention to students in socially vulnerable situations at E@D so that it is inclusive, giving the opportunity to integrate knowledge with reality and not making this student feel increasingly excluded. A pivotal point is to involve colleagues in work groups, and/or class, to make them part of the integration, trying to reduce this possible inequality that the student may feel.

The E@D must be inclusive, respecting the differences of each region, proposing actions and measures that aim to ensure the improvement of the quality of education, the investment in training by the teachers, the removal of physical barriers and changes in attitude, the planning and preparation of resources materials that are necessary for an effective E@D must be prepared by teachers using access to virtual learning environments (Moodle and others), which were eventually already used to support presential classes. And all the preparation of the Videoconferencing tool (MSTeams, ZOOM, GoogleClassRoom, etc ...) that meanwhile was chosen to be used for classes by videoconferencing (synchronous), chat, tasks, etc. (asynchronous).

5. CONCLUSIONS

In this new world scenario, a new pulmonary disease, created a Covid-19 Pandemic. With unprecedented speed and worldwide dissemination, caught several governments off-guard, even though WHO (2020) kept disease data updated (as one can expect in a time of upmost uncertainty), disseminating disease evolution status, trying to prevent mass uncontrolled infection.

Portugal, as a mitigating action, establishes in a council of ministers from 13 March 2020, that presential classes should be cancelled, while recommending remote work, followed by a strict social isolation policy.

In the Higher Education context, the direct application of such policies had a heavy impact, as one should expect, even considering pre-existing social vulnerabilities.

- We can now say that, we were all caught off-guard with overall activity shutdown. While transforming course into E@D is a challenge itself, even more when the timeframe is so short, and so little margin for error. The semester should maintain context, in content and grading. Provided tools should be solid and also user-friendly. The teacher's commitment and overtime dedicated this few days after lockdown, were crucial for semester continuity, and even more important, academic continuity.
- There was no questionnaire. The authors are, in firsthand, reporting class students' comments and feedback. In general, students agreed to the E@D found solution. As every class is different, each Teacher restructured the class towards a format more compatible with their students, offering live or postponed lessons, reading documents or quizzes, reflection papers or group work, and so on. Students found diversity and they liked it - some students complained in the past that some classes were too "demonstration oriented" - so work was more practical, more team based. Individual work was now more flexible, and teachers were all online, most of the time, so, more accessible.
- Teachers have an active role in detecting social vulnerability. Social isolation stresses areas untouched until now. Students with no compatible or up-to-date equipment, bad internet or expensive connections. Working students should maintain their expenses, and even, in some cases, invest in equipment to keep studying. Some students had complex family situations (little children, elderly or even handicap relatives) that now lost their outside support. This teacher "new" role, is a relevant one on preventing that complex situations became worst.
- Since March 2020, the teacher's spend most of its time feeding the chosen platform with the remaining of the course data, while adapting evaluation and exams.
- Now interaction happen 24/7, questions are asked at any hour, in any format (chat, group forum, phone or video call), replies are made ASAP. This one to one process personalizes the follow-up, making it effective and assertive.
- This home-based class system as a negative effect on costs, as it increases consumption of water, electricity, gas, internet and so on.
- Some more complex situations were detected where students could not adapt to E@D. A small group of students quitted classes or even the hole course – group partners complained about lack of or even no communication with dropped out students. Others reported that online courses implied a bigger workload, incompatible with their family routines. Others had to maintain their jobs (first line work, needed in times of COVID-19), complicating all aspects of E@D even further.

- On last but very important reference, E@D classes were home-based classes during isolation, which is expected, however, the format is maintained now, after isolation obligation is over. Exams will occur in E@D environment, which, in our opinion, is a very relevant finding.

E@D is here to stay. It is already considered a *de facto* solution for learning, whatever the distance. The information and assets accessibility as had an unprecedented leap forward. These initiatives empowered the school to accelerate and conclude the opening of several new courses, some with E@D features. Fully, partially or specific case oriented. E@D will allow remote students to keep tabs with learning while allowing to invite teachers and professionals, from all over the globe for inputs, interaction or even course classes. This is a new dawn for E@D, in the expectation this dawn leads us to a COVID-19 free future.

ACKNOWLEDGEMENT

We would like to show our gratitude with ISEP – Instituto Superior de Engenharia do Porto for providing us all the information needed to compile this work.

REFERENCES

Camacho, A. C. L. F., Joaquim, F. L., Menezes, H. F. & Sant' Anna, R. M. (2020). A tutoria na educação à distância em tempos de COVID-19: orientações relevantes. Research, Society and Development, 9(5), e30953151.

Carmo, R. O. S., & Franco, A. P. (2019). Da docência presencial à docência online: aprendizagens de professores universitários na educação a distância. Educação em Revista, 35, e210399.

Cunha, J. M. P., Jakob, A. A. E., Hogan, D. J. & Carmo, R. L. (2016). *A vulnerabilidade social no contexto metropolitano: o caso de Campinas.* ABEP, Retrieved em 21 de May, 2020, http://www.abep.org.br/publicacoes/index.php/anais/article/viewFile/1425/1390

Dambros, I. B. (2018). Desconectados e desqualificados: os desafios da capacitação profissional EAD de jovens em vulnerabilidade socioeconômica. *Iluminuras*, 19(47), 142- 161.

General Directorate of Health (2020), online: https://covid19.min-saude.pt/. Retrieved in several dates.

Maia, J. F., Bokums, R. M. (2018). Educação a Distância (EaD) no Brasil: uma reflexão a respeito da inclusão social. *Diálogo*, 38(3), 99-111.

Marcolino, T. Q., Mizukami, M. G. N. (2008). Narratives, reflective processes and professional practice: contributions towards research and training. *Interface - Comunicação, Saúde, Educação*. 12(26), 541-547.

National Health Service (2020) online: https://www.sns.gov.pt/?cpp=1. Retrieved in several dates.

Presidency of the Council of Ministers, (2020). Decreto-Lei 10-A/2020, pag22-(2) a 22-(13), Diário da República n.º 52/2020, 1º Suplemento, Série I de 2020-03-13. Online: https://data.dre.pt/eli/dec-lei/10-A/2020/03/13/p/dre. Retrieved in 28 May, 2020.

Ramos, R. C. G. (2009). Design de material didático on line: reflexões. Editora UNESP, Retrieved in 03 de May, 2020, http://books.scielo.org/id/px29p/pdf/soto-9788579830174- 06.pdf

Rother, E. T. (2007). Revisão sistemática X Revisão narrativa. Ata Paulista de Enfermagem, 20(2), v.

Ribeiro, V. M., Vóvio, C. L. (2017). Desigualdade escolar e vulnerabilidade social no território. Educar em Revista, Edição Especial (2), 71-87.

Santos, B. S. (2020). A Cruel Pedagogia do Vírus. Coimbra: Almedina.

World Health Organization (2020). *Coronavirus disease 2019 (COVID-19): Situation Report –51.* OMS, Retrieved in 22 April, 2020, https://www.who.int/docs/default- source/coronaviruse/situation-reports/20200311-sitrep-51-covid-19.pdf?sfvrsn=1ba62e57_10

ECOPOLYTECHNIC: A SUSTAINABLE AND FLEXIBLE E-LEARNING SYSTEM FOR AGILE SMART LEARNING SCENARIOS

Michele Angelaccio
University of Rome "Tor Vergata" - Management Engineering Dept, Via del Politecnico 1, 00100 Rome, Italy

ABSTRACT

The rapid change of technological and human-machine co-evolutionary processes due to smart working and smart industries, present several issues that are also influencing the world of e-learning systems. Nowadays is quite hard to distinguish between learning spaces/systems/organizations and working organizations especially when smart working and tele-monitoring are becoming widespread. In this work we analyze smart learning concepts that are leading to a new emerging scenario in which the distinction between learning and working activities is dynamic and in evolution. In particular we present an integrated smart learning model called EcoPolytechnic which aims to redesigns the organization model of a Polytechnic by introducing several concepts of agile learning and project-based learning. The model is built upon the notion of smart learning cell that replaces in a flexible and sustainable way the notion of set of courses and can be used in a better way in smart learning scenarios. The result is a complete and easy to be configured smart learning organization system for which a comparative analysis is carried out. The benefits in terms of innovation and adaptive learning performance are given by using agile learning analysis.

KEYWORDS

Data Science, Smart Learning, Agile Learning

1. INTRODUCTION

Technology is transforming jobs and skills faster than the ability of organizations or people to adapt to them. Coursera's Global Skills Index 2019 found that two-thirds of the world's population is falling behind in critical skills. Research from the World Economic Forum suggests that the core skills required to perform most roles will change by 42% on average within 2022. At this level of disruption, companies are scrambling to identify and source the skills they need in order to stay competitive. The availability of key skills is now one of the top three business threats for CEOs globally, according to a recent PwC survey. Driven by these impulses, new scenario of learning systems (Figure 1) are emerging, in which online courses are required in several ways and at different places with the aim of yielding digital skills capabilities in an effective way and often as soon as possible. Moreover interdisciplinary approaches besides typical engineering sectors as for instance social science, are leading to consider a new knowledge base of social data science extending the role of scientific data science (see Lifelong learning schema in Figure 1- discussed in *Piano Scuola* Digital).

In this way, we can say that a new era of smart learning activities is becoming a reality. Unfortunately the traditional model of university campus with physical or virtual online learning activities carried out in a fixed place and with a long-range organization system, does not seem to satisfy well this change, because it hardly cope with dynamic digital skills required by several stack holders and smart industries (Kavasakalis & Lioss, 2019; Angelaccio & Buttarazzi, 2010 and Angelaccio & Buttarazzi, 2016).

As noted in Sonetti, Lombardi, and Chelleri (2016), in order to obtain a new approach for green campuses, there is the need to propose "clusters of different university typologies", and to this purpose they remarked at micro-scale, the need for revising and replacing current eco-efficiency-driven indicators with more life cycle and user-centric related metrics.

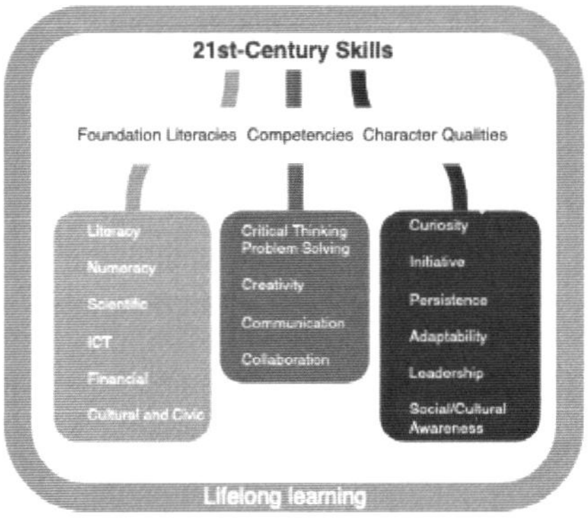

Figure 1. New Vision for Education (World Economic Forum 2013)

In this paper we try to explore this direction of new modeling with user-centric approach and outline a different approach for smart learning system more adequate to digital competencies and skills.

2. ECOPOLYTECHNIC DESCRIPTION

2.1 Smart Learning Concepts and EcoPolytechnic Organization

Typical Engineering Learning Activities performed in a so-called Polytechnic System, are characterized by Multiple Engineering Sectors shared among the same students and researchers with the aim to be very interdisciplinary.

Figure 2 shows the traditional organization schema of a campus performing learning and research activities in synergy with external communities by focusing on the smart city context (Polytechnic organization and smart city).

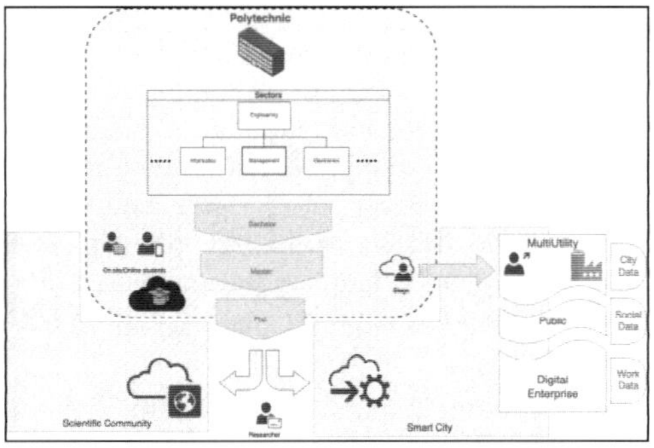

Figure 2. Traditional Polytechnic organization schema

To overcome this organization scheme and provide a different organization for e-learning in a smart scenario, we introduce a smart learning organization built upon a set of hybrid educational/coworking islands where it will be possible to learn and apply digital technologies. These are called smart learning cells (SLC) and allow an easy configuration in several places and in several ways, with little organizing effort. Basically they are composed by web notebooks working on datasets incoming from real environment (IoT datasets for example) and targeted to particular learning outputs matching some of the real needs. Each cell acts as a minimal learning space involving a working group assigned to a data project related to a smart city subfield. Tutor starts the activities, but after an initial scrum period the SLC will proceed autonomously and will be monitored independently. After a minimal learning activity, the cell will output a set of digital results hosted by the cloud lab platform. The main novelty, compared to previous models, concerns the fact that the resulting learning system works as a virtual organization box that could be embedded in a real scenario depending on the original dataset and the corresponding set of learning objectives, without the need of a particular physical space as a Campus or University Building. This is the main reason for the choice of the eco prefix label used in the Organization Model name presented here, and it must to be considered as a further step beyond well-known concepts used in e-learning technologies (online course, webinar, etc.).

In particular, there is a need to reinforce the motivation of a new Model based on a more agile learning phases obtained via optimization of staging and online courses better suited to industry and working needs.

To this purpose, it occurs to change the overall process to reach a more flexible and dynamic organization level, in which small learning units are definable in a suitable way and customizable to different working needs in an easy way but at the same time by ensuring a minimal knowledge base in the learning curricula.

Figure 3 gives an example of learning organization that could be implemented by a different Polytechnic system called **eco-Polytechnic** in which the organization is based on cells (subfigure (a)), called Smart Learning Cell (SLC) in which, through the use of notebooks, agile learning with data science paradigms yields a scrum process that monitors learning activity.

In this way the learning organization could be reconfigured on the basis of learning goals and depending on the external scientific data and corresponding working context (subfigure (b)). This adaptability to the context and the capability for a single cell to be implemented in a flexible way both in a campus or in other place will introduce the novel schema and its property to be eco-sustainable in the sense that it works in accord to smart working and smart learning objectives.

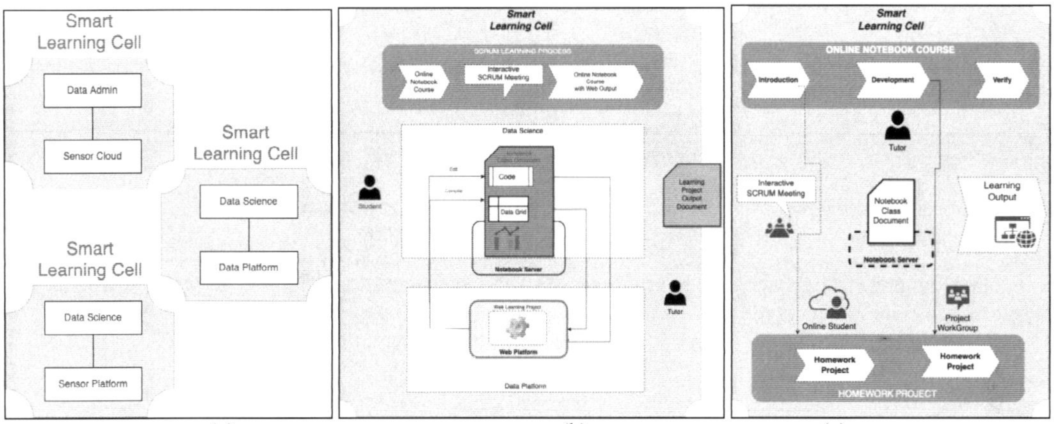

(a) (b) (c)

Figure 3. EcoPolytechnic organization schema: (a) Smart Learning Cells, (b) SLC Description, (c) SLC Workflow

The data science topics are organized in two main blocks (Content and Platform) by using the notion of web notebook with interactive learning sections useful to learn in an autonomously and flexible way all digital foundations and using real data example downloaded by internet.

In this way active learning becomes a reality in data science course through notebooks due to the following main reasons:

- Notebooks can be used without requiring particular preliminaries on digital skills that could be easily integrated in the same notebook.
- Learning output are easily managed without the need of a different web learning platform
- Agile development of learning output and results for certifying digital skills could be easily deployed in terms of web platforms described through notebook code examples with digital repositories.

In this way we obtain a small organization learning box system which is more flexible and suitable to be used in a cellular based learning system thanks to the capability to be connected in several way to obtain a chain of Smart learning Cells for Smart learning Scenarios (see Workflow description in (subfigure (b)).

In the next section we give some example of smart learning thrugh SLC, to evidence the capability to accelerate learning outputs in interdisciplinary socio technological sectors like Smartourism and Smart City.

2.2 Smart Learning Scenarios Examples

Digital Skills for Smart City technologies often require an interdisciplinary approach for which a flexible and dynamic e-learning approach must kept into account (Smart Learning Scenarios). In these cases it could be useful to focus on project-based learning designed on the basis of common data science topics since public open data are the common source of required digital skills and competencies for which there is the main attention by stakeholders (Kavasakalis, & Lioss, 2019).

This activity is quite independent from other learning activities and can be executed in a project-based framework without the need to be considered simply as a set of lessons.

The required learning re-organization will put research and students at the nexus of neighborhood networks (see Figure 4). EcoPolytechnic could be used to engage students in external community and enterprises having a common data science paradigm.

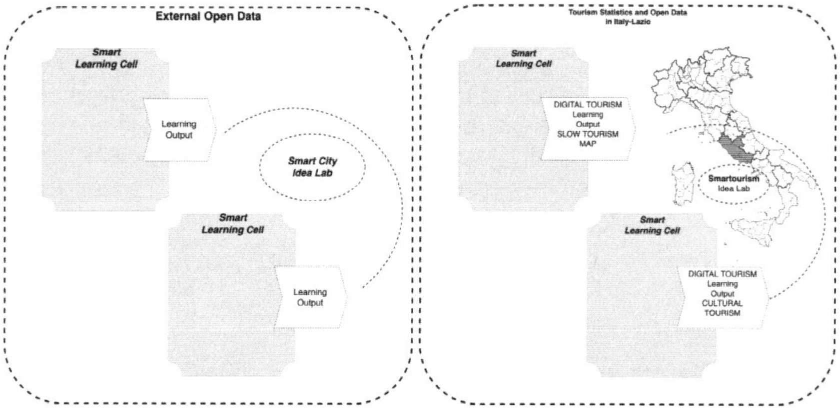

Figure 4. EcoPolytechnic Cellular Organization for Smart City data science

As example of this interaction, Figure 4 (on the right) outlines the case of smart learning scenario resulting by the application of a two learning cells designed to approach data science for smartourism for which the referenced data are taken by touristic places aroud Rome in Italy (Lazio Region).

REFERENCES

Angelaccio, M. & Buttarazzi, B. (2016) *Enhancing web programming learning through mobile ecommerce paradigms* in atti di Didamatica 2016, Udine, 19-21 aprile 2016, ISBN: 978889809144.

Angelaccio, M. & Fanti, A. (2011), *Design of active learning strategy through agile development methodologies: a technological view*, in: CECIIS-2011.

Angelaccio, M. & Buttarazzi, B. (2010) *A social network based-enhanced learning system*, in: S. Reddy (Ed.), 19th IEEE International Workshopson Enabling Technologies: Infrastructures for Collaborative Enterprises,WETICE 2010, Larissa, Greece, 28-30 June 2010, Proceedings, IEEEComputer Society, 2010, pp. 94–95.

Kavasakalis, A. & Lioss, F. (2019) *Lifelong Learning Policies: The Case of Work-Based Learning*, July 2019 DOI:10.5296/jet.v6i2.14804 Journal of Education and Training ISSN 2330-9709 2019, Vol.6, No.2

Piano Scuola Digitale (*Italian Digital School Program*) https://www.miur.gov.it/scuola-digitale

Sonetti, G., Lombardi, P. & Chelleri, L. (2016). *True Green and Sustainable University Campuses? Toward a Clusters Approach.* in Sustainability 8(1):83 January 2016.

Taylor, K & Negron, R & Bell, C & Riesland, A & Taylor, Katie & Silvis, Deborah & Cramer, C.. (2019). *Supporting Public-Facing Education for Youth: Spreading (Not Scaling) Ways to Learn Data Science With Mobile and Geospatial Technologies*

TESTING AND USING "tiSb-Albania" (TRANSPARENT INTERACTIVE SCREEN-BOARD) DURING COVID19

Romeo Teneqexhi[1] and Loreta Kuneshka[2]
[1]*Ex Director of Distance Education Centre, Lecturer of Electrotechnics, Polytechnic University of Tirana, Albania, Sheshi "Nënë Tereza", No 4. Tirana, Albania*
[2]*Lecturer of Statistics, Medical University of Tirana, Albania, Rruga e Dibres, Tirana, Albania*

ABSTRACT

Due to the coronavirus, almost all teachers around the world are teaching through the Internet from their homes, sitting in chairs, in most cases even without showing their faces to the students. Most of the students do not like this. They want the teacher to stand on his feet and to explain by pointing on his notes on the blackboard and making gestures with his hands according to the lesson, like they have historically done. Using the "tiSb-Albania" system, everyone can teach the right way. Moreover, you never turn your back to the students even when you write on the blackboard (which is transparent in this case) during the lecture. You will be, during the whole lecture, face to face with the students watching them in real time. This makes them more focused on the lesson despite the fact that they are following it from their homes. Learning in this form "shortens" the distance between the students and the teacher. "tiSb-Albania" is an implant where several hardware devices and software have been assembled, which serves for making and recording the lectures in real-time in a very special form. "tiSb-Albania" is the acronym for Transparent Interactive Screen-Board. The beginnings of this system were presented at the 10th e-Learning conference organized by IADIS in Madeira 2016 (Teneqexhi and Kuneshka, 2016). The system was presented with many new features at the 13th e-Learning conference organized by IADIS in Porto 2019 (Teneqexhi and Kuneshka, 2019), in which we announced that work was underway to build the prototype for ordinary users. The COVID19 created an appropriate ground for further experimentation and completion with other necessary features of the system for such situations. The use of "tiSb-Albania" during the pandemic period as well as other developments in Albanian schools and universities make us draw some conclusions and give some recommendations, we believe it is useful for achieving the teaching process in extraordinary situations, so why not implement it even for normal situations.

KEYWORDS

Transparent Interactive Screen-Board (tiSb), DTSE (Daily Twice Short Exams), Semi-Virtual Classroom (SVC)

1. MAIN PORTABLE CONSTRUCTION OF tiSb-Albania

All hardware devices explained in "Making virtual classrooms of google platform more real using transparent interactive screen-board" (2) are assembled in the construction of first prototype "tiSb-Albania" as shown in Figure 1. This system is now portable and easily implementable in every traditional classroom.

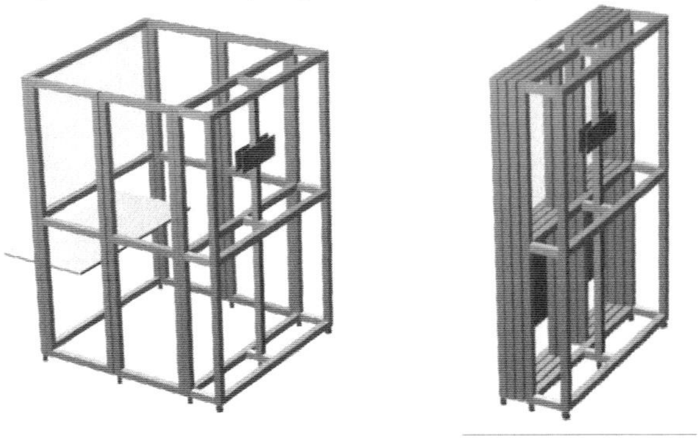

Figure 1. Main construction of tiSb-Alnbaia

2. TWO EXPERIMENTS WITH tiSb-Albania BEFORE AND AFTER CLOSING SCHOOLS BECAUSE OF COVID-19

In Albania, due to an educational reform undertaken in recent years, Distance Education is no longer available. Our work on the "tiSb" project has started before the decision of closing distance education schools. Of course, we never liked this decision but we couldn't do anything to prevent it. In a way we needed to test the prototype in all its parameters with real students. In fact, among other things, we had another strong reason to do an experiment. Actually, we never thought that one day would come when schools would be closed due to a virus. But due to a strong earthquake on November 26 in Albania, the schools were closed for 2 weeks and during this time teaching process was paused. We wanted to show the education authorities that we should be prepared to be able to continue the teaching process without interruption even in the future if schools are closed due to other natural disasters.

For this we used an anniversary day, The opening of the first Albanian language school, March 7, 1887. On March 7, 2020, as a sign of gratitude for my former teachers, I conducted a homage lecture through the system "tiSb-Albania" where most of the students attended it live from home via YouTube while they were logged in the "eBeam Scrapbook" platform. The lecture was very successful in all technical parameters. Figure 2. a/b. (Watch this video at: https://www.youtube.com/watch?v=G5gsAgHlyio&t=856s)

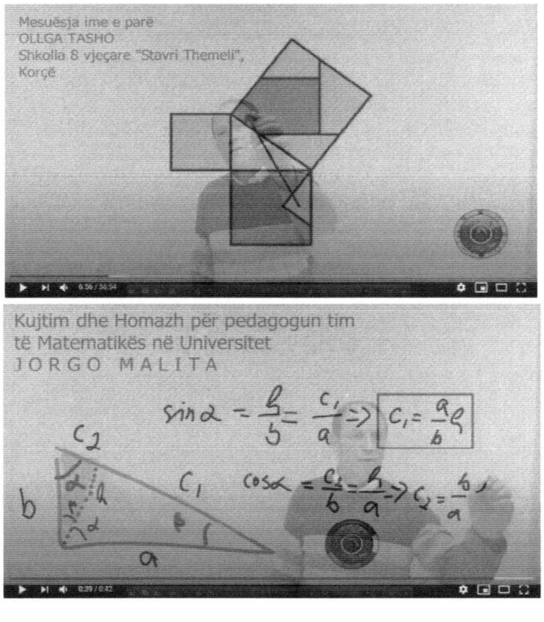

Figure 2a/b. Teaching standing on foot during pandemic time

Ironically, 2 days later, on March 9, 2020, the Albanian government closed schools after the first case of COVID-19 was confirmed in Albania. Covid-19 found Albania totally unprepared to continue the learning process online. Although we notified the education authorities about the existence of the tiSb system, large-scale implementation could not be carried out for many reasons. However, I used and continued to use the "tiSb-Albania" system with great success, perfecting its special features intertwined with existing platforms such as Zoom and Meet.

Immediately after the government closed the schools, we decided to do another big experiment involving as many student as we could, this time to show the educational authorities how the teaching could be organized through the Internet, mainly for primary schools. Through the teaching secretaries, we informed all the students of the Polytechnic University of Tirana to become part of a large virtual classroom to attend a single lecture. We also made the invitation public on Facebook. To ensure participation in the experiment, we invited a well-known Albanian cartoonist, asking him to make for our lecture a cartoon without the title. With this cartoon, through a material stimulus for the participating students, we wanted to test the so-called DTSE ideas (we'll talk about that later). The other reason of the cartoon was the treatment of the lecture with humor and optimistic notes, very important during the pandemic lockdown.

Well-known Albanian cartoonist Bujar Kapexhi made a very interesting cartoon which we are publishing (Figure 3) hoping the cartoon will orient us towards the answers of some questions that concern the whole academic world of today. About 540 students expressed the desire to participate in our experiment. The video was livestreamed on You Tube. Some students logged in eBeam Scrapbook. Many other students just watched the livestream, but they, and not only them, were able to download slides from the lecture any time. All you have to do is to connect via eBeam Scrapbook meeting ID 352 724 420 (slides are on the cloud; ID is on the right up corner of video Figure 4.a. / 3.b.). Through this experiment we retested "tiSb-Albania" in all technical terms including so-called DTSE (Daily Twice Short Exams). It was a really successful experiment. You can watch this video at: https://www.youtube.com/watch?v=PIdK-prQjpE (full version, Albanian language) or at: https://www.youtube.com/watch?v=lJyMJyy5OF4 (short version, music background). After this experiment I have personally used and continue to use the "tiSb-Albania" system. I record every lecture and upload it for the students in their respective Google Classroom. So, my students never lose the lecture even if they have not followed it in real time. I should mention that I have recorded with this system lab-courses using different software simulators.

Figure 3. Friendly cartoon with PM and Minister of Education

Figure 4a. Daily short MCQ exam

Figure 4b. Individual Question Results

3. "tiSb-Albania" LIVESTREAM IN YOUTUBE VS ZOOM PLATFORM

During pandemic time we used two different platforms for transmitting livestream, YouTube and Zoom. In both cases we used eBeam Scrapbook software for four important reasons. First eBeam Scrapbook gives us the possibility to have interactive screen-board. Second, we can use prepared slides or create and edit new ones during the lecture. Third, all these slides are downloadable for the students after the lecture via the eBeam Scrapbook meeting's ID. Forth and most importantly, it is possible to make "short fast exams" during the lecture with MCQ (Multiple Choice Question) or essay type questions using eBeam Scrapbook. Teacher can save in a Data Base all the results of this short exam-type and use them for the final assessment. Zoom platform is very useful for video meeting but does not give you the possibility for MCQ. Zoom annotating tool also does not offer more than one slide. On the other hand, we have notice most of the students do not want to open the camera for privacy reasons. But some time they just log in Zoom meeting and go away (because no MCQ during lecture). A significate difference between streaming in YouTube and Zoom platform is the delay in time (some seconds depending on the internet speed) because of streaming. In the first case the student has the possibility to ask the teacher only via eBeam Scrapbook chat tool. Any way in both cases recording of lecture is important.

4. WHAT ABOUT EXAMS DURING SCHOOL CLOSING TIME?

Due to COVID-19 schools were closed almost all over the world. Teachers changed the way of doing lectures, via internet, without knowing when the schools would reopen. Everyone was engaged with lectures and almost forgot that the schools could have been closed even at the time when the exams would normally take place. Now all universities have a big challenge ahead: How will the exams be done. We want to share our experience by suggesting something that sounds unusual "school without traditional exams". How is it possible? We were confident that the school would remain closed even during the exam period and doing exams in traditional form would be difficult and maybe even dangerous. So, we organize every teaching class with two "short exams" before and after the lecture. At the beginning of the lecture, there is a short, up to 10 minutes exam, with MCQ related to the previous lecture. After the lecture, we do another short exam with problems related to what we just explained in the lecture. eBeam Scrapbook application offers this option, but it can also be done using Google Form in Google Classroom. This gives the lecturer the opportunity to evaluate the student in two very important components, how much he has understood from today's lecture and how much he learned after reviewing the lecture at home. On the other hand, it is a great advantage that "forces" the student to study systematically as there is no exam at the end of the semester but only DTSE (Daily Twice Short Exams) every day in the lecture.

5. CONCLUSIONS

-We strongly believe that the recording of lectures should be done even in normal times. "tiSb-Albania" infrastructure makes it possible. For this, the system must be installed in each lecture classroom and the teacher will do nothing more than usual other than just clicking a button at the beginning and at the end of the lecture. The student should be free to choose to follow the lecture in the same room with the teacher or at home or somewhere else for as long as he is online with the teacher. The second version saves the student a lot of time and money by getting a much better service from the school. We would like to call this kind of combination "Semi-Virtual Classroom", some students are in the class, others at home or somewhere else being involved with other tasks that do not require much commitment.

-Recording of lectures and saving them on different platforms of the departments will become a powerful mechanism for improving the quality of teaching and will increase, in a good sense, academic competition, just because of the transparency of the recorded materials.

- DTSE (Daily Twice Short Exams) every lecture day is an option for substituting some of the traditional exams even in normal situation (without pandemics).

- All of the above are our opinions and conclusions. An extensive survey with students after pandemic would be of great interest for "ACADEMIA POST COVID19".

REFERENCES

Teneqexhi, R. and Kuneshka, L. (2016). Virtual & Real Face to Face Teaching. In MCCSIS 2016, 1-4 July, Madeira, Portugal ISBN: 978-989-8533-51-7, pp. 227-230.

Teneqexhi, R. and Kuneshka, L. (2019). Making virtual classrooms of Google platform more real using transparent interactive Screen-board (tiSb-Albania). In MCCSIS 2019, 16-19 July, Porto, Portugal ISBN: 978-989-8533-88-3, pp. 333-336.

THE EXPANDING ROLE OF IMMERSIVE MEDIA IN EDUCATION

Emre Erturk and Gabrielle-Bakker Reynolds
Eastern Institute of Technology, 501 Gloucester Street, Taradale, Napier 4112, New Zealand

ABSTRACT

This paper seeks to understand the impact of immersive media, in particular augmented reality, within the education sector. A small experimental methodology was adopted alongside a current literature review. Three research questions were posited as follows: (1) What are the affordances of immersive media within education? (2) What are the barriers to immersive media in education? (3) How may immersive media be implemented?
Affordances of immersive media include greater content customisation, increased creativity with less risk, promoting student interaction, enhanced motivation and engagement, and the chance for students to engage in extraordinary experiences. In 2020, many students around the world are staying home and studying in isolation, as a result of the COVID-19 pandemic. In this emergency context, mobile applications can offer interesting experiences that can make life and learning less difficult and more pleasant.
The mobile web application Metaverse was used to exemplify in two different ways how immersive media can be appropriately used as a tool in a university level education setting. The first prototype was a short quiz on general knowledge about New Zealand, to help orient new international students. The second prototype was a quick poll to feel the pulse and understand the mood of students while at home and physically away from the campus and their lecturers. In summary, the authors present an updated review of this technology and present their own new examples of applications that serve additional purposes.

KEYWORDS

Immersive Media, Augmented Reality, Mobile Learning, Home Learning, Educational Technology

1. INTRODUCTION

Immersive media can be understood as any technology that blends computer generated content with the physical environment, creating a sense of immersion and stimulating the human senses through interactive multimedia. For instance, virtual reality aims to occlude the physical environment. In contrast, augmented reality may involve overlaying content the upon physical world. The Virtuality Continuum (see Figure 1) was created in 1994 by Milgram and Kishino as cited in Milman (2018) to show the various modes on a scale.

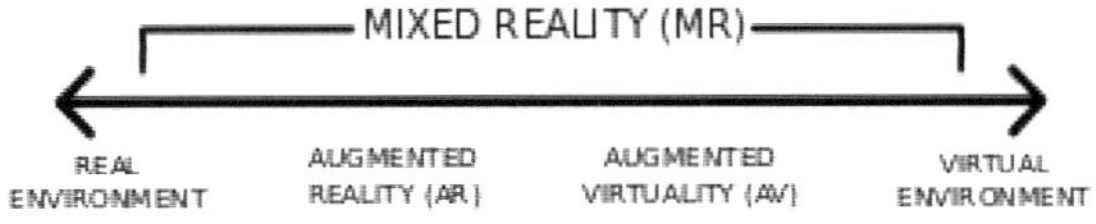

Figure 1. The Virtuality Continuum

Since immersive media's use within the educational sector is still relatively recent, the objective of this paper is to explore its role by discussing its pedagogical affordances and barriers, and provide examples of its practical use. Common previous applications of augmented reality were for younger students and children, or for teaching high school and university students application development and visual design. This paper takes a broader approach in a different context in 2020 where virtual engagement is important.

2. LITERATURE REVIEW

The literature review examined peer-reviewed sources. Keywords used to find sources include *"immersive media," "immersive technologies," "immersive media and education," "augmented reality and education" "virtual reality and student learning," "mixed reality and education" and "AR, VR, MR, and education."*

Jensen & Konradsen (2018) undertook research about the use of virtual reality head-mounted displays in education and training and their findings demonstrated several instances where virtual reality assisted in skills acquisition related to cognitive abilities. Furthermore, Sirakaya (2018) explored the effects of augmented reality use on achievement, misconception, and course engagement among 118 seventh grade students within six different classes. They concluded that students' levels of engagement were not necessarily affected by the implementation of augmented reality. Nevertheless, overall, the students' achievement levels were increased by augmented reality, while reducing any misconceptions from theoretical learning.

Harper et al. (2018) developed a mixed reality game made for simulation-based training, specifically, stonemasonry. Currently, vocational training can be restricted by regulations that do not permit the use of power tools, such as an angle grinder. So, the use of cyber-physical systems allows students to learn without the safety risks. A prototype of a mixed reality, vocational educational training (VET) game was created using Microsoft HoloLens, receiving positive feedback during the trials.

Team-based teaching is another possible approach. Denholm et al. (2013) conducted a study on the value of team-based mixed reality games in higher education on international students. Results demonstrated that not only did 75% of students believe that the mixed reality games improved team collaboration, but over 60% indicated that participation in mixed-reality games were more useful than lectures.

Furthermore, Cascales et al. (2013) examined parents' perceptions of the use of didactical augmented reality in preschool education. They categorised parents' perceptions into elements: writing, reading, knowledge, motivation, degree of satisfaction, and creativity. Although findings showed differences among the participants, the majority of parents believed that augmented reality offered benefits.

3. METHODOLOGY

The first part of Section 4 covers two questions based on a literature review. To address these questions, the authors examined a range of case studies, industry-based information, and educator perspectives. The method of search utilised different resources and online databases such as Google Scholar, ProQuest, and ERIC. Section 4.2 summarizes the experimental project for the third question by investigating the use of the augmented reality platform Metaverse Studio, which is an open-source web platform that allows users to create interactive experiences without the need for coding. Two applications have been created to show how Metaverse may be used as an educational tool. The research questions for the next section are: (1) What are the affordances of immersive media within education? (2) What are the barriers to immersive media within education? and (3) How may immersive media be implemented in the education sector?

4. FINDINGS

4.1 Affordances of Immersive Media and the Barriers

Findings suggest that the pedagogical benefits of immersive media in education include greater customisation, increased creativity and less risk, promotion of student interaction, enhanced motivation and engagement, and extending traditional learning by offering experiences that would otherwise be impossible.

Fernandez (2017) investigated how virtual reality can be used as a tool in representing abstract concepts. Virtual reality is able to be programmed so that situations can be controlled, as well as contexts in which students act. Applications can be tailored to suit a diverse range of subjects and geographical locations. Augmented reality increases creativity among students because it offers fewer risks. Within teaching health, an image of a human body may be superimposed in a classroom environment and split into different segments. In engineering, a digital model of an engine may be superimposed and examined in different ways.

Khan et al. (2019) researched the impact of augmented reality on the learning motivations of health science students at the University of Cape Town. Results supported the notion that augmented reality assists in terms of motivation, and helps bring an increase in students' attention, confidence, and satisfaction.

Google Cardboard, a virtual reality platform, can be used for learning (https://arvr.google.com/cardboard/). For instance, the Expeditions application offers tours around the world, allowing teachers to take students on virtual field trips (https://edu.google.com/products/vr-ar/expeditions/). This enables students to undergo experiences that would otherwise be dangerous, impossible, or costly, such as swimming with sharks or visiting space. It allows a level of customisation that would not be possible with physical tours, and in turn can be more engaging for student learning. Reinforcing this, Foote (2017) found that immersive technologies such as Google Cardboard are valuable tools for teaching geography because they may increase engagement and heighten students' motivation to learn. Lastly, Knierim et al. (2018) explored mixed reality in education, highlighting (1) the personalisation of learning, (2) strengthening of ubiquitous learning through spatially distributed knowledge, and (3) enrichment of learning by amplifying students' understanding of course materials. These findings may be more representative of how students react to a new technology, and less representative of whether the benefits may continue in the long term.

Overall, a final significant affordance of immersive media may be how it enables learning experiences that would otherwise be costly. This may be considered as an incentive for its adoption in education.

Barriers to immersive media include lack of teacher competencies and pedagogical structure in some applications, cognitive overload among students, inflexibility of immersive applications, and technical issues.

Martins et al. (2015) investigated the challenges of using augmented reality within music education, noting that barriers towards augmented reality's adoption include technological issues. For instance, designing applications is not a competence that all teachers have. Augmented reality applications in the educational sector are often influenced by game developers and may not always be pedagogically structured.

Furthermore, Wu et al. (2013) examined the challenges that come with employing augmented reality within education, noting that learning issues may be a barrier. For instance, students have reported feeling overwhelmed. Some tasks in augmented reality applications may be challenging if instructions are missing. This points to another issue teachers may face: the inflexible design of some augmented reality applications.

In relation to the challenges, Akçayır & Akçayır (2017) conducted a systematic literature review, noting technical issues as a hindrance, e.g. location-based applications using GPS may miscalculate directions or locations. Some applications offer low sensitivity in trigger detection. Similar issues are pointed out in Knierim et al.'s (2018) research into the use of mixed-reality, e.g. lack of comfortability with prolonged wear and limited field of view. Hands-free interaction is scarcely supported; hand gestures and speech are often required, and mid-air hand gestures may cause fatigue. Overall, because the technology is constantly improving, what is learned from past studies is not conclusive and new research is expected on this topic.

4.2 Immersive Media Implementation

In this section, the authors demonstrate recent uses of augmented reality in a university level education setting. Both sample applications were created using the web platform Metaverse (https://studio.gometa.io/). The requirement for users is that they need to have the Metaverse app on their mobile device to scan a QR code to play the experiences, which overlays the multimedia elements over the physical environment.

The idea behind the first experience was an enjoyable quiz on general knowledge and trivia about New Zealand, especially for new international students. The questions are not easy; therefore, this quiz can be played by the general public as well. A friendly cartoon face is overlaid on the mobile device screen and asks the questions one by one – allowing students to guess again before moving on to the next question if they give an incorrect answer. Students can also end the experience if they wish. The quiz adds the points for each user, and generates a leaderboard (scoreboard). This provides an incentive to play again.

According to the feedback, there have been two advantages to this augmented reality approach (as opposed to having a web browser-based quiz). First, the students can run this without requiring a computer, and in any comfortable setting with their phones, for example, outdoors. Secondly, this experience can be enjoyed together with others. In the case of a mature student, this can be their family (e.g. spouse and child).

The second experience is a poll taken during the 2020 global pandemic and the ensuing lockdown, when students have found themselves in a situation that is also different from ordinary online study. For example, most students studying online would still have access to campus or education centre resources and face-to-face advisors, which are now lacking. Therefore, the authors released an augmented reality app to take the pulse of postgraduate IT students. In the app, the camera turns on and an interactive friendly robot is overlaid and floats around in the room. It conducts a quick poll, and gives each student advice based on their mood.

Both applications have been tested with users, successfully without technical issues. The tests can be discussed in a longer paper in the future. The results of the poll are anonymous, and have shown most students to be happy or normal in their study bubble. The experience offers them the chance to call someone if they are feeling unhappy or having issues; although students have not selected this option. Another lesson learned from both apps is that creating an augmented reality experience is not difficult in Metaverse. This is not only an educators' tool, but also a tool that students can use as a general creative outlet away from school.

5. CONCLUSION

Immersive media has benefits such as: enhanced motivation, and extending traditional teaching practices by engaging students in different ways. The literature and numerous trials support the idea that immersive media offers new opportunities to interact. Barriers such as lack of teacher competencies and lack of pedagogical structure and inflexibility of applications may be a result of a divide between educators and developers. Therefore, it is recommended to have more communication between teachers and developers. Lack of certain competencies can be addressed by technical training for teachers. This project has also trialed different practical uses of immersive media and illustrated its value. Although the work continues to progress, the authors have prepared to share screenshots of their current applications during the conference. If new applications are created, they will boost educators' experience and increase the implementation in this realm.

REFERENCES

Akçayır, M. and Akçayır, G. (2017). Advantages and Challenges Associated with Augmented Reality for Education: A Systematic Review of the Literature. *Educational Research Review,* Vol. 20, pp. 1-11. https://doi.org/10.1016/j.edurev.2016.11.002

Cascales et al. (2013). Study on Parents' Acceptance of the Augmented Reality Use for Preschool Education. *Procedia Computer Science,* Vol. 25, pp. 420-427. https://doi.org/10.1016/j.procs.2013.11.053

Denholm et al. (2013). The Value of Team-based Mixed-reality (TBMR) Games in Higher Education. *International Journal of Game Based Learning,* Vol. 3, No 1, pp. 18-33.

Fernandez, M. (2017). Augmented Virtual Reality: How to Improve Education Systems. *Higher Learning Research Communications,* Vol. 7, No. 1, pp. 1-15. https://doi.org/10.18870/hlrc.v7i1.373

Foote, C. (2017). Mobile technology goes virtual: using virtual reality in education. *Internet at Schools,* Vol. 24, No. 3.

Harper et al. (2018). Development of a Mixed Reality Game for Simulation Based Education. *Proceedings of 12th European Conference on Games Based Learning.* Sophia Antipolis, France, pp. 212-220.

Jensen, L. and Konradsen, F. (2018). A Review of the Use of Virtual Reality Head-mounted Displays in Education and Training. *Educational Technology, Research and Development,* Vol. 66, No. 5, pp. 1515-1529.

Khan et al. (2019). The Impact of an Augmented Reality Application on Learning Motivation of Students. *Advances in Human-Computer Interaction.* https://doi.org/10.1155/2019/7208494

Knierim et al. (2018). Challenges and Opportunities of Mixed Reality Systems in Education. https://dx.doi.org/10.18420/muc2018-ws07-0471

Martins et al. (2015). Challenges and Possibilities of Use of Augmented Reality in Education Case Study in Music Education. *Proceedings of 15th International Conference on Computational Science and Applications.* Banff, Canada, pp. 223-233.

Milman, N. (2018). Defining and Conceptualising mixed reality, Augmented Reality, and Virtual Reality. *Distance Learning,* Vol. 15, No. 2, pp. 5-58.

Sirakaya, M. (2018). The Effect of Augmented Reality Use on Achievement, Misconception and Course Engagement. *Contemporary Educational Technology,* Vol. 9, No. 3, pp. 297-314.

Wu et al. (2013). Current Status, Opportunities and Challenges of Augmented Reality in Education. *Computers and Education,* Vol. 62, pp. 41-49. https://doi.org/10.1016/j.compedu.2012.10.024

DESIGN OF A SERIOUS GAME FOR THE USE OF FOREIGN LANGUAGES: TOWARDS A RELEVANT DIDACTIC SYSTEM

Lizandro Becerra and Georges Antoniadis
LIDILEM Laboratory, Grenoble Alpes University, France
Bâtiment Stendhal CS40700-38058 Grenoble cedex 9

ABSTRACT

Our reflection paper is the continuation of an ongoing R&D project and focuses on the design and development of a didactic system for second language learning. This didactic system is based on the potential of the edutainment scenario for language learning. The system aims at practicing Spanish as a second language in a French secondary school. We consider that the combination of computer science, linguistics, language didactics and natural language processing (NLP) issues could offer operational solutions to language learners. We have therefore proposed an edutainment scenario capable of integrating the potential of serious games. The scenario has been designed and developed according to the linguistic needs of learners. In this paper, we propose to focus on four notions that make part of the design and development process of our edutainment scenario: serious games, teacher mediation, dictation and formative feedback.

KEYWORDS

Didactic System, Serious Games, Edutainment Scenario, Dictation, Feedback

1. INTRODUCTION

Advances in technology have changed learners' learning behaviors and reshaped teaching methods (Prensky, M. 2001). This has transformed the experience of learning processes in the teaching of foreign languages. As a result, language didactics, computer science, linguistics and natural language processing (NLP) are coming together to provide language learners with operational solutions. On the one hand, these systems are capable of offering didactic added value compared to conventional systems (Antoniadis, 2008). On the other hand, serious games have the potential to provide serious content in a playful way (Alvarez, J. & Djaouti, D. 2012; Fenouillet, F. 2016; Oblinger, D.C. 2004). We have therefore proposed an edutainment scenario capable of integrating the potential of serious games in order to offer a relevant solution to second language learners. Thus, this issue is at the crossroads of two main areas concerning language learning: digital game-based language learning (DGBLL) and computer-assisted language learning (ICALL). First, we propose to explore some relevant elements of the available literature; second, we want to describe the adopted model of our system; third, we will see some important notions of our didactic system such as: serious games, teacher mediation, dictation and formative feedback; fourth, we want to explain our didactic system; and finally, we would also like to present some perspectives on the method and evaluation of our system.

2. BACKGROUND

Video games for language learning have been studied by various researchers (Chen, H. & Yang, T. 2013; Yong-Ming. H. 2015; Schmoll, L. 2016; Loiseau, M., & al 2016; Alyaz, Y. & al, 2017) to name a few. The positive impact of the DGBLL tools has been reported in terms of improving learners' listening and writing skills (Alyaz, Y. & al., 2017). On the basis of the available literature, there seems to be a scientific consensus that a game alone does not allow learning if it is not accompanied by pedagogical measures (O'Neil & al., 2005). We also know that well-designed games are capable of motivating and engaging players by introducing them to compelling narratives and communicative complexity beyond what many traditional learning activities are capable of achieving (Reinhardt, J., & al., 2014).

3. EDUTAINMENT SCENARIO

The logic of designing a learning video game leads us to start from the learning objectives on which we will graft the gameplay more or less adapted to the learning needs of second language learners. To do this, we want to focus on the edutainment scenario model designed as a stage of linguistic performance and restitution of linguistic knowledge, based on alternative reality video games (Schmoll, L. 2016). The structure of an edutainment scenario takes into account both the framework of the interactive story (integrating the mechanisms of the game) and the pedagogical planning. Such a scenario is based on a first stage: the preparation sessions that would begin outside the serious game (tasks necessary for linguistic and playful understanding) and the second stage: the immersion stage with the serious game. On the one hand, our choice to adopt this model is justified because we consider the time spent using the serious game as a stage of language practice. Games that offer the possibility of transferring previously acquired knowledge to new problems, including those that require an adaptation of previous knowledge, with accompanying measures, should lead to better performance (O'Neil & al. 2005). On the other hand, we chose the edutainment scenario because we seek to include the teacher as mediator; before, during and after the use of the technical system. We want to highlight four important elements of our edutainment scenario: serious play, mediation, dictation and feedback.

3.1 Serious Game

A serious game is a computer application, whose initial intention is to combine coherently the serious aspects (serious) in a neither exhaustive nor exclusive manner, with instruction, learning, communication or further on information, assorted with the playing aspect of video games (Alvarez, 2007). Thus, a serious game is a way to integrate an educational scenario into a video game. Concerning the serious game design, we considered the prerequisites necessary when designing a video game to expect a state of flow (optimal experience) from the player: a challenging activity, clear goals, clear feedback and the paradox of having control in an uncertain situation (Salen, K. & Zimmerman, E. 2004).

3.2 Teacher Mediation

The notion of mediation/mediator is polysemic. At the level of the teacher, pedagogical mediation refers to the teacher's activity of relaying knowledge to learners. It therefore refers to the accompaniment of a human being by another human being. This notion of mediation is to be put in relation with the concept of the Proximal Development Zone (Vygotsky, 1967), which postulates that a subject progresses more rapidly in contact with a person of a higher level of development. In our project, the teacher retains a determining role because, in a pedagogical aim linked to the curriculum, play is not an end in itself (Musset, M. & Thibert, R., 2009). For us, there is no education without mediation. Thus, the teacher's role is first and foremost that of a mediator; one who verbalizes experience and knowledge to ensure successful acquisition. In terms of ICT integration, the teacher can be a designer, expert, tutor and evaluator at the same time (Klein, A. & Godinet H. 2000).

3.3 Dictation

We're concerned about dictation / transcription as a positive method for training linguistic skills: spelling, grammar and conjugation. Dictation / transcription as learning and training activities are not new; but what could be new to the considerations in our implementation is the combination with the potentiality of a serious game (Alyaz, Y. & al., 2017), mediation and formative feedback. Dictation works in a number of different ways, depending on how long segments are. A good strategy is the scaffolding dictation; making chunks of different lengths in order to adapt them to the learner (Buck, G. 2001).

3.4 Feedback

We are interested in the potential for automatic, direct and immediate feedback. We want to help the learner to identify and correct the error himself when using the serious game (Chen, 2003). Instead of giving a binary response (correct or incorrect), it may be more interesting to provide automatic, direct and immediate feedback.

Feedback in the ICALL system allows students to learn at their own pace and causes less frustration for learners (Kilickaya, 2007). Although more specific feedback can generally be better than less specific feedback. However, if feedback is too long or too complicated, many learners will simply ignore it, making it useless (Valerie J. S. 2008).

4. EDUTAINMENT SCENARIO PROPOSITION

We proposed an edutainment scenario adapted to the needs of second language learners (listening comprehension and writing skills). The target is Spanish as a second language (L2) in France. To do so, we designed five class sessions and a debriefing session; and we defined an immersion session corresponding to the serious game. The project is aimed at students of a French public secondary school (13 and 14 years old). The learners are at levels A1 and A2 of the CEFR (Common European Framework of Reference for Languages). As far as the theme to be dealt with is concerned, we have chosen the notion: Encounter with other cultures from the French curriculum (2018). When using the technical system, we aimed at dictation as a pedagogical and scaffolding method. We also proposed to help the learner to identify and correct the error himself through automatic formative feedback. In this way, any misspelled words will be automatically underlined.

4.1 Design Model and Technical Structure

We followed the steps of the PLOT model (Public, playful, Language Objectives and Tasks) since all the steps are in dialogue and therefore all are iterative (Schmoll, L. 2016). We defined the needs of the learners, then the gameplay (the story, the dialogues, the player's actions and the non-player's actions), after the specific linguistic objectives and finally the preparation tasks outside the technical system. We included the role of the teacher as tutor/mediator during the preparation sessions, the immersion game and the debriefing session. Concerning the technical aspects, we developed a 3D exploration video game with a First Person Perspective (FPP) in order to offer more field exploration elements and visibility. There is a Non Player Character (NPC) as a guide and speaker of the L2. In that way, player performs the right action (listening comprehension skills) and writes the right text (writing skills) in order to progress through the game. Regarding the structure of the scenario, we have opted for a nested event structure (Koster, 2005) that allows the subject to choose which area he will explore first and thus the corresponding task. The mission of the player/learner is to make an inventory of species in a virtual logbook. The player/learner must explore the terrain and perform actions such as searching for species, taking photos, freeing the animals (playful tasks) and writing down the characteristics of the species (language task). This information is provided by the NPC orally. The structure of the dialogues is still based on the Boolean type. However, it does not start from an instruction or a question formulated by the NPC, but from an event triggered by the player who initiates an interaction.

5. PERSPECTIVES

We would like to adopt the triangulation mixed method combining a quantitative and a qualitative approach (Creswell, J. W., et al., 2007). This, in order to answer the first research question; How could our didactic system provide operational and relevant solutions to the needs of language learners? We planned to collect and analyses quantitative and qualitative data and then compare the results in order to develop a complete understanding. In this way, we would like to test and experiment our first edutainment scenario for the use of Spanish as a second language. In order to evaluate our system, we propose to adopt an interactionist approach to foreign language learning, which would focus on five criteria: language learning potential, adaptation to the learner, focus on meaning, impact, authenticity and practicality (Chapelle, 2001). We chose this evaluation approach because for us evaluating the serious game is also to evaluate the preliminary instructions given by the teacher, the help he gives in class and the clarity of the restitution following the game session. Rather than questioning the possible performances for the learning of the serious game object itself, it is therefore necessary to seek the good adequacy of the tool to the needs of the teacher and the learners (All, A. & al., 2014).

REFERENCES

All A., Nuñez Castellar E. P. & Van Loy, J. 2014. Measuring Effectiveness in Digital Game-Based Learning: A Methodological Review, *International Journal of Serious Games*, vol. 1, n° 2.

Alvarez, J. 2007. Du jeu vidéo au Serious game. Approches culturelle, pragmatique et formelle. *Thèse de Doctorat en Science de la communication et de l'information*. Université de Toulouse II et III.

Alvarez, J. & Djaouti, D. 2012. *Introduction au serious game.* 2e Revue et augmentée. Questions Théoriques, Paris.

Alyaz, Y., Dorothea S. W., Esim, G. A. 2017. Study on Using Serious Games in Teaching German as a Foreign Language. *Journal of Education and Learning*; Vol. 6.

Antoniadis, G. 2008. Du TAL et son apport aux systèmes d'apprentissage des langues. *Contributions. Spécialité : Industries de la langue*. Habilitation à diriger des recherches, laboratoire LIDILEM. Université Stendhal - Grenoble 3.

Buck, G. 2001. *Assessing listening*. Cambridge: CUP.

Chapelle, C. A. 2001. *Computer applications in second language acquisition*. New York: Cambridge.

Chen, J. 2007. Flow in games (and everything else). *In Communications of the ACM*, vol. 50, n°4. 31-34. https://www.jenovachen.com/flowingames/p31-chen.pdf

Creswell, J. W. & Plano Clark, V. L. 2007. *Designing and conducting mixed methods research*. Thousand Oaks, CA: Sage.

Fenouillet, F. 2016. *Les théories de la motivation*. Dunod, Paris.

Guichon, N. 2012. *Vers l'intégration des TIC dans l'enseignement des langues.* Didier. Paris.

Kilickaya, F. 2007. The Effect of Computer Assisted Language Learning on Turkisk Learners. Achievement on The TOEFL Exam.

Klein A. & Godinet H. 2000. The teacher as a mediator in a networked society. In: Watson D.M., Downes T. (eds) Communications and Networking in Education. IFIP — *The International Federation for Information Processing*, vol 35. Springer, Boston, MA. pp 157-164.

Koster, R. 2005. A grammar of gameplay – Game atoms: can games be diagrammed? Sony Online Entertainment. Futurevision. *Game Developers Conference*. San Francisco.

Musset, M. & Thibert, R. 2009. Quelles relations entre jeu et apprentissages à l'école ? Une question renouvelée. Dossier d'actualité de la VST, n° 48.

Oblinger, D.G. 2004. The Next Generation of Educational Engagement. *Journal of Interactive Media in Education.* p. Art. 10.

O'Neil, H. F., Wainess, R. & Baker, E. L. 2005. Classification of learning outcomes: Evidence from the computer games literature. *The Curriculum Journal,* 16(4).

Prensky, M. 2001. Digital Natives, Digital Immigrants. *On the Horizon*, vol. 9, n° 5, octobre.

Reinhardt, J., Warner, C., Lange, K.: Digital games as practices and texts: New literacies and genres in an L2 German classroom. University of Arizona (USA). *Calico Monograph series*. Volume 12. Chapter 7, 159-177 (2014).

Salen, K. & Zimmerman, E. 2004. *Rules of Play - Game Design Fundamentals.* Massachusetts London, England: The MIT Press Cambridge.

Schmoll, L. 2016. Concevoir un scénario de jeu vidéo sérieux pour l'enseignement-apprentissage des langues ou comment dominer un oxymore. *Thèse de doctorat en Sciences du langage* – linguistique. Université de Strasbourg.

Valerie J. S. 2008. Focus on Formative Feedback. *Review of Educational Research*, vol. 78, 1: pp. 153-189. , First Published March 1.

Vygotski, Lev S. 1967. *Play and its role in the mental development of the child. In Soviet psychology*, vol. V, n°3, printemps.

AUTHOR INDEX